P9-CKD-205

WOMEN AND PSYCHOTHERAPY

616.8914
B7852

WOMEN
AND
PSYCHOTHERAPY

An Assessment of Research

and Practice

Edited by
ANNETTE M. BRODSKY
University of Alabama
and
RACHEL T. HARE-MUSTIN
Harvard University

WITHDRAWN

LIBRARY ST. MARY'S COLLEGE

THE GUILFORD PRESS
New York

© 1980 The Guilford Press, New York
A Division of Guilford Publications, Inc.

All rights reserved

No part of this book may be reproduced, stored in a retrieval system, or transmitted, in any form or by any means, electronic, mechanical, photocopying, microfilming, recording, or otherwise, without written permission from the Publisher

Printed in the United States of America

Last digit is print number 9 8 7 6 5

LIBRARY OF CONGRESS CATALOGING IN PUBLICATION DATA

Main entry under title:

Women and psychotherapy.
    "Based on the work of the participants of a conference held March 20-22, 1979, in Washington, D.C. . . . The conference was part of a contract by the National Institute of Mental Health to the American Psychological Association."
    Includes bibliographies and index.
    1. Women—Mental health—Congresses.   2. Psychotherapy—Philosophy—Congresses.   3. Psychotherapy—Research—Congresses. I. Brodsky, Annette M. II. Hare-Mustin, Rachel T., 1928–   III. United States. National Institute of Mental Health. IV. American Psychological Association. [DNLM: 1. Psychotherapy—Congresses. 2. Women—Congresses. WM420 W872 1979]
RC451.4.W6W65   616.89'1'088042   80-14842
ISBN 0-89862-605-6
ISBN 0-89862-909-8 paperback

Contributors

ELAINE A. BLECHMAN, Ph.D. Department of Psychology, Wesleyan University, Middletown, Connecticut

ANNETTE M. BRODSKY, Ph.D. Department of Psychology, University of Alabama, Tuscaloosa, Alabama

DIANNE L. CHAMBLESS, Ph.D. Psychology Clinic, Department of Psychology, University of Georgia, Athens, Georgia

LUCIA ALBINO GILBERT, Ph.D. Department of Educational Psychology, University of Texas at Austin, Austin, Texas

ALAN J. GOLDSTEIN, Ph.D. Department of Psychiatry, Temple University Medical School, Philadelphia, Pennsylvania

ALAN S. GURMAN, Ph.D. Department of Psychiatry, University of Wisconsin School of Medicine, Madison, Wisconsin

RACHEL T. HARE-MUSTIN, Ph.D. Program in Counseling and Consulting Psychology, Graduate School of Education, Harvard University, Cambridge, Massachusetts

KENNETH I. HOWARD, Ph.D. Department of Psychology, Northwestern University, Evanston, Illinois

MARILYN JOHNSON, Ph.D. Department of Psychology and Social Sciences, Rush University, Chicago, Illinois

ALEXANDRA G. KAPLAN, Ph.D. Department of Psychology, University of Massachusetts, Amherst, Massachusetts

MARJORIE H. KLEIN, Ph.D. Department of Psychiatry, University of Wisconsin School of Medicine, Madison, Wisconsin

DIANE KRAVETZ, Ph.D. School of Social Work, University of Wisconsin, Madison, Wisconsin

JEANNE MARECEK, Ph.D. Department of Psychology, Swarthmore College, Swarthmore, Pennsylvania

SARAH LYNNE MCMAHON, M.S. Women in Transition, West Philadelphia Mental Health Consortium, Philadelphia, Pennsylvania

CAROL NADELSON, M.D. Department of Psychiatry, Harvard Medical School and Tufts–New England Medical Center, Boston, Massachusetts

MALKAH T. NOTMAN, M.D. Department of Psychiatry, Harvard Medical School and Beth Israel Hospital, Boston, Massachusetts

DAVID E. ORLINSKY, Ph.D. Social Science Collegiate Division, University of Chicago, Chicago, Illinois

JULIA SHERMAN, Ph.D. Madison Psychiatric Associates, Madison, Wisconsin

LENORE E. WALKER, Ed.D. Department of Psychology and Battered Women Research Center—Domestic Violence Institute, Colorado Women's College, Denver, Colorado

MYRNA M. WEISSMAN, Ph.D. Departments of Psychiatry and Epidemiology, Yale University School of Medicine, and Depression Research Unit, Connecticut Mental Health Center, New Haven, Connecticut

DORIS Y. WILKINSON, Ph.D. Department of Sociology, Howard University, Washington, D.C.

ORLAND W. WOOLEY, Ph.D. Department of Psychiatry, University of Cincinnati College of Medicine, Cincinnati, Ohio

SUSAN C. WOOLEY, Ph.D. Department of Psychiatry, University of Cincinnati College of Medicine, Cincinnati, Ohio

LORRAINE YASINSKI, M.A. Department of Psychology, University of Massachusetts, Amherst, Massachusetts

Acknowledgments

Much enthusiastic work went into the planning of the project from which this book evolved. We would like to acknowledge the contributions of those persons involved in the project and those who aided the development of the current volume, which represents an expansion of the original project.

Our National Institute of Mental Health Project Officer, Irene Elkin Waskow, became a strong voice behind the scenes in shaping the project, from the selection of authors and organization of content areas to the final chapter, which is a revised version of the project report. Irene put a great deal of personal care and love into her input, and we wish to formally thank her for her challenging ideas and persuasive influence on the project and its report.

To Alan Gurman, our able and decisive editor, we extend our gratitude for helping to resolve issues related to the content of the manuscript. He has been particularly helpful in confronting problem areas and offering useful suggestions for overall format and for revisions of various chapters.

Nancy Felipe Russo, of the Women's Program Office of the American Psychological Association, helped to implement the project through her role as manager of the administrative aspects of the conference. For her dedication we are indeed grateful.

Also, we are indebted to Cathy Hall Shelton, the Project Director's secretary, for competence and loyalty above and beyond the call of duty. Her professional and emotional support was greatly appreciated.

Finally, we wish to acknowledge the cooperation of the many authors, some of whom were invited to prepare chapters after the completion of the National Institute of Mental Health project. Our contributing authors were understanding of our pressure to complete the manuscript with necessary revisions in the most timely fashion possible. They were a wonderful, stimulating group to work with, and we are delighted to have had the opportunity to get to know them through the course of this venture.

Annette M. Brodsky
Rachel T. Hare-Mustin

Preface

Practitioners and researchers alike have recognized the need for a volume that could pull together the scattered research literature on psychotherapy and women. This book is based on the work of the participants in a conference held March 20–22, 1979, in Washington, D.C., to assess the state of the art of research on psychotherapy and women and to develop recommendations for future research priorities.

The conference was part of a contract awarded by the National Institute of Mental Health to the American Psychological Association. The assessment of the state of the art of psychotherapy and women was based on 15 background papers prepared by leaders representing various disciplines in the field of psychotherapy research. The conference also included representatives of 20 organizations with interests relevant to psychotherapy with women. All participants were invited to discuss the papers and have input into the development of the report and recommendations presented to the National Institute of Mental Health as the product of the contract. The meeting of researchers and organizational representatives provided the first opportunity for experts with a variety of perspectives to come together to discuss the current thinking, criticism, evaluation, and priorities for research on women's issues in psychotherapy.

By necessity, the focus was selective. Five major areas were identified within which specific topics became focal points:

1. research on gender differences in therapy—emphasizing therapists' attitudes, the process of therapy, and therapy outcomes
2. traditional approaches—focusing on psychodynamic and behavioral perspectives and the use of medication as treatment
3. high-prevalence disorders—including depression, anxieties and phobias, and marital and family conflicts
4. crisis intervention—evaluating the status of interventions for crises of violence against women, such as rape and incest; reproductive-system crises, including pregnancy, mastectomy,

and menopause; and crises of marital transition, such as widowhood and divorce

5. alternative approaches—considering nontraditional therapeutic
   treatments such as feminist therapy, consciousness-raising
   groups, and self-help approaches

These areas were expanded to include three additional papers commissioned after the project report. Papers on eating disorders, battered
women, and minority women were not included in the conference,
but these topics were of special interest and concern in the discussions
and recommendations so that chapters on these three areas are included
in this volume.

All chapters are original contributions commissioned expressly for
the project or the book. Only the final chapter, which is based on the
original National Institute of Mental Health report, has been published
elsewhere.

This book is organized according to the five content areas identified
at the conference. The first part considers research on gender differences
in therapy. Orlinsky and Howard's chapter on outcome variables sets the
stage for consideration of the rest of the chapters by presenting the
theoretical issues that confront all psychotherapy research, but it can be
seen as specifically applied to psychotherapy and women. Other issues of
concern to research on gender differences in psychotherapy addressed
primarily by Orlinsky and Howard regard the need to demonstrate a
causal link between psychotherapy and outcome and the identification
of standards in interpreting outcome.

Sherman's chapter on therapists' attitudes looks at the issues surrounding stereotyping of clients, particularly the apparent trend toward
a moderating of such stereotyping in recent years. Sherman examines
the problem of a lack of conceptual understanding of the issues by
researchers. She also draws attention to the differences between results
of analogue studies and those of naturalistic or survey studies.

In addressing process variables and gender, Marecek and Johnson
note that there are almost no "true" process studies in which actual
therapy material is studied. They include in their analysis of the literature such issues as therapist preferences for clients, perceptions of
therapy, empathy, and gender differences in distress of clients entering
therapy.

The second part includes chapters on disorders of high prevalence
among women. A major question considered is how women's roles may
predispose them to mental illness. Weissman examines the research on
depression in women, noting that the sex difference in prevalence is a

real difference, not an artifact of labeling. Some myths are challenged, but other suspected associations of women's roles and depression are supported. Psychosocial factors become important variables in studying depressions, particularly because marriage appears to have a protective effect on men, but a detrimental effect on women, in terms of rates of depression.

Chambless and Goldstein address both hysteria and agoraphobia as high-prevalence disorders. The issues they raise about hysteria regard problems in diagnosis and the differences in treated versus nontreated hysterics. They note that multiple factors appear to be involved in agoraphobia, such as socialization, separation anxiety, and family history. Treatment results have been found to differ when short-term versus long-term criteria are used, as agoraphobics are characterized by relapses after short-term improvement.

Wooley and Wooley's chapter on eating disorders looks at a problem that has recently received considerable interest from clinicians and researchers. They make a case for the importance of considering the social context as well as medical explanations when eating becomes a problem and draw attention to the problems associated with attempting to achieve a weight that may be more socially desirable than physically necessary or even possible.

In looking at the research on marital and family conflict, Gurman and Klein discuss the inadequacy of marital status as a researchable concept. They raise questions about the need to clarify what is dysfunctional in a family. Their chapter considers the relationship of marriage and depression as well as new parenting roles and division of labor in the family that are of recent origin.

Traditional and alternative approaches to psychotherapy are the subject matter of the next part. Kaplan and Yasinski discuss the psychodynamic approaches and raise questions about insight therapies when applied to women. In Blechman's chapter on behavior therapies, questions about outcome criteria are discussed in terms of appropriateness of therapy goals and goals for systems changes as they may affect women. These chapters on traditional approaches note that competency has been neglected as a central theoretical issue for therapy outcome for women. Consideration is given to the need for measuring devices for sex-bias evaluation.

Feminist therapy is addressed by Gilbert and consciousness-raising by Kravetz. These alternative therapeutic approaches draw attention to the question of who their clients are and for whom these alternatives are particularly effective. Research is reviewed on self-report and behavioral changes in clients who participate in these treatment approaches. The few comparative examinations of different approaches have not led to any data that would support one approach over any other with regard to special benefits for women in general. The authors of many chapters look at the interactions of therapists and clients in attitudes toward sex roles, theoretical orientations, and other social variables.

Minority women have been particularly ignored as a research focus, so there is little research literature available to review. The chapter by Wilkinson considers attitudes toward minorities and women concerning treatment and the need to confront this issue.

The final part deals with crisis intervention. Notman and Nadelson provide a wealth of information about reproductive issues for women that include life-stage crises as well as trauma from physical events. Walker looks at battered women from both a theoretical and an applied perspective, with a view toward having the emerging research deal with the situation as it appears during stages of the battering cycle. As examined by McMahon, women in marital transition confront different issues that need research and treatment considerations. For example, she points out that divorced and widowed women may not be helped by the same techniques. Victims of crises appear to differ in their needs and their responses to treatment.

The chapters in each of the five topic areas and the discussions growing out of them were the basis for the editors' final chapter, based on their report and recommendations to the National Institute of Mental Health. While the recommendations reflect the sense of the conference participants, they also involve the independent assessment of the editors. In addition, many comments, recommendations, and issues were raised that could not be comprehensively covered for practical reasons. Thus, several other topics relating to women's issues in psychotherapy were considered but are not included as separate chapters in this book, such as epidemiology, diagnosis, prevention, risk factors, cognitive and humanistic approaches, older women, and lesbian women.

Contents

PART TWO: DISORDERS OF HIGH PREVALENCE

WOMEN AND PSYCHOTHERAPY

PART ONE

The Influence of Gender on Research

CHAPTER 1

Gender and Psychotherapeutic Outcome

DAVID E. ORLINSKY

KENNETH I. HOWARD

Introduction

The study of therapeutic outcome requires that we know about something happening outside therapy as a result of something else happening inside therapy. The actual interchanges of patient and therapist inside therapy are usually referred to as the therapeutic process. What happens outside therapy, in the lives of the patient and the therapist and of any others directly affecting or affected by their work, comprises the functional context or environment of psychotherapy. The influence of that environment on the events of therapy can be viewed as the input of context to process. The influence of therapy on events in its functional environment can be viewed as the output of process to context. Questions pertaining to therapeutic outcome fall within the purview of functional output but more narrowly concern the impact of therapeutic process on the life and person of the patient. Questions might also be raised concerning the impact of therapy on the therapist, on the mental health professions, and on the community or the culture at large, but those are of less practical concern and are hardly ever the subject of research.

Questions of outcome, however, are not simply matters of fact. They are also inevitably matters of value. One needs to know not only that something in the patient's life or personality has changed as a result of therapy, but that it has changed for better or worse. This judgment must be made with respect to some specific value standard or criterion, by parties who inevitably have some interest, one way or another, in the

David E. Orlinsky. Social Science Collegiate Division, University of Chicago, Chicago, Illinois.
Kenneth I. Howard. Department of Psychology, Northwestern University, Evanston, Illinois.

outcome. It is possible to determine that something about the patient's life or person has changed with a substantial measure of scientific objectivity. It is also possible to establish a plausible causal link between aspects of therapeutic process and patient change by scientific research. However, what such a change is worth in the realm of value in principle cannot be settled scientifically. It is a practical, even a political, matter to be settled among various interested parties. The best that one can expect for this aspect of outcome research is an explicit, reasoned, public procedure that is susceptible to critical review (for which the institutions of legal judgment might provide a model).

The study of therapeutic outcome is, therefore, a complex, not to say delicate, undertaking. The study of women's influence on psychotherapy, and of psychotherapy's influence on women, is likewise a complex and delicate matter. It raises a number of questions: How do men and women differ? What does it mean to be a woman? What exactly is gender—as a social, psychological, or cultural variable—beyond one of many ways of classifying people? No doubt, there are very important practical consequences contingent on gender classification; but no one is simply a woman, or simply a man, without further qualification. Women differ significantly among themselves (as do men) by age and generation, by ethnicity and culture, by socioeconomic status and family status, by intelligence and appearance, and by other social or personal characteristics. A thoughtful analysis must find ways to take these factors and their interactions with gender into account. It will take a considerable effort just to decide how to ask meaningful questions about therapeutic outcome, about women and men, and about the differential impact of gender on therapeutic outcome. It will take a little further effort still to accumulate some meaningful answers.

We will try to make a start toward these goals by discussing, in turn, the general perspective from which we view psychotherapy research, the basic logic of outcome evaluation, and the nature of gender as a variable in psychotherapy research. We will then go on to review the sparse research literature dealing with the effects of gender on outcome and to report some more recent findings on the subject that should serve to stimulate further research.

A Functional Perspective for Psychotherapy Research

Logically, the study of psychotherapy can be divided into three parts. First, there is the functional context or environment prior to therapy, including the patients, with their problems and resources; the therapists, with their skills and orientations; the institutions that bring patients and therapists together; and the beliefs and values held by patients, therapists, and others in the community regarding what these problems, people, and institutions are and ought to be. Questions concerning these matters focus on the functional inputs to therapy, that is, on the potential determinants of therapeutic process and the potential predictors of therapeutic outcome.

The second division in therapy research pertains to the unfolding sequence of events and experiences that constitute psychotherapy as a systematic phenomenon: the intentions and actions, perceptions and feelings, satisfactions and frustrations of patients and therapists; the organization, schedules, and circumstances of their meetings; and the meanings they conceive and the forms of conversation by which they express these meanings to each other. Questions concerning these matters focus on processes which are potential determinants (and, in early phases, predictors) of therapeutic outcome.

Third, there is the functional context or environment subsequent to therapy: the further life and personal condition of the patient, as well as the state of the therapist, of the therapeutic art, and of the institutions and cultural attitudes relevant to therapy. Questions concerning these matters focus on functional outputs, that is, on the possible consequences or effects of therapeutic process. Preeminent among these for practical purposes are the effects that may be observed in the lives and persons of patients. What sort of effects might there be? How soon do they develop? How long do they last? Do they cumulate or dissipate? Above all, do they seem beneficial or harmful—and to whom, by what standards, judging on whose behalf? When focused on the patient, and when judged in relation to standards of value, output can be interpreted as therapeutic *outcome*.

This input–process–output conception permits us to consider the variety of psychotherapy studies in a systematic fashion. In addition to studies that focus simply on input, process, or output/outcome questions, there are also studies that deal with the relation of input to process, that is, which describe the ways that prior context (e.g., patient diagnosis or therapist orientation) may become active as determinants of therapeutic process (e.g., the quantity or content of patient and therapist communications). There are studies that relate input to output/outcome in order to distinguish which aspects of prior context (e.g., patient and therapist gender) are meaningful predictors of subsequent context (e.g., symptom reduction). Further, there are studies of process in relation to outcome the aim of which is to specify the aspects of patient–therapist interchange (e.g., patient self-exploration or therapist empathy) that become active as determinants of subsequent context (e.g., patient self-regard). The most complex and ambitious studies are those which trace the systematic interrelations of input, process, and output (or outcome). Since outcome is our principal theme, let us be more precise about what that means.

The Logic of Outcome Evaluation

Outcome evaluation is in part a descriptive task and in part a value judgment. The descriptive task involves establishment of a probable causal relationship between a specific treatment process and specific changes in the life or personality of the patient. The value judgment involves comparison of those specific changes by some interested party with whatever ideal standards that party deems relevant as criteria of the desirable or undesirable. These components of outcome evaluation are presented in Figure 1.

Insofar as we ourselves value clarity in our research operations, it seems desirable that the different components be explicitly implemented as separate steps and undesirable that they be carried out implicitly in a way that confounds description with value judgment. A prime instance of the latter is the common practice of using global evaluative ratings of therapeutic outcome made by patients, therapists, or outside persons. Very little actual information is obtained by this method beyond the unelucidated opinion of the observer. If we want meaningful evaluations of psychotherapy, we will have to approach the problem with greater circumspection.

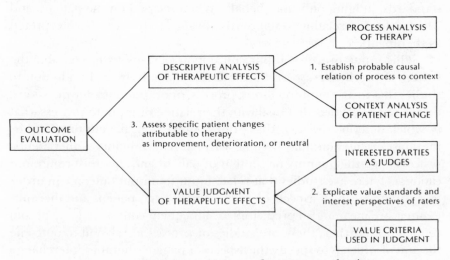

Figure 1.   Logical components of outcome evaluation.

The descriptive task involves demonstrating a causal relationship between a specific therapeutic process and specific changes in the patient. We may leave aside the question of how therapeutic processes are to be described, since we have recently dealt with that in detail elsewhere (Orlinsky & Howard, 1978). The problem we have yet to deal with is specifying the particular aspects of the patient's life and person in which change might occur.

The relationship between the patient's life and person is intimate and reciprocal, but not wholly circular. The patient is a physical person who carries on, in conjunction with others, an intersubjective life. The person shapes, and is shaped by, her life. The two are nevertheless distinguishable. The physical person is both a functioning psychosomatic body and a distinctive adapting personality mediating and integrating a series of interpersonal relationships. The intersubjective life is both a subjective autobiography unfolded in the person's experiences of self and others and an objective biography consisting of impressions formed and retained in the minds of others whose own lives have in some part included and been included in the person's. (The former aspect might be called the person's life-in-self, and the latter her life-in-others.)

The Patient as Physical Person

The conceptualization of the patient as a physical person is presented in Figure 2. As a living being, the person is a functioning psychosomatic body and a distinctive adapting personality. The psychosomatic body can be construed at a relatively microscopic level as a psychophysiologic organism, observable mainly by means of special instrumentation. This is the body as known to scientific biology. Consideration of the patient as a person in this sense is most relevant to the psychosomatic and psychophysiologic disorders (e.g., hypertension) and to the recently developed biofeedback and meditative therapies. At a relatively macroscopic level, on the other hand, the person as psychosomatic body can be viewed as a psychophysical character whose features are explicitly discernible to the appropriately trained observer through bodily configuration (in the sense of posture and physique) and through kinetic self-utilization (in terms of energy and coordination or of "effort/shape," in the technical language of dance notation; Dell, 1977). Interpretation of, and intervention directed at, bodily configuration relative to psychophysical character is a central feature of bioenergetic and other body therapies (Lowen, 1975). The approach to psychophysical character through kinetic self-utilization is common to methods such as Alexander training (Alexander, 1974) and dance or expressive movement therapies.

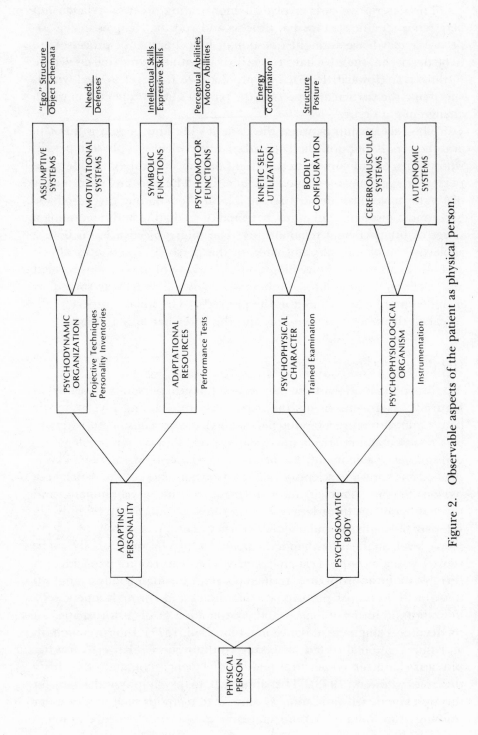

Figure 2. Observable aspects of the patient as physical person.

8

More traditional measures of the person in psychology have concentrated on the individual as an adapting personality. The adapting personality can be viewed, in one sense, as a repertoire of adaptational resources for which various psychometric assessments of symbolic (expressive and intellectual) skills and psychomotor (perceptual and performance) skills have been devised. The adapting personality can be viewed, in another sense, as a psychodynamic organization whose features as an assumptive system of self and object schemata, and as a motivational system of needs and defenses, can be inferred from a variety of projective measures and personality inventories. The techniques for measuring personality as psychodynamic organization are particularly popular in studies of therapeutic outcome but tend to subtly confound description and value judgment. Klein (1976) has shown how carefully these instruments must be scrutinized for value biases, especially in relation to assessment of outcome with women.

The Patient's Intersubjective Life

The other main target area for descriptive analysis of patient change is the life that the patient experiences and shares, in experiencing, with others (see Figure 3). The patient's life-in-self is subjective autobiography insofar as it consists of her own perceptions and understandings, and the patient's life-in-others is objective biography insofar as it consists of others' perceptions and understandings of her. The patient's life as objective biography is derived primarily from the testimony of privileged observers, including both personal intimates who are directly involved in her everyday relationships and expert witnesses who have had some reason to observe and interview her. Other sources of data concerning the patient's life as objective biography are peripheral observers such as casual acquaintances or hearsay witnesses who know the patient only by reputation. Outcome studies often rely on data provided by privileged observers (expert witnesses such as the therapist or an independent diagnostician and personal intimates such as parents or spouse); they rarely utilize data drawn from peripheral observers.

The patient's life as subjective autobiography is derived primarily from patient reports, sometimes in written forms such as diaries or questionnaires, sometimes in oral forms such as the psychotherapeutic or research interview. Self-reports typically confound description and evaluation, since hedonic reactions are such a salient and pervasive feature of experience (cf. the ubiquitous "evaluation" factor of Osgood, Suci, & Tannenbaum, 1957), but these two aspects can frequently be separated by the researcher, if not by the patient herself. Generally

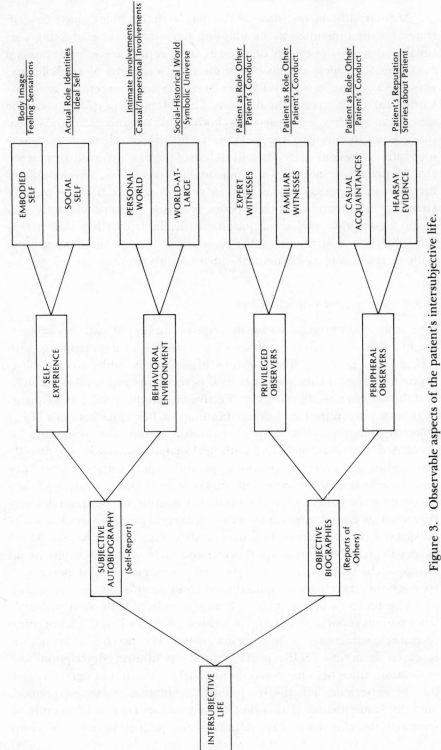

Figure 3. Observable aspects of the patient's intersubjective life.

speaking, the individual's subjective autobiography is organized in terms of self-experience (i.e., perceptions and understandings of oneself) and perceptions and understandings of one's surroundings (what the an- thropologist A. I. Hallowell, 1967, has called the individual's behavioral environment).

Self-experience is distinguishable phenomenologically into an em- bodied self (body image and affective impulses) and a social self (actual and idealized role identities). One's role identities reflect and organize experiences in social relationships and tend to formulate social conduct into a series of interpersonal projects (McCall & Simmons, 1966). The patient's experience as an embodied self overlaps with but is not identical to the patient's person viewed as a psychosomatic body by trained obser- vers or special instrumentation; these are subjective and objective pre- hensions of the same phenomena. A physician who initially asks her patient about his physical complaints (embodied self) will normally go on to directly examine and test him physically (psychosomatic body) in order to diagnose the person's condition. (The physician in this example would be acting both as a trained observer in the context of physical personality and as an expert witness in the context of the patient's inter- subjective life.)

Most patients who come voluntarily for psychotherapy probably do so because of what seems to them inconsistent or intolerable features of their self-experience. Most psychodynamic, interpersonal, and cognitive therapists work to a great extent with their patients' reported self- experiences. Some researchers, mostly in the client-centered tradition, have even used patients' self-experiences (actual vs. ideal self) as a basis for evaluating therapeutic outcome. While patients' self-experiences cannot by themselves answer all questions regarding outcome, it seems unlikely that their contents and organization can be left altogether out of any satisfactory accounting of therapeutic effects.

The complement to the individual's self-experience in subjective autobiography is the behavioral environment, that is, the patient's per- ceptions and understandings of the world around her. The behavioral environment can be conceptualized as a concentrically organized field in which the self is centered. The broad inner region of that field—the realm of persons, objects, and locales in which the self routinely moves, and of which she has direct knowledge—may be called the individual's personal world. Immediately outside herself are intimate others and objects; somewhat more distant are casual or impersonal involvements. The surrounding outer region of the field, which the individual con- strues on the basis of indirect knowledge (e.g., received opinion) but which frames and stabilizes her personal world, is her representation of the world-at-large. This includes the wider social-historical world of human affairs and the transcendental or "ultimate" symbolic context in which all takes place. Because the patient's personal world is directly shared and jointly created by the patient with her intimates and others who have influence (including her therapist), it is the realm that is most directly susceptible to her efforts at therapeutic change. Insofar as the patient can change the circumstances, quality, and variety of her relationships with others, she can change a basic core area of her life. The patient's world-at-large can also change, though mainly by means of symbolic redefinition or reinterpretation which is fostered and sustained by changes in group membership and participation (e.g., consciousness-raising), unless the patient is one of those rare individuals who becomes a significant actor on the stage of history.

Time Frames in Outcome Analysis

Conceptions of the patient's life and person can be further refined toward the specificity necessary to make them observational categories by reference to the time frames within which changes might be revealed. Successively longer and more inclusive time frames are the patient's momentary state, measurable in fractions or multiples of hours; the patient's current condition, measurable in fractions or multiples of months; the progressing phase, measurable in fractions or multiples of years; and the total sequence or history, measurable for adults in fractions or multiples of generations (assuming that one generation = approximately 30 years). For the physical person, these time frames might be rendered as personal state, personal condition, developmental phase, and developmental history. For the intersubjective life, the corresponding time frames might be called the immediate life space, the current life pattern, the progressing life passage, and the cumulative life history.

   With respect to outcome analysis, one can see that changes in the patient's personal state or immediate life space might result from individual sessions or events within them (e.g., an effective insight or emotional catharsis). In themselves, such changes are usually too evanescent to be convincing indices of outcome, but they are most directly observable and may gradually cumulate into more enduring changes in the patient's personal condition or current life pattern. Changes in condition, by definition, occur over a greater length of time and are longer lasting. It is not uncommon for the patient's personal condition or life pattern to change several times in the course of long-term treatment, although brief crisis-oriented therapies are usually geared to bring about one specific change in condition. Improvements or deteriorations in the patient's condition provide a sufficient scope for a clinically meaningful outcome evaluation. So, too, do successes and failures in the patient's negotiation of a significant developmental phase (e.g., resolution of Oedipal conflicts) or progressing life passage (e.g., departure from one's parents' home and establishment of autonomous living arrangements). By contrast, the total sequence of the patient's personal developmental history or cumulative life history is a much larger time frame than a single course of psychotherapy (with the possible exception of Woody Allen's analysis) and, therefore, not so easily utilized in outcome evaluation. Nevertheless, as Ricks, Wandersman, and Poppen (1976) have indicated, it is possible to evaluate the effects of therapy undergone in childhood or adolescence in relation to events in the patient's subsequent history (e.g., psychiatric hospitalization, mortality).

The basic observational grid for descriptive analysis of patient changes can be visualized by cross-tabulating the four time frames (state, condition, phase, history) with the specific target aspects of the patient's physical person (organism, character, adaptational process, psychodynamic organization) and the patient's intersubjective life (self-experience, behavioral environment, privileged observers, peripheral observ-

Observable Aspect / Time Frame			State	Condition	Phase	History
Physical Person	Adapting Personality	Psychodynamic Organization				
		Adaptational Resources				
	Psychosomatic Body	Psychophysical Character				
		Psychophysiological Organism				
Intersubjective Life	Subjective Autobiography	Self-Experience				
		Behavioral Environment				
	Objective Biographies	Privileged Observers				
		Peripheral Observers				

Figure 4. Descriptive grid for outcome assessment.

ers), as shown in Figure 4. No single cell of this grid by itself can validly represent the patient as a target in outcome research. Proper assessment requires the sampling of variables for all cells that are theoretically relevant to the patients and to the therapies being studied.

The Causal Relation of Process and Outcome

Having observed specific changes in the patient as a concomitant of therapy, the next major step in outcome evaluation involves establishing a probable causal link between the observed changes and the patient's participation in therapy. If no such link can be established, then the observed changes are irrelevant as indices of therapeutic outcome. There are always many other involvements in a patient's life, and other processes in the patient's person, that might have brought about the observed changes. If a patient feels better while in therapy because she meets someone with whom she falls in love, to what extent is her transformation (e.g., in embodied self and in psychodynamic organization) attributable to therapy rather than to the fortuitous change in her life situation? The most realistic approach is probably to allow for a multiplicity of determinants of patient change (including psychotherapy) and to aim at estimating the proportion of variance in the observed changes that are attributable to each. The reader is referred to Gottman and Markman (1978) for further references and a discussion of issues related to experimental design.

Value Judgment in Outcome Research

Even having determined that therapeutic processes contributed a statistically and clinically significant proportion of the variance in observed patient changes, there remains the further problem of evaluating these changes as improvements or deteriorations (or as value-neutral). This is the part of outcome research that requires the making of value judgments. Who has the right and the qualifications to make such judgments? What are their interests regarding therapy, and how are those interests affected by having a positive or negative evaluation of therapy established? What value criteria do they employ, and what standards of comparison?

The logical elements of value judgment are outlined in Figure 5. There are interested parties applying value criteria to patient changes that are consequences of therapy. A preliminary distinction among interested parties can be drawn between service consumers and service providers, but each category can be further divided. Service consumers

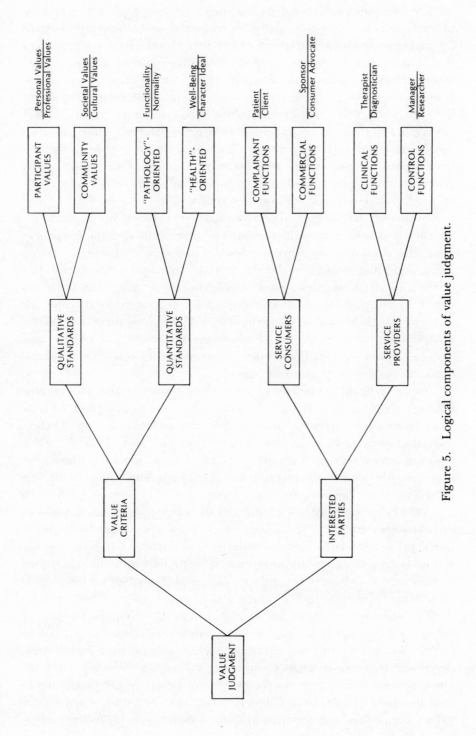

Figure 5. Logical components of value judgment.

include the patient, defined as the target or recipient of therapeutic procedures; the client, who instigates treatment and whose interests are ostensibly served by it; the sponsor, who provides the financial resources that make therapy possible; and the consumer advocate, who undertakes to monitor how well the interests of patient, client, and sponsor are being served. All of these parties may be comprehended in a single individual, as in the case of a well-informed, voluntary patient who is paying for her own therapy and is alert to its effects on her. Alternatively, the client may be someone other than the patient (e.g., the patient's spouse or parent), the sponsor may be an insurance company or a governmental agency, and the consumer advocates may be a self-selected group of social or political activists.

Similarly, the category of service providers can be distinguished into the therapist, who personally conducts or directs the therapeutic procedure; the diagnostician, who assesses the patient's condition at various times, including intake and termination; the manager, who controls the terms and circumstances under which therapy is given; and the researcher, who gathers and analyzes information concerning therapy. All of these functions may be performed by a single individual, such as the independent private practitioner who keeps systematic case records and studies various aspects of her practice, or these functions may be distributed among several persons or agencies.

It is important to identify which of the interested parties (or combinations) are actually making the value judgments in any piece of outcome research, since their evaluative concerns and their frames of reference are bound to be somewhat different. Krause and Howard (1976), who discuss evaluation research in terms of these several parties, give some consideration to the methodologic problems entailed in attempting to balance their various partisan interests.

Whichever party is, in fact, making the value judgments, the procedure requires that the observed patient changes be compared with directional value criteria so as to be adjudged as changes for better or for worse. Both qualitative and quantitative standards must be taken into consideration. Qualitative standards can be differentiated into participant values and community values. Participant values, in turn, can be distinguished into personal values (e.g., strength or happiness) such as patients might naturally employ and professional values (e.g., educational value or scientific interest) most likely to be operating in therapist, diagnostician, or researcher. Community values, on the other hand, include societal values (e.g., deviance control or economic productivity) that sponsors, clients, or managers might find congenial, and cultural values (e.g., ethical commitment or esthetic activity) that consumer advocates or researchers might espouse. Perhaps the most reasonable approach is to use a variety of qualitative value criteria in outcome research, providing, of course, that they are not confounded with one another.

Quantitative criteria can be differentiated into "pathology"-oriented standards and "health"-oriented standards. In terms of pathology-oriented standards, the most extreme degrees of mental and emotional disorder are those in which patients are incapable of autonomous functioning (e.g., catatonia). Considerable success might be achieved by simply helping such patients to overcome their incapacitation and to become functional, even though they were to remain grossly deviant in mood or manner. Next on the pathology-oriented scale are patients who are capable of autonomous functioning but in so deviant a fashion that they would be considered psychotic or borderline psychotic. Success with patients in this category would involve a remission of psychosis or attainment of approximate normality, even though they were still to feel significantly impaired in effectiveness and emotional balance.

Health-oriented standards are more salient when viewing the other end of the spectrum. There are, for instance, many patients who enter psychotherapy even though approximately normal in the gross aspects of mood, thought, and action, because they suffer what they believe to be unnecessary impairments in the subtler aspects of their functioning. For them, success in therapy would require overcoming the restrictions and dis-ease imposed by symptomatic or character neuroses and the attainment of a fuller measure of well-being. Finally, there are some who become patients in therapy even though at a reasonable level of well-being in their lives and personal functioning. These are persons who, because of their advantaged positions, their sophistication, or the demands of their vocation, feel dissatisfied with their undeveloped potential and seek to perfect their interpersonal skills and their emotional responsiveness or to maintain these in a finely tuned state. Patients such as these (including many professional therapists) would be judged successful to the extent that they overcame their "normosis" and approximated to a cultural character ideal in their personal functioning.

Obviously, patient changes must be evaluated in relation to their quantitative level of functioning at the beginning and end of therapy, whatever qualitative value standard is employed. Some patients in therapy may be starting out at a higher level than others might ever hope to achieve, yet the latter might be considered successful while the former may not. A basic evaluative grid for outcome research can be constructed by cross-tabulating the various party perspectives (patient, client, sponsor, advocate; therapist, diagnostician, manager, researcher) with the various qualitative and quantitative value criteria, as shown in Figure 6. To make fully explicit evaluations of therapeutic outcome, one or more of the cells defined by the evaluative grid (Figure 6) must be applied to changes caused by therapy that are recorded in those particular cells of the observational grid (Figure 4) that are theoretically relevant to the patients and the therapeutic methods being studied.

Gender as a Variable in Psychotherapy Research

What meaning can be assigned to gender in the context of outcome research? Viewed in the framework of a functional perspective on psychotherapy, patient gender and therapist gender have significance

Value Criteria	Party Perspective	Patient	Client	Sponsor	Consumer Advocate	Therapist	Diagnos-tician	Manager	Researcher
Personal Values	Functional								
	Normal								
	Well								
	Ideal								
Professional Values	Functional								
	Normal								
	Well								
	Ideal								
Societal Values	Functional								
	Normal								
	Well								
	Ideal								
Cultural Values	Functional								
	Normal								
	Well								
	Ideal								

Figure 6.   Evaluative grid for outcome assessment.

mainly as input variables. Singly or in combination, patient and therapist gender might be found to be determinants of therapeutic process; they might also be found to have utility as predictors of therapeutic outcome. It is important to recognize that patient and therapist gender in themselves cannot be direct determinants of outcome and that the process of therapy must intervene in order to realize whatever causal potential for outcome the gender variables may possess. If, however, convincing causal linkages can be demonstrated between gender as an input variable and some specific features of therapeutic process, and between those process variables and outcome, then gender could, indeed, be regarded as an indirect determinant of therapeutic outcome. Even then, one would want to know what there is about being a man or woman that could have such an effect. The social, cultural, and psychological concomitants of gender, rather than the demographic category in itself, constitute the real focus of interest.

Gender, of course, is not the only input variable that is a prominent feature of the prior functional context of psychotherapy. Men and women do not constitute homogeneous subpopulations in our society, and the report of gender unqualified by other characteristics gives a limited amount of information about an individual. How much do lower-upper class, college-educated, white liberal Protestant women with one or two children, married to business executives or successful professionals and living in exclusive suburbs have in common with lower-middle class, high-school-educated, white Catholic women with four or five children living in traditional ethnic city neighborhoods, or with their black inner-city counterparts, or with young business and professional women living independently in fashionable high-rise apartment complexes? It would be rather surprising if the gender variable were found to act alone rather than in conjunction with other input variables. It seems plausible to expect more "interaction effects" than "main effects" of gender in our research results.

What, then, are the meaningful subpopulations of women and of men in our society from which patients come to psychotherapy and to which the results of our studies may be referred? Defining these subpopulations is one of the more urgent tasks awaiting researchers in this field. We can begin, at least, by noting the various characteristics that differentiate individuals as members of the general population. These refer mainly to the niches occupied by individuals in the social and cultural system facets of the community (Howard & Orlinsky, 1972; Orlinsky & Howard, 1978). In addition to gender, other biologically conditioned characteristics include age status, physical type (height, weight, somatotype, "condition," and culturally standardized esthetic qualities), and biocultural origin (race, ethnicity, and religious background). There are also various sociohistorical characteristics that differentiate individuals, including generation, habitat (residential and occupational ecology, and geographic mobility), socioeconomic status (income, occupation, social prestige, and political influence), and sociocultural status (education and religious, political, or associational affiliations). Finally, there are differential features of the individual as a social participant, including family background (birth order, number and spacing of siblings, parental characteristics, family constellation, and history), current sociosexual or family status (psychosexual orientation, marital status, parental status, family constellation, and domestic arrangements), community involvement (especially occupational and associational activities and standing), and subcultural orientation (lifestyle, e.g., consumer habits, dress and grooming style, leisure habits). The foregoing categories describe differential input characteristics of patients (beyond the more individual personal features discussed in the preceding section). Facts in these 12 categories overlap with aspects of the patient's objective biography and are usually easily ascertained. They are coexistent with gender and seem likely to interact with gender in varying ways that may obscure or potentiate gender effects in therapy; therefore, they should be taken explicitly into account in analyzing gender data in relation to therapeutic process or outcome.

Though a population context variable, gender is not alterable as a result of psychotherapy and is not in itself an outcome variable. (The decision to undergo a sex-change operation may be reached as a result of therapy, and psychosexual orientation might be changed as a result of therapy, but these are clearly different matters.) Gender is nevertheless relevant to the assessment of therapeutic outcome, with regard to both the descriptive analyses and the value judgments that must be made. Gender is relevant to the descriptive analysis of patient effects, insofar as the lives and persons of women are different from the lives and persons of men. The assumption of parental status, for example, tends to have rather different meanings and consequences for the lives of the two sexes. Similarly, the different reproductive biologies that men and women must integrate into their social adaptations and self-experiences as physical persons require the researcher to ask somewhat different questions in designing research. There are many other less obvious ramifications of gender that must be thoughtfully explored in order to determine which descriptive dimensions are especially relevant for the assessment of change in male and female patients.

Gender is also relevant to outcome research in terms of value judgments, insofar as there are different value criteria applicable to changes in the lives and persons of women and men, and especially insofar as there are divergently interested parties making evaluations from their separate perspectives. Klein (1976) has shown how antifeminist value biases covertly enter a number of standard outcome assessment instruments. Feminists, perhaps acting as consumer advocates, would no doubt apply different value criteria to changes observed in female patients than might traditional sponsors or clients.

A major requirement for future research on gender in relation to therapeutic outcome is a searching clarification of (1) the basic descriptive dimensions differentiating the lives and persons of men and women, (2) the prevalent value standards by which changes along these dimensions may be judged, and (3) the various partisan interests overtly or covertly represented by those who actually make or seek to make assessments of therapeutic outcome. One could do worse than to set a task force directly to work on these issues.

Research on Women and Therapeutic Outcome

What is known, to date, about the relation of gender to therapeutic outcome? A decade ago, Meltzoff and Kornreich (1970), in an exhaustive review of research on therapeutic outcome, wrote as follows:

> Do males or females as a class, with all other things being equal, do equally well, better or worse as therapists? Do same-sex pairings do better, worse, or equally well as opposite-sex pairings? More specifically, do male or female therapists perform differentially when paired with patients of the same or opposite sex? Are there any particular kinds (other than sex) of patients with whom male or female therapists have noteworthy success or difficulty? Do personality, style, and approach affect the success of therapists working with same- or opposite-sex patients? All these questions are eminently researchable. Nevertheless, direct experimental work that could put speculations to rest is meager. (p. 294)

Their questions are still pertinent; the research is still meager.

Concerning some 20 studies[1] loosely relevant to outcome and patient gender, Meltzoff and Kornreich concluded, "On balance, the sex of

[1]Meltzoff and Kornreich cite D. S. Cartwright (1955); Ellis (1956); Esterson, Cooper, and Laing (1965); Friedman (1950); Gluck, Tanner, Sullivan, and Erickson (1964); Hamilton, Varney, and Wall (1942); Hare (1966); Katahn, Strenger, and Cherry (1966); Kaufman, Frank, Friend, Heims, and Weiss (1962); Lazarus (1963); Levitt, Beiser, and Robertson (1959); Luff and Garrod (1935); Rachman (1965); Rodriguez, Rodriguez, and Eisenberg (1959); Rogers and Dymond (1954); Rosenbaum, Friedlander, and Kaplan (1956). Rosenthal and Frank (1958); Schmidt, Castell, and Brown (1965); Sobel (1962); and Warren (1965).

the patient does not seem to be a crucial variable in the success of psychotherapy" (p. 237). Citing only one study bearing directly on outcome and therapist gender, plus a few others bearing indirectly on the issue, Meltzoff and Kornreich noted:

> In summation, we find that the very few studies available on patient improvement showed no differences between male and female therapists. ... At present there is no clear basis for preferential assignment of a patient of either sex to a therapist of either sex. No statements can be made with confidence about the relative benefits of selected pairings with given types of patients. (p. 299)

Only 2 years ago, two major reviews in the new Garfield and Bergin (1978) *Handbook of Psychotherapy and Behavior Change* came to basically similar conclusions. Dealing with patient gender, Garfield (1978) cited six studies[2] and commented, "The prevailing evidence with regard to sex and outcome appears to indicate that there is no clear relationship. Most of the studies show no differences in outcome" (p. 213). Parloff, Waskow, and Wolfe (1978), reviewing 15 more or less relevant studies[3] on therapist gender with considerable attention to feminist concerns, likewise remarked, "There is very little evidence to support any conclusions of the effects of same-sex versus opposite-sex pairs on outcome" (p. 264).

Our own search for empirical studies on gender effects and outcome, concentrating on the last six years, has revealed three additional studies. Strassberg and Anchor (1977) found that male therapist trainees made more favorable ratings of improvement in their student clients of both sexes than did female therapist trainees, but the trend in this direction was not statistically significant. Goldenholz (1976) studied 494 adult clients of both sexes who were treated by an undisclosed number of male and female therapists at two outpatient clinics and found no significant differences in sex composition of therapeutic dyads and outcome of treatment. Finally, Norkus (1976) explored the effects of assignment or nonassignment to a therapist of preferred sex (whether male or female) on improvements in self-esteem for a relatively small sample of female

[2]Garfield cites D. S. Cartwright (1955); Gaylin (1966); Hamburg, Bibring, Fisher, Stanton, Wallerstein, Weinstock, and Haggard (1967); Knapp, Levin, McCarter, Wermer, and Zetzel (1960); Mintz, Luborsky, and Auerbach (1971); and Seeman (1954).

[3]Parloff, Waskow, and Wolfe cite R. D. Cartwright and Lerner (1963); Geer and Hurst (1976); Grantham (1973); Hill (1975); Howard, Orlinsky, and Hill (1970); Johnson (1976); Kirshner, Hauser, and Genack (1979); Linehan, Goldfried, and Goldfried (cited in Parloff *et al.*, 1978); Mintz, O'Brien, and Luborsky (1976); Orlinsky and Howard (1975, 1976); Pardes, Papernik, and Winston (1974); Persons, Persons, and Newmark (1974); Scher (1975); and Sullivan, Miller, and Smelser (1958).

undergraduates and found a positive relationship between preferred assignment and outcome. A recent review of sex differences in psychiatric evaluation and treatment (Zeldow, 1978) for some reason fails even to mention the issue of therapeutic outcome. Similarly, an otherwise most impressive handbook of research concerning the characteristics and functioning of psychotherapists (Gurman & Razin, 1977) has no listing for "sex" or "gender" in its subject index. We are left to echo the conclusions of other commentators: not much directly relevant research, not much consistent quality, and not much by way of results. The impression thus far sustained is that gender, by itself, is not a powerful or consistent predictor of therapeutic outcome.

The question that suggests itself is why, with the multitude of outcome studies that have been published, so very few have examined outcome with respect to gender. It is not because women have been excluded from such studies, at least as patients; nor is it because reliable and valid measures of patient or therapist gender are undeveloped. The answer (which, of course, is no real answer) is simply that researchers have not wanted or have not thought to ask the questions posed in 1970 by Meltzoff and Kornreich and now again being addressed in this volume. Personally, we are inclined to believe that researchers just have not thought to ask the question, since they have never shown great reluctance to study anything, important or trivial, that could be easily measured. We suspect that the problem lies in the fact that researchers have followed the dominant cultural and professional tendency to view psychotherapy as a technical medical or psychological procedure, that is, as something persons trained in a body of knowledge and skills do to other persons who require their services. Viewed in this perspective, the role attributes (e.g., orientation or diagnosis) of the therapists and patients seem most salient, while the person attributes (e.g., gender) appear to be peripheral.

There does exist an indeterminately large body of outcome data in the files of researchers who are sufficiently compulsive or honest not to have destroyed their records once their results were published. Very probably the sex of the patients and therapists in these samples was recorded, along with other salient demographic characteristics. It should be easy enough for these researchers to reanalyze their data, and tempting enough if another publication could be wrung from them. We urge them to do so and, in the same spirit, urge investigators in ongoing or contemplated outcome studies to do the simple statistical analyses that will bring forth new information on the relation of gender to therapeutic outcome.

New Findings from Old Data: Therapist Sex
and Patient Outcome

To show that our last suggestion is made in good faith, and to offer an
example of what can be done by reanalyzing existing data, we present
some new results from data originally collected between 1965 and 1967
at the Katharine Wright Clinic in Chicago, Illinois (Howard, Orlinsky, &
Hill, 1969; Orlinsky & Howard, 1975). The original study focused prin-
cipally on psychotherapeutic process and on input variables predictive of
various types of therapeutic experience. All of the approximately 150
patients studied were women, simply by the historical accident that Dr.
Wright initially established the clinic at the Women's and Children's
Hospital (it is currently part of the Illinois Masonic Medical Center), and
the therapists who treated them were 16 men and 10 women. In 1964,
when the project was conceived, active concern with women's issues was
not very strong either in the public mind or in our own (the "movement"
then was the civil rights movement), and we thought of our research
subjects as patients and therapists rather than as women and men. Ten
years later, women's issues were much on our minds, and we undertook
to reanalyze our process data from this perspective (Orlinsky & Howard,
1976).

     At about the same time, we began to rue our initial disinclination to
collect outcome data and tried to see what could be recovered in that
domain. The patients in our sample could not be found in sufficient
numbers, due in part to the distressing habit that women have of changing their names when they change their marital status. We were left to
work as best we could from clinic case records, which typically included
separate diagnostic evaluations at intake by a social worker and a psychiatrist, a diagnosis and treatment recommendation made by the clinic
director at the initial case conference, along with the therapist's session-
by-session process notes, quarterly treatment summaries, closing note,
and ratings of patient condition and prognosis at termination. To quantify the information contained in these records, we devised a series of
scales for use by two independent clinical raters. These were (1) assessments of specific problems or symptoms at intake and at termination; ratings of the degree to which patients achieved (2) insight or
understanding of their problems and (3) relief from emotional distress;
ratings of (4) the degree of patients' personal integration and (5) the
quality of their interpersonal relationships; and (6) a global outcome
assessment by the independent raters. Interrater reliabilities on the
separate components (1 through 6) ranged from +.74 to +.82 (median
$r = +.76$); intercorrelations among specific components ranged from

+.60 to +.83 (median r = +.70); correlations of the specific components (2 through 5) with global outcome ranged from +.84 to +.91. The final outcome measure used was an equally weighted composite of (1) symptom improvement and (6) global outcome. It is based primarily on observations recorded by therapists and diagnosticians and is accordingly selectively biased by their perspective, but it is *not* a rating made directly by the therapists. Outcome measured in this way was found to be positively and significantly (though moderately) correlated with patients' own global ratings of their condition in their final sessions.

This is not an elegant outcome measure. It falls far short of the ideal for outcome evaluation that we have advanced earlier in this chapter. The measure confounds descriptive analysis and value judgment in the usual way and leaves both relatively nonspecific. But it is at least comparable (even favorably comparable) with outcome measures found in most published research, and it has the merit of permitting us to explore some interesting questions.

Outcomes for 147 patients who had at least three sessions of therapy were rated, and the composite measure showed 7% "worse," 13% "unchanged," 76% "improved," and 35% (of the total) "considerably improved." These figures do not distinguish between women treated by male and female therapists. For 91 patients treated by 16 male therapists, 8% were worse, 21% unchanged, 71% improved, and 31% (of the total) considerably improved. For 56 patients treated by 10 female therapists, 5% were worse, 14% unchanged, 81% improved, and 40% (of the total) considerably improved. Thus, we have a modest deterioration and a respectable improvement rate, with a statistically nonsignificant trend for more women to improve, and to improve more, when treated by women therapists. This finding in itself is unremarkable and rather like those of other studies, but the matter becomes more interesting when interactions between outcome, gender, and other input variables are considered.

In the reanalysis of our process data (Orlinsky & Howard, 1976), we distinguished patients according to diagnostic and life-status categories in order to see if having a male or female therapist had a differential impact for various types of female patients. Following the same procedure with our outcome data, we obtained the results shown in Tables 1 and 2. (Diagnostic and life-status categories were cross-tabulated and appeared to be relatively unconfounded.) Table 1 shows outcome by sex of therapist for patients diagnosed as depressive reactions (46% of the sample), anxiety reactions (14%), schizophrenics (15%—both ambulatory schizophrenics and schizoids), and personality disturbances (25%—both personality disorders and passive–aggressive personalities). In our

Table 1. Outcome for Male and Female Therapists by Patient Diagnosis

Diagnosis	n^a	% worse	% same	% improved	% considerably improved
Depressive reaction					
Male therapist	43	5	23	72	30
Female therapist	26	8	23	69	31
Anxiety reaction					
Male therapist	13	15	15	69	46
Female therapist	8	0	12	88	63
Schizophrenic					
Male therapist	14	14	43	43	14
Female therapist	9	0	11	89	56
Personality disturbance					
Male therapist	24	4	12	83	33
Female therapist	14	7	7	86	43

[a] Number of patients.

process data, patients diagnosed as depressive reactions showed the most marked sensitivity to therapist gender (women with female therapists had the most positive experiences), but in terms of outcome the patients treated by male and female therapists were virtually equally well off. So, too, were patients diagnosed as personality disturbances. These two

Table 2. Outcome for Male and Female Therapists by Patient Life Status

Life status	n^a	% worse	% same	% improved	% considerably improved
Young single women					
Male therapist	36	14	19	67	36
Female therapist	11	9	0	91	27
Single women					
Male therapist	16	0	31	69	25
Female therapist	8	0	38	62	50
Young family women					
Male therapist	13	0	46	54	23
Female therapist	8	0	12	88	38
Family women					
Male therapist	11	0	9	91	36
Female therapist	10	10	0	90	70
Single parents					
Male therapist	8	12	0	88	50
Female therapist	12	8	17	75	33

[a] Number of patients.

diagnostic categories account for a reassuring majority of cases in our sample. However, there was a marked advantage for the anxiety reactions, and a very dramatic advantage for the schizophrenic women, in having a female therapist. Of the 23 schizophrenic women, 14% were worse with male therapists and 0% with female therapists; 43% were unchanged with male therapists but only 11% with female therapists; 43% were improved with male therapists, while 89% with female therapists improved; and only 14% (of the total) with male but 56% with female therapists were considerably improved. The numbers involved are small and the criterion is less than ideal, but a minority of such patients were improved at all with male therapists, whereas a majority were considerably improved with female therapists. That seems impressive enough to merit further study.

The life-status categories consisted of an ad hoc grouping of female patients by age, marital status, and parental status into the following types: young single women (32%—age 18-24, not married, not mothers); single women (16%—age 25-31, not married, not mothers); young family women (14%—age 20-30, married, mothers); family women (14%—age 32-60, married, mothers); and single parents (14%—age 22-52, not married, mothers). All but a few patients fit into one or another of these groups. Table 2 shows the differential effects on outcome for these women of having a male or female therapist. Interestingly, the only women who fared better with a male therapist than with a female were the single parents. Family women did about as well with male as with female therapists in overall improvement, but 70% of those with females as opposed to 36% of those with males were considerably improved. Those women who most clearly benefitted from having a female therapist were the single women and the young single women, which confirms the impression left by the comparable analysis of our process data. A similar but less dramatic trend appeared with the young family women.

Since these results tended to favor female over male therapists, we thought it desirable to know how uniform the effect was within groups. Table 3 shows the average outcome ratings for patients of individual male and female therapists, each of whom treated three or more cases. It is instantly obvious that some male therapists were as good with women as their female colleagues but that the women were much more consistent. Following the lead of *Consumer Reports* magazine, we decided to set some arbitrary standards for therapist quality. Those therapists of whose patients at least 70% were improved, at least 33% considerably improved, and less than 10% worse were "√-rated" as reasonably safe and effective. Those who met that standard, but of whose patients at least

Table 3.   Outcome for Individual Therapists

Therapist	n^a	% worse	% same	% improved	% considerably improved	"Consumer" rating
Male
A	3	0	0	100	67	√+
B	16	0	12	88	38	√
C	6	0	17	83	50	√+
D	6	0	17	83	33	√
E	11	9	9	82	55	√+
F	5	0	20	80	40	√+
G	4	0	25	75	25	
H	3	0	33	67	0	
I	3	0	33	67	0	
J	9	11	33	56	0	
K	8	13	37	50	25	X
L	4	25	25	50	50	X
M	7	14	43	43	14	X
N	3	33	33	33	0	X
Female
O	7	0	0	100	43	√+
P	3	0	0	100	33	√
Q	3	0	0	100	33	√
R	7	0	14	86	29	
S	13	8	7	85	38	√
T	4	0	25	75	25	
U	4	0	25	75	25	
V	11	9	18	73	73	√+
W	3	33	33	33	0	X

^{a} Number of patients.

50% were considerably improved, or at least 40% were considerably improved with none at all worse, received a "√+" rating. Finally, those of whose patients 50% or less were improved and more than 10% were worse were "X-rated" as therapists whom women should probably avoid. By these arbitrary but practical standards, six male therapists were √-rated (four √+) and four were X-rated; five female therapists were √-rated (two √+) and only one was X-rated.

Since it is obviously impossible to publish the names of these therapists, we tried to find some other way of distinguishing between the better and worse, especially among males. Profession was not a factor: The best women were psychiatrists and social workers (no female psychologists happened to be in the sample); and while the four X-rated males were all psychiatrists, the best male therapists included psychiatrists and psychologists. Nor was age a factor. However, we found that level of experience made a definite difference in outcome among male

Table 4. Outcome for Male and Female Therapists by Experience

Therapist	n^a	% worse	% same	% improved	% considerably improved
Male					
2–6 years	52	12	29	60	21
7+ years	39	3	10	87	44
Female					
2–6 years	24	4	17	79	29
7+ years	32	6	12	81	50

[a] Number of patients.

therapists. Table 4 presents outcome data for male and female therapists who were highly experienced (7 or more years) or moderately experienced (2–6 years). Six years was the median level of experience among therapists in the sample; there were no really inexperienced therapists. It is clear that highly experienced males were as good as female therapists, that moderately and highly experienced female therapists did about equally well, and that all three of these groups were reassuringly effective (4% worse, 13% unchanged, 83% improved, 42% considerably improved). The moderately experienced males had at least twice the others' rate of worse and unchanged patients and half the others' rate of considerably improved patients.

To see if experience counted for the poorer performance of male therapists with patients in specific diagnostic and life-status categories, we recomputed outcome within these groups separately for patients of moderately and highly experienced male therapists (see Table 5). The numbers are relatively small with so fine a breakdown, but it does appear that experience level among male therapists made a substantial difference in our sample. Highly experienced male therapists did very well with anxiety reactions and fairly well with schizophrenic women, in both cases much better than their moderately experienced counterparts. Similarly, highly experienced male therapists did very well with single women and young single women and fairly well with young family women.

On whom are male therapists to practice until they become highly experienced? Perhaps on male patients, although we cannot say this from our own data. Our data do suggest that they are relatively safe and helpful with family women and single parents, especially with women who are older than they are, and perhaps with those who also show relatively low levels of manifest anxiety (depressive reactions and personality disturbances rather than anxiety reactions and schizophrenics).

Table 5.   Outcome for Male Therapists by Experience and by Patient Diagnosis and Life Status

Patient category	n^a	% worse	% same	% improved	% considerably improved
Depressive reaction					
2–6 years	17	6	29	65	29
7+ years	23	4	13	83	35
Anxiety reaction					
2–6 years	10	20	20	60	40
7+ years	3	0	0	100	67
Schizophrenic					
2–6 years	11	18	46	36	9
7+ years	3	0	33	67	33
Personality disturbance					
2–6 years	14	7	21	71	7
7+ years	10	0	0	100	60
Young single women					
2–6 years	22	23	23	54	23
7+ years	14	0	14	86	57
Single women					
2–6 years	11	0	46	54	0
7+ years	5	0	0	100	80
Young family women					
2–6 years	7	0	57	43	14
7+ years	6	0	33	67	33
Family women					
2–6 years	5	0	20	80	60
7+ years	6	0	0	100	17
Single parents					
2–6 years	4	25	0	75	50
7+ years	4	0	0	100	50

[a] Number of patients.

Special training to familiarize these therapists with the psychology of women's experiences might also be worth a test.

A similar trend of interaction between therapist gender and experience level in relation to outcome was found in another imperfect but comparatively large-scale study by Kirshner et al. (1979). Of former patients at the Harvard University health service, both male and female, 189 responded to a retrospective questionnaire concerning their treatment with 17 male and 5 female therapists (all but 2 being psychiatrists). Kirshner et al. found that patients' ratings of satisfaction with their therapy were approximately equal for junior and senior female therapists and for senior male therapists but noticeably lower for junior male therapists. As with our own sample, senior therapists were highly experienced (more than 10 years), while junior therapists were moderately experienced (2–5 years), and the numbers involved did not permit reaching impressive levels of statistical significance. Two differences between the studies were that the outcome measure used by Kirshner *et al.* was a global rating made by patients and that patients with whom the effect was found were both male and female.

Two swallows do not make a summer, but they do make a gulp. One might not, therefore, rush to change clinical practice on the basis of such tentative findings, but they should at least provide an incentive for planning more extensive and more sophisticated research on the apparently complex relation of gender to psychotherapeutic outcome.

Recommendations for Future Research

1. Review and reconstruct outcome evaluation procedures generally, in order (a) to separate descriptive analysis from value judgment as task components; (b) to fairly sample the various descriptive categories of the patient's life and person that are relevant to the type of patients and the therapeutic methods being studied—before, during, and after treatment, so as to establish the proportion of variance in patient changes that is plausibly attributable to specific aspects of therapeutic process; and (c) to identify the partisan interests and the qualitative and quantitative value standards used by them in judging patient changes resulting from therapy.

2. Identify the descriptive dimensions of the patient's life and person that are salient for women and men as patients, as well as those that are differentially relevant to men and women in contemporary society.

3. Identify the probable value biases in various partisan perspectives as these are likely to differentially affect evaluative judgments of changes in men and women, in relation to both the qualitative standards they employ and the quantitative standards of achievement that they expect.

4. Recognize the likelihood that the gender variable operates in conjunction with other characteristics of patients and therapists, that interaction effects rather than main effects of gender are to be expected. For example, interactions between patient gender and diagnostic and life-status categories and between therapist gender and experience seem, on the basis of preliminary evidence, to be promising targets for further research.

5. Identify the significant subpopulations of males and females who become participants in psychotherapy as patients and as therapists by exploring the intercorrelations among various input variables, so that valid and generalizable comparisons can be made between truly comparable groups of men and women and between diverse groups of women (or men).

6. Encourage new research projects on therapeutic outcome (e.g., those being funded by the National Institute of Mental Health) to include analyses of gender effects in their design.

7. Test the feasibility of recovering and reanalyzing data relevant to gender effects from the better research projects that have been completed during the past two or three decades.

References

Alexander, F. M. *The resurrection of the body.* New York: Delta, 1974.

Cartwright, D. S. Success in psychotherapy as a function of certain actuarial variables. *Journal of Consulting Psychology,* 1955, *19,* 357-363.

Cartwright, R. D., & Lerner, B. Empathy, need to change, and improvement with psychotherapy. *Journal of Consulting Psychology,* 1963, *27,* 138-144.

Dell, C. *A primer for movement description.* New York: Dance Notation Bureau Press, 1977.

Ellis, A. The effectiveness of psychotherapy with individuals who have severe homosexual problems. *Journal of Consulting Psychology,* 1956, *20,* 191-195.

Esterson, A., Cooper, D. G., & Laing, R. D. Results of family-oriented therapy with hospitalized schizophrenics. *British Medical Journal,* 1965, *2,* 1462-1465.

Friedman, J. H. Short-term psychotherapy of "phobia of travel." *American Journal of Psychotherapy,* 1950, *4,* 259-278.

Garfield, S. Research on client variables in psychotherapy. In S. Garfield & A. Bergin (Eds.), *Handbook of psychotherapy and behavior change.* New York: Wiley, 1978.

Garfield, S., & Bergin, A. (Eds.). *Handbook of psychotherapy and behavior change.* New York: Wiley, 1978.

Gaylin, N. Psychotherapy and psychological health: A Rorschach structure and function analysis. *Journal of Consulting Psychology,* 1966, *30,* 494-500.

Geer, C. A., & Hurst, J. C. Counselor–subject sex variables in systematic desensitization. *Journal of Counseling Psychology,* 1976, *23,* 276-301.

Gluck, M. R., Tanner, M. M., Sullivan, D. F., & Erickson, P. Follow-up evaluation of 55 child guidance cases. *Behaviour Research and Therapy,* 1964, *2,* 131-134.

Goldenholz, N. The effect of the sex of therapist–client dyad upon outcome of psychotherapy. *Dissertation Abstracts International,* 1976, *36,* 4687B-4688B.

Gottman, J., & Markman, H. J. Experimental designs in psychotherapy research. In S. Garfield & A. Bergin (Eds.), *Handbook of psychotherapy and behavior change.* New York: Wiley, 1978.

Grantham, R. J. Effects of counselor sex, race, and language style on black students in initial interviews. *Journal of Counseling Psychology* 1973, *20,* 553-559.

Gurman, A., & Razin, A. (Eds.). *Effective psychotherapy.* New York: Pergamon, 1977.

Hallowell, A. I. *Culture and experience.* New York: Schocken, 1967.

Hamburg, D. A., Bibring, G. L., Fisher, C., Stanton, A. H., Wallerstein, R. S., Weinstock, H. I., & Haggard, E. Report of Ad Hoc Committee on Central Fact-Gathering Data of the American Psychoanalytic Association. *Journal of the American Psychoanalytic Association,* 1967, *15,* 841-861.

Hamilton, D. M., Varney, H. I., & Wall, J. H. Hospital treatment of patients with neurotic disorders. *American Journal of Psychiatry*, 1942, *99*, 243–247.

Hare, M. K. Shortened treatment in a child guidance clinic: The results in 119 cases. *British Journal of Psychiatry*, 1966, *112*, 613–616.

Hill, C. E. Sex of client and sex and experience level of counselor. *Journal of Counseling Psychology*, 1975, *22*, 6–11.

Howard, K. I., & Orlinsky, D. E. Psychotherapeutic processes. *Annual Review of Psychology*, 1972, *23*, 615–668.

Howard, K. I., Orlinsky, D. E., & Hill, J. A. Content of dialogue in psychotherapy. *Journal of Consulting Psychology*, 1969, *16*, 396–404.

Howard, K. I., Orlinsky, D. E., & Hill, J. A. Patients' satisfaction in psychotherapy as a function of patient–therapist pairing. *Psychotherapy: Theory, Research, and Practice*, 1970, *7*, 130–134.

Johnson, M. An approach to feminist therapy. *Psychotherapy: Theory, Research, and Practice*, 1976, *13*, 72–76.

Katahn, M., Strenger, S., & Cherry, N. Group counseling and behavior therapy with test-anxious college students. *Journal of Consulting Psychology*, 1966, *30*, 544–549.

Kaufman, I., Frank, T., Friend, J., Heims, I. W., & Weiss, R. Success and failure in the treatment of childhood schizophrenia. *American Journal of Psychiatry*, 1962, *118*, 909–913.

Kirshner, L. A., Genack, A., & Hauser, S. T. Effects of gender on short-term psychotherapy. *Psychotherapy: Theory, Research, and Practice*, 1979, *15*, 158–167.

Klein, M. H. Feminist concepts of therapy outcome. *Psychotherapy: Theory, Research, and Practice*, 1976, *13*, 89–95.

Knapp, P. H., Levin, S., McCarter, R. H., Wermer, H., & Zetzel, E. Suitability for psychoanalysis: A review of 100 supervised analytic cases. *Psychoanalytic Quarterly*, 1960, *29*, 459–477.

Krause, M., & Howard, K. I. Program evaluation in the public interest. *Community Mental Health Journal*, 1976, *12*, 291–300.

Lazarus, A. A. The results of behavior therapy in 126 cases of severe neurosis. *Behavior Research and Therapy*, 1963, *1*, 69–79.

Levitt, E. E., Beiser, H. R., & Robertson, R. E. A follow-up evaluation of cases treated at a community child guidance clinic. *American Journal of Orthopsychiatry*, 1959, *29*, 337–349.

Lowen, A. *Bioenergetics*. New York: Penguin, 1975.

Luff, M. C., & Garrod, M. The after-results of psychotherapy in 500 adult cases. *British Medical Journal*, 1935, *2*, 54–59.

McCall, G. J., & Simmons, J. L. *Identities and interactions*. New York: The Free Press, 1966.

Meltzoff, J., & Kornreich, M. *Research in psychotherapy*. New York: Atherton, 1970.

Mintz, J., Luborsky, L., & Auerbach, A. H. Dimensions of psychotherapy: A factor-analytic study of ratings of psychotherapy sessions. *Journal of Consulting and Clinical Psychology*, 1971, *36*, 106–120.

Mintz, J., O'Brien, C. P., & Luborsky, L. Predicting the outcome of psychotherapy for schizophrenics. *Archives of General Psychiatry*, 1976, *33*, 1183–1186.

Norkus, A. G. Sex of therapist as a variable in short-term therapy with female college students. *Dissertation Abstracts International*, 1976, *36*, 6361B–6362B.

Orlinsky, D. E., & Howard, K. I. *Varieties of psychotherapeutic experience*. New York: Teachers College Press, 1975.

Orlinsky, D. E., & Howard, K. I. The effect of sex of therapist on the therapeutic experiences of women. *Psychotherapy: Theory, Research, and Practice*, 1976, *13*, 82–88.

Orlinsky, D. E., & Howard, K. I. The relation of process to outcome in psychotherapy. In S. Garfield & A. Bergin (Eds.), *Handbook of psychotherapy and behavior change*. New York: Wiley, 1978.

Osgood, C. E., Suci, G. J., & Tannenbaum, P. H. *The measurement of meaning*. Urbana, Ill.: University of Illinois Press, 1957.

Pardes, H., Papernik, D. S., & Winston, A. Field differentiation in inpatient psychotherapy. *Archives of General Psychiatry,* 1974, *31,* 311–315.

Parloff, M. B., Waskow, I. E., & Wolfe, B. E. Research on therapist variables in relation to process and outcome. In S. Garfield & A. Bergin (Eds.), *Handbook of psychotherapy and behavior change.* New York: Wiley, 1978.

Persons, R. W., Persons, M. K., & Newmark, I. Perceived helpful therapists' characteristics, client improvements, and sex of therapist and client. *Psychotherapy: Theory, Research, and Practice,* 1974, *11,* 63–65.

Rachman, S. Studies in desensitization: I. The separate effects of relaxation and desensitization. *Behaviour Research and Therapy,* 1965, *3,* 245–251.

Ricks, D. F., Wandersman, A., & Poppen, P. J. *Humanism and behaviorism: Dialogue and growth.* New York: Pergamon, 1976.

Rodriguez, A., Rodriguez, M., & Eisenberg, L. The outcome of school phobia: A follow-up study based on 41 cases. *American Journal of Psychiatry,* 1959, *116,* 540–544.

Rogers, C. R., & Dymond, R. F. (Eds.). *Psychotherapy and personality change.* Chicago: University of Chicago Press, 1954.

Rosenbaum, M., Friedlander, J., & Kaplan, S. M. Evaluation of results of psychotherapy. *Psychosomatic Medicine,* 1956, *18,* 113–132.

Rosenthal, D., & Frank, J. D. The fate of psychiatric clinic outpatients assigned to psychotherapy. *Journal of Nervous and Mental Disease,* 1958, *127,* 330–343.

Scher, M. Verbal activity, sex, counselor experience, and success in counseling. *Journal of Counseling Psychology,* 1975, *22,* 97–101.

Schmidt, E., Castell, D., & Brown, P. A retrospective study of 42 cases of behavior therapy. *Behaviour Research and Therapy,* 1965, *3,* 9–19.

Seeman, J. Counselor judgments of therapeutic process and outcome. In C. R. Rogers & R. F. Dymond (Eds.), *Psychotherapy and personality change.* Chicago: University of Chicago Press, 1954.

Sobel, R. The private practice of child psychiatry: A ten-year study. *American Journal of Psychotherapy,* 1962, *16,* 567–579.

Strassberg, D. S., & Anchor, K. N. Ratings of client self-disclosure and improvement as a function of sex of client and therapist. *Journal of Clinical Psychology,* 1977, *33,* 239–241.

Sullivan, P. L., Miller, C., & Smelser, W. Factors in length of stay and progress in psychotherapy. *Journal of Consulting Psychology,* 1958, *1,* 1–9.

Warren, W. A study of adolescent psychiatric inpatients and the outcome six or more years later: II. The follow-up study. *Journal of Child Psychology and Psychiatry,* 1965, *6,* 141–160.

Zeldow, P. B. Sex differences in psychiatric evaluation and treatment. *Archives of General Psychiatry,* 1978, *35,* 89–93.

CHAPTER 2

Therapist Attitudes
and Sex-Role Stereotyping

JULIA A. SHERMAN

This review deals with therapists' attitudes toward women and sex-role stereotyping of women, particularly in their role as patient. There are several other reviews, commentaries, and critiques of this literature (Abramowitz & Dokecki, 1977; APA Task Force, 1975; Gingras-Baker, 1976; Rauch, 1978; Schlossberg & Pietrofesa, 1973; Stricker, 1977; Tanney & Birk, 1976; Voss & Gannon, 1978; Zeldow, 1975). Some preview of the findings may be gained from the conclusion of Zeldow (1975): "The results . . . are sufficiently diverse and ambiguous as to be interpretable both as strong and weak evidence for sexism in the mental health field, depending on the point of view of the interpreter. The fairest statement that can probably be made at present is that" (p. 93).

Studies of effects of the sex of the therapists and sex-related differences among therapists will not be included in this review (see Kirshner, 1978; Parloff, Waskow, & Wolfe, 1971). Results of therapist sex-related differences in attitudes toward women, however, will be noted. Studies of judgments from test results or personality judgments of "normal" individuals also will not be included (Haan & Livson, 1973; see also Werner & Block, 1975), nor will studies that have used undergraduates or other nontherapists as subjects. Results from studies of therapists in training will be included, however. "Therapist" has been broadly defined, including psychiatrists, psychologists, counselors, and social workers. Some samples also included nurses, teachers, and medical students. Subjects, however, have been described as accurately as possible so that the reader may differentiate between these subject groups if desired. Questions of sexual contact with the patient and of sex bias as additionally related to social class, ethnic group, sexual orientation, age, and handicap are beyond the scope of this review.

Julia A. Sherman. Madison Psychiatric Associates, Madison, Wisconsin.

This review is organized historically and by topic. Over 50 studies are included. First the work of Broverman and her colleagues (Broverman, Broverman, Clarkson, Rosenkrantz, & Vogel, 1970) and studies using a similar technique are reviewed, and then studies of direct assessments of therapists' attitudes are considered. Before proceeding to a review of the analogue studies, the reaction to the first two sets of studies is discussed, and research strategies are examined for their relevance to the question. Finally, the analogue studies are reviewed, conclusions drawn, and recommendations given for further research.

Sex-Role Stereotyping of Mental Health Standards

Sixteen studies were located which investigated sex-role stereotyping of mental health standards, not counting studies of undergraduate students. Studies with undergraduate students as subjects were not included (in the table or in the review), since results from such studies could not reasonably bear on *therapists'* attitudes. The 16 studies are charted in Table 1. For this and all other tables, studies are listed chronologically by publication date, with studies of clinicians in training listed last. A published paper was presumed to supersede an unpublished one, and both are not included. The subjects and relevant results are described as accurately as possible, often using language from the paper itself. Subjects were of both sexes unless otherwise indicated. Some omissions and vagueness are a reflection of the reports themselves. For Tables 1 and 2, if clinicians of one sex were reported to have stereotyped significantly more than the other ($p < .05$), the sex doing so is indicated by an "M" or "F" after the results. When the original document could not be inspected, the source of information has been indicated. In the case of nearly all dissertations, only the abstracts could be examined. Interested readers are advised to obtain fuller information from the dissertations themselves.

The current interest in the topic of sex-role stereotyping of mental health standards seems to have begun with a presentation by Neulinger, later published by Neulinger, Stein, Schillinger, and Welkowitz (1970). They had 114 psychotherapists rank descriptions of Murray's needs for "optimally integrated" males and females. Therapists ranked dominance and achievement higher for males and nurturance and succorance higher for females.

The study by the Broverman team (Broverman *et al.*, 1970; Broverman, Vogel, Broverman, Clarkson, & Rosenkrantz, 1972), however, proved to be the grandmother of successive studies. They had 79 clinicians rate the Stereotype Questionnaire to describe a healthy, mature, socially competent adult, man, and woman. They found that clinicians' ratings for "healthy women differ from healthy men by being more submissive, less independent, less adventurous, more easily influenced, less aggressive, less competitive, more excitable in minor crises, having their feelings more easily hurt, being more emotional, more conceited about their appearance, less objective, and disliking math and science" (Broverman *et al.*, 1970, p. 4). It was pointed out that while there had been no difference between clinicians' descriptions of a mentally healthy (sex unspecified) adult and a mentally healthy male, the description of the mentally healthy female was different from and less healthy than that of the mentally healthy adult. It was also noted that women were in a double bind. They could be healthy and masculine or less healthy and feminine. The findings of this study became known as demonstrating a double standard of mental health.

As reported in Tanney and Birk (1976), these essential findings were confirmed by in-depth interviewing of 15 counselors (Siechta, Note 1). Counselors showed marked similarities in the terms they used to describe "typical women" and neurotic symptoms (even though over two-thirds of the subjects maintained that there were no personality differences between men and women).

Fabrikant and his colleagues (Fabrikant, 1974; Fabrikant, Landau, & Rollenhagen, 1973) conducted a series of studies which included asking therapists to assign adjectives to either the male or female role. Results of the 1973 study are not readily available but are briefly reported in Fabrikant (1974). Therapists rated 68–70% of the words assigned to the female role negatively, while 67–71% of the words assigned to the male role were rated positively. In another study, 31 therapists were asked to rate adjectives as descriptive of the male or female role. Once again, male role characteristics were seen as positive and female role characteristics as "strongly negative," though Fabrikant thought he saw some evidence of fewer prejudicial attitudes than in the previous study, suggesting more liberal attitudes over time. Goldberg (1973), however, found no marked prejudicial sex-linked attitudes toward mental health standards among 184 clinical psychologists. Essentially negative findings were also reported by Maxfield (1976) and Kahn (1976), both of whom used the Stereotype Questionnaire with 129 and 264 therapists, respectively. Kahn, however, found that male therapists stereotyped more than female therapists, a result also obtained by Aslin (1977) using the Stereotype Questionnaire with 212 therapists.

Delk and Ryan (1975, 1977) found stereotyping related to "A–B" status and sex. "A" therapists (more authoritarian?) and male therapists

Table 1. Studies of Sex-Role Stereotyping of Mental Health Standards by Subjects and Chronology[a]

Study and subjects	Method	Results and comment
Neulinger et al. (1970) Psychotherapists (n = 114)	Ranked Murray needs for optimally integrated males and females	Males higher for dominance, achievement; females for nurturance and succorance
Broverman et al. (1970) Clinicians (n = 79)	Rated Stereotype Questionnaire for healthy, mature adult, man, woman	For example, women more submissive, less independent, less aggressive, more emotional, less objective
Siechta (Note 1) (1971) Therapists (n = ?)	Interview	"Marked similarities between the terms . . . to describe 'typical women' and . . . neurotic symptoms" (Tanney & Birk, 1976, p. 29)
Fabrikant et al. (1973) Therapists (n = ?)	Assigned adjectives to either male or female role	Therapists rated 68–70% of female words negatively and 67–71% of male words positively (Fabrikant, 1974)
Goldberg (1973) Clinical psychologists (n = 184)	Questionnaire about mental health standards	"No marked prejudicial . . . sex-linked attitudes"—M (p. 1018B)
Fabrikant (1974) Therapists (n = 31)	Rated adjectives as descriptive of male or female role	"Male characteristics . . . seen as positive, female as strongly negatively" (p. 105)
Cowan (1976) Therapists (n = 30)	Stereotype Questionnaire rated for which pole a problem for average male and female clients	Female clients seen as too feminine

Study	Part of Stereotype Questionnaire	Results[a]
Kahn (1976) Therapists ($n = 129$)	Part of Stereotype Questionnaire	"Today's clinicians more likely to expect same characteristics"—M (p. 3613B)
Maxfield (1976) Division 29 therapists ($n = 264$)	Stereotype Questionnaire	"No overall bias against women" (p. 1914B)
Aslin (1977) Therapists ($n = 212$)	Stereotype Questionnaire	"Male therapists perceived mentally healthy adults in more male-valued terms"—M (p. 537)
Billingsley (1977) Therapists ($n = 64$)	Stereotype Questionnaire	More feminine treatment goals *not* assigned female protocol
Delk & Ryan (1977) Therapists ($n = 80$)	Stereotype Questionnaire (adapted)	"Male subjects stereotyped significantly more"—M (p. 253); therapists stereotyped less than students, patients
Delk & Ryan (1975) Therapists, nursing and medical students ($n = 76$)	Stereotype Questionnaire (adapted)	Stereotyping related to "A-B" status "A" stereotype more
Maslin & Davis (1975) Counselors in training ($n = 90$)	Stereotype Questionnaire	"Male subjects . . . held a more stereotypically feminine standard for healthy females"—M (p. 87)
Harris & Lucas (1976) Social work students ($n = 345$)	Stereotype Questionnaire	No difference between healthy man, woman, person—M
Dreman (1978) Israeli therapists ($n = 60$)	Stereotype Questionnaire	"Healthy female . . . more stereotypically feminine"—F (p. 961)

[a] If one sex stereotyped significantly more than the other, $p < .05$, the sex doing so is indicated by an "M" or "F" after the results.

stereotyped more. Among counselors in training, Maslin and Davis
(1975) found that male subjects held a more stereotypically feminine
standard for healthy females (using the Stereotype Questionnaire).
Using the same classic method, Harris and Lucas (1976) also found that
male social work students stereotyped more but found no difference in
the overall group among ratings for healthy man, woman, or person.
Among Israeli therapists, females stereotyped more (Dreman, 1978).
The limits of stereotyping were demonstrated by Cowan's (1976) study
of 30 therapists, mostly male. Asked to rate which pole of the adjective
pairs of the Stereotype Questionnaire were problems for their average
male and female clients, the therapists' responses indicated that they saw
their female clients as too feminine. Similarly, Billingsley (1977) found
that more feminine treatment goals were *not* assigned to females.

Considering the 15 studies with North American subjects, only one
study (Maxfield, 1976) was apparently completely negative in the sense
of showing neither evidence of stereotyping nor evidence that males
stereotype more than females. Maxfield's research has been criticized
because of the low response rate (29%), imprecision of design (Delk,
1977), and the probability that the intent of the study was obvious to the
subjects, members of Division 29 (Gilbert, 1977). It is important to note,
however, that the double standard of mental health is not a dichoto-
mous, mutually exclusive standard of mental health, but rather a matter
of the degree to which healthy characteristics are considered as important
for females as for males (Stricker, 1977). In demonstrating this point,
the Cowan and Billingsley studies can be said to delineate the limits of
stereotyping rather than to be negative in the sense of demonstrating
that stereotyping does not exist among therapists. Male subjects did not
always stereotype more than females, but this was the case in several
studies, and there seemed to be some evidence that stereotyping declined over time. These tentative conclusions were also supported by the
results of the next set of studies which used a different methodology.

Attitudes toward Women among Therapists and Counselors

Ten studies were found that directly measured therapists' attitudes by
using questionnaires. They are charted in Table 2. Information on several studies was not sufficient to permit much more discussion of them
than is present in the table. Males were more conservative in their attitudes than females in five of the ten studies. Five studies made a particular point that attitudes about working mothers tended to be particu-

larly conservative. Four reports presented actual questionnaire items (Bingham & House, 1973; Brown & Hellinger, 1975; Engelhard, Jones, & Stiggins, 1976; Sherman, Koufacos, & Kenworthy, 1978).

As reported by Rabkin (1977), there is direct confirmation of the existence of sex-role stereotypes among therapists. Roche Laboratories (1974) sent every sixth American psychiatrist a questionnaire about attitudes toward women's liberation. Most of them (73%) believed that psychiatrists have a stereotype of the "normal healthy male" role and "normal healthy female" role, and 66% believed that psychiatrists attempt to influence their patients to "adjust" to the psychiatrists' own stereotype.

Bingham and House (1973) received responses from 126 New Jersey secondary school counselors (66% response rate). Of this group, 75% of the male counselors and 50% of the female counselors disagreed with the statement, "Employment practices clearly discriminate against women." Half of the information items were responded to incorrectly by half or more of the respondents. Some of this information had been so widely publicized that the authors speculate that negative attitudes may have influenced a selective perception process. Males were significantly less well informed than females (see also Sherman *et al.*, 1978, discussed later).

Four studies noted that counselor attitudes were more liberal than traditional. Helwig (1976) gave the Attitudes toward Women Scale (Spence, Helmreich, & Stapp, 1973) to 80 employment counselors in Wisconsin (60 males and 20 females) during in-service training meetings. The average score for males was 63; for females, 70. These scores were considerably higher (more liberal) than the normative scores for Texas college students (males 45, females 50; fathers of students 39, mothers 42). These differences are doubtless partly regional. For several reasons, however, it is unwise to assume that liberal attitudes are typical of therapists and/or counselors. None of the samples reported was a representative national sample, and in some cases samples were probably biased in a liberal direction. Also, if therapists were not going to be frank in their responses, it seems more likely that they would misrepresent themselves in a liberal rather than a conservative direction.

Engelhard *et al.* (1976) found evidence of more liberal attitudes over time. They presented data for the years 1968, 1971, and 1974 from three cross-sectional random samples of Minnesota guidance counselors. There was an unknown degree of overlap between samples, but they were treated statistically as independent samples. Questionnaires were sent by mail, return rate 82–100%. The samples ranged from 74 to 78%

Table 2. Studies of Attitudes toward Women among Therapists and Counselors[a]

Study and subjects	Method	Results and comment
Brogan (Note 2) Therapists (n = ?)	Questionnaire	"Therapists assumed a significantly liberal orientation" (Brown & Hellinger, 1975, p. 266)
Roche Laboratories (1974) Psychiatrists ($n \approx 1500$)	Questionnaire	Seventy-three percent believed psychiatrists stereotype and 66% believed this affects treatment (Rabkin, 1977)
Brown & Hellinger (1975) Canadian therapists (n = 274)	Questionnaire	"Fifty percent of all therapists . . . held a relatively traditional stance."—M (p. 270)
Sherman et al. (1978) Therapists (n = 184)	Therapists' Information about Women Scale and Therapists' Attitudes toward Women Scale	Attitudes more liberal than stereo-typed—M; females better informed; thirty-eight percent of factual items missed by half or more of subjects
Cline-Naffziger (1971) Counselors (American School Counselor Association) (n = ?)	Survey	"Counselors project women as supportive and vicariously achieving" (p. 3021A)

Bingham & House (1973) School counselors ($n = 126$)	Questionnaire of information and attitudes toward women (latter not reported)	Half of factual items missed by half or more of subjects; males less informed
Lesser (1974) School counselors ($n = 197$)	Questionnaire	Results unclear because of design problems; most conservative about childrearing responsibility
Engelhard et al. (1976) Vocational guidance counselors (1968, $n = 139$; 1971, $n = 143$; 1974, $n = 179$)	Questionnaire	Attitudes most conservative about Working Mother factor; more liberal over time—M
Helwig (1976) Employment counselors ($n = 80$)	Attitudes toward Women Scale	Generally liberal—M
Davenport & Reims (1978) Students in social work, family counseling ($n = 114$)	Brown & Hellinger (1975) scale, modified	"Responses . . . more contemporary than traditional"—M (p. 308)

[a] If one sex stereotyped significantly more than the other, $p < .05$, the sex doing so is indicated by an "M" or "F" after the results.

male. The scale measured three factors: Working Mother, Sex-Role Definition, and Societal Impact (expectation that women have a contribution to make to society). Attitudes were most conservative for the Working Mother factor. Attitudes were more conservative in 1968 than later; males were more conservative than females, and older counselors were somewhat more conservative than younger ones. These data support the general impression that attitudes have become more liberal, though it is not clear how much change could be attributed to cohort effects and how much to developmental effects. It is also unwise to assume, without supporting evidence, that attitudes will continue to become more liberal.

Sherman *et al.* (1978) reported responses of 184 Wisconsin therapists, about 29% of the listed psychologists, psychiatrists, and social worker therapists in the state. The sample was believed to be biased in the direction of more liberal persons, and, indeed, the therapists' overall attitudes were more liberal than stereotyped. The fact, however, that their information about the psychology of women did not reflect equally up-to-date views underscores the fact that response to attitude scales basically reflects what people want to tell you. Over half the subjects, all practicing clinicians with advanced degrees, failed to give the correct response to 38% of the items. In the long run, it might prove more useful to measure therapists' information about women than to measure their attitudes toward women. Information tests could easily be included in licensing, certification, and ABEPP examinations and would at least insure consumers that therapists have certain kinds of basic knowledge. An important aspect of the Therapists' Attitudes toward Women Scale and the Therapists' Information about Women Scale is that the items were based on attitudes and information relevant to therapy and sensitive to bias. The items reflected information emerging from the American Psychological Association Task Force on Sex Bias and Sex-Role Stereotyping in Psychotherapeutic Practice (1975). Female therapists were significantly better informed ($p < .01$) and more liberal in their attitudes ($p < .05$) than male therapists.

The results of these studies are consistent with those in the Broverman tradition—there is evidence of stereotyping. Most of the studies showed at least some evidence of stereotyping, and many showed evidence that males stereotype more than females. There was also some evidence that older persons and those with a Freudian theoretical orientation have more conservative views. Therapists' attitudes toward women do seem to have become more liberal over time, a change which probably reflects overall developments in the culture. Therapists' lack of information underscores the need for educational improvement.

Bias about Bias?

From the point of view of the sociology of knowledge, it is instructive to note the role of values in the way in which research in sex-role stereotyping has been assessed (Sherif, 1979). In the field of sex-related differences in cognition, the point has frequently been made that it is not possible to prove a null hypothesis, hence, impossible to prove that females are not inferior to males in intellectual functioning (for further discussion, see Sherman, 1978). Studies that did not show sex-related differences in cognition have often been discounted or disbelieved (or not even published to begin with). In the area of sex bias in psycho-therapeutic practice, however, one finds a willingness to ignore even results with a .05 probability, a practice rare in psychological research (though not *necessarily* inappropriate). Many studies have examined the question of sex bias with irrelevant variables (or definitions of concepts) and then announced that they have "refuted contentions of bias." Hypotheses must emerge from relevant observation. Further research needs to apply these insights to cogently constructed research designs.

One important reaction took the form of, "There may be evidence of bias in attitudes or stereotyping of mental health, but there is no evidence that this actually adversely affects the outcome of therapy". On the surface, this seems to be a reasonable response, until one reflects upon the fact that psychologists generally assume that what people think affects their behavior, albeit not in any one-to-one fashion. Demands for proof that sex bias adversely affects the outcome of psychotherapy become even more questionable when one realizes that many hard-minded persons do not think that there is any convincing evidence that psychotherapy does anyone any good. Is it reasonable, then, to expect demonstration of such a relative nuance as that sexist therapy damages women or is not as effective for them as nonsexist therapy? Later on, I will discuss research strategies; let me now note, however, that *no* study was found relating sexist therapy to outcome, and *no* process studies of actual therapists dealing with actual patients were found.

Studies of Actual Therapists and Patients

Two of the earliest studies are the only ones that approached a methodology giving information about how real clinicians deal with real clients. The first study, by Pietrofesa and Schlossberg (1970; Schlossberg & Pietrofesa, 1973), had 16 male and 16 female counselor trainees interview a bogus female client who ostensibly could not decide between a career in teaching or a career in engineering. The interviews were audiotaped and rated for bias. Of the total biased statements, 81% were against the client entering an engineering career and 19% for it. Both male and female counselors showed evidence of bias against a woman entering the "male" profession of engineering.

The study by Fabrikant (1974) and his colleagues, however, is the only one dealing with actual therapists and actual patients. For this reason, it will be described in some detail, and difficulties in conducting this kind of study will be noted. While 50 therapists were asked to participate, twice as many male as female therapists actually participated, introducing a potential source of bias. Each therapist was asked to have both a male and female patient participate, but twice as many female as male patients participated, another potential source of bias. Therapists were asked to respond to both a list of questions and a list of words describing the sex-role traits, rating the intensity of each word as it applied to either or both male and female (results in Table 1). Each therapist was also asked to have both a male and female patient complete the same form as the therapist, as well as to answer additional questions as to *how the therapist came across to the patient,* and to return them to the research team without discussion with the therapist. One potential source of bias stemmed from the therapists' selection of the patients and another from the fact that Fabrikant received twice as many responses from female patients as male.

The data of greatest interest here are the females' descriptions of their therapists in regard to the therapists' views of marriage and sex role in general and the discrepancies between the views of therapists and patients. These patients had been in therapy for an average of 5.7 years, so they had ample opportunity to learn of their therapists' views. For example, male therapists stated that the majority of women can be satisfied and fulfilled by the wife/mother role and that a decision on abortion should be a joint one between husband and wife, but female patients (and therapists) disagreed. Therapists and patients differed in their perceptions of the therapists' beliefs. Therapists felt that, if one is married, then the marriage should be a partnership. Female patients, however, reported that the therapists' attitude was that the male should dominate the marital relationship. The patients also did not believe that therapists held a single standard of sexual behavior for marital partners, despite therapists' verbalizations to that effect. These results highlight potential areas of conflict between the values of therapists and their female patients.

Fabrikant observed that both the women therapists and the women patients had been in therapy much longer than their male counterparts (male therapists 1.8 years, female therapists 3.5 years; male patients 2.3 years, female patient 5.7 years). From this observation, Fabrikant concluded, "The overall results most strongly support the feminist viewpoint that females in therapy are victimized by a social structure and therapeutic philosophy which keeps them dependent for as long as possible. There is no rationale for a continuation of this practice, and psychotherapists of all persuasions must reexamine their philosophy, practices, and goals in the light of these findings" (Fabrikant, 1974, p. 97). While Fabrikant does seem to have a point, can we simply assume that differences in the way male and female patients are treated can be attributed to bias?

Differences in Treatment between Males and Females: Correlational Studies

In many discussions of biased treatment of women in relationship to mental disturbance, inferences of bias have been drawn on the basis of differences or apparent differences in the treatment of women. Chesler (1972), for example, cited statistics to indicate that more women than men have been institutionalized in mental hospitals and that more women than men have been outpatients at mental health facilities. These general facts have been confirmed by others (e.g., Gove and Tudor, 1973); however, there are several problems in interpreting these facts. It is extremely important to note that the statistics for institutionalization cited by Chesler and by Gove and Tudor refer only to persons institutionalized for purely psychic distress problems, not including, for example, those who are aggressive, alcoholic, or drug users. The excluded categories tend to be those in which males predominate, and they are also those in which the disposition may well be prison rather than psychiatric hospital. The statistics used by Chesler and by Gove and Tudor are, therefore, misleading if one infers that more females than males are institutionalized in mental hospitals or if one infers that more females than males are locked up in our society.

There are numerous other problems with statistics of institutionalization. Records are often incomplete and not comparable from time to time or place to place, and, since women live longer than men, it is necessary to take this fact into account in making comparisons. One must distinguish between incidence and prevalence, taking care not to count people who go in and out of hospitals the same as new cases. Assuming, however, that Gove and Tudor have correctly demonstrated an excess of women hospitalized with psychic distress during the recent period, note should also be made that it is not at all clear that this has been the case in the past or in other countries.

Accepting the Gove and Tudor statistics, however, can we infer that biased treatment has been accorded to women, in that a comparably ill man was not institutionalized while the woman was? Perhaps more women than men were actually ill; perhaps more men than women evaded institutionalization. While the statistics may be accurate, such data do not allow us to infer that there is something in our recent society that is making more women than men sick in these ways. Studies of sex-related differences in treatment cannot directly shed light on the attitudes of therapists toward women and their sex-role stereotyping (see Abramowitz & Dokecki, 1977). For this reason, such studies will not be included in this review.

A closer look at one of the correlational studies will illustrate the difficulties. Abramowitz, Abramowitz, Roback, Corney, and McKee (1976) in a paper titled, "Sex-Role Related Countertransference in Psychotherapy," observed the following facts from their data: Male therapists saw female patients longer than male patients, but female therapists did not see male patients longer than female patients. (Apparently, the length of time that male and female therapists saw female patients was not compared.) Male therapists saw more female than male clients, and female therapists saw more female clients. From such material, the inferences were made that male therapists might be prolonging therapy out of sexual curiosity (recall that Fabrikant, 1974, attributed the longer therapy of females to the desire to keep them dependent) and that female therapists might be avoiding treatment situations likely to arouse their sexual curiosities. In this sample, as in many others, female therapists had less training than male therapists. Because of this obvious confounding, inferences of sex-related differences are unjustified.

Abramowitz and Dokecki (1977) noted that correlational research has lower validity than other kinds of research, and for the purposes of drawing inferences of bias, this would certainly appear to be the case. Abramowitz and Dokecki described the positive results of the studies of sex-role stereotyping (Table 1) and the correlational findings (studies such as that described above and including some of the studies of diagnostic testing which are beyond the scope of this review) as the most positive evidence of bias in clinical practice to the detriment of women. In contrast, they concluded that the evidence from analogue studies was largely negative.

Counseling and Clinical Analogue Studies

The analogue study derives from experimental social psychology. It attempts to create an analogy of an actual situation, in this case, a clinical situation. The strategem permits control of factors not controllable in naturalistic circumstances, but the method has its own pitfalls. Ratings of materials are made by clinicians who presumably do not know that the aim is to look for evidence of bias. Given the popularity of the method, however, this assumption is increasingly questionable. Variations of material have been made along the dimension of sex-role appropriateness in order to test for bias, but materials often have not been checked to see that the manipulation was successful. For example, crying may be stereotypically female, but is depression? Depression, however, has been used as a stereotypical female condition. Unfortunately, the materials usually are not described in sufficient detail so that readers can form their own opinions. Some designs also vary the traditionalism of the clinician raters. If the more traditional raters show more bias, the validity of the inference that *bias* is responsible for the responses is increased (Abramowitz & Dokecki, 1977).

All studies that reported measures of traditionalism or other measures of attitudes toward women found that clinician samples were *less* traditional than the normative groups. Since the response rate was typically low, samples studied may well have been biased in being more liberal than the overall group of clinicians. While the sex of the clinician rater was varied, in most studies the number of females was smaller than the number of males, and the sex of the clinician tended to be confounded with profession differences. For this reason, little mention will be made of such findings. In general, the number of subjects per cell was often small, and, given the complex interaction effects, many of the studies may simply have found negative effects because of lack of power in the design. The dependent measures were themselves not very reliable; for example, a clinician might be asked to rate the protocol for degree of maladjustment on a four-point scale. Would the clinician rate the same way next week? We do not know.

Probably the most serious problem with many of the analogue studies, however, is their lack of cogency to the question of therapists' attitudes toward women and therapists' sex-role stereotyping of women. Some writers have confused misogyny with stereotyping and, having found that therapists do not rate women more severely or like them less than men, believe that they have "refuted" claims for their being a problem. (Publications of the Abramowitz group tend to be particularly ambivalent, sometimes noting bias, sometimes denying it.) What these studies have shown is that women qua women are not discriminated against in terms of severity, for example, of diagnosis, judgment of maladjustment, or prognosis. These studies perhaps bear on the more dramatic charges of Chesler (1972), but, as already discussed, there have been many reasons to be skeptical of those charges without doing any studies. It should be noted that many studies contain multiple dependent variables with little apparent forethought as to what a significant effect involving the variables might mean (see also Zeldow, 1975). Consequently, the results contribute little to our knowledge. In spite of these misgivings, all relevant studies have been included in this review, since most discussions of the topic have included them.

Table 3 contains eight counseling analogue studies, while Table 4 charts 16 clinical analogue studies. As with the other tables, only the aspects of the studies most relevant to the purposes of this review have been included. As before, unless otherwise noted, all studies included clinician raters of both sexes.

Some of the earliest studies came from counseling. Of the five counseling analogue studies which are judged to engage sex-role stereotyping and which showed no obvious methodological problems, all showed evidence of sex-role stereotyping. Thomas and Stewart (1971), for example, had 62 counselors listen to a tape of a female voice describing either traditional vocational goals or nontraditional ones (e.g., engineering). The woman represented by the sex-role discrepant protocol was rated as needing more counseling. Likewise, Abramowitz, Weitz, Schwartz, Amira, Gomes, and Abramowitz (1975) found that the protocol of a female aspiring to go to medical school was rated more maladjusted by traditional counselors than was the protocol of her male counterpart. Persons (1972) found that male counselor trainees predicted higher-prestige occupations for male compared to female protocols, and especially for the black male compared to the black female. Magnus (1975) concluded that graduate students viewing videotapes of traditional and nontraditional marital interactions were biased in favor of traditional interactions.

Some studies manipulated sex of the analogue, but were not judged to engage sex-role appropriateness very effectively. For example, one study varied the sex (male/female) and symptoms (anger/sadness) of the protocol. The latter, however, is a questionable manipulation of symptoms related to sex-role stereotyping. The dependent measures were counselor behaviors such as empathy and warmth. Here again, the dependent measures seem unlikely to engage the sex-role dimension. Findings were negative, but even the author questions the method (Stengel, 1976). Another study (Shapiro, 1975) used 16 graduate students to rate behavior of a live-acted client playing typical and atypical sex-role conditions. Counselor behaviors were found to be biased in favor of the bogus client in the *atypical* sex-role conditions. Insufficient detail is presented, however, to evaluate the result. For example, what were the conditions? Were they alike in social desirability? Was there a manipulation check of their typicality? Another study (Hayes & Walleat, 1978) apparently expected that sex-role stereotyping would be manifested by clinicians (in this case, graduate students) giving more feminine stereotypical ratings to the protocol of a female voice while giving more masculine stereotypical ratings to the male voice, but the method was suspect and the results difficult to interpret.

On the whole, there is evidence of bias from the counseling analogue studies that can be judged relevant and sound. Bias was noted in occupational matters as well as in traditionalism of marital interaction.

Of the 16 clinical analogue studies charted in Table 4, nine clearly showed results consistent with bias and sex-role stereotyping; other studies were unclear and/or negative. This tally does not agree with that of Abramowitz and Dokecki (1977), who stated, "Clinical analogues that have afforded a more direct test of the notion of evaluative prejudice against women have for the most part refuted it" (p. 467). The "it" they referred to cited the Broverman-type studies, but, as already indicated, evaluative prejudice and sex-role stereotyping of mental health standards are two different matters, as will be clarified in the discussion of the individual studies. Abramowitz and Dokecki cited seven studies to support their view. Three of those studies are not included here, since they dealt with clinical assessment of test data; however, the other four studies (all by the Abramowitz group) are included. It is not at all clear that these results are negative (and/or relevant). Table 4 also includes 12 studies not in their review.

Two positive studies not included in Abramowitz and Dokecki (1977) are Miller (1974) and Bowman (1976). Miller (1974) found that 67 clinicians rated a very passive protocol as better adjusted when the protocol was labeled female than when it was labeled male. Rather than interpret this as positive bias toward the female, Miller pointed out that a double standard of mental health would lead to just such an expectation, standards being higher for the male than for the female. Even more telling is the fact that there was a significant difference in the focus of therapy for the bogus male and female clients. More therapists chose passivity as the focus of therapy when the protocol was labeled male than when it was labeled female. Bowman's (1976) results are similar. She found that active as opposed to passive responses were discouraged by therapists for female protocols.

Table 3. Counseling Analogue Studies

Study and subjects	Method	Results and comment
Thomas & Stewart (1971) Counselors (n = 62)	*Independent variable:* audiotape analogue—goals appropriate and not appropriate to female role *Dependent variable:* Need for counseling	Sex-role-discrepant protocol rated as needing more counseling
Pringle (1973) High school counselors (n = 254)	*Independent variables:* subject—sex; written analogue—dependent and independent, high-achieving and low-achieving *Dependent variables:* 6 ratings	Results positive but complex
Abramowitz et al. (1975) Counselors and graduate students (n = 22)	*Independent variables:* subject—traditionalism; written analogue—sex, medical-school-aspiring or not *Dependent variables:* ratings of adjustments	Medical-school-aspiring female rated more maladjusted by traditional counselors
Persons (1972) Counselor trainees (n = 32)	*Independent variables:* subject—sex; written analogue—sex, black, and white *Dependent variable:* predicting occupation	Male counselors predicted higher-prestige occupations for male male protocol, especially black male compared to female

52

Magnus (1975) Graduate students ($n = 67$)	*Independent variables:* subject—sex, age; videotape analogue of marital couples—traditional and non-traditional *Dependent variables:* ratings	"Bias existed in favor of traditional interaction patterns" (p. 2635A)
Shapiro (1975) Graduate students ($n = 16$)	*Independent variables:* subject—sex; live-acted analogue—typical and atypical female role *Dependent variable:* rating	More behavioral bias *for* atypical bogus clients
Stengel (1976) Graduate students ($n = 60$)	*Independent variables:* subject—sex; videotape analogue—sex, angry, and sad *Dependent variables:* counselor behavior (e.g., empathy, warmth)	Sex of protocol had no effect (question method)
Hayes & Walleat (1978) Graduate students ($n = 40$)	*Independent variables:* subject—sex; audiotape analogue—sex *Dependent variable:* rating on Stereotype Questionnaire	Female protocol rated more masculine (question method)

53

Table 4. Clinical Analogue Studies[a]

Study and subjects	Method	Results and comment
Abramowitz et al. (1973) Professionals ($n = 71$)	*Independent variables*: subject—sex, political orientation; written analogue—sex, political orientation *Dependent variable*: rating of maladjustment	Left-oriented female client judged more maladjusted than her male counterpart by the less, but not by the more liberal clinicians
Miller (1974) Clinicians ($n = 67$)	*Independent variables*: subject—sex; written analogue of very passive person—sex *Dependent variables*: clinical judgments	Male seen as less healthy; passivity judged more focus of therapy for males
Libbey (1975) Psychotherapists ($n = 60$)	*Independent variables*: subject—sex; audiotape analogue—sex *Dependent variables*: 3 dimensions of therapist response	On one of two analogues, therapists showed greater positive emotion to female than male
Schwartz & Abramowitz (1975) Psychiatrists ($n = 102$)	*Independent variables*: subject—sex, experience, traditionalism; written analogue—sex, race *Dependent variables*: 8 ratings (e.g., maladjustment, prognosis, treatment recommendations)	Less traditional psychiatrists recommended less insight therapy for women than men; more experienced psychiatrists recommended drugs more for women than for men
C. V. Abramowitz et al. (1976) Professionals, very mixed ($n = 58$)	*Independent variables*: subject—sex, sex-role ideology (AWS); written analogue—sex, sex role *Dependent variables*: 4 ratings (e.g., maternal–paternal blame, need for treatment)	Subjects untraditional; mothers more to blame for feminine-role symptoms; female professionals recommended more treatment focus on mother than father; therapy recommended more for mothers of boys by sex-role-traditional professionals and by professionals as a group. Overall more maternal than paternal attribution

Abramowitz, Roback et al. (1976) Group therapists ($n = 130$)	*Independent variables*: subject—sex, values; written analogue—sex *Dependent variables*: 25 ratings (e.g., clinical impressions, responses to group-therapy incident)	Prognosis rated *better* for female; group therapy less recommended for women than men; female patient elicited more behaviorally focused reaction from traditional female therapists
Bowman (1976) Psychotherapists ($n = 61$)	*Independent variables*: subject—sex, sex-role ideology (AWS); written analogue—sex, activity–passivity *Dependent variables*: clinical assessment, therapy recommendations	Conservative therapists more stereotyped in issues would explore, goals set; "discouragement of activity in women" (p. 5779B)
Fischer *et al.* (1976) Social workers, Hawaii ($n = 135$)	*Independent variables*: subject—sex; written analogue—sex, aggressivity–passivity *Dependent variables*: 11 clinical judgments	Female protocol elicited more positive reaction, rated more mature, intelligent, needing less home and family involvement, *nondirective* therapy, *more emotional expression*; no effect of aggressivity–passivity
Goldberg (1975) Mental health practitioners ($n = 380$)	*Independent variables*: subject—sex, profession; written analogue—sex, sex-role conventionality of solution *Dependent variables*: 3 (e.g., solution preferred)	No difference in choice of sex-role-conventional solution; validity of study questioned
Gomes & Abramowitz (1976) Psychotherapists ($n = 182$)	*Independent variables*: subject—sex, sex-role ideology (AWS); written analogue—sex, sex role *Dependent variables*: 6 clinical judgments	Attitudes untraditional; female protocol judged more mature, better prognosis by males; more traditional clinicians rated females higher in social adjustment; sex-role-inappropriate female evoked less empathy from less traditional female clinicians
Oppedisano-Reich (1976) Therapists ($n = 44$)	*Independent variables*: written analogue—sex, race, social class, neurotic–psychotic	High-SES females rated more motivated than low-SES females; neurotic–psychotic variation powerful effect

(continued)

55

Table 4 (*continued*).

Study and subjects	Method	Results and comment
Abramowitz (1977) Professionals, very mixed (*n* = 48)	*Dependent variables:* 6 clinical judgments *Independent variables:* subject—sex, sex-role ideology (AWS); written analogue—sex, sex role congruency, sex role *Dependent variables:* 2 ratings (maternal–paternal attribution)	Attitudes untraditional; mother (especially of girls) blamed more and rated more in need of treatment
Johnson (1978) Psychologists (*n* = 40)	*Independent variables:* subject—sex; videotape analogue—sex, depressed or aggressive *Dependent variables:* total of 8; 4 ratings of their subjective reactions	No effects of sex of protocol
Feinblatt & Gold (1976) Graduate students in clinical and school psychology (*n* = 27)	*Independent variables:* written analogue—sex, sex role (active-passive) *Dependent variables:* 3—severity, treatment recommendation, prediction success	Chid protocol with sex-role-inappropriate symptoms seen as more maladjusted and less likely to have future success (results consistent with study of parents and correlational study)
Hobfall & Penner (1978) Graduate students in clinical psychology (*n* = 16)	*Independent variables:* audiotape-videotape, sex, attractiveness *Dependent variable:* rating self-concept	Self-concept of attractive protocol rated better; and better under videotapes than audiotapes, especially for females
Schwartz & Abramowitz (in press) Male graduate students in clinical and counseling (*n* = 32)	*Independent variables:* videotape analogue—female attractive-unattractive, severity of problem *Dependent variables:* several process and clinical judgment reponses	More attractive analogue elicited more social response, not likely to terminate prematurely

[a] Abbreviations: AWS, Attitudes toward Women Scale; SES, Socioeconomic Status.

The studies that Abramowitz and Dokecki (1977) cited in their negative evaluation and which appear positive or equivocable include that of Abramowitz, Abramowitz, Jackson, and Gomes (1973), which found that a hypothetical left-oriented female client was judged more maladjusted than her male counterpart by the less, but not by the more liberal examiners. (Perhaps this was the part of their findings *not* "refuting" evaluative prejudice.) Schwartz and Abramowitz (1975) found that less traditional psychiatrists recommended less insight therapy for female than for male protocols, but one hardly knows how to interpret such a finding. More clearly indicative of bias is the fact that more experienced psychiatrists recommended drug treatment more for the female protocol than for the male, yet this study was apparently counted as providing no evidence of biased behavior.

Gomes and Abramowitz (1976) also obtained complex results difficult to interpret. They found that the female protocol was judged more mature and as having a better prognosis (by males). The more traditional clinicians rated females higher in social adjustment. The sex-role-inappropriate female protocol evoked less empathy from the less traditional female clinicians. Except for the last findings, the results sound like positive bias unless, like Miller, Chesler, and the Broverman team, one predicts that clinicians have lower standards for the mental health of females. In that case, one would interpret the results as consistent with a double standard of mental health. The authors, however, considered the results as "refuting allegations of covert sex-related discrimination perpetrated under the aegis of psychological appraisal" (Gomes & Abramowitz, 1976, p. 1).

The study of Abramowitz, Roback, Schwartz, Yasuna, Abramowitz, and Gomes (1976) announced their opinion of the results in the title, "Sex Bias in Psychotherapy: A Failure to Confirm." The female protocol was given a better prognosis; group therapy was recommended less for women than for men, and the female protocol elicited more behaviorally focused reactions from traditional female therapists. There were 25 dependent variables. How is one to interpret these results? What findings would one expect to indicate bias (Zeldow, 1975)? The conceptualization of studies such as these is not sufficiently clear that one can be sure that a dimension relevant to sex-role stereotyping has been tapped.

Other unclear and/or negative studies include those of Libbey (1975) and Fischer, Dulaney, Fazio, Hudak, and Zivotofsky (1976). On one of two analogues, Libbey found that therapists showed greater positive emotion toward the female than the male protocol. What does this mean about sex-role stereotyping? The study of Fischer *et al.* asked, "Are social workers sexists?" and answered, "No." Again, however, they did not successfully manipulate a sex-role variable. These investigators attempted to engage the sex-role variable by varying analogues for both sex and an aggressivity–passivity dimension of symptoms. For dependent variables, they used 11 clinical judgments. There was apparently no check of the aggressivity–passivity experimental manipulation, and the dimension showed no effects. They found that the female protocol elicited a more positive reaction and was rated more mature and more intelligent. In contrast to her male counterpart, the female protocol was rated as needing less home and family involvement, as more suited for nondirective therapy, and as needing more emotional expression. The results are certainly a mixed bag, and, in view of the lack of conceptual clarity in the framing of the study, they are hard to interpret. Is the more positive reaction a reflection of a lower standard for women's mental health? Is there no sex-role stereotyping about recommending *more* emotional expression for the female, but not for the male protocol? How does being more suited for nondirective therapy relate to sexism? The rating of the female as needing less home and family involvement does sound contrary to sex-role stereotypy, but the rest of the results are by no means clear in their meaning, and, in fact, some of them could be interpreted as supporting sex-role stereotyping.

Other studies which could potentially be counted as evidence not supporting the view that sex-role stereotyping exists in psychotherapeutic practice include the dissertations of Goldberg (1975) and Oppedisano-Reich (1976). In the first study, 380 mental health practitioners chose the same solution to a problem posed regarding a male or female protocol, regardless of the sex-role conventionality of the solution. The author, however, notes that there is question about the external validity of the study. The Oppedisano-Reich (1976) dissertation (cited by Stricker, 1977) found that 44 mental health professionals differentiated not on the basis of the sex label of the protocols, but on the basis of symptomatology described as neurotic or psychotic. Treatment recommendations that would vary by sex labeling in the face of the very different treatments possible for neurotic compared to psychotic symptoms (major tranquilizers, hospitalization, electroshock therapy) would not constitute evidence of sex-role stereotyping, but evidence of gross incompetence. It is reassuring, however, to know that merely by being female we will not be treated as psychotic when we are only neurotic.

Johnson (1978) explored responses of 40 experienced psychologists to videotaped clients alike except for variations of sex (male or female) and symptoms (angry or depressed). The verbal reactions of counselors at certain points during the tapes were recorded and rated, for example, for sympathy or feeling of identification with the client. Counselors themselves rated four variables, for example, empathy. None of the ratings seemed necessarily relevant to the dimension of sex-role stereotyping. Neither sex of protocol nor the anger/depression dimension of symptomatology yielded any significant effects, though there were a couple of effects related to sex of the therapist. If the angry female had been rated as eliciting less empathy than the angry male protocol, this might have been evidence of the effects of sex-role stereotyping. Such a finding would depend on a significant interaction effect. With five subjects per cell in a between-subjects design with measures of dubious reliability, one can hardly be surprised by negative findings (see Delk, 1977).

The study by Feinblatt and Gold (1976) was conceptually well thought out. They were interested in the hypothesis that children who exhibited behavioral characteristics inappropriate to their sex would be more likely to be referred to psychiatric facilities than would children who exhibited behavioral characteristics appropriate to their sex. In a preliminary study, they found that the records of an outpatient child-guidance clinic were in accord with the hypothesis. More girls than boys were referred for being defiant and verbally aggressive. In two subsequent studies, samples of parents and graduate students (sample charted in Table 4) read hypothetical case studies in which identical behavior problems were attributed either to a boy or to a girl. The data from both samples were consistent with the hypothesis. Data from graduate students indicated that the child exhibiting the behavior inappropriate to his/her sex was seen as more severely disturbed and less likely to have a successful future than the child exhibiting sex-role-appropriate behaviors. The authors offered the perspective that these data do *not* permit the generalization that such children would be locked up. Children who were, in fact, in a state mental hospital were characterized by far more serious disturbances which were *not* sex-typed. This caveat aside, the authors concluded that there was definite evidence of the influence of sex-role stereotyping in mental health practice.

Four studies dealt with variables which are clearly relevant to sex-role stereotyping in psychotherapeutic practice (APA Task Force, 1975). These variables are exaggerated blaming of the mother for a child's emotional difficulties and the attractiveness or unattractiveness of the female client and its biasing effects, particularly on the male therapists. These four studies all provided evidence of sex-role stereotyping.

Abramowitz (1977) found that mothers, especially mothers in the protocol labeled female, were blamed more than fathers for a child's psychopathology. Mothers, more than fathers, were rated in need of treatment for themselves. In a second study (Abramowitz, Abramowitz,

Weitz, & Tittler, 1976), there was more maternal than paternal attribution of responsibility for the children's psychopathology as described in the protocols. In both samples, the clinician subjects were relatively untraditional. More striking findings might well be forthcoming from more traditional subjects (if one could get them to participate in such a study).

Regarding physical attractiveness, Hobfall and Penner (1978) found that the self-concept ratings of protocols of attractive females increased significantly from the audiotape to the videotape conditions, whereas the ratings of all the other stimulus persons remained the same. This suggested that self-concept ratings were unduly influenced by the female's attractiveness. Finally, Schwartz and Abramowitz, in an analogue study (in press), found that the more attractive female (shown on videotape) elicited more social responsiveness from 32 male graduate students and a judgment that she would be less likely to terminate therapy prematurely than the unattractive female (same woman with glasses, etc.).

Conclusions

Data provide evidence that therapists' sex-role values are operative during therapy and counseling. Data indicate there is sex-role stereotyping in mental health standards and that sex-role-discrepant behaviors are judged more maladjusted. Clinical judgments of women do not appear to be more severe than those accorded their male counterparts. This does not mean that there is no sex-role stereotyping, since part of sex-role stereotyping has been a lower standard of mental health for females. These data do provide reassurance that, under the controlled conditions selected by researchers so far, women were not, for example, judged more "crazy." Even with these data, one must add that many analogue studies were not maximally constructed to demonstrate a bias effect. Maximal conditions would present an ambiguous case history in order to leave room for prejudice to operate. Supposed manipulations of behaviors not congruent with traditional sex role often lacked face validity, let alone manipulation checks. No study was found investigating the situation of the patient presenting with vague physical symptoms. It is a classic female experience to have such symptoms discounted and labeled neurotic. It would be interesting to see whether there was a difference between the sexes in the frequency with which they would be referred for the purpose of ruling out physical disease.

While samples of clinicians tested were probably biased in the liberal direction, there was no evidence that therapists were generally conservative nor that they served as watchdogs or enforcers of conventionality. Of course, even if therapists are no more conservative than the general population, if they use their power on the side of conventionality, they nonetheless play such a role. One also cannot ignore the difference between an analogue study and real life. One of the most obvious facts of female life is less power in status, economics, and physical strength. Studies so far tell us nothing about clinical judgment and treatment as applied to women, for example, when the mental health workers are under pressure from powerful others (e.g., disenchanted husband), nor do they tell us of the prevalence of a problem in this area.

The foremost need in promoting better research in this area is more cogent conceptualization ("theory" is too grandiose a term in this context). A reasonable hypothesis needs to be submitted to a test in a fair manner. If we are looking for evidence of sex-role stereotyping, let us be sure that we engage a relevant variable. Collecting data on many irrelevant variables merely adds confusion. Research designs need to include manipulation checks. We must be sure that materials of analogue studies are not so specific as to swamp any bias effect attributed to gender. Analogue materials should be described and made available. Analogue studies are subject to the problem of persons guessing the intent of the study and, therefore, not revealing their true feelings. Delk (1977), in recommending within-subjects design, points out that many persons consciously differentiate in their treatment of males and females. He suggests that a frank within-subjects design is preferable to a between-subjects design that is probably patently obvious in its intent. Methods to obtain more complete and less biased sampling of populations are needed, and studies need to have adequate power to demonstrate effects, if any are present. Power can be improved by more subjects per cell and/or increased use of within-subjects design. Studies confounding sex of clinician and level of training should not draw conclusions attributing results to the sex of the subject.

Recommendations for Further Research

If we want to know the answer to the questions discussed because we want to remedy any existing inequity, then we need to know if policymakers find the existing evidence adequate to require changes such as curriculum that deals with psychology of women, values, and sexualized countertransference; licensing/certification procedures which reflect these changes; and postdoctoral workshops dealing with these questions. A survey of policymakers to see if they perceive a need for these changes would be useful.

If one wished to gain more information, in addition to replications, one might consider some new research strategies. Knowledge of the prevalence of bias against women and sex-role stereotyping in psychotherapy might be obtained from surveys of women's groups. Groups could be of various kinds, for example, church groups as well as the National Organization for Women. An entire group could be enlisted as subjects to help avoid bias in respondents. Needless to say, the questions on the survey would need to reflect an intelligent understanding of the issues involved.

A second approach would attempt to pursue the method by which therapists give questionnaires to their patients. The problem of biases, however, might still be introduced in therapist participation, which patients they picked, and which patients returned questionnaires. Using the Kinsey group method, therapists could be enlisted to gather data from all of their patients. In this way, less bias would be introduced in the response rate.

Pietrofesa and Schlossberg (1970) had student clinicians interview a bogus client. This method could be replicated with clinicians using different sex-role-relevant problems, for example, to get an abortion or to seek a career while the mother of small children. Recording of such interviews with randomly or representatively selected therapists would doubtless prove interesting. For example, clinicians could agree in advance to permit recording of an interview with a bogus client but be unaware of the full purpose of the study until debriefing.

Real-life process studies of therapists, although desirable, are no cure-all, since they have all the potential biases of the Fabrikant (1974) study and would be immensely expensive. Since the effect of psychotherapy itself has yet to be demonstrated to the consensual satisfaction of the scientific community, it would appear folly indeed to embark on outcome studies testing whether sexist therapy has a poorer outcome than nonsexist therapy. In view of the many pitfalls such studies encounter, it would be far more appropriate to spend the effort on implementing needed changes.

If we are interested in the questions of sex-role stereotyping in psychotherapy from a theoretical viewpoint, then that theory needs to be delineated. The issue does not seem to be a theoretical one. Rather, the issue rubs the interface of science and values. Without further clarification and consensus about how value issues can be handled in psychotherapy, there is a limit to the contributions science can make.

Reference Notes

1. Siechta, J. B. *Women in therapy as perceived by mental health personnel or down the primrose path with a "blind" therapist.* Paper presented at the meeting of the Rocky Mountain Psychological Association, 1971.
2. Brogan, C. *Changing perspectives on the role of women.* Unpublished master's degree report, Smith College School for Social Work, 1971.

References

Abramowitz, C. V. Blaming the mother: An experimental investigation of sex-role bias in countertransference. *Psychology of Women Quarterly,* 1977, *2,* 25-34.

Abramowitz, C. V., Abramowitz, S. I., Weitz, L. J., & Tittler, B. Sex-related effects on clinicians' attributions of parental responsibility for child psychopathology. *Journal of Abnormal Child Psychology,* 1976, *4,* 129-138.

Abramowitz, C. V., & Dokecki, P. R. The politics of clinical judgment: Early empirical returns. *Psychological Bulletin,* 1977, *84,* 460-476.

Abramowitz, S. I., Abramowitz, C. V., Jackson, C., & Gomes, B. The politics of clinical judgment: What nonliberal examiners infer about women who do not stifle themselves. *Journal of Consulting and Clinical Psychology,* 1973, *41,* 385-391.

Abramowitz, S. I., Abramowitz, C. V., Roback, H. B., Corney, R., & McKee, E. Sex-role related countertransference in psychotherapy. *Archives of General Psychiatry,* 1976, *33,* 71-73.

Abramowitz, S. I., Roback, H. B., Schwartz, J. M., Yasuna, A., Abramowitz, C. V., & Gomes, B. Sex bias in psychotherapy: A failure to confirm. *American Journal of Psychiatry,* 1976, *133,* 706-709.

Abramowitz, S. I., Weitz, L. J., Schwartz, J. M., Amira, S., Gomes, B., & Abramowitz, C. V. Comparative counselor inferences toward women with medical school aspirations. *Journal of College Student Personnel,* 1975, *16,* 128-130.

American Psychological Association Task Force. Report of the Task Force on Sex Bias and Sex-Role Stereotyping in Psychotherapeutic Practice. *American Psychologist,* 1975, *30,* 1169-1175.

Aslin, A. L. Feminist and community mental health center psychotherapists' expectations of mental health for women. *Sex Roles,* 1977, *3,* 537-544.

Billingsley, D. Sex bias in psychotherapy: An examination of the effects of client sex, client pathology, and therapist sex on treatment planning. *Journal of Consulting and Clinical Psychology,* 1977, *45,* 250-256.

Bingham, W. C., & House, E. W. Counselors view women and work: Accuracy of information. *Vocational Guidance Quarterly,* 1973, *21,* 262-268.

Bowman, P. R. The relationship between attitudes toward women and the treatment of activity and passivity (Doctoral dissertation, Boston University School of Education, 1976). *Dissertation Abstracts International,* 1976, *36,* 5779B. (University Microfilms No. 76-11, 644)

Broverman, I. K., Broverman, D. M., Clarkson, F. E., Rosenkrantz, P. & Vogel, S. R. Sex-role stereotypes and clinical judgments of mental health. *Journal of Consulting Psychology,* 1970, *34,* 1-7.

Broverman, I. K., Vogel, S. R., Broverman, D. M., Clarkson, F. E., & Rosenkrantz, P. S. Sex-role stereotypes: A current appraisal. *Journal of Social Issues,* 1972, *28,* 59-78.

Brown, C. R., & Hellinger, M. L. Therapists' attitudes toward women. *Social Work,* 1975, *20,* 266-270.

Chesler, P. *Women and madness.* Garden City, N.Y.: Doubleday, 1972.

Cline-Naffziger, C. A survey of counselors' and other selected professionals' attitudes towards women's roles (Doctoral dissertation, University of Oregon, 1971). *Dissertation Abstracts International*, 1971, *32*, 3021A. (University Microfilms No. 72-955)

Cowan, G. Therapist judgments of clients' sex-role problems. *Psychology of Women Quarterly*, 1976, *1*, 115-124.

Davenport, J., & Reims, N. Theoretical orientation and attitudes toward women. *Social Work*, 1978, *23*, 306-309.

Delk, J. L. Differentiating sexist from nonsexist therapists, or my analogue can beat your analogue. *American Psychologist*, 1977, *32*, 892-893.

Delk, J. L., & Ryan, T. T. Sex-role stereotyping and A-B therapist status: Who is more chauvinistic? *Journal of Consulting and Clinical Psychology*, 1975, *43*, 589.

Delk, J. L., & Ryan, T. T. A-B status and sex stereotyping among psychotherapists and patients. *The Journal of Nervous and Mental Disease*, 1977, *164*, 253-262.

Dremen, S. B. Sex-role stereotyping in mental health standards in Israel. *Journal of Clinical Psychology*, 1978, *34*, 961-966.

Engelhard, P. A., Jones, K. O., & Stiggins, R. J. Trends in counselor attitude about women's roles. *Journal of Counseling Psychology*, 1976, *23*, 365-372.

Fabrikant, B. The psycotherapist and the female patient: Perceptions and change. In V. Franks & V. Burtle (Eds.), *Women in therapy*. New York: Brunner/Mazel, 1974.

Fabrikant, B., Landau, D., & Rollenhagen, J. Perceived female sex role attributes and psychotherapists sex role expectations for female patients. *New Jersey Psychologist*, 1973, *23*, 13-16.

Feinblatt, J. A., & Gold, A. R. Sex roles and the psychiatric referral process. *Sex Roles*, 1976, *2*, 109-122.

Fischer, J., Dulaney, D. D., Fazio, R. T., Hudak, M. T., & Zivotofsky, E. Are social workers sexists? *Social Work*, 1976, *21*, 428-433.

Gilbert, L. A. The sexist psychotherapist: An ephemeral species. *American Psychologist*, 1977, *32*, 888-889.

Gingras-Baker, S. Sex role stereotyping and marriage counseling. *Journal of Marriage and Family Counseling*, 1976, *2*, 355-366.

Goldberg, B. J. Mental health practice as social control: Practitioners' choices of therapy goals as a function of sex of client, situations, and other practitioners' opinions (Doctoral dissertation, State University of New York at Stony Brook, 1975). *Dissertation Abstracts International*, 1976, *36*, 5256B. (University Microfilms No. 76-7570)

Goldberg, L. H. Attitudes of clinical psychologists toward women (Doctoral dissertation, Illinois Institute of Technology, 1973). *Dissertation Abstracts International*, 1974, *35*, 1017B-1018B. (University Microfilms No. 74-16, 997)

Gomes, B., & Abramowitz, S. I. Sex-related patient and therapist effects on clinical judgment. *Sex Roles*, 1976, *2*, 1-13.

Gove, W. R., & Tudor, J. F. Adult sex roles and mental illness. *American Journal of Sociology*, 1973, *78*, 812-835.

Haan, N., & Livson, N. Sex differences in the eyes of expert personality assessors: Blind spots? *Journal of Personality Assessment*, 1973, *37*, 486-492.

Harris, L. H., & Lucas, M. E. Sex-role stereotyping. *Social Work*, 1976, *21*, 390-395.

Hayes, K. E., & Walleat, P. L. Effect of sex in judgment of a simulated counseling interview. *Journal of Counseling Psychology*, 1978, *25*, 164-168.

Helwig, A. A. Counselor bias and women. *Journal of Employment Counseling*, 1976, *13*, 58-67.

Hobfall, S. E., & Penner, L. A. Effect of physical attractiveness on therapists' initial judgments of a person's self-concept. *Journal of Consulting and Clinical Psychology*, 1978, *46*, 200-201.

Johnson, M. Influence of counselor gender on reactivity to clients. *Journal of Counseling Psychology*, 1978, *25*, 359-365.

Kahn, L. G. Effects of sex and feminist orientation of therapists on clinical judgments (Doctoral dissertation, Columbia University, 1976). *Dissertation Abstracts International*, 1977, *37*, 3613B. (University Microfilms No. 76-29, 598)

Kirshner, L. A. Effects of gender on psychotherapy. *Comprehensive Psychiatry*, 1978, *19*, 79–82.

Lesser, E. K. Counselor attitudes toward male and female students: A study of "helpers" in conflict (Doctoral dissertation, University of Rochester, 1974). *Dissertations Abstracts International*, 1975, *36*, 708A.

Libbey, M. D. Sex-stereotyping in psychotherapist responses in an analogue therapy situation (Doctoral dissertation, Columbia University, 1975). *Dissertations Abstracts International*, 1975, *36*, 1441B.

Magnus, E. C. Measurement of counselor bias (sex-role stereotyping) in assessment of marital couples with traditional and nontraditional interaction patterns (Doctoral dissertation, University of Georgia, 1975). *Dissertations Abstracts International*, 1975, *36*, 2635A.

Maslin, A., & Davis, J. L. Sex-role stereotyping as a factor in mental health standards among counselors-in-training. *Journal of Counseling Psychology*, 1975, *22*, 87–91.

Maxfield, R. B. Sex-role stereotypes of psychotherapists (Doctoral dissertation, Adelphi University, 1976). *Dissertations Abstracts International*, 1976, *37*, 1914B. (University Microfilms No. 76–22, 816)

Miller, D. The influence of the patient's sex on clinical judgment. *Smith College Studies in Social Work*, 1974, *44*, 89–100.

Neulinger, J., Stein, M. I., Schillinger, M., & Welkowitz, J. Perceptions of the optimally integrated person as a function of therapists' characteristics. *Perceptual and Motor Skills*, 1970, *30*, 375–384.

Oppedisano-Reich, M. T. The effect of a patient's social class, race and sex on mental health professionals' diagnoses, prognoses and recommendations for treatment (Doctoral dissertation, Adelphi University, 1976). *Dissertations Abstracts International*, 1976, *37*, 3157B–3158B. (University Microfilms No. 76–29, 259)

Parloff, M. B., Waskow, I. E., & Wolfe, B. E. Research on therapist variables in relation to process and outcome. In A. E. Bergin, & S. L. Garfield (Eds.), *Handbook of psychotherapy and behavior change: An empirical analysis.* New York: Wiley, 1971.

Persons, W. E. Occupational prediction as a function of the counselor's racial and sexual bias (Doctoral dissertation, The University of Florida, 1972). *Dissertations Abstracts International*, 1973, *34*, 139A–140A. (University Microfilms No. 73–15, 533)

Pietrofesa, J. J., & Schlossberg, N. K. *Counselor bias and the female occupational role.* Detroit: College of Education, Wayne State University, 1970. (ERIC Document Reproduction Service No. CH 006 056)

Pringle, M. B. The responses of counselors to behaviors associated with independence and achievement in male and female clients (Doctoral dissertation, University of Michigan, 1973). *Dissertation Abstracts International*, 1973, *34*, 1627A. (University Microfilms No. 73–24, 659)

Rabkin, J. G. Therapists' attitudes toward mental illness and health. In A. S. Gurman & A. M. Razin (Eds.), *Effective psychotherapy: A handbook of research.* New York: Pergamon Press, 1977.

Rauch, J. B. Gender as a factor in practice. *Social Work*, 1978, *23*, 388–395.

Roche Laboratories. Report of a survey of psychiatric opinion on the social issue—"Women's liberation." *Psychiatric Viewpoints Report.* Nutley, N.J.: Hoffman–LaRoche, 1974.

Schlossberg, N. K., & Pietrofesa, J. J. Perspectives on counseling bias: Implications for counselor education. *Counseling Psychologist*, 1973, *4*, 44–54.

Schwartz, J. M., & Abramowitz, S. I. Value-related effects on psychiatric judgment. *Archives of General Psychiatry*, 1975, *32*, 1525–1529.

Schwartz, J. M., & Abramowitz, S. I. Effects of female client physical attractiveness on clinical judgment. *Psychotherapy: Theory, Research, and Practice,* in press.

Shapiro, J. F. Socialization of sex roles in the counseling setting: Differential counselor behavioral and attitudinal responses to typical and atypical female sex roles (Doctoral dissertation, Stanford University, 1975). *Dissertations Abstracts International*, 1976, *36*, 5839A. (University Microfilms No. 76-5801)

Sherif, C. W. Bias in psychology. In J. A. Sherman & E. T. Beck (Eds.), *The prism of sex: Essays in the sociology of knowledge*. Madison, Wis.: University of Wisconsin, 1979.

Sherman, J. *Sex-related cognitive differences: An essay on theory and evidence*. Springfield, Ill.: Charles C Thomas, 1978.

Sherman, J., Koufacos, C., & Kenworthy, J. A. Therapists: Their attitudes and information about women. *Psychology of Women Quarterly*, 1978, *2*, 299-313.

Spence, J. T., Helmreich, R., & Stapp, J. A short version of the Attitude Toward Women Scale (AWS). *Bulletin of the Psychonomic Society*, 1973, *2*, 219-220.

Stengel, J. B. Counselor response as a function of client's sex, counselor's sex, and client's presenting affect (Doctoral dissertation, Boston University School of Education, 1976). *Dissertations Abstracts International*, 1976, *36*, 5819B. (University Microfilms No. 76-11, 831)

Stricker, G. Implications of research for psychotherapeutic treatment of women. *American Psychologist*, 1977, *32*, 14-22.

Tanney, M. F., & Birk, J. M. Women counselors for women clients? A review of the research. *The Counseling Psychologist*, 1976, *6*, 28-32.

Thomas, A. H., & Stewart, N. R. Counselor response to female clients with deviate and conforming career goals. *Journal of Counseling Psychology*, 1971, *18*, 352-357.

Voss, J., & Gannon, L. Sexism in the theory and practice of clinical psychology. *Professional Psychology*, 1978, *9*, 623-632.

Werner, P. D., & Block, J. Sex differences in the eyes of expert assessors: Unwarranted conclusions. *Journal of Personality Assessment*, 1975, *39*, 110-113.

Zeldow, P. B. Clinical judgment: A search for sex differences. *Psychological Reports*, 1975, *37*, 1135-1142.

CHAPTER 3

Gender and the Process of Therapy

JEANNE MARECEK

MARILYN JOHNSON

In this chapter, we review studies of the influence of gender on the process of therapy. Our review covers three broad areas: (1) evidence of the influence of therapists' and clients' gender on the process of therapy; (2) studies of the influence of sex-role stereotypes on therapists' behavior toward their clients; and (3) evidence of the incidence of sexist statements and actions by therapists during the course of therapy.

There are several reasons why it is important to study the ways in which gender affects the process of therapy. First, given the extensive literature accumulated by social psychologists on ways in which one's expectations, perceptions, and reactions are shaped by the gender or presumed gender of an interaction partner, it is highly probable that therapists, like people in general, are influenced by the gender of their clients. Furthermore, many therapists were educated in the psychoanalytic tradition, a belief system that promulgates a stereotypical view of the psychology of men and of women (cf. Miller, 1973, pp. 379–406; Schafer, 1974). It is doubtful that most of these therapists have had corrective educational experiences subsequent to their early training.

It is not only therapists' expectations and attitudes about clients that influence the process of therapy; clients' expectations and perceptions of their therapists also shape therapy interactions. Thus, our review includes ways in which the gender of the therapist appears to affect the contribution of the client to therapy. Yet a third way in which gender affects psychotherapy is through its channeling influence on the experiences and life situations common to women and to men. For example,

Jeanne Marecek. Department of Psychology, Swarthmore College, Swarthmore, Pennsylvania.
Marilyn Johnson. Department of Psychology and Social Sciences, Rush University, Chicago, Illinois.

women who enter treatment for psychological disorders tend to be in different life situations, to experience different life crises, and to express different symptoms than men (e.g., Gove & Tudor, 1973; Marecek, 1978; Radloff, 1975). Though there is an overlap in men's and women's complaints, more women than men experience problems of depression, and more men than women become involved in aggressive behavior and substance abuse. This contrast in disorders has been elaborated by Gove (1980) into a theory that "feminine" syndromes are socially defined as illness, while "masculine" syndromes are defined as social deviance. It seems doubtful that practicing clinicians would agree with Gove's distinction. Nonetheless, gender differences resulting from social roles and socialization histories will affect clients' contributions to the therapy process.

An understanding of gender-related influences on psychotherapy can improve our understanding of how therapy works and, ultimately, can make therapy more successful. Gender biases in therapy may prevent clients from deriving maximum benefit from therapy. Results of studies of gender bias might be used to show therapists ways in which they inadvertently treat female and male clients differently. In addition, those who train therapists might find such information useful in designing coursework or supervisory experiences.

Information on gender-related influences on the therapy process may also provide us with improved knowledge about the effectiveness of various gender pairings. This knowledge would help us to make referrals that enhance chances for productive therapeutic alliances. The research we will review below indicates that the effects of gender pairings are mediated by factors such as age, marital status, and, possibly, client's personality (cf. Heilbrun, 1974; Orlinsky & Howard, 1976). Thus, recommendations for matching client and therapist are likely to be complex.

Not only the practice of therapy but also research on therapy can benefit from a fuller understanding of the effects of gender on the process of therapy. Failing to take gender differences into account may raise the error variance in studies of therapy process and outcome and thus mask significant effects (e.g., Mendelsohn & Rankin, 1969).

Overview

Concerns about the effects of gender and sex-role stereotypes on therapy are fairly recent. Thus, the 1971 edition of the *Handbook of Psychotherapy and Behavior Change* (Bergin & Garfield, 1971) indexes only one entry under the heading "sex of counselor" and does not contain headings referring to "sex of client" or to "gender." Much of the existing literature consists of exhortations for increased sensitivity and for non-sexist attitudes on the part of counselors. However, this review covers only empirical work on psychotherapy, counseling, and behavior therapy.

There is some literature on gender-related influences on other forms of psychological treatment, for example, on the prescribing of psychotropic medication (Brink, 1972; Cooperstock, 1971), on admitting individuals as psychiatric inpatients (Gross, Herbert, Knatterud, & Donner, 1969), and on recommendations for specific treatment programs (Doyle & Levy, Note 1). There is also a substantial literature on gender influences on psychological testing and clinical judgment (e.g., Harris & Masling, 1970; Masling & Harris, 1969). Though these aspects of mental health services are related to therapy, our review does not include them. It is limited to studies of the therapy process.

Nearly all the research on gender influences on therapy pertains to individual psychotherapy. Furthermore, there are virtually no relevant studies on the process of behavior therapy, probably because few behavior therapists consider process factors to be important components of their therapeutic method. Surprisingly, there is only a small amount of literature concerning gender influences on the process of marital and family therapy. Therapy involving couples or families seems like an ideal setting for observing therapists' reactions to clients of different genders. Furthermore, marriage and family life is the central area in which stereotypical notions of masculine and feminine roles have been promulgated (cf. Hare-Mustin, 1978). Finally, there are few studies of gender-related effects on the process of group therapy. We have augmented these by including studies of small groups formed for purposes of interpersonal exploration or self-study.

This review is restricted to literature on adults (including college students) in therapy. We are not aware of any relevant studies of therapy with children. Research on child therapy may well require different conceptual frameworks from those that appear useful for interpreting the findings on therapy with adults. For example, some theorists have suggested that stereotypes of powerlessness and dependency may play an important role in defining therapists' attitudes and behavior toward female clients (e.g., Chesler, 1972; Marecek, 1976). However, these traits are common to all children, not just girls. Thus, if children's gender is shown to influence therapists' behavior, sex-role stereotypes of powerlessness and dependency are not likely to provide an adequate explanation for the observed effects.

We have adopted conservative criteria for the methodologies of studies that are included in this review. We have restricted the survey to studies using therapists and counselors currently in practice or in training. We have omitted several studies of peer counseling processes (e.g., Persons, Persons, & Newmark, 1974; Wyrick & Mitchell, Note 2) on the grounds that their results cannot be generalized to therapists. We have included both naturalistic therapy studies and analogue studies. Unfortunately, there are very few naturalistic studies. There are many analogue studies, but they vary widely in the plausibility and realism of the simulations involved. As we point out, the evidence on the validity of the analogue methodology is not reassuring (cf. Kushner, 1978). In two of the three instances in which replications of analogue studies have been attempted in naturalistic settings, the agreement between their results was not good. There are numerous reasons why this lack of agreement might occur: the "set" of the participants; their awareness of being in a study or of not really being in therapy; differences in the nature of the experimental task; and high nonresponse rates in studies using mailed questionnaires. Analogue studies generally seem most valuable as ways of gaining preliminary information to be verified subsequently in naturalistic studies.

Table 1 shows the areas of the therapy process that are included in this review. By extratherapeutic processes we refer to aspects of therapists' or clients' behavior that occur outside the therapy session yet

Table 1.   Outline of Areas under Review

Extratherapeutic Processes

Therapists' behavior
1.   Selection or referral of clients for therapy
2.   Preferences for clients' gender
3.   Judgments of clients' need for treatment
4.   Duration of theraу

Clients' behavior
1.   Likelihood of seeking therapy
2.   Preferences for therapists' gender
3.   Early termination

Therapy Processes

Therapists' behavior
1.   Perceptions of and feelings toward clients
2.   Empathy
3.   Intervention style
4.   Manifest content of interventions
5.   Seduction of clients

Clients' behavior
1.   Perceptions of therapy and of their therapists
2.   Manifest content and interaction styles
3.   Affective experiences in sessions

strongly affect how (and if) therapy is carried out. Therapy processes are aspects of therapists' and clients' behavior in actual therapy transactions. In each section, we first describe studies of therapists' behavior and then studies of clients' behavior.

Extratherapeutic Processes

Selection of Clients for Therapy

Three studies bear on the question of whether therapists are more likely to select women as clients for therapy than men. Brown and Kosterlitz (1964) studied the records of a large number of individuals seeking treatment at an outpatient psychiatric clinic. Though twice as many women as men applied for treatment, equal proportions (75%) of each sex were accepted. Marital status strongly affected women's likelihood of being accepted for treatment but had no effect for men. Married women had a much higher rate of acceptance into treatment than single, divorced, separated, and widowed women (91% vs. 67%). Two studies (Rosenthal & Frank, 1958; Kirshner, Hauser, & Genack, Note 3) found that women were favored as individual therapy patients. The study of Kirshner *et al.* was limited to first-year college students seeking help at a student counseling service.

These three studies were conducted during different decades and in different mental health settings. Given their divergences, it seems unwise to attempt to integrate their results. We need additional studies in the area. Furthermore, the finding that marital status and gender interact in predicting acceptance into therapy suggests the need to consider other factors in addition to gender. Studies of psychiatric diagnosis and treatment disposition (e.g., Gross *et al.*, 1969) have shown that clients' race, social class, and behavior at intake also affect whether practitioners wish to work with them. These factors, as well as presenting complaints, should be taken into account in studies of selection for therapy.

Schwartz and Abramowitz (Note 4) asked whether gender influences therapists' referrals of clients for insight therapy versus supportive therapy. They mailed questionnaires accompanied by simulated case histories to therapists. The results showed that therapists with traditional values were more likely to recommend insight therapy for women than for men, while nontraditional therapists made opposite recommendations. Unfortunately, the sample on whom these results were based was highly self-selected, because less than 25% of the potential respondents actually returned the questionnaires. Thus, it seems unwise to draw firm conclusions from this study. However, the authors' hypothesis that therapists' sex-role beliefs may influence their treatment recommendations for women and men and that clients' gender may influence therapists' recommendations about the specific types of therapy suitable for them merits further exploration.

Therapists' Preferences for Clients' Gender

A number of studies have examined therapists' caseloads as an indirect measure of their preferences for women versus men. An early questionnaire study (Schofield, 1964) assessed random samples of psychiatrists, psychologists, and social workers. Less than half of the psychiatrists and psychologists reported that their caseloads were composed mainly of clients of one gender. However, among practitioners whose caseloads were single-gender, 75% of the psychiatrists saw only women. Psychologists with single-gender caseloads were equally likely to have all-female as all-male clientele. Among social workers, 75% reported that their caseloads were composed predominantly of clients of one gender; however, roughly equal numbers reported all-female and all-male caseloads. Schofield noted the dramatic differences in gender composition of the three groups of professionals: 90% of the psychiatric sample were men, 66% of the psychologists were men, and 66% of the social workers were women. However, he did not examine the relationship between a therapist's gender and his or her caseload. A later study of archival data noted a trend for female therapists to see more women than men (Abramowitz, Abramowitz, Roback, Corney, & McKee, 1976). A similar trend was reported by Barocas and Vance (1974).

There are serious problems with inferring therapists' preferences for clients' gender on the basis of caseload information. One problem is that the majority of therapy clients are women and most psychiatrists and clinical psychologists are men. Thus, male therapist–female client pairings can be expected to occur most frequently, even in the absence of preference or intent. A second problem is that many therapists in agency settings (and, to a lesser extent, those in private practice) have little control over the makeup of their caseloads. Thus, caseloads may reveal little about actual preferences.

A few studies from the 1960s deal directly with the question of therapists' preferences. Schofield (1964), in the questionnaire study reported above, asked therapists to indicate the characteristics of the "ideal patient," that is, "the kind of patient with whom you feel you are efficient and effective in your therapy" (p. 130). Roughly one-third of the psychiatrists and half of the psychologists expressed a preference for the gender of the "ideal" clients. (Schofield does not report the proportion of social workers with preferences.) For all three professions, therapists who had preferences tended to prefer women. The effect was most marked for psychiatrists: Among those who had preferences, 67% preferred women. Among psychologists and social workers who expressed preferences for gender, there was only a slight margin of preference for female clients. Unfortunately, Schofield did not report whether therapists' gender was related to preferences for the gender of their clients.

In a later study, Rice (1969) reported that among college students applying for outpatient psychotherapy at a university health clinic, equal proportions of men and women were accepted. Interestingly, Rice also found that the males who were accepted into therapy had more symptoms and reported more problems than those not accepted for therapy; among the females, being accepted into therapy was not related to symptom level or number of problems.

There is too little information on therapists' preferences from which to draw any generalizations. We need research that not only addresses whether therapists prefer women as clients, but also addresses whether such preferences are modified by other client characteristics such as age, marital status, presenting complaint, and interaction style. Were we to find evidence for therapists' preferences, additional research questions would arise. What are the motivations and expectations underlying therapists' preferences? Are preferences based on the presumed likelihood of success or on the "interest value" of the client? Are there therapist characteristics (such as age, orientation, or marital status) or attitudes (such as attitudes about women or sex roles) that predict preferences for male or female clients? Finally, do therapists with preferences for the gender of their clients behave differently toward women and men in treatment?

Therapists' Judgments of Clients' Need for Treatment

This section summarizes studies of therapists' judgments about the urgency of clients' need for treatment, their prescriptions for the length, intensity, or type of treatment needed, and their estimations of the benefits to be derived from treatment.

An interesting addition to the literature can be found in two linked studies. The first was an analogue study that examined female and male therapists' judgments of two female clients (Hill, Tanney, Leonard, & Reiss, 1977). The second study (Helms, 1978) examined the same variables using actual clinical data. In each study, the independent variables were age of client, type of problem, and gender of therapist.

In the analogue study, therapists observed videotapes of female clients and evaluated the probable duration of therapy and the severity of the problem. The female "clients" were either 20 or 35 years old, with either vocational or personal–social problems. In the naturalistic study, four groups of clients corresponding to those used in the study of Hill *et al.* were drawn from the case files of a university counseling service. Both studies used both male and female therapists. In the study of Hill *et al.*, the therapists included students in a masters' degree program, counselors, and faculty members in psychology and counseling. In Helms' study, the therapists were counseling center staff members.

The results of the two studies showed a fair amount of agreement. In both studies, therapists of both genders agreed that for the 35-year-old woman, the personal problems were more important than the vocational problems. In the analogue study (Hill *et al.*), vocational issues were regarded as more serious for the 35-year-old woman than the 20-year-old woman. However, the effect was reversed in Helms' study. Furthermore, Helms found that female therapists perceived the female clients as having more problems than did the male therapists. Also, the female therapists saw the clients for more sessions than did the male therapists. While the findings of these two studies are not identical, there is considerable agreement. More real-life extensions of analogues are to be encouraged.

In the study of Hill *et al.*, the comparison of therapists' responses to portrayals of conflicts over vocational problems was especially interesting. The woman whose problem concerned a nontraditional career did not differ from traditional-career women in judgments of severity of problem, length of therapy required, or predicted therapeutic benefits. However, the work of Thomas and Stewart (1971) is in sharp contrast to the findings of Hill *et al.* They studied counselors' responses to an actress playing a high school student who expressed a desire either for a traditional feminine career or for a nontraditional career (engineering). Therapy was recommended more often for the young woman with the nontraditional vocational goals. The discrepancy between the two sets of findings may have been due to a number of factors such as the time elapsed between the two studies, differences between the two samples of counselors (high school counselors vs. students and counselors in university settings), or differences in the age and life status of the two hypothetical clients.

C. V. Abramowitz (1977) conducted a study of family therapists attending a family therapy conference. Most of them were social workers

(50%) or psychologists (25%). Practitioners' judgments of parents' contributions to children's problems were studied using vignettes describing a girl or boy with a problem either in a stereotypically masculine domain (athletic incompetence) or in a stereotypically feminine domain (carelessness about appearance and obesity). The respondents judged the extent of each parent's responsibility for the child's problem and each parent's need for treatment.

Overall, mothers of disturbed girls were judged to need more treatment than mothers of disturbed boys. Practitioners with traditional sex-role attitudes showed this effect more strongly than practitioners with nontraditional sex-role attitudes. The traditional practitioners also viewed mothers of the "feminine-inadequate" (i.e., obese) children as requiring more treatment effort than mothers of "masculine-inadequate" children.

These studies do not lend themselves to any straightforward conclusions. Both gender and gender-role appropriateness of the client may modify therapists' judgments of the client's need for treatment. Furthermore, therapists' judgments appear to be modified by their own gender and their attitudes about sex roles. Viewed chronologically, the studies suggest that practitioners are becoming more liberal in their attitudes and behaviors toward women's career aspirations. However, direct tests are needed to confirm this.

With the exception of Helms' study, all of the work reviewed here measures therapists' reactions to brief vignettes, either written, taped, or "live." There are at least two drawbacks to this design. Therapists' awareness that they are participating in a study may affect their judgments. Furthermore, it is conceivable that the effects of a client's gender are strongest when little additional information about the client is available. These effects might be tempered as therapist and client come to know each other through their work together. More studies that make use of information about the entire treatment history and that access therapists' behavior as well as their a priori recommendations are needed.

Duration of Therapy

It has been suggested that therapists inadvertently foster dependency in their female clients by keeping them in treatment relationships longer than male clients (Chesler, 1971; Fabrikant, 1974). Harris' (1971) review of the numerous studies on length of stay in therapy shows that the majority of studies found no difference between women and men (e.g., Chesler, 1971; Garfield & Affleck, 1959; Kirshner, Hauser, & Genack,

1979; Mendelsohn, 1966). However, a fair number of studies found that women remained in therapy longer than men (e.g., Abramowitz, Abramowitz, Roback, Corney, & McKee, 1976; Lowinger & Dobie, 1968). In only two studies did men appear to remain in therapy longer than women (Brown & Kosterlitz, 1964; Safer, 1973). In Safer's study, the effect of client's gender was sharply qualified by interactions with therapist's gender and frequency of sessions. Male client–male therapist pairs persisted longer in twice-weekly psychodynamic therapy sessions than any other gender pairing; however, this effect did not hold for clients and therapists with once-a-week contact. Furthermore, male client–female therapist pairs ended therapy sooner than any other gender pairing.

Studies on the duration of therapy have two implications. First, it appears that clients' gender does not have a consistent effect on the duration of therapy. The other implication bears on future studies of the duration of therapy. Safer's work suggests that other variables such as therapists' gender and frequency of therapy sessions interact with clients' gender in determining the duration of therapy. Other variables such as the therapists' age and experience, the type of therapy, and the nature of the clients' problems may also have effects.

Two conceptual problems with studies on the duration of therapy need to be mentioned. First, length of stay in therapy is not wholly determined by the therapist. It is erroneous to assume that if women remain in therapy longer than men, the reason is that therapists "keep" women in therapy longer. Women might choose to remain in therapy longer than men, possibly because they feel they are deriving more benefit from it. The point is that studies comparing the length of time that women and men remain in therapy will tell us only whether differences exist. They cannot tell us how or why such differences occur.

The second conceptual issue concerns the relationship of early termination of therapy to overall duration of therapy. Early termination refers to dropping out of therapy before a therapeutic alliance has been formed. By definition, early termination is a unilateral action on the part of the client, and, thus, it reflects different processes from those of the normal termination procedure. Early termination should be treated as a separate research issue. Clients who drop out of therapy after the first few sessions should be eliminated from studies on the duration of therapy. Otherwise, the results of such studies may be misleading.

Clients' Likelihood of Seeking Treatment

Many theorists have suggested that women and men differ in their likelihood of seeking therapy. These conjectures derive from two sources. First, there is fairly consistent evidence that the ratio of women to men entering therapy is roughly 2:1 (e.g., Brown & Kosterlitz, 1964; Davidson, 1976; Schofield, 1964). Second, it has been theorized that the traditional feminine role is more compatible with help-seeking than the traditional masculine role (Nathanson, 1975). Kirshner (1978) presented evidence consistent with the idea that help-seeking is "easier" for women than for men. He found that among college students, women sought help from the counseling service at an earlier stage of their distress than men did. Neither line of reasoning provides direct evidence that, given comparable levels of distress, women are more likely to enter therapy than men. Though the hypothesis is plausible, we know of no demonstration that such a gender difference exists.

Clients' Preferences for Therapists' Gender

Clinicians have long been interested in why their clients preferred therapists of one gender or the other. In 1938, Clara Thompson pointed out the interplay of psychodynamic factors—some positive, some maladaptive—that shapes a client's desire to have a woman or man for a therapist. These factors were thought to foster or to impede the development of transference. More recently, the rationale for studying clients' preferences for the gender of their therapists has shifted. Many researchers now interpret clients' preferences as a reflection of their sex-role socialization or as an indication of societal sexism.

Most of the studies on clients' preferences for the gender of their therapists have used college students as research subjects. Some of these studies (e.g., Boulware & Holmes, 1970) used random samples of students who were not therapy clients. However, two studies (Fuller, 1963; Walker & Stake, 1978) showed that students who were simply research volunteers expressed very different preferences from students who were actually seeking therapy. Thus, we will review only studies of actual clients.

An early study of clients' preferences found that most college students entering the counseling service preferred to see therapists of their own gender (Koile & Bird, 1956). However, the majority of clients with preferences for a therapist of the opposite gender were women. A later study by Fuller (1964) found that clients in a student counseling service preferred male therapists over female therapists. Finally, results of a recent study (Walker & Stake, 1978) suggest that dramatic changes in college students' preferences may have occurred. Walker and Stake found that roughly 50% of clients had preferences for their therapists' gender. Of these, 92% of the women chose female therapists; the men were evenly divided in their choices of male and female therapists.

Two large-scale studies of clients in outpatient therapy clinics are available. Chesler (1971) interviewed 1001 clients seeking therapy at a middle-income clinic in New York City during 1965–1969. About 25% of them spontaneously expressed their preferences (or lack of preference) for the gender of their therapists. Of those who spoke to the issue, 26% had no preference, 45% preferred male therapists, and 29% preferred female therapists. Among female clients, the modal choice was a male therapist (40%); 35% had no preference, and only 25% preferred female therapists.

Davidson (1976) studied clients seeking therapy at a middle-income clinic in Texas during 1973–1974. Each client completed a self-administered questionnaire in the clinic waiting room prior to intake. The questionnaire asked the client to indicate a preference or no preference for the therapist's gender and ethnicity. If a preference was indicated, the client was asked to complete a checklist of reasons for his or her preference. The results showed that 50% of the clients had no preferences, 35% preferred male therapists, and 15% preferred female therapists. "Older" clients (ages 28–68 years) were more likely to prefer male therapists and less likely to prefer female therapists than were younger clients. Among both female and male clients, persons who were married least often expressed preferences for therapists of the other gender, and those who were separated, divorced, or widowed most often expressed such preferences. Overall, female clients more frequently expressed preferences for cross-gender therapists than did male clients.

The second portion of Davidson's questionnaire dealt with reasons for choosing a female or a male therapist. Unfortunately, the design of the questionnaire allowed only limited analyses to be undertaken. The reasons most commonly given for a gender preference were "feeling comfortable" and "able to talk freely" in the presence of the therapist. Clients who preferred female therapists were more likely than those who preferred male therapists to feel that the therapist "would understand their problems better." (This is of interest in light of the discussion of therapists' empathy which follows.) Clients who preferred male therapists were more likely to cite past experience with and general preferences for male doctors as reasons for their choices. Among clients preferring female therapists, men were more likely than women to cite the therapist's attractiveness and intelligence as reasons for their choices.

One final study is of interest because it deals with a client population very different from those mentioned heretofore. Eldred and Washington (1975) studied 158 heroin addicts in an urban outpatient clinic. Very few had preferences for the gender of their therapists: 86% of the male clients and 72% of the female clients had no preferences.

Those who had preferences were evenly split in their choices of female or male therapists.

Although the studies in this area differ to some extent in experimental design, some generalizations are possible. It appears that the modal client does not have a preference for the gender of his or her therapist. Among those who have preferences, better-educated individuals, younger individuals, and women are more likely than their counterparts to prefer female therapists. Finally, viewing the studies chronologically suggests that the number of clients—especially women—who prefer female therapists is increasing.

It would be of interest to study the motives underlying the apparent growing interest among women (at least, young women) in having a woman as a therapist. There is also anecdotal evidence that a growing number of women seek out therapists who are feminists (Johnson, 1976; Kirshner *et al.*, 1979). Both trends may reflect a growing awareness of the need to discuss sex-role-related issues in therapy.

Early Termination of Therapy

Most of the research on clients' gender and early termination of therapy has been carried out by Alfred Heilbrun, using clients at a college counseling service. A series of his studies (e.g., Heilbrun, 1961, 1970, 1973, 1974) explored the personality traits of women and men who terminated therapy early. He also addressed the paradoxical finding that dependent women appear to be at special risk for terminating therapy early. His recent studies suggested that nondirective therapeutic styles provoke early termination in women who score low on a Counseling Readiness Scale. These women were more likely to remain in therapy with a directive therapist than with a nondirective therapist. Among women who scored high on the Counseling Readiness Scale, the opposite effect occurred. Not surprisingly, clients' gender per se did not predict the likelihood of early termination. However, intervention style appeared to interact with gender to promote dropping out versus remaining in therapy. It is to such interactions that future attention should be directed.

Other researchers have studied therapists' gender and early termination. Two studies (Hiler, 1958; McNair, Lorr, & Callahan, 1963) found that female therapists appeared more successful than male therapists in retaining male clients. The study of McNair *et al.* showed that female therapists experienced fewer early terminations by male clients than did male therapists. The study by Hiler showed that female therapists retained more male clients who had been identified as potential early terminators. However, Hiler's study also showed that, compared to male therapists, female therapists lost more male clients who had been identified as likely to remain in therapy.

We need more studies of early termination of therapy before the phenomenon can be understood. Our knowledge would be enhanced greatly if some studies sought information directly from the client on why he or she quit therapy. It is possible that not all of the "early terminators" were dissatisfied with the help they got. Some may have felt able to resolve their problems after only a brief encounter with a therapist.

Therapy Processes

Therapists' Perceptions of and Feelings toward Their Clients

The few studies of therapists' perceptions of their clients focus on therapists' liking and sympathy for their clients and on therapists' judgments of their clients' ability to self-disclose. Lowinger and Dobie (1968) reported that a group of 16 psychiatric residents (gender unspecified) judged their female clients to possess greater ego strength, greater ability to communicate, and greater physical attractiveness than their male clients. Not surprisingly, female clients were also better liked. Ehrlich and Bauer (1967) examined therapists' liking and sympathy for inpatients whom they were treating with intensive short-term psychotherapy. Therapists' perceptions of their clients were obtained in interviews held during the third or fourth week after the clients' hospitalization. Neither liking nor sympathy for clients differed as a function of therapists' gender or clients' gender. Furthermore, there were no differences in liking or sympathy due to other demographic characteristics of the clients, a finding that contradicts much other evidence in the literature. Finally, Strassberg and Anchor (1977) asked 26 trainees in a university counseling center to rate their clients' levels of self-disclosure on a seven-point scale of "willingness to share." These ratings were completed after each therapy session. Overall, male therapists regarded their clients as more willing to share than did female therapists. Therapists of both genders gave more ratings indicating low self-disclosure to female clients than to male clients.

All of these studies have several shortcomings in common. They failed to obtain independent assessments of the qualities that the therapists judged. Therefore, we cannot know whether the therapists' perceptions reflect accurate appraisals of clients' characteristics or biases due to sex-role stereotyping. They all use inexperienced therapists—residents and counseling trainees. Finally, all used convenience samples of therapists, and, in some cases, these samples are too small to permit appropriate analysis. Further studies in the area must employ more sophisticated experimental approaches.

The question of therapists' affective responses to female and male clients has been addressed in only a few studies. The earliest of these (Fuller, 1963) simply reported that more feelings were expressed in client–therapist pairs containing a female, regardless of her role. As part of a larger study, Johnson (1978) collected the immediate reactions of female and male therapists to videotaped clients. Judges rated this material on four dimensions: sympathy, defensiveness, identification, and anger. The videotapes showed clients who were male or female, depressed or angry. Female therapists were judged to feel significantly more anger toward all clients than were male therapists. None of the other dimensions yielded significant effects. The use of global ratings rather than sentence-by-sentence content analysis or other microanalytic techniques may have obscured some gender effects. Nonetheless, eliciting spontaneous, open-ended reactions from therapists yielded rich material. This method may be fruitful in future studies.

Howard, Orlinsky, and Hill (1969) studied the feelings engendered by female clients in 19 therapists. The therapists averaged 6 years of experience. The clients were also experienced: Two-thirds had been in therapy previously. Most (55%) of the clients were diagnosed as neurotic, 29% were diagnosed as personality disorders, and the remainder were schizophrenic. The therapists' feelings were recorded on the Therapy Session Report (TSR) after each session. Overall, male therapists reported more frequent unpleasant and "personal" (vs. "professional") feelings than female therapists. The correlations of therapists' and clients' TSR ratings showed strong, fairly consistent differences between male and female therapists. Female therapists appeared "more sensitive and responsive to the emotional–expressive component" of the therapy relationship than the male therapists did. For instance, female therapists felt "nurturant warmth" in response to clients' painful self-exploration; they felt a sense of failure when clients expressed rejection or dislike. The category of clients' feelings labeled "Erotic Transference Resistance" evoked particularly interesting reactions. Male therapists tended to feel "disturbing sexual arousal," while female therapists reported mainly feelings of "uneasy intimacy" and, secondarily, positive affect, feelings of resignation, and nurturant warmth.

These studies suggest that female therapists experience and express more feelings in interactions with clients than do male therapists. The study by Howard *et al.* further suggests that female therapists may be more aware of their clients' affect as well as more responsive to it. However, this study was limited to female clients; it is possible that the greater responsiveness of female therapists is conditioned by clients' gender. Overall, this area suffers from a sheer lack of research. This lack is particularly regrettable in view of the intriguing findings of Howard *et al.*

Empathy

A variety of different techniques and designs have been used to study gender differences in empathy. Breisinger (1976) asked graduate students in a counselor education program to respond to videotaped clients. Ratings of their responses showed no gender differences in empathy. Interestingly, Breisinger's study failed to replicate a previous study of empathy that used college students instead of therapists (Olesker & Balter, 1972); the previous study had found gender differences. Another pair of studies was conducted with beginning-level practicum students in clinical psychology and with therapy trainees (Abramowitz, Abramowitz, & Weitz, 1976). Subjects observed videotapes of clients presenting their problems and then wrote down the responses they considered helpful. In both studies, judges evaluated the responses made by women as more empathic than the responses made by men. Johnson (1978) asked experienced therapists to respond to several videotaped portrayals of clients (male or female, depressed or angry). Female therapists' self-ratings on empathy were higher than those of male therapists, regardless of clients' gender or affect. Commenting on the finding that the female therapists described themselves as quite empathic even with the client toward whom they felt most negative, Johnson suggested that the female therapists may have believed that they *should* be empathic toward all clients.

There are several naturalistic studies of gender differences in therapists' empathy, and they have yielded different results from those of the analogue studies described above. Cartwright and Lerner (1963) found that therapists obtained higher empathy ratings when working with cross-gender rather than same-gender clients. However, this difference diminished over the course of therapy. Furthermore, therapists' experience level was found to have a significant effect: Experienced therapists achieved high empathy toward same-gender clients, while inexperienced therapists achieved high empathy toward opposite-gender clients. A recent attempt to replicate this study (Andrews, 1975) found no gender effects on empathy. Furthermore, another recent study (Hill, 1975) found that both experienced and inexperienced therapists were more empathic toward clients of their own gender.

It is difficult to draw conclusions about gender and empathy from these studies. Methods, therapist characteristics, and findings are too divergent to assemble into a coherent picture. It is important to note, however, that there appear to be distinct differences between the results of analogue studies and the results of naturalistic studies. The analogue studies suggest that female therapists are more empathic than male therapists. However, the naturalistic studies imply that gender-matching and the experience level of the therapist may be more important determinants of empathy. This disparity requires caution in generalizing from analogue research. In the future, researchers studying empathy might be wise to focus on natural therapy situations or, at least, to construct analogues that are as naturalistic as possible.

Intervention Style

Two studies of therapists' interventions suggest that the gender of the client may influence the therapist's style of intervening. Parker (1967) studied tape-recorded therapy sessions of 16 male therapy trainees, each treating a male client and a female client. An analysis of the number of directive therapist responses (e.g., direct questions, giving information) and of nondirective responses (e.g., simple acceptance, restatement) indicated that the therapists made more nondirective responses to women than to men. The numbers of directive responses to males and to females were approximately equal. Gamsky and Farwell (1966) had 15 male and 15 female counseling trainees interview four individuals whom they believed to be real clients: males and females, who were either friendly or hostile. Judges' ratings of therapists' statements indicated that the hostile male client elicited more nondirective responses (e.g., agreement, reflection) than did the hostile female. The interpretation of these two studies is unclear, as their results are somewhat contradictory. Future research should examine the styles of female therapists as well as male therapists. In general, inexperienced therapists make more directive interventions than experienced therapists (cf. Auerbach & Johnson, 1978). Thus, studies of intervention style should consider possible interaction effects of gender and experience.

Manifest Content of Therapists' Interventions

There have been very few studies of the content of therapists' interventions, though this has been a major area of feminist concerns. The Task

Force on Sex Bias and Sex-Role Stereotyping of the American
Psychological Association (APA Task Force; 1975) collected anecdotal
evidence of sexist or sex-role-stereotyped content in therapy. These
statements were grouped into four categories: fostering traditional sex
roles; biased expectations and devaluation of women; sexist use of
psychoanalytic concepts; and responding to women as sex objects. The
survey did not deal with the incidence or prevalence of sex-biased content. Nonetheless, it points the way for future studies to do so.

In an unusual study, Shapiro (1977) studied the responses of 16
male and female counseling trainees to female "clients" who portrayed
either a conventional "feminine" role or a "masculine" one. The counselors believed the clients to be volunteers relating authentic problems.
Videotapes of the interviews were rated for the numbers of "positively
reinforcing" versus "extinguishing" responses made by the counselors in
response to cues in the clients' script. Overall, female counselors gave
more positively reinforcing responses and fewer extinguishing responses than male counselors. Furthermore, female counselors showed
less sex-role stereotyping in their choice of which cues to reinforce positively and which cues to extinguish. Surprisingly, a measure of counselors' sex-role attitudes failed to predict responses to stereotypical and
counterstereotypical cues.

This is clearly an area demanding researchers' attention. It was
identified as a high-priority area of research at the 1974 Society for
Psychotherapy Research workshop (cf. Waskow, 1976). Yet, only one
relevant study has been reported in the intervening 5 years. The need
for empirical work is urgent.

Seduction of Clients

The occurrence of sexual contact between therapist and client within the
therapeutic relationship is not a therapeutic process, but it nonetheless
deserves mention here, because it is of considerable import to women in
therapy. Holroyd and Brodsky (1977) surveyed therapists concerning
their participation in sexual relations with clients. Seventy percent of
therapists queried returned the questionnaire. The results showed that
6% of male therapists and 0.06% of female therapists had engaged in
sexual relations with clients. Furthermore, therapists who engaged in
erotic contact tended to do so with more than one client. Chesler (1972)
reported anecdotal evidence that, for some therapists, the seduction of
female clients may be habitual.

The survey conducted by the Task Force on Sex Bias and Sex-Role
Stereotyping of the American Psychological Association (APA Task

Force, 1975) indicated that sexual contact between client and therapist is considered exploitive by female professional psychologists. For psychologists and psychiatrists, such behavior is unethical. Nonetheless, as Davidson (1977) pointed out, few practitioners, including supervisors and administrators, take steps to intervene when a colleague or trainee is engaged in such behavior. Perhaps research documenting the deleterious consequences of sexual contact in therapy is necessary before the professions take action (cf. Taylor & Wagner, 1976).

Clients' Perceptions of Therapy and of Their Therapists

Two studies of clients' perceptions of therapy are available, and neither found gender differences. Feifel and Eels (1963) administered questionnaires to clients in a Veterans Administration mental health clinic. Clients were asked to describe changes they had undergone, to state what had been helpful or not helpful in therapy, and to suggest ways in which therapy could be improved. Results revealed that clients' responses did not differ according to their therapists' gender. Using Yalom's Q-sort of curative factors, Rohrbaugh and Bartels (1974) studied participants' perceptions of their experiences in group therapy and human relations groups. There were no differences due to clients' gender; differences due to therapists' gender were not studied.

Studies of clients' perceptions of their therapists have yielded fragmentary and inconsistent results. Apfelbaum (1958) studied 100 clients in a university outpatient clinic. Prior to entering therapy, they completed a Q-sort to measure their "best guess as to what the therapist would be like"; they were told to assume that the therapist would be male. Analyses of the Q-sort data revealed three clusters of expectations: (1) that the therapist would nurture, support, and protect; (2) that he would be diplomatic, well-adjusted, and accepting; and (3) that he would be cold, critical, and unemotional. Male clients were more likely to expect their therapists to be of either the first or third type; female clients expected their therapists to be of the second type.

The discussion of therapists' behaviors thus far has focused on one-to-one therapy. Very little work exists on gender-related processes in therapies involving cotherapists. Strauss (cited in Wright & Gould, 1977) investigated perceptions of female and male cotherapists of each other's role. She found that women were seen as providers of warmth and affective support to the group, while male cotherapists were assigned the task of actually leading the sessions. In one anecdotal account, the female cotherapist's role included making and serving coffee weekly to group members (Mintz, 1974). Similarly, some family theorists have urged cotherapy teams to adopt sex-stereotyped roles in order to model "appropriate" behaviors for family members (Boszormenyi-Nagy & Spark, 1973). Clearly, empirical work on the effects of role-modeling by cotherapists is needed.

Interaction Style

A few researchers have addressed the topic of how clients respond in therapy. Scher (1975) found that female clients spoke more in therapy sessions than male clients. In contradiction to this, Siegman (Note 5) found that undergraduate males volunteering for a study of interview processes were more productive than females in responding to intimate questions, though the two were similar in responses to neutral questions. Siegman also studied the effect of interviewers' warmth on interviewees' productivity. In same-gender dyads, warmth had no effect, nor did it have any effect on male interviewees. However, female interviewees were more reticent when talking with warm male interviewers than with reserved male interviewers. Possibly the warm male interviewers led the young women to experience discomfort stemming from sexual feelings (cf. Orlinsky & Howard, 1976).

Affective Experiences in Sessions

A popular belief is that women are more emotionally expressive than men. Is this true in the therapy situation? Fuller (1963) studied initial therapy sessions conducted in a university counseling center and found that more feelings were expressed in client–therapist pairs containing either a female client or a female therapist. Furthermore, clients of both genders expressed more feelings with female counselors than with male counselors (Fuller, 1964). Brooks (1974) replicated this latter finding but found that, overall, female clients did not disclose more feelings than male clients. Grantham's (1973) study of black clients at a college counseling center found that clients were more self-revealing in initial interviews when the counselor was female rather than male.

A study of feelings expressed in human relations groups (Aries, 1976) showed that women expressed and elicited more feelings than men. Groups composed of female college students shared personal information and feelings, while the interactions in all-male groups were competitive, nondisclosing, and self-aggrandizing. In mixed-gender groups, men dominated the interactions, but they talked more about feelings than did men in all-male groups.

Hill (1975) studied the interaction of therapists' experience level and clients' gender on the expression of feelings in therapy. She obtained ratings of segments of therapy sessions conducted in a university counseling center. The ratings showed that both experienced and inexperienced therapists focused on feelings more with same-gender clients than with opposite-gender clients; inexperienced therapists elicited more feelings from same-gender clients than opposite-gender clients.

Hill's study also points out a source of bias in studies of clients' affect. Raters' judgments of clients' expression of feelings indicated that the females were more expressive than the males. However, objective counts of affective self-referents (a behavioral measure of expressiveness) revealed no gender difference. This discrepancy points to the need for measurement procedures that circumvent raters' expectations.

Clients' level of experiencing—defined as the awareness and expression of strong immediate feelings—was examined in a large-scale therapy study (Auerbach, Luborsky, & Christoph, Note 6). When audiotapes of segments of sessions were rated for clients' level of experiencing, women's levels were higher than men's.

Orlinsky and Howard (1976) also carried out an analysis of clients' affect in the psychotherapy study already described. They analyzed several hundred TSRs completed by 118 female clients and their therapists at the end of each therapy session. Overall, the women who had female therapists perceived the therapeutic process as a comfortable and supportive experience. However, women with male therapists viewed the process as a tense one in which they felt self-critical and unsure of themselves. Sexual feelings toward the male therapists were also reported and may have led to some of the feelings of tension. Despite these differences, the gender of the therapists was not related to women's perceptions of the benefits of therapy.

The second step of the analysis was to categorize clients into six groups according to age and life status: (1) younger single women (age 18–22, never married; (2) single women (age 23–28, never married); (3) independent women (age 29 or older, not currently married); (4) young married mothers (age 23–25, currently married, with children; (5) young divorced mothers (age 23–25, formerly married, with children); and (6) family women (age 36–45, married or formerly married, with children). The first two groups (never-married women, 18–28 years old) showed the greatest reactivity to the gender of the therapists. In fact, most of the differences found in the total sample could be attributed to these two groups. Furthermore, women diagnosed as depressed showed the strongest reactivity to the gender of their therapists, with female therapists fostering more positive therapy processes than male therapists. Orlinsky and Howard interpret their findings not as reflections of actual differences in the behavior of female and male therapists, but rather as reflections of the culturally based value and significance of men qua men for young, unattached women. If so, the reactions of female clients to male therapists may be relatively independent of the behaviors and practices the therapists employ.

Gender appears to be a strong determinant of the expression of affect in therapy. However, though each of these studies found gender effects, no generalization about the nature of the effects is consistent with all of them. One reason for the inconsistency in results might be the diversity of conceptualizations and measurements of affective experiences across the studies. Furthermore, the studies use clients drawn from a variety of backgrounds and life statuses. Orlinsky and Howard's work suggests that some affective experiences may be relevant only to specific subpopulations of clients. The work reported thus far provides strong justification for continued efforts in this area.

Recommendations and Conclusions

Three recent reviews of sex roles and therapy (Abramowitz & Dokecki, 1977; Whitely, Note 7; Zeldow, 1978), as well as this review, highlight the striking absence of true process studies in this area. The other three reviews failed to include any naturalistic studies of trained therapists treating actual clients; we have located only a handful.

If one examines the frequency with which various topics are investigated, it appears that levels of research interest are more a function of the ease of conducting studies than of the centrality of the topic to our understanding of the therapy process. Studies relying on archival records or on questionnaire data are numerous. Analogue studies requiring interviews or experimental sessions with therapists or clients are done less frequently. Process studies of actual therapy are seldom carried out. Such studies require access to therapy session material and lengthy, painstaking analysis. Though the cost of such studies in terms of experimenters' efforts and research dollars may seem prohibitive, we strongly recommend that more efforts be directed toward process studies.

Specific recommendations are as follows:

1. Insofar as possible, studies should employ actual clients and therapists, rather than individuals engaging in role-play. Because professional socialization can exert an effect on sex-role attitudes, it is difficult to generalize from volunteer subjects to trained therapists. Making the decision to enter therapy may arouse in clients strong expectations

about therapy and the therapists, so it may be misleading to generalize from volunteers to committed clients.

2. Caution must be exercised in accepting the results of analogue studies as valid. More replications of analogue studies in naturalistic settings need to be undertaken. The results of such replications to date suggest that analogue studies are only of limited usefulness.

3. In studying actual therapy process, ways to minimize reactivity to being studied need to be found. The creative use of unobtrusive measures is one possibility. Greater use of extant data is also recommended, especially in light of the expense and time commitment entailed in large-scale therapy studies. Another possibility is to incorporate studies of gender influence into ongoing studies of therapy process or outcome.

4. Measurement techniques that eliminate the possibility of contamination due to raters' gender biases need to be developed. Increased reliance on behavioral measures rather than global judgments might help control possible measurement artifacts. Disguising the gender of the therapist or the client is another way to circumvent rater bias.

5. Simple comparisons of women and men are of limited interest to researchers or to practitioners.

6. We need to distinguish among therapy modalities and among therapists. We have found virtually no evidence pertaining to modes of therapy other than psychoanalytic or Rogerian approaches. There are few studies of therapies involving more than one therapist or groups of clients. There is also fairly little differentiation made among therapists. Experience level needs to be considered more frequently. The relation of therapists' sex-role attitudes to their behaviors in therapy also needs to be examined. Finally, nearly all of the studies reviewed here pertain to therapists practicing in clinics or university settings. Attention needs to be addressed to private practitioners as well.

7. There is a need for more complex experimental designs and more sophisticated multivariate statistical approaches. Many variables—such as presenting complaints, life stresses, and life status—appear to be severely confounded with the gender of therapy clients, thus leading to serious multicolinearity problems. Analytic techniques that account for multicolinearity must be used if we are to understand how strong the effects of gender are and through what mechanisms they operate.

Reference Notes

1. Doyle, K. M., & Levy, S. J. *The female client: How treated in drug abuse programs?* Paper presented at the meetings of the American Psychological Association, Chicago, August 1975.

2. Wyrick, T. J., & Mitchell, K. M. Relationship between accurate empathy, warmth and genuineness and perceived resident assistant effectiveness. *Discussion Papers,* Arkansas Rehabilitation: Research and Training Center, University of Arkansas, 1969, 12.
3. Kirshner, L. A., Hauser, S. T., & Genack, A. *Male and female freshmen in a university mental health clinic.* Unpublished study, Harvard University Health Services, 1976.
4. Schwartz, J., & Abramowitz, S. I. *Effects of psychiatrist values and patient race and sex on clinical judgment.* Paper presented at the meetings of the American Psychological Association, New Orleans, August 1974.
5. Siegman, A. W. *Effects of cross-gender pairing on vocal behavior.* Paper presented at the meetings of the American Psychological Association, San Francisco, August 1977.
6. Auerbach, A., Luborsky, L., & Christoph, P. *Sex differences in the University of Pennsylvania Psychotherapy Study.* Paper presented at the annual meeting of the Society for Psychotherapy Research, Toronto, June 1978.
7. Whitely, B. *Sex roles and psychotherapy: Where they stand now.* Unpublished manuscript, University of Pittsburgh, 1978.

References

Abramowitz, C. V. Blaming the mother: An experimental investigation of sex-role bias in countertransference. *Psychology of Women Quarterly,* 1977, *2,* 24–34.
Abramowitz, C. V., Abramowitz, S. I., & Weitz, L. J. Are men therapists soft on empathy? Two studies in feminine understanding. *Journal of Clinical Psychology,* 1976, *32,* 434–437.
Abramowitz, C. V., & Dokecki, P. R. The politics of clinical judgment: Early empirical returns. *Psychological Bulletin,* 1977, *84,* 460–476.
Abramowitz, S., Abramowitz, C. V., Roback, H., Corney, R., & McKee, E. Sex-role related countertransference in psychotherapy. *Archives of General Psychiatry,* 1976, *33,* 71–73.
American Psychological Association Task Force. Report of the Task Force on Sex Bias and Sex-Role Stereotyping in Psychotherapeutic Practice. *American Psychologist,* 1975, *30,* 1169–1175.
Andrews, S. B. The effect of sex of therapist and sex of client on termination from psychotherapy (Doctoral dissertation, University of Illinois, 1975). *Dissertation Abstracts,* 1976, *36B,* 3687B–4237B.
Apfelbaum, B. *Dimensions of transference in psychotherapy.* Berkeley: University of California Press, 1958.
Aries, E. Interaction patterns and themes of male, female and mixed groups. *Small Group Behavior,* 1976, *7,* 7–18.
Auerbach, A., & Johnson, M. Research on the therapists' level of experience. In A. Gurman & A. Razin (Eds.), *The therapist's contribution to effective psychotherapy: An empirical assessment.* New York: Pergamon Press, 1978.
Barocas, R., & Vance, F. Physical appearance and personal adjustment counseling. *Journal of Counseling Psychology,* 1974, *21,* 96–100.
Bergin, A. E., & Garfield, S. L. *Handbook of psychotherapy and behavior change.* New York: Wiley, 1971.
Boszormenyi-Nagy, I., & Spark, G. M. *Invisible loyalties: Reciprocity in intergenerational family therapy.* New York: Harper and Row, 1973.
Boulware, D., & Holmes, D. Preferences for therapists and related expectancies. *Journal of Consulting and Clinical Psychology,* 1970, *35,* 269–277.
Breisinger, G. D. Sex and empathy reexamined. *Journal of Counseling Psychology,* 1976, *23,* 289–290.
Brink, P. J. Behavioral characteristics of heroin addicts on a short-term detoxification program. *Nursing Research,* 1972, *21*(1), 38–45.

Brooks, L. Interactive effects of sex and status on self-disclosure. *Journal of Counseling Psychology,* 1974, *21,* 469–474.

Brown, J., & Kosterlitz, N. Selection and treatment of psychiatric outpatients. *Archives of General Psychiatry,* 1964, *11,* 425–437.

Cartwright, R. D., & Lerner, B. Empathy, need to change, and improvement with psychotherapy. *Journal of Consulting Psychology,* 1963, *27,* 138–144.

Chesler, P. Women as psychiatric and psychotherapeutic patients. *Journal of Marriage and the Family,* 1971, *33,* 746–759.

Chesler, P. *Women and madness.* Garden City, N.Y.: Doubleday, 1972.

Cooperstock, R. Sex differences in the use of mood-modifying drugs: An explanatory model. *Journal of Health and Social Behavior,* 1971, *12,* 238–244.

Davidson, V. Patient attitudes toward sex of therapist: Implications for psychotherapy. In J. L. Claghorn (Ed.), *Successful psychotherapy.* New York: Brunner/Mazel, 1976.

Davidson, V. Psychiatry's problem with no name: Therapist–patient sex. *The American Journal of Psychoanalysis,* 1977, *37,* 43–50.

Ehrlich, H. J., & Bauer, M. L. Therapists' feelings toward patients and patient treatment and outcome. *Social Science and Medicine,* 1967, *1,* 283–292.

Eldred, C. A., & Washington, M. N. Female heroin addicts in a city treatment program: The forgotten minority. *Psychiatry,* 1975, *38,* 75–85.

Fabrikant, B. The psychotherapist and the female patient: Perceptions, misperceptions, and change. In V. Franks and V. Burtle (Eds.), *Women in therapy.* New York: Brunner/Mazel, 1974.

Feifel, H., & Eels, J. Patients and therapists assess the same psychotherapy. *Journal of Consulting Psychology,* 1963, *27,* 310–318.

Fuller, F. Influence of sex of counselor and of client on client expressions of feeling. *Journal of Counseling Psychology,* 1963, *10,* 34–40.

Fuller, F. Preferences for male and female counselors. *Personnel Guidance Journal,* 1964, *42,* 463–467.

Gamsky, N. R., & Farwell, G. F. Counselor verbal behavior as a function of client hostility. *Journal of Counseling Psychology,* 1966, *13,* 184–190.

Garfield, S. L., & Affleck, D. C. An appraisal of duration of stay in outpatient psychotherapy. *Journal of Nervous and Mental Disease,* 1959, *129,* 492–498.

Gove, W. Mental illness and psychiatric treatment among women. *Psychology of Women Quarterly,* 1980, *4,* in press.

Gove, W., & Tudor, J. F., Adult sex roles and mental illness. *American Journal of Sociology,* 1973, *78,* 812–831.

Grantham, R. J. Effects of counselor sex, race and language style on black students in initial interviews. *Journal of Counseling Psychology,* 1973, *20,* 553–559.

Gross, H., Herbert, M., Knatterud, G., & Donner, L. The effect of sex on the variation of diagnosis and disposition in psychiatric emergency rooms. *Journal of Nervous and Mental Disease,* 1969, *148,* 638–642.

Hare-Mustin, R. T. A feminist approach to family therapy. *Family Process,* 1978, *17,* 181–194.

Harris, S. The influence of patient and therapist sex in psychotherapy. *Comments on Contemporary Psychiatry,* 1971, *1,* 17–27.

Harris, S., & Masling, J. Examiner sex, subject sex and Rorschach productivity. *Journal of Consulting and Clinical Psychology,* 1970, *34,* 60–63.

Heilbrun, A. B. Male and female personality correlates of early termination in counseling. *Journal of Counseling Psychology,* 1961, *8,* 31–36.

Heilbrun, A. B. Toward a resolution of the dependency–premature termination paradox for females in psychotherapy. *Journal of Consulting and Clinical Psychology,* 1970, *34,* 382–386.

Heilbrun, A. B. History and self disclosure in females and early defection from psychotherapy. *Journal of Counseling Psychology,* 1973, *20,* 250–257.

Heilbrun, A. B. Interviewer style, client satisfaction and premature termination following the initial counseling contact. *Journal of Counseling Psychology,* 1974, *21,* 346-350.

Helms, J. Counselor reactions to female clients: Generalizing from analogue research to a counseling setting. *Journal of Counseling Psychology,* 1978, *25,* 193-199.

Hiler, E. W. An analysis of patient-therapist compatibility. *Journal of Consulting Psychology,* 1958, *22,* 341-347.

Hill, C. Sex of client and sex and experience level of counselor. *Journal of Counseling Psychology,* 1975, *22,* 6-11.

Hill, C., Tanney, M. F., Leonard, M. M., & Reiss, J. A. Counselor reactions to female clients: Type of problem, age of client, and sex of counselor. *Journal of Counseling Psychology,* 1977, *24,* 60-65.

Holroyd, J. C., & Brodsky, A. M. Psychologists' attitudes and practices regarding erotic and nonerotic physical contact with patients. *American Psychologist,* 1977, 843-849.

Howard, K. I., Orlinsky, D. E., & Hill, J. A. The therapist's feelings in the psychotherapeutic process. *Journal of Clinical Psychology,* 1969, *25,* 83-93.

Johnson, M. An approach to feminist therapy. *Psychotherapy: Theory, Research, and Practice,* 1976, *13,* 72-76.

Johnson, M. Influence of counselor gender on reactivity to clients. *Journal of Counseling Psychology,* 1978, *25,* 359-365.

Kirshner, L. A. Effects of gender on psychotherapy. *Comprehensive Psychiatry,* 1978, *19,* 79-82.

Kirshner, L. A., Hauser, S. T., & Genack, A. Effects of gender on short-term psychotherapy. *Psychotherapy: Theory, Research, and Practice,* 1979, *15,* 158-167.

Koile, E., & Bird, D. Preferences for counselor help on freshman problems. *Journal of Counseling Psychology,* 1956, *3,* 97-106.

Kushner, K. On the external validity of two psychotherapy analogues. *Journal of Consulting and Clinical Psychology,* 1978, *46,* 1394-1402.

Lowinger, P., & Dobie, S. The attitude of the psychiatrist about his patients. *Comprehensive Psychiatry,* 1968, *9,* 627-732.

Marecek, J. Powerlessness and women's psychological disorders. *Voices: Journal of the American Academy of Psychotherapists,* 1976, *12,* 50-54.

Marecek, J. Psychological disorders in women: Indices of role strain. In I. H. Frieze, J. Parsons, P. Johnson, D. Ruble, & G. Zellman (Eds.), *Women and sex roles: A social psychological perspective.* New York: Norton, 1978.

Masling, J., & Harris, S. Sexual aspects of TAT administration. *Journal of Consulting and Clinical Psychology,* 1969, *33,* 166-169.

McNair, D. M., Lorr, M., & Callahan, D. M. Patient and therapist influences on quitting psychotherapy. *Journal of Consulting Psychology,* 1963, *27,* 10-17.

Mendelsohn, G. Effects of client personality and client-counselor similarity on the duration of counseling: A replication and extension. *Journal of Counseling Psychology,* 1966, *13,* 228-234.

Mendelsohn, G., & Rankin, N. D. Client-counselor compatibility and the outcome of counseling. *Journal of Abnormal Psychology,* 1969, *74*(2), 157-163.

Miller, J. B. *Psychoanalysis and women.* New York: Brunner/Mazel, 1973.

Mintz, E. E. What do we owe today's woman? *International Journal of Group Psychotherapy,* 1974, *24,* 273.

Nathanson, C. A. Illness and the feminine role: A theoretical review. *Social Science and Medicine,* 1975, *9,* 57-62.

Olesker, W., & Balter, L. Sex and empathy. *Journal of Counseling Psychology,* 1972, *19,* 559-562.

Orlinsky, D., & Howard, K. Female clients' perceptions of psychotherapy process. *Psychotherapy: Theory, Research, and Practice,* 1976, *13,* 82-88.

Parker, G. Some concomitants of therapist dominance in the psychotherapy interview. *Journal of Consulting Psychology,* 1967, *31,* 313-318.

Persons, R. W., Persons, M. K., & Newmark, I. Perceived helpful therapists' characteristics, client improvements and sex of therapist and client. *Psychotherapy: Theory, Research, and Practice,* 1974, *11*(1), 63–65.

Radloff, L. Sex differences in depression. *Sex Roles,* 1975, *1*(3), 249–265.

Rice, D. Patient sex differences and selection for individual therapy. *Journal of Nervous and Mental Disease,* 1969, *148,* 124–133.

Rohrbaugh, M., & Bartels, B. D. Participants' perceptions of "curative factors" in therapy and growth groups. *Small Group Behavior,* 1974, *6,* 430–456.

Rosenthal, D., & Frank, J. The fate of psychiatric clinic outpatients assigned to psychotherapy. *Journal of Nervous and Mental Disease,* 1958, *127,* 330–343.

Safer, J. Effects of sex of patient and therapist on length of therapy. *International Mental Health Research Newsletter, 1973,* 12–13.

Schafer, R. Problems in Freud's psychology of women. *Journal of the American Psychoanalytic Association,* 1974, *22,* 459–485.

Scher, M. Verbal activity, sex, counselor experience and success in counseling. *Journal of Counseling Psychology,* 1975, *22,* 97–101.

Schofield, W. *Psychotherapy: The purchase of friendship.* Englewood Cliffs, N.J.: Prentice-Hall, 1964.

Shapiro, J. Socialization of sex roles in the counseling setting: Differential counselor behavioral and attitudinal responses to typical and atypical female sex roles. *Sex Roles,* 1977, *3,* 173–184.

Strassberg, D. S., & Anchor, K. N. Rating of client self-disclosure and improvement as a function of sex of client and therapist. *Journal of Clinical Psychology,* 1977, *33,* 239–241.

Taylor, B. J., & Wagner, N. N. Sex between therapists and clients: A review and analysis. *Professional Psychologist,* 1976, *7,* 593–601.

Thomas, A. H., & Stewart, N. R. Counselor responses to female clients with deviate and conforming career goals. *Journal of Counseling Psychology,* 1971, *18,* 352–359.

Thompson, C. Notes on the psychoanalytic significance of the choice of the analyst. *Psychiatry,* 1938, *1,* 205–216.

Walker, E. F., & Stake, J. E. Changes in preferences for male and female counselors. *Journal of Consulting and Clinical Psychology,* 1978, *46,* 1153–1154.

Waskow, I. E. Summary of discussion following the workshop. *Psychotherapy: Therapy, Research, and Practice,* 1976, *13,* 96–98.

Wright, F., & Gould, L. J. Recent research on sex-linked aspects of group behavior: Implications for group psychotherapy. In L. R. Wolberg and M. L. Aronson (Eds.), *Group therapy '77: An overview.* New York: Stratton Intercontinental Medical Book Corp., 1977.

Zeldow, P. Sex differences in psychiatric evaluation and treatment. *Archives of General Psychiatry,* 1978, *35,* 89–93.

PART TWO

Disorders of High Prevalence

CHAPTER 4

Depression

MYRNA M. WEISSMAN

Introduction

It is most appropriate that a volume on women and psychotherapy should include within a section on high-prevalence disorders a chapter devoted to the discussion of depression. There is little question that depression is a high-prevalence disorder of women and that psychotherapy is an important method of treatment with reasonably established efficacy for depression.

Having made these definite statements, I would like to point out contradictions in the understanding and treatment of depression and the discrepancy between our understanding of treatment and the actual clinical practice of the treatment of depression. Knowledge of the complexity and heterogeneity of a disorder is a positive sign of activity and progress in scientific understanding.

In this chapter, I will present evidence for higher rates of depression among women than men and show that the reasons are biologic as well as psychosocial. I will review the evidence—and gaps in the evidence—for the efficacy of the treatments for depression and show that the treatments are both pharmacologic and psychotherapeutic. Lastly, I will describe the discrepancy between scientific understanding and clinical practice to show that, despite the growing body of evidence for the efficacy of a wide variety of treatments, many depressed women are either poorly treated or untreated.

Depression as a Symptom

Depression covers a broad spectrum of moods and behaviors that ranges from the disappointment and sadness of normal life to bizarre suicidal

Myrna M. Weissman. Departments of Psychiatry and Epidemiology, Yale University School of Medicine, and Depression Research Unit, Connecticut Mental Health Center, New Haven, Connecticut.

acts of severe melancholia. There are at least three meanings to the term—a mood, a symptom, and a syndrome.

Depression as a normal mood is a universal and transient phenomenon which none of us escapes. As a symptom or abnormal mood, depression is also common, and the differentiation between the normal and the pathologic can be indistinct. Depression of mood that is unduly persistent and pervasive is generally considered to be pathologic. Depressive symptoms are common. They occur in many persons who do not have psychiatric disorders, as well as in those with medical disorders or with psychiatric disorders other than depression (Weissman, Pottenger, Kleber, Ruben, Williams, & Thompson, 1977).

Depression as a Clinical Syndrome

Depression as a clinical syndrome is our concern in this discussion. A syndrome includes a number of specific symtpoms of certain severity and persistence that produce impairment and/or disorders which may better explain the condition.

Table 1 lists the Research Diagnostic Criteria (RDC) for the syndrome of major depression (Spitzer, Endicott, & Robins, 1978). These include dysphoric mood, at least five other symptoms, persistence for at least 2 weeks, resultant impairment of functioning or necessity of treatment, and occurrence in the absence of schizophrenia or other disorders which may better explain the symptoms. There are further subclassifications of the depressive syndrome (e.g., unipolar, bipolar, primary, secondary) which are of considerable research interest but are not critical for this discussion.

Evidence and Explanations for the Preponderance of Women among Depressives

Evidence

In a review of the sex differences in the epidemiology of depression reported by Gerald L. Klerman and myself, covering a span of more than 40 years and including about 30 Western countries, we found few exceptions to the observation that depression is more common among women than among men.[1] This finding was consistent in studies of hospitalized cases, studies of cases seen in outpatient clinics, and com-

[1]For a complete review of the evidence and explanations for the sex differences in the rates of depression, see Weissman and Klerman (1977).

Table 1. Research Diagnostic Criteria (RDC) for a Depressive Syndrome[a]

A through F are required for the episode of illness being considered.
A. Dysphoric mood which is prominent and relatively persistent.
B. At least five of the following symptoms are required for definitive diagnosis:
  1. Poor appetite or weight loss, or increased appetite or weight gain.
  2. Sleep difficulty or sleeping too much.
  3. Loss of energy, fatigability, or tiredness.
  4. Psychomotor agitation or retardation.
  5. Loss of interest or pleasure in usual activities, or decrease in sexual drive.
  6. Feelings of self-reproach or excessive or inappropriate guilt
  7. Complaints or evidence of diminished ability to think or concentrate, such as slow thinking or mixed-up thoughts.
  8. Recurrent thoughts of death or suicide, including of wishing to be dead.
C. Dysphoric features of illness lasting at least 2 weeks.
D. The subject sought help from someone during the dysphoric period or had impaired functioning.
E. None of the following which suggests schizophrenia is present:
  1. Delusions of being controlled or of thought broadcasting, insertion, or withdrawal.
  2. Nonaffective hallucinations of any type throughout the day for several days or intermittently throughout a 1-week period.
  3. Auditory hallucinations in which either a voice keeps up a running commentary on the subject's behavior or thoughts as they occur, or two or more voices converse with each other.
  4. At some time during the period of illness the subject had more than 1 month during which he or she exhibited no prominent depressive symptoms but had delusions or hallucinations.
  5. Preoccupation with a delusion or hallucination to the relative exclusion of other symptoms or concerns.
  6. Definite instances of marked formal thought disorder, accompanied by either blunted or inappropriate affect, delusion or hallucinations of any type, or grossly disorganized behavior.
F. Does not meet the criteria for Schizophrenia, Residual Subtype.

Spitzer, Endicott, and Robins (1978).

munity surveys of both treated and untreated persons (Weissman & Klerman, 1977).

Using the new RDC developed by Spitzer, Endicott and Robins, Jerome K. Myers and I conducted a study in New Haven, Connecticut, in 1976 and found essentially the same results. Women preponderate in the rates of depression; moreover, the rates are relatively high. The current-point prevalence rate/100 in New Haven was 5.2 for women and 3.2 for men, a sex ratio of 1.6:1 (Weissman & Myers, 1978).

Explanations

The preponderance of females with depressive syndrome has gained the attention of biologists, geneticists, epidemiologists, sociologists, and feminists, and a number of explanations have been offered. One set of explanations questions whether the finding is real and hypothesizes the likelihood that it is an artifact attributable to women's perceptions of stress and coping responses, their willingness to express affective symptoms, and the high frequency with which they seek medical help. The artifact hypothesis proposes that women perceive, acknowledge, report, and seek help for stress and symptoms differently from men and that these factors account for the sex-ratio findings. Alternatively, the finding is considered to be a real phenomenon related biologically to women's genetic or endocrine susceptibility or to social causes.

AN ARTIFACT

Our review of the various artifactual evidence led us to conclude that women do not have more stressful life events and do not judge life events as more stressful. While women more frequently acknowledge having symptoms and affective distress than do men, it does not appear to be because they feel less stigma or because they wish to win approval (Clancy & Gove, 1974).

Women and men have different help-seeking patterns (Hinkle, Redmont, Plummer, & Wolfe, 1960). However, increased female utilization of health care would not account for the preponderance of depressed women in community surveys wherein most "cases" are not in psychiatric treatment either at the time of the interview or in the past.

There is no question that more men than women have alcohol-abuse problems (Gomberg, 1974), and it is probable that some unknown proportion of depressed men appear in the alcoholism rates but are not identified as depressed. It could be debated, however, as to whether or not these men are really depressed. Accurate diagnostic assessments are needed to determine the morbid risk of depression and the time sequence of onset in relationship to the alcoholism. Pending future research to test this possibility, it remains an interesting but unproven hypothesis. When all of these possibilities are considered, my conclusion is that the female preponderance is not an artifact.

A REAL FINDING

I regard the sex differences as real findings and will examine the possible biologic and psychosocial explanations.

Genetic Reasons.   There are mainly four sources of evidence for the genetic hypothesis to explain the higher rates of depression among women: family-aggregation studies comparing illness rates within and between generations of a particular family on the basis that family members share the same genes to varying degrees; studies of twins comparing illness rates in monozygotic and dizygotic twins; cross-rearing studies; and linkage studies, in which known genetic markers are used to follow other traits through several generations or in siblings. The majority of genetic studies in depression are concerned with evidence from the first two types of studies.

The available evidence from several investigators (Gershon, Dunner, & Goodwin, 1971) shows an increased morbid risk of depression in the first-degree relatives of diagnosed depressives as compared to the general population and a higher concordance rate in monozygotic than in dizygotic twins. Summarizing all of the studies, there is reasonable evidence for a genetic factor operating in some types of depressive disorders. However, the samples studied are still small, and the more mildly ill outpatients have not yet been reported (Kidd & Weissman, 1978).

Endocrine Reasons. Interest in the possible relationship between female depression and sex hormones derives from observations that clinical depression tends to occur in association with events in the reproductive cycle, such as menstruation, use of contraceptive drugs, the postpartum period, and menopause.

The pattern of the relationship of endocrine to clinical states is inconsistent. There is good evidence that premenstrual tension and use of oral contraceptives have the effect of increasing rates of depression, but the effect is probably of small magnitude (Neu & DiMascio, 1974; Weissman & Slaby, 1973). There is excellent evidence that the postpartum period does induce an increase in depression (Paffenberger & McCabe, 1966). Contrary to widely held views, there is good evidence that menopause has no stimulatory effect on rates of depression (Weissman, 1979).

There is little evidence to relate these mood changes and clinical states to altered endocrine balance or specific hormones. However, it must be emphasized that I could find no reported study correlating clinical state with female endocrines and utilizing modern endocrinologic methods or sensitive quantitative hormonal assays. Here is an area for fruitful collaboration between endocrinology and psychiatry.

Psychosocial Reasons. Sociologists, psychologists, feminists, and others with a concern for women have become increasingly occupied with explaining why more women than men become depressed. The conventional wisdom is that the long-standing disadvantaged social status of women has psychosocial consequences that are depressing, thereby explaining the long-term trends of female preponderance in the rates of depression.

Two main pathways whereby women's disadvantaged status might contribute to clinical depression have been outlined. One emphasizes the low social status and the legal and economic discrimination against women; the other emphasizes women's internalization of role expectations, leading to learned helplessness.

The first pathway, called the "social-status hypothesis," is widely accepted in the recent discussions on social discrimination against women. Many women find their situation depressing because real social discrimination makes it difficult for them to achieve mastery by direct action and self-assertion, further contributing to their psychological distress. Applied to depression, it is hypothesized that these inequities lead to legal and economic helplessness, dependency on others, chronic low self-esteem, low aspirations, and, ultimately, clinical depression.

The second pathway, called the "learned-helplessness hypothesis," which is derived from the work of Seligman (1974), proposes that socially conditioned, stereotypical images produce in women a cognitive set against assertion, which is reinforced by social expectations. In this hypothesis, the classic "femininity" values are redefined as a variant of the learned helplessness that is characteristic of depression. Young girls learn to be helpless during their socialization and thus develop a limited response repertoire when under stress. These self-images and expectations are internalized in childhood so that the young girl comes to believe that the stereotype of femininity is expected and normal.

The most convincing evidence that social role plays a part in the vulnerability of women to depression is the data that suggest that marriage has a protective effect for men but a detrimental effect for women (Radloff, 1975). This supports the view that elements of the traditional female role may contribute to depression.

Further understanding of social stress and its interactions with components of female vulnerability in the traditional role is a promising area of research. This research would need to take into account intervening variables such as women's employment and the quality of the marriage. Any comprehensive theory proposed to account for the preponderance of depression among women, even the biologic theories, must explain both long-term rates and recent changes in rates.

Conclusions

The male–female differences in the rates of depression are real, and the evidence in support of them is best established in Western industrialized societies. Further studies need to be conducted in non-Western countries, particularly Africa and Asia, before any conclusions can be drawn about the universality of these differential rates.

There is little doubt, however, that the sex differences found in rates of depression are a promising lead that requires considerably broader-based inquiry into epidemiology. It is highly unlikely that any one of the explanations already described will be the sole factor accounting for the sex differences or that all types of depression will be associated with the same risk factors. As was shown, the explanations cross such a wide variety of disciplines that rarely are all interactions entertained by any one group. There has been an unfortunate tendency for fragmentation, so that the investigators in genetics, social psychology, or endocrinology are not specifically aware of attempts by their scientific colleagues to deal with similar phenomena. My purpose has been to assess different positions and, hopefully, to guide future research. The salient areas of needed research include (1) broad, community-based epidemiologic studies that use consistent and operationalized diagnostic criteria and overcome the problem of reporting and response sets; (2) further studies on the genetics of depression, including the nonbipolar and less severe forms of the disorder, and examination of the rates of depression among first-degree relatives of depressed patients to see if they fit frequencies and patterns consistent with a particular mode of inheritance; (3) endocrine studies on the relationship between hormones and mood; (4) cross-cultural epidemiologic studies, using consistent and similar diagnostic criteria, to examine the suggestion that depression may occur less frequently among women in nonindustrialized countries; (5) longitudinal studies of help-seeking patterns and rates of depression of women who do not assume the traditional female roles, especially in countries where women have achieved increased emancipation; and (6) close surveillance of changes in rates by sex and marital status.

In summary, I have reviewed the evidence critically and believe that the sex differences in rates of depression in Western society are, in fact, real and not an artifact of reporting or health care behavior and that the reasons for these sex differences are heterogeneous and include both biologic and psychosocial factors.

Progress and Gaps in Understanding the Efficacy of Treatments for Depression

Progress

Over the last two decades, evidence for the efficacy of various treatments for depression has increased dramatically. Recent developments in psychiatry have resulted in better specification of the treatment and of patients and in improved scientific standards for conducting clinical trials. The standards of research for investigating the efficacy of pharmacotherapy and psychotherapy have been clarified by the independent efforts of the Psychopharmacology and the Clinical Research Branches of the National Institute of Mental Health in sponsoring study groups and workshops that have led to key publications of therapeutic evaluation, including guidelines for the principles and problems in establishing the efficacy of psychotropic drugs, guides for designing clinical trials of psychotherapy, and catalogues of standardized change and outcome measures.

PHARMACOTHERAPY

The result of these efforts is excellent evidence for the treatment of depression. In numerous well-designed, placebo-controlled clinical trials using random assignment, it has been demonstrated that tricyclic antidepressants reduce the acute depressive syndrome (Hollister, 1978; Morris & Beck, 1974). In addition, there is good evidence from at least three clinical trials that maintenance treatment with tricyclic antidepressants for 6–8 months prevents relapse, once the clinical syndrome has been alleviated (Klerman, DiMascio, Weissman, Prusoff, & Paykel, 1974). Moreover, over 80% of persons with a depressive syndrome will respond to a tricyclic antidepressant in 1–4 weeks. Their sleep and appetite will improve, energy and interest will increase, and suicidal feelings and helplessness will diminish.

PSYCHOTHERAPY

The overwhelming evidence for the efficacy of psychopharmacologic agents does not preclude the importance of psychotherapy. There is also good evidence for the efficacy of psychotherapy, especially in enhancing interpersonal satisfaction and functioning. Contrary to the concerns of a decade ago, no negative interactions of combined drugs and psychotherapy have been found. In fact, the advantage of combined treatment for the depressive syndrome is striking and represents an additive effect of the two treatments (Weissman, 1979).

Thus far, five types of psychotherapy (group, marital, interpersonal, cognitive, and behavioral) have been tested in clinical trials which have included homogeneous samples of ambulatory adult depressed patients, usually women. In all of the studies, psychotherapy was more efficacious than a nonactive treatment control group.

The results of studies comparing drugs to psychotherapy were equivocal. One study found psychotherapy to be more efficacious than drugs, one study found them about equal, and three studies found that drugs and psychotherapy effected different outcomes. These three latter studies found that drugs improved the symptoms of depression and that psychotherapy had more of an effect on social functioning.

Four studies examining the combination of drugs (tricyclic antidepressants) and psychotherapy found the combination to be additive; that is, both treatments together were more effective than either treatment alone. No negative interactions between the treatments were noted.

In general, these studies demonstrate the efficacy on symptom reduction of psychotherapy alone, in comparison with pharmacotherapy, and in combination with pharmacotherapy for the acute ambulatory depressive (Weissman, 1979).

Several of the psychotherapies have been sufficiently operationalized in procedural manuals, and training programs are being conducted so that some comparability between therapists and replication of results may be achieved. Because of these technical advances and the promising evidence for efficacy, the Clinical Research Branch of the National Institute of Mental Health is initiating a large-scale collaborative trial of the treatment of depression including various psychotherapies and pharmacotherapy.

Gaps in the Evidence

While there has been rapid progress in psychotherapy trials, and the evidence suggests that the advantages of combined treatments for depression are additive, there are many issues which render the studies inconclusive. Some of these issues are related to understanding the treatment of depression in general, others to depressed women in particular. Since the majority of ambulatory depressives are women, any limitation in information on efficacy is important for the health of women. I would like to summarize briefly the gaps in the evidence which suggest future research directions.

SCANTINESS OF DATA

I have identified 17 clinical trials that include homogeneous samples of depressed patients (mostly women) and meet reasonable scientific standards, including randomized assignment of treatment (Weissman, 1979). These 17 studies represent five different types of psychotherapy (cognitive, interpersonal, behavioral, marital, group), so that information on any one treatment is sparse.

There is little question that further testing of all five therapies among depressed patients is indicated. Group and marital therapies require further testing, particularly as acute treatment, since to date these therapies have been tested in only one trial each and only as maintenance treatment. Future studies of the behavioral and cognitive therapies should include larger samples as well as drug comparison and combination groups. Moreover, many treatments that are potentially useful for depressed women, for example, assertiveness training and conjoint marital therapy, have not been tested in a clinical trial (Weissman, 1979).

DIAGNOSTIC HETEROGENEITY

Operationalized diagnostic criteria and standardized clinical assessments of signs and symptoms are quite recent developments in psychiatric research and were not available or in wide use when the studies I reviewed were initiated (Spitzer *et al.*, 1978). The studies completed have, for the most part, included heterogeneous samples of depressed patients. This diagnostic heterogeneity and imprecision obscure a major question about differential treatment response which would allow us to identify which types of depressed women should receive drugs or psychotherapy alone or in combination, and which psychotherapy.

ABSENCE OF DATA ON THE SEVERELY ILL DEPRESSED WOMAN

To date, clinical trials of psychotherapy have included only ambulatory patients. There are currently no published data from clinical trials on the psychotherapy of the hospitalized, severely ill, psychiatrically depressed, or bipolar patient.

ABSENCE OF LONG-TERM STUDIES

The studies testing psychotherapy have been short-term, usually lasting less than 4 months and often only 1 month. Since psychotherapy may have a late onset of therapeutic action and since many women have long-standing problems associated with the development of depression, the efficacy of long-term psychotherapy (e.g., 1 year) should be examined, particularly for the prevention of future depressions.

THE ROLE OF WOMEN'S SELF-HELP GROUPS

There have been at least two systematic studies of consciousness-raising groups (Lieberman & Bond, 1976; Weitz, Note 1), and neither of these studies examined their efficacy with regard to depression. Both studies found that the majority of respondents were dissatisfied with their personal lives and had experienced significantly more symptoms of depression and anxiety than a normative sample (although this may not necessarily have been the syndrome of major depression). There are many similar types of self-help groups which are reported by women to be quite helpful. Further study of the efficacy of women's self-help groups in treating depression or perhaps in preventing development of the full-blown depressive syndrome would be of value.

TREATMENT FOR MARITAL DIFFICULTIES

Marital difficulty is the most commonly reported event in the 6 months prior to the onset of depression and the most frequent problem presented and discussed by depressed women coming for outpatient treatment (Paykel, Myers, Dienelt, Klerman, Lindenthal, & Pepper, 1969). Moreover, these problems appear to be enduring, even with traditional psychotherapy. In a 4-year follow-up of depressed patients who had received 8 months of treatment (drugs and/or psychotherapy), marital problems remained for the formerly depressed patient in comparison with her normal neighbor, although the formerly depressed woman was functioning well in other areas (Bothwell & Weissman, 1977). Lastly, in a community study of women living in the Camberwell area of London, Brown and Harris found that a confiding, intimate relationship with the spouse was the most important protection against depression in the face of life stress (Brown & Harris, 1978). Thus, clinical trials of psychotherapy should concentrate on techniques to strengthen marital relations, to resolve or dissolve an irreparable and destructive marriage, and to strengthen the woman's vulnerability to depression in the absence of an intimate, confiding relationship and help her to seek alternatives.

Based on uncontrolled studies, there is some suggestion that conjoint marital therapy may be more efficacious than individual therapy (Gurman & Kniskern, 1979). A clinical trial testing this hypothesis is timely. However, the results must be considered in light of the fact that a couple willing to undergo conjoint therapy may have a potentially more viable marriage than a couple who refuses. Any results from such a study cannot be generalized beyond a sample of willing partners. Moreover, even if the results show the efficacy of conjoint over individual therapy, they should not be interpreted to mean that a depressed woman whose spouse refuses to enter conjoint marital treatment should be denied individual treatment.

NEGLECTED GROUPS: THE DEPRESSED OLDER WOMAN

Women in the 65-and-over age group are the fastest-growing segment of the United States population (Fact Sheet, Note 2). Women over 65 are living much longer than men. The gap in life expectancy between the sexes will continue to widen into the next century. In 1920, older women lived an average of 1 year longer than men. Today, the older woman lives about 4–7 years longer. The reasons for this difference between male and female life expectancy are not known, but its impact on the older woman's family, social life, income, and emotional health has been enormous (Fact Sheet, Note 2).

Compounding the life-expectancy differential between men and women is the fact that most women are younger than the men they marry. If the woman is 5 years older, then her chances of widowhood are 3 in 4. Therefore, the vast majority of women who marry, even if the marriage does not end in divorce, can expect to spend about 10 years alone as a widow.

Moreover, the older woman can expect to have financial difficulties. In 1976, about 18% of women over age 65 lived at or below the poverty level. For elderly black women, the percent jumped to about 40%. The older woman living alone as a widow and experiencing financial problems is vulnerable to depression.

In a survey of the New Haven, Connecticut, community (Weissman & Myers, 1978), it was found that the lifetime rates of depressive reactions associated with grief were sixfold higher in women than in men, probably due to the fact that most women outlive their spouses. Moreover, the rates were considerably higher in women in the lower social classes—21.1% in class 5 as compared to 8.1% in classes 1 and 2. Women, and especially those in the lower social classes, are at high risk for depressive reactions associated with grief as well as for depressive reactions associated with loneliness, isolation, loss of status, etc.

How do the therapeutic advances that I have described apply to the health of the older woman? Here, the information diminishes dramatically. In every one of the 17 trials that have tested psychotherapy for depression, the elderly have been excluded. The cutoff age for inclusion into the studies usually has been age 60—often 55. In practice, the patients studied usually have been between the ages of 20 and 40.

Similar situations exist for the trials examining the efficacy of psychotropic drugs alone, except in a few instances where special studies of geriatric patients have been conducted; for example, Raskin, in a recent review on the efficacy data of psychotropic drugs in psychogeriatrics, found only two placebo-controlled trials of a tricyclic antidepressant in geriatric patients (Raskin, in press).

Many questions concerning the treatment of depression are now ready to be tested. Does pharmacotherapy have similar efficacy during the acute phase of depression and as maintenance treatment in the depressed elderly as has been reported for younger groups? Why are the depressed elderly less frequently offered psychotherapy? Is there any evidence for less efficacy? What about the role of self-help and support groups?

The loss of social supports through death or loss of roles would seem to make psychotherapy even more important in the elderly in order to overcome grief, to increase self-esteem, and to assist in the search for alternative social supports. Further study of these approaches in the depressed older woman is required.

Conclusions

The purpose of this section has been to highlight the considerable progress made in the testing and development of a range of useful treatments for depressed women. In addition to the range of psychotherapeutic approaches which I discussed somewhat briefly, there are a number of antidepressant medications in use which I have not discussed. Moreover, there is not a contradiction in use between apparently contradictory treatments, drugs and psychotherapy. Despite the considerable research on efficacy, gaps still exist in our understanding, with precision, the right treatment for the right person. Certain groups of women at high risk for depression—particularly older women—have been excluded from the studies.

Gaps between Research Evidence and Clinical Practice

While there is reasonable evidence for the efficacy of a variety of treatments for depression, and although the magnitude of depression among women in the community is quite high, we have, in fact, found in our surveys of the New Haven, Connecticut, community that most depressions are either poorly treated or untreated.

We have found that few women (8.7%) with a major depression saw a psychiatrist. Only 43.5% received any treatment for an emotional problem from anyone, and quite often (21.9%) the treatment they received was from a non-mental health professional. Depressed women were high users of nonpsychiatric physicians; 78.3% with a current depression made three or more visits during the year. While over half received a psychotropic drug, this was usually a minor tranquilizer (Valium or Librium). Only 15.8% received a tricyclic antidepressant.

In summary, the majority of depressed women are in the health care system but not the *mental* health care system. They are seen primarily by non-mental health professionals or tend to make multiple visits to nonpsychiatric physicians for symptomatic complaints which they do not identify as emotionally or psychiatrically related. Consequently, few depressed women receive psychotherapy or antidepressants, and nearly one-half of them receive minor tranquilizers for the treatment of depression.

Conclusions

In general, the evidence suggests that research must be broadly based and should not be the exclusive domain of any one discipline. Understanding the sex differences in the rates of depression requires studies in genetics, endocrinology, sociology, and psychology.

With regard to treatment, the major needs now are in understanding the efficacy of specific, well-defined psychotherapies, alone and in combination with the tricyclic antidepressants; treating well-defined subtypes of depressed women; and expanding the data base both for the range of psychotherapies studied and for the range of women included. Special attention should be given to including older depressed women in these studies.

With regard to clinical practice, further efforts must be made to reduce the discrepancy between what is known about treatment and what is actually prescribed. Part of the discrepancy might be related to limited access, stigma, or acceptance of treatment by patients, but it can be only a small part, since depressed women do seek treatment in the health care system, albeit not the *mental* health care system. It is incumbent upon the nonpsychiatric physician and the mental health professional to learn how to detect depression and how to treat it properly.

Depression is of current scientific and therapeutic interest. This interest is a reflection of the rapid developments in understanding and has led to more precise, yet, at times, apparently contradictory answers. The information that will come from continued research on depression will help to improve the health of women.

ACKNOWLEDGMENTS

Part of the research reported here was supported by USPHS research grants 1 R01 MH25712 and 1 R01 MH26466 from the Center for Epidemiologic Studies and the Clinical Research Branch, National Institute of Mental Health, Alcohol, Drug Abuse and Mental Health Administration, Rockville, Maryland. The community survey was conducted in collaboration with Jerome K. Myers, Ph.D., Department of Sociology, Yale University.

Reference Notes

1. Weitz, R. *Feminist consciousness raising, self-concept and depression.* Unpublished doctoral dissertation, Yale University, 1978.
2. Fact Sheet. *The older woman: Continuities and discontinuities.* Conference sponsored by the National Institute on Aging and the National Institute of Mental Health, Bethesda, Md., September 15, 1978.

References

Bothwell, S., & Weissman, M. M. Social impairments four years after an acute depressive episode. *American Journal of Orthopsychiatry,* 1977, *47,* 231-237.

Brown, G. W., & Harris, T. *The social origins of depression: A study of psychiatric disorder in women.* London: Tavistock Publications, 1978.

Clancy, K., & Gove, W. Sex differences in mental illness: An analysis of response bias in self reports. *American Journal of Sociology,* 1974, *80,* 205-216.

Gershon, E. S., Dunner, D. L., & Goodwin, F. K. Toward a biology of affective disorders. *Archives of General Psychiatry,* 1971, *25,* 1-15.

Gomberg, E. S. Women and alcoholism. In V. Franks & V. Burtle (Eds.), *Women in therapy.* New York: Brunner/Mazel, 1974.

Gurman, A. S., & Kniskern, D. P. Research on marital and family therapy: Progress, perspective and prospect. In S. L. Garfield & A. E. Bergin (Eds.), *Handbook of psychotherapy and behavior change: An empirical analysis* (2nd ed.). New York: Wiley, 1979.

Hinkle, L. E., Redmont, R., Plummer, N., & Wolfe, H. G. An explanation of the relation between symptoms, disability, and serious illness in two homogeneous groups of men and women: II. *Journal of Public Health,* 1960, *50,* 1327-1336.

Hollister, L. E. Tricyclic antidepressants. *The New England Journal of Medicine,* 1978, *299* (20), 1106-1109.

Kidd, K. K., & Weissman, M. M. Why we do not yet understand the genetics of affective disorders. In J. Cole, A. F. Schatzberg, & S. H. Frazier (Eds.), *Depression: Biology, dynamics, treatment.* New York: Plenum, 1978.

Klerman, G. L., DiMascio, A., Weissman, M. M., Prusoff, B. A., & Paykel, E. S. Treatment of depression by drugs and psychotherapy. *American Journal of Psychiatry,* 1974, *131,* 186-191.

Lieberman, M., & Bond, G. R. The problem of being a woman: A survey of 1700 women in consciousness raising groups. *Journal of Applied Behavioral Science,* 1976, *12,* 363-379.

Morris, J. B., & Beck, A. T. The efficacy of antidepressant drugs: A review of research (1958 to 1972). *Archives of General Psychiatry,* 1974, *30,* 667-674.

Neu, C., & DiMascio, A. Variations in the menstrual cycle. *Medical Aspects of Human Sexuality,* February 1974, pp. 164-180.

Paffenberger, R. S., & McCabe, L. J. The effect of obstetric and perinatal events on risk of mental illness in women of childbearing age. *American Journal of Public Health,* 1966, *56,* 400-407.

Paykel, E. S., Myers, J. K., Dienelt, M., Klerman, G. L., Lindenthal, J. J., & Pepper, M. P. Life events and depression: A controlled study. *Archives of General Psychiatry,* 1969, *21,* 753-760.

Radloff, L. Sex differences in depression: The effects of occupation and marital status. *Sex Roles,* 1975, *1,* 249-269.

Raskin, A. A selected review of anxiolytics, neuroleptics and antidepressants in psychogeriatrics. In *Proceedings of the IXth Congress of the Collegium Internationale Neuro-Psychopharmacologicum,* Vienna, July 1978, in press.

Seligman, M. E. Depression and learned helplessness. In R. J. Friedman & M. M. Katz (Eds.), *The psychology of depression: Contemporary theory and research.* Washington, D.C.: Winston, 1974.

Spitzer, R. L., Endicott, J., & Robins, E. Research diagnostic criteria: Rationale and reliability. *Archives of General Psychiatry,* 1978, *35,* 773-785.

Weissman, M. M. The psychological treatment of depression: Research evidence for the efficacy of psychotherapy alone, in comparison and in combination with pharmacotherapy. *Archives of General Psychiatry,* 1979, *36,* 1261-1269.

Weissman, M. M. The myth of involutional melancholia. *The Journal of the American Medical Association,* 1979, *242,* 742-744.

Weissman, M. M., & Klerman, G. L. Sex differences and the epidemiology of depression. *Archives of General Psychiatry,* 1977, *34,* 98-111.

Weissman, M. M., & Myers, J. K. Affective disorders in a United States community: The use of research diagnostic criteria in an epidemiological survey. *Archives of General Psychiatry,* 1978, *34,* 1304-1311.

Weissman, M. M., Pottenger, M., Kleber, H., Ruben, H. L., Williams, D., & Thompson, W. D. Symptom patterns in primary and secondary depression: A comparison of primary depressives with depressed opiate addicts, alcoholics, and schizophrenics. *Archives of General Psychiatry,* 1977, *34,* 854-862.

Weissman, M. M., & Slaby, A. E. Oral contraceptives and psychiatric disturbance: Evidence from research. *British Journal of Psychiatry,* 1973, *123,* 513-518.

CHAPTER 5

Anxieties: Agoraphobia and Hysteria

DIANNE L. CHAMBLESS

ALAN J. GOLDSTEIN

The concept of the hysterical personality type has been largely rejected by feminist psychotherapists due to the denigrating use of the term "hysterical" by professionals and lay people alike. We risk reintroducing this term in this chapter, as we are to consider two problems which occur primarily in women who might be so described.

Generally, hysterics are described as demandingly dependent, overly dramatic, scatterbrained, and sexy but frigid. Krohn (1978), in the most comprehensive modern work on hysteria, has defined the hysterical personality largely in terms of ego qualities. He stresses the hysteric's vague and global cognitive style, especially notable in the context of affect-laden issues. In very charged situations, blocking and mild "fogging" of thoughts and perceptions occur. These characteristics are thought to result from a heavy reliance on repression and denial as defenses.

Similarly, Goldstein and Chambless (1978) have emphasized the hysteric's inability to link emotional experiences with the events actually eliciting them. Thus, the hysterical style is, "Don't think, don't know, and don't feel." This style may be learned when a child is regularly punished for the expression of strong feelings. Alternatively, one may learn to fear affect vicariously by seeing others lose control. Any one or all emotions may be negatively conditioned and targeted for supression, including sadness and sexual and aggressive feelings.

Freud (*passim*) initially proposed that females are more likely to show hysterical traits because they tend to repress rather than resolve the

Dianne L. Chambless. Psychology Clinic, Department of Psychology, University of Georgia, Athens, Georgia.
Alan J. Goldstein. Department of Psychiatry, Temple University Medical School, Philadelphia, Pennsylvania.

conflicts of the phallic–Oedipal period. Should later events stir incestuous longings, these may be expressed in symbolic language through "body talk," that is, through a conversion symptom. Should displacement occur as well, a phobia may result. In later years, Freud considered the possibility that females might be more frightened of loss of love than of castration. This is more consistent with interpersonal interpretations of hysterical behavior.

Based on studies of infant perception, Krohn (1978) has advanced the hypothesis that females may be innately more attuned to the human face and more responsive to it. This might foster the tendency to be more dependent on the reactions of others, a key attribute of hysterical development. Wolowitz (1971) and Halleck (1967) have offered sociocultural explanations. Both writers have noted that the hysterical personality is but an exaggeration of the female stereotype and suggest that girls are trained to have careers as hysterics. Girls are taught to overemphasize the importance of others' reactions and, in more extreme cases, develop histrionic, manipulative behavior to obtain attention and approval.

On the basis of studies of parent–child interaction to date (reviewed by Maccoby & Jacklin, 1974), one cannot conclude that girls are shaped by their parents to respond in the fashion described by Wolowitz and Halleck, with the exception of flirtatiousness. Nevertheless, girls do seem to be more obedient than boys, with both their parents and their teachers; this would tend to support the hypothesis that girls might be more attuned to others' needs and approval.

For women, a hysterical personality mode does not of itself constitute pathology, since a hysterical adjustment is highly congruent with the female sex-role stereotype. Nevertheless, this personality style provides an ideal matrix for the development of serious psychiatric problems. Under stressful circumstances, hysteria, defined as "neurotic conflict in a hysterical personality" (Krohn, 1978, p. 213), may develop. Hysterical symptoms may take a variety of culturally determined forms, but the two most common appear to be agoraphobia (anxiety hysteria) and conversion reactions.

Conversion Hysteria

When psychological conflicts are experienced as physical illness which has no organic basis, one is said to be suffering a conversion reaction. Conversion symptoms reflect "somatic imaging," memories of prior bodily sensations derived from one's own experiences or from observation of others (Beck, 1976; Engel, 1970). Behavioral symptoms may result from these sensations. If one feels unable to breathe, she may gasp repeatedly for air. If she feels weakness in a limb, she may cease to move it. Actual physical complications may ensue from these reactions; for instance, a hysterically paralyzed limb may atrophy from disuse, or hyperventilation may result in physiologically induced lightheadedness as well as numbness and tingling in the limbs. The variety of conversion symptoms is great. Though such symptoms are frequently described as being limited to bodily symptoms under voluntary, central nervous system control, more often the problem is sensory in nature. Thus, pain is cited as the most frequent complaint today (Engel, 1970; Stefansson, Messina, & Meyerowitz, 1976), while other common symptoms are hyperventilation, fainting, convulsions, paralysis, blindness, globus hystericus (imaginary lump in the throat), and anorexia.

It is extremely difficult to assess the general incidence of conversion reactions, as the syndrome is difficult to diagnose, and its sufferers would steadfastly maintain its organic nature to the hapless interviewer attempting such a survey. Estimates in Greece (Stefanis, Markidis, & Christodoulou, 1976) and the United States (Ziegler, Imboden, & Meyer, 1960) suggest that about 3% of psychiatric patients are diagnosed as conversion hysterics. Given hysterics' denial of psychological problems, it is unlikely that such patients will voluntarily seek psychiatric consultation. Consequently, it is not surprising that the incidence of conversion reactions among general medical hospital patients is higher, ranging from 4.5% (Stefansson *et al.*, 1976) to 13% (Ziegler *et al.*, 1960). From the vantage point of an internist/psychiatrist, Engel (1970) has estimated that 20–25% of patients admitted to a general medical service have shown conversion symptoms at some time in their medical history. In a survey of 1000 applicants for Social Security disability payments, Stephens and Kamp (1962) found over 10% to be diagnosed as conversion hysterics on the basis of mandatory psychiatric consultation. These figures debunk the common belief that the current incidence of conversion hysteria is negligible. The most carefully conducted survey indicates that the incidence has remained a stable 3% of the psychiatric population over the past 50 years (Stephens & Kamp, 1962). This figure may be inflated in times of great sociocultural stress. For instance, Stefanis *et al.* (1976) found that immediately after World War II, when Greece was in chaos, conversion reactions accounted for 6% of psychiatric cases. Conversion reactions have, however, changed their form, becoming more subtle and difficult to detect (Krohn, 1978). Commonly, the most transparent symptoms are now found in poorly educated, rural people (Engel, 1970).

Engel suggests that conversion symptoms develop under conditions of psychological stress when the individual feels helpless and frustrated. Common stresses are grief, interpersonal conflict, and sexual threats or temptations. The overwhelming feelings are somaticized, with the particular symptom determined in a number of ways. The symptoms chosen frequently have been experienced during a previous physical illness or were manifested by someone else close to the hysteric. The most famous example of the latter is Freud's case of Dora, whose hysterical cough mimicked that of her father's mistress (Freud, 1905/1963). Symptoms may also reflect in body language the repressed feelings or may represent bodily harm wished on another. To the degree that the conversion fills its primary role (expression of the conflictual impulses), *la belle indifférence* will be expressed. Since only a minority display this attitude (Stephens & Kamp, 1962), one must conclude that the conversion solution is an inefficient one.

Perhaps the most solidly established fact about conversion hysterics is that the majority are women. Estimates of female predominance range from 2:1 to 4:1 (Engel, 1970; Stefansson *et al.*, 1976; Stephens & Kamp, 1962; Ziegler *et al.*, 1960); however, during wartime, the incidence of conversion reactions among males increases (Buss, 1966). It has been suggested above that individuals with a hysterical personality are susceptible to the development of conversion reactions; thus, it is to be expected that many conversion hysterics would be female. Other factors must also pertain, as a considerable number of conversion hysterics manifest other personality styles. A number of explanations have been proffered, ranging from absurd to plausible but unproven.

In ancient times, conversion reactions were thought to result from the meanderings of the uterus throughout the female body. Clearly, all hysterics had to be female according to this scheme. Organs or parts of the body against which the uterus pressed would become symptomatic. For example, the still common conversion sensation of choking or inability to breathe emerged when the errant uterus lodged against the lungs and throat. Though the term "hysteria" (after *hystera,* meaning womb) originated with the Greeks, the concept is even older and was borrowed from Egyptian physicians (Veith, 1965). Generally, the wandering uterus was thought to be searching for sexual gratification or for a child. The putative connection between conversion hysteria and frustrated sexuality thus antedates Freud by centuries.

A less dramatic but more plausible explanation is that the "sick" role is more acceptable for women in this culture in line with their stereotyping as frail creatures. The imaginary illness often renders the conversion hysteric incapable of carrying out her responsibilities and renders her dependent on her family. These behaviors as well are more easily tolerated in women and may cause less conflict for the hysteric and her family than would an overt rejection of onerous duties. Thus, once begun, symptoms may be reinforced in complex ways.

Empirical Investigations and Treatment

Though theoretical papers and case studies abound, actual research is scarce and at a primitive methodological level. Nevertheless, some consistent findings have emerged. In three studies, hysterics were found to have had a high frequency of gynecological surgery (Blinder, 1966; Lazare & Klerman, 1968; Winokur & Leonard, 1963); in addition, they were likely to have had children earlier (Lazare & Klerman, 1968) than women in a control group. Marital and sexual difficulties were common. Blinder and Winokur and Leonard found reports of deteriorating sexual satisfaction after marriage, and the hysterics in Lazare and Klerman's study reported having more extramarital affairs than the nonhysterics. A high incidence of alcoholism among fathers of hysterics was noted in two investigations (Blinder, 1966; Lazare & Klerman, 1968). These findings were based on the clients' report, but Arkonac and Guze (1963) obtained similar findings by interviewing relatives of hysterics. Of male relatives interviewed, 33% were determined to be alcoholics or sociopaths. About 15% of female relatives were diagnosed as hysterics themselves.

In the best-controlled study to date, Bendefeldt, Miller, and Ludwig (1976) studied cognitive functions in conversion hysterics on an inpatient service as compared to other nonpsychotic patients. Hysterics were found to be more suggestible and field-dependent. They performed poorly on tests of recent memory, vigilance, and attention when compared to other subjects. When these tests were given under stress conditions, 16 out of 17 hysterics could be differentiated from the control subjects on the basis of these cognitive tasks alone. These results are somewhat difficult to interpret, since the factor of intelligence was not controlled. However, Rapaport, Gill, and Schafer (1968) have reported similar findings on individual psychological testing where intrasubject comparisons are made.

A meaningful synthesis of theory and research on conversion is hampered by the diffuse nature of the category itself. Careful delineation of the population to be studied seems to be a prerequisite for systematic investigation.

In ancient times, conversion hysteria was treated by fumigating the vulva of the victim with pleasant fragrances while applying noxious odors to the nose. This procedure was designed to drive the roaming uterus away from its resting place and to entice it back to its proper site (Veith, 1965). In light of the statistics on gynecological surgery among hysterical women (Blinder, 1966; Lazare & Klerman, 1968; Winokur & Leonard, 1963), one wonders if modern practices are qualitatively different. Psychotherapeutic interventions with this disorder are only slightly better validated.

Given the historical significance of conversion hysteria in the development of psychotherapy, it is striking that so little empirical evidence is available on the effectiveness of psychotherapy with this syndrome. The reluctance of these clients to accept referrals for psychotherapy undoubtedly hampers systematic study. Though psychoanalysis has been advocated, no outcome study has indicated that this approach is useful. Behaviorists have reported the successful treatment of individual cases, but, of course, failures will not find their way into print.

In only one case of behavioral treatment reviewed (Munford, Reardon, Liberman, & Allen, 1976) did the writers demonstrate that treatment procedures were responsible for the change observed, as opposed to some nonspecific treatment effect. Using an ABA design with a hospitalized adolescent, Munford *et al.* showed hysterical coughing to diminish and be replaced by appropriate behavior (speech) only when such changes were reinforced with trips home. Several behaviorists have emphasized the importance of withdrawing any reinforcers maintaining the hysterical behavior. It is notable that effective behavioral treatment has largely been carried out on an inpatient basis, where the daily reinforcement of "sick" behavior, particularly, attention from family members, can be eliminated. Shaping of normal behaviors is also common (e.g., Brady & Lind, 1961). Assertiveness training, vocational counseling, and family therapy may be included to help the client resolve the stresses that may have precipitated the symptoms initially (Meichenbaum, 1966; Munford *et al.*, 1976). On the basis of etiologic formulations, these additional procedures seem of likely value, but more controlled observations are required.

Though studies involving group comparisons are improbable due to the lack of willing subjects, progress can be made through the use of single-case design (see Hersen & Barlow, 1976). Perhaps the more difficult question is how to motivate the conversion hysteric to seek psychological treatment. The growing field of behavioral medicine may provide an opening to the hysteric's defenses. At special clinics in medical settings, patients are treated for the psychological components of physical problems whether functional or organic in basis. In such centers, psychological treatment may be begun without the hysteric's having to agree with her doctor that the problem is "all in her head."

Agoraphobia

More than a million American women find their lives restricted by agoraphobia syndrome.[1] Though the existence of this problem has been documented throughout written history, it remains something of a mystery. People with agoraphobia comprise the bulk of those seeking psychiatric treatment for phobias (Goldstein & Chambless, 1978; Marks, 1970c); yet, despite the common notion that phobias are simple problems to treat, effective treatments for agoraphobia had not been devised until the 1970s. The available treatments remain only moderately effective.

The label "agoraphobia" has contributed to the confusion about the syndrome. While a literal translation would be "fear of the marketplace," the usual dictionary definition is "fear of open spaces." Each of these definitions represents a fraction of the situations agoraphobics fear, which include crowds, bridges, tunnels, public places and conveyances, elevators, expressways, being distanced from home, or being separated from a trusted companion. The theme throughout this array of phobias is that the agoraphobics fear any situation in which escape to safe territory or to a trusted companion might be hindered; the more confining the situation, the more anxiety-provoking.

The degree of restriction varies widely. Generally, the agoraphobic defines an area around her home as a safety zone and ventures beyond this area only with a trusted friend or, in many cases, not at all. The safety zone may be as small as her home or as large as 100 miles. The extent to which a companion's presence expands the safety zone is also highly individualistic. Some agoraphobics can travel worldwide with a selected companion even though they may avoid stepping out their front doors alone. Others travel more freely with a trusted person but limit movement to within an hour of their homes. A minority, estimated at 5% of all agoraphobics by Marks (1970a), find no comfort in the presence of another; frequently, these are male agoraphobics who seem to reject forming a dependent relationship with a phobic companion. To add further to the confusion, particular places within the safety zone may be avoided, as they are experienced as particularly confining, for example, crowded stores, beauty shops, or busy streets.

[1]Based on a population estimate of 6.3/1000 by Agras, Sylvester, and Oliveau (1969).

There is, however, considerable individual consistency in what a given individual defines as dangerous entrapment. While agoraphobics fluctuate in the extent to which they will venture on a particular day, each individual's rank ordering of perceived confinement across situations remains stable. The fluctuations in the severity of the syndrome have puzzled workers in the field and have created suspicion among family members that the agoraphobic's restrictions are faked. With some clients, there is a cyclical nature to the severity of the symptoms. Frequently, women report increased symptomatology at certain points of the menstrual cycle; others describe circadian cycles. More bewildering are those who experience severe symptoms for years, gradually or markedly improve, only to precipitously relapse years later. These erratic improvements have reinforced superstitious behaviors among therapists who believe that they have found a cure at last. Since clients frequently seek another therapist on relapse, workers who are unaware of the course of the syndrome may persist with treatment methods actually unrelated to the client's improvement. Transient improvements aside, once the symptoms begin, they generally persist a lifetime with fluctuating severity (Marks, 1970a). Roberts (1964) followed the progress of agoraphobics posttreatment for up to 16 years and reported that only 23.7% achieved stable full recovery.

The syndrome is not limited to a multiplicity of phobias. Other common symptoms not found with other phobias are high levels of chronic anxiety, depression, depersonalization, derealization, and, most importantly, panic attacks (Marks, 1970a; Snaith, 1968). Conversion symptoms, for example, globus hystericus, are common. Substance abuse may further compound the agoraphobic's difficulties, and vocational maladjustment is common. Family members are usually strained in caring for the dysfunctional person; for example, children of agoraphobic mothers are more likely to be school-phobic (Berg, 1976).

Though panic attacks are not limited to agoraphobia (severe social phobics and anxiety neurotics also report these experiences), they are sufficiently important to the development of the syndrome to warrant further explication. Panic attacks are described as terrifying episodes during which the victim may experience tachycardia, faintness, difficulty in breathing, a powerful urge to urinate or defecate, and a desire to scream or run. Typically, these seem to strike "out of the blue." Agoraphobics construe these sensations as evidence of impending doom. The most frequent appraisals are that one is dying of a heart attack or stroke, is going crazy, or is going to faint and cause a scene.

Agoraphobia is further differentiated from other phobias by its pattern of onset (Goldstein, 1973; Snaith, 1968). Rather than a history of conditioning events or of fears since childhood, one finds that agoraphobia begins with a period of generalized anxiety and seems in part to be a stress reaction. While the most frequent stressor is marital dissatisfaction (Goldstein, 1973), other precipitants include bereavement, physical illness (particularly hypoglycemia), childbirth, and moving to a strange setting. Stressful situations such as these are also implicated in relapses.

Empirical Investigations

In a number of studies agoraphobics have been compared to people complaining of other phobias. Based on their model of agoraphobia, Goldstein and Chambless (1978) selected nine items from the Fear Survey Schedule (Wolpe & Lang, 1964) on which they predicted agoraphobics would differ from other phobics. Four of these items reflected sensations and cognitions associated with panic attacks: heart palpitations, loss of control, fainting, and thoughts of mental illness. Agoraphobics rated themselves significantly more fearful of all these occurrences. Analyses of three other Fear Survey Schedule items showed agoraphobics to be more fearful of criticism, rejection, and disapproval. Since these items are typically rated high by socially anxious people, these scores are consistent with therapists' ratings of agoraphobics as more socially anxious and less expressive and aggressive. In an effort to assess general coping skills unrelated to the phobias, responses on items concerning taking responsibility and making decisions were compared along with therapists' ratings of coping skills, the Bernreuter Self-Sufficiency Scale, and the Willoughby Personality Inventory (general neuroticism). Agoraphobics scored in the direction of higher pathology on all these scales compared to other phobics.

Similarly to Goldstein and Chambless, Marks (1967) reported that agoraphobics score higher on the Neuroticism scale of the Eysenck Personality Inventory and on the Cornell Medical Index than do specific phobics. Social phobics, however, were not significantly different from agoraphobics on these scales which measured depression, exhaustion, irritability, and social anxiety. Data collected by Emmelkamp and Cohen-Kettenis (1975) indicate that agoraphobics show a more external locus of control than normal subjects, but statistical comparisons are not reported. Factor analyses have yielded distinct factors in questionnaire data obtained from agoraphobics which are not found with normal subjects or with other phobic and neurotic clients (Hallam & Hafner, 1978; Marks, 1967). These factors seem to be comprised of items related to the places agoraphobics fear and to the sensations and fears associated with panic attacks. Psychophysiologic studies further identify agoraphobics as more generally anxious than specific phobics (reviewed by Marks, 1970b).

FAMILIAL FACTORS

Although clinical impressions from various settings are fairly consistent in describing agoraphobics' families of origin, little objective evidence is available. These families are typically pictured as being either over-protective or rejecting (e.g., Goldstein & Chambless, 1978), and a high incidence of separation of the child who becomes agoraphobic from her attachment figure in early childhood has been noted. Snaith (1968) attempted to test these assertions by comparing the family histories of agoraphobics to those of other phobics. Families of agoraphobics were found to have been significantly more unstable compared to the other families surveyed. Snaith did not, however, find support for the overprotection–rejection hypothesis. His findings appear to have been based on retrospective information obtained from the phobic subjects and therefore constitute a weak test. Solyom, Silberfield, and Solyom (1976) actually tested mothers of agoraphobics on a questionnaire designed to measure overprotection. These mothers scored markedly higher than not only normal mothers but also overprotective mothers on whose responses the questionnaire norms had been established. The mother's degree of anxiety was related to the prevalence of her child's fears. As Solyom *et al.* note, their findings do not demonstrate a causal or even sequential chain of events, since the mothers were tested after their children had grown to adulthood and developed pathologic fears. It is possible, therefore, that the mothers were simply responding to their children's debilitated state.

According to data collected by Marks and Herst (1970), 19% of British agoraphobics surveyed reported having a close relative who was agoraphobic. As this information was based on questionnaire data, these figures are probably spuriously low. Clients in our program have been asked to question family members, or family members themselves have been interveiwed concerning this issue. Frequently, we find that parents have experienced episodes of agoraphobia but had never informed the client. While we have yet to tabulate these data, the incidence appears to be considerably higher than 19%.

DEMOGRAPHIC DATA

A striking characteristic of this syndrome is that the great majority of agoraphobics are female (about 80%), although this is not the case for social phobias (Marks, 1970b). They are usually married (Marks, 1970a), hence the label "housewives' disease." Since most agoraphobics are of a hysterical personality type, it is to be expected that most would be women. Several additional factors have been postulated.

One investigator has suggested that panic attacks and/or separation anxiety may be linked to estrogen disorders. There is some indirect support for this hypothesis: Postpartum onset is common, intensified symptoms are reported on particular days of the menstrual cycle, and the emergence of agoraphobia before puberty is rare. A different, yet still hormonal, explanation is that agoraphobia, indeed most fears, may be more frequent among women because they have lower levels of testosterone, a hormone which has been related to dominance and aggressive behavior (Money & Ehrhardt, 1972). Thus, passively avoiding rather than approaching and conquering a feared situation might be more typical of women.

While agreeing that women are, indeed, less likely to attempt to master feared situations, Fodor (1974) has argued that the basis for this behavior lies in a woman's sex role, not her physiology. If women are not encouraged to become competent, self-assertive, and self-reliant human beings, Fodor asserts, they are more helpless in the face of stress and more easily trapped in situations from which they see no escape. Klein (in Zitrin, Klein, Lindeman, Tobak, Rock, Kaplan, & Ganz, 1976) has suggested that agoraphobia may be a variant of the affective disorders because of its fluctuating severity. On the basis of family histories, we suspect that agoraphobia is related to the depression/alcoholism factor. This is a postulated genetic predisposition, which is said to be expressed differently in males and females of a family, with males susceptible to alcoholism and females to endogenous depression. In addition to such histories, we find that the acute-onset phase of agoraphobia is extremely similar to a state of agitated depression. For these reasons, we are inclined to think that there may be a genetic predisposition toward having panic attacks under conditions of prolonged stress. Whether agoraphobic symptoms develop will depend on other factors to be described below. It may well be that females and males respond differently to these physical signs of stress according to sex-role stereotyping, with women developing avoidance behavior and men "acting-out" behavior, for example, alcoholism.

Age at onset differentiates agoraphobia from animal phobias which begin in childhood and persist and from social phobias which generally start in early adolescence. Studies in the United States and England have found a bimodal distribution of the age at which agoraphobic symptoms make their appearance. The modes are at late adolescence and at the late

20s–early 30s (Marks, 1970b; Mendel & Klein, 1969). Clients who experience the earlier onset are more likely to have been school-phobic as
children and to be more severely neurotic in general (Berg, Marks,
McGuire, & Lipsedge, 1974). Distinguishing features in intelligence,
socioeconomic class, and religious affiliation have not been noted
(Marks, 1970a).

Thus, agoraphobia emerges as a distinct syndrome on the basis not
only of clinical data but also of questionnaire and psychophysiologic
data. Though sharing many components of social anxiety and general
anxiety states, agoraphobia may be discriminated from these conditions
by sex incidence, age at onset, physiologic measures, and clustering on
factor analyses.

A Theoretical Model for Agoraphobia

Both psychoanalytic and learning models of agoraphobia suffer from
reductionism, such that important aspects of the syndrome are ignored
to make the data fit the theory rather than the opposite. Freudian theory
attempts to found all of the phobic's problems in sexual conflicts, while
behavior theorists have looked for simple conditioned responses. It
seems more appropriate to abandon a priori notions and create a model
for agoraphobia which attempts to account for the clinical and experimental evidence that has been obtained and to subject this model to
empirical test. The following model represents such an attempt and is
largely based on formulations by Goldstein and Chambless (1978) in
their paper entitled, "A Reanalysis of Agoraphobia."

FEAR OF FEAR

Goldstein and Chambless (1978), among others (e.g., Weekes, 1976),
have argued that the principal phobic component of agoraphobia syndrome is neither a fear of places nor a fear of separation from an attachment figure. Rather, it is a fear of panic attacks and their fantasized
consequences—a fear of fear. This is consonant with the observation that
agoraphobics fear places to the degree that they feel panic attacks cannot
be aborted therein and also with the finding of day-to-day fluctuations in
the degree of avoidance and discomfort. Thus, a particular place may be
avoided some days but not others depending on the phobic's assessment
of the likelihood of panics that day. If this hypothesis be correct, interventions that reduce the intensity and frequency of panic attacks should
be more effective than those than aim to desensitize anxiety to a particular place. Klein and his colleagues have reported marked improvement

in agoraphobics with the use of imipramine, a psychotropic drug purported to reduce the frequency and intensity of panics (Klein, Zitrin, & Woerner, 1978). In a study that compared systematic desensitization with supportive therapy plus imipramine (among other comparisons), Zitrin, Klein, and Woerner (1978) found that, indeed, the group receiving imipramine fared better.

Goldstein and Chambless further suggest that the panic attack acts as an unconditioned stimulus, so that stimuli associated with attacks become themselves elicitors of high anxiety and even panics. The most consistent stimuli are interoceptive ones, the client's own physiologic signs of arousal. Because feelings of anxiety may arise in many situations, the phobia generalizes widely, with particular places attaining some power to elicit anxiety through higher-order conditioning. An important discriminative stimulus in this process of anxiety evocation is the phobic's assessment of whether a particular situation is an entrapping one. This hypothesis of interoceptive conditioning is indirectly supported by outcome studies. Goldstein and Chambless suggest that systematic desensitization is ineffective with agoraphobics because in maintaining clients in a relaxed state, the therapist does not expose them to the putatively crucial cues of physiologic arousal.

Flooding, on the other hand, has been effective, and it is hypothesized that this is precisely because flooding involves the evocation and maintenance of anxiety responses until habituation or extinction occurs. Furthermore, Watson and Marks (1971) found that even irrelevant flooding was beneficial to agoraphobics, and Goldstein and Chambless suggest that this is because even irrelevant flooding elicited the crucial interoceptive cues of sensations associated with anxiety. Irrelevant flooding has not been found to be helpful for other kinds of phobias (McCutcheon & Adams, 1975; Prochaska, 1971). This finding is consistent with the hypothesis that simple phobics are chiefly fearful of external stimuli, not of internal states. More direct support for the fear-of-fear hypothesis comes from two recent studies in which the experience of interoceptive anxiety cues during flooding was diminished through the use of drugs (Chambless, Foa, Groves, & Goldstein, 1979; Hafner & Milton, 1977). In both studies, improvement was impaired in clients taking the drug compared to clients flooded in the usual manner.

One difficulty with the fear-of-fear hypothesis is that panic attacks are not unique to agoraphobia. Social phobics and people suffering from anxiety states are also plagued by these attacks. Clinically, agoraphobics are differentiated from these other syndromes by inferences they draw from panic experiences, for example, "I am going crazy"; "I am dying." In addition, they are distinguished by particular fears of being trapped, of not being able to escape panicky feelings due to external confinement; this, in turn, leads to the pattern of avoidance.

PERSONALITY VARIABLES

On the whole, agoraphobics have been described as passive, dependent people who lack the ability to appropriately express their feelings and needs (Andrews, 1966; Goldstein & Chambless, 1978; Terhune, 1949). There is some empirical validation for this picture and some support for the notion that frequently they have been parentally overprotected. Clinical observations verify Bowlby's assertion (1973) that separation anxiety or anxious attachment is an important variable. Firmer data are available only in the form of the high incidence of separation and bereavement as precipitating factors in the onset or worsening of symptoms.

Despite accumulating evidence that this passive, dependent personality type is basic to agoraphobia, it does not seem sufficient, as it does not discriminate between agoraphobia and anxiety states, leading some to suggest that the distinction is meaningless (Bowlby, 1973; Snaith, 1968). The strong avoidance patterns in agoraphobia, however, do set it apart and require specific treatment interventions. Goldstein and Chambless suggest that the remaining defining characteristic of the agoraphobic personality is a "hysterical response style." Indeed, Freud (1936/1964) alternatively labeled agoraphobia as "anxiety hysteria" because he viewed the syndrome as having elements of both anxiety states and conversion reactions. Hysterical personality has been descriptively defined above as the inability to accurately connect feeling states with their eliciting stimuli or even to appropriately label current feeling states. Hence, agoraphobics who appear sad or angry frequently describe themselves as anxious instead. A common example is the report of an anxiety attack out of the blue which follows the phobic's having been treated badly by a spouse or parent. The agoraphobic interprets the arousal which another might label "anger" as anxiety and displaces the cause of the feeling to the environment, that is, "I feel trapped by this elevator" rather than "I feel trapped by my inability to refuse unreasonable demands." It is this displacement process that led Freud to link agoraphobia with hysteria. Another example of mislabeling which leads to agoraphobics' distress is the interpretation of any intense feeling as a sign of mental illness. Thus, potentially pleasurable feelings become anxiety-evoking. As noted by analytical writers, these feelings may be sexual, particularly in the case of a strong extramarital attraction, or angry ones. An important omission in the analytical reports is that these feelings frequently are of intense grief. The content, therefore, seems less important than the overall pattern of suppressing recognition of a strong reaction, mislabeling it as anxiety or "craziness" (a perception which elicits considerable anxiety), and misattributing the eliciting stimuli. This misattribution leads to avoidance as a type of superstitious behavior.[2]

Given this hysterical response style, the agoraphobic is prevented from identifying sources of distress in her environment and, consequently, from initiating efforts to resolve the difficulties leading to outbreaks of anxiety. Along with the generalization of interoceptive conditioning, this lack of problem resolution leads to chronic high anxiety which perpetuates the cycle of panic attacks, avoidance, and increased fear. Unfortunately, despite the importance of this characteristic, there is no objective evidence on the frequency of the hysterical response style in agoraphobia compared to similar syndromes such as anxiety states and social phobias.

STRESS

In some ways, agoraphobia may be viewed as a stress syndrome. Just as some people suffer from migraine headaches or gastrointestinal distress as a result of chronic anxiety, agoraphobics are inflicted with panic attacks. The analogy breaks down at this point, however, for clients with other psychosomatic symptoms do not necessarily evolve an entire lifestyle based on their complaints. Agoraphobics do, and the secondary gain and interpersonal factors involved are more comparable to those of conversion hysterics. While many people cope with panic attacks without developing a superstructure of symptomatology, the personality factors described in the preceding section render others vulnerable to the formation of conditioned fears and avoidance behavior. These individuals, Goldstein and Chambless contend, are those likely to develop agoraphobia.

Marks (1970a) has suggested that since almost any kind of stress may be the precipitating event in the onset of agoraphobia, categorizing or interpreting particular stressors may be irrelevant. Chambless and Goldstein (1980) have challenged this notion and have claimed that the type of precipitant generally reflects the underlying conflicts which need to be resolved for a particular client; therefore, different precipitants should point to different treatment interventions.

By far, the most common category is that of threatened or actual separation from important attachments. As noted by Bowlby (1973),

[2]We are indebted to Jesse Milby, Ph.D., for this observation.

many agoraphobics appear to suffer from anxious attachment, perhaps as a result of childhood events. Thus, it is understandable that a very common time of onset is late adolescence, when issues of separating from one's family must be faced. Frequently, the first panic attacks occur around making the decision to go to college or actually leaving for college. Rather than being qualitatively different, those who develop agoraphobia appear to experience a more severe form of normal separation anxiety at these times. Those who do not go to college often go through a similar experience of panicking while making vocational decisions or while traveling to their new place of employment.

The other common time of onset is during the late 20s and early 30s. Agoraphobics in this age group are usually unhappily married women with small children. More often than not, they never experienced a period of autonomous functioning but transferred dependency on parents to dependency on an authoritarian, dominant husband. They often remain close by their parents and sometimes are in conflict because of divided loyalties between their new family and the family of origin. More frequently, however, the conflict centers on unhappiness with their marriages and resentment of the spouse's domination. Given their hysterical response style, they do not strive to solve the marital problems. Rather, these difficulties are denied, for separation is so anxiety-provoking that thoughts of it are immediately suppressed. In most cases, separation is difficult, not only psychologically but also realistically, as such individuals have never learned the skills required to function autonomously. In not a few cases, however, the individual is quite capable objectively but for emotional reasons is terrified of being alone. For adolescent and adult onset under threatened separation, the avoidance symptoms are operantly reinforced in several ways. First, there is the negative reinforcement derived from avoiding the noxious situations, that is, the identified phobic stimuli as well as the core fear of leaving home and being on one's own. Second, there is generally covert positive reinforcement from parents or spouse for remaining dependent, as they tend to view independent functioning as threatening to the survival of the relationship. (See Hafner, 1977a, for the effects of the client's improvement on her spouse.) Third, there is the punishment the conflicted person receives for appropriate autonomous behavior in the form of subtle or blatant abuse from significant others.

Other forms of separation which lead to outbreaks of anxiety and subsequent agoraphobia are the death or threatened death of a significant person (Mendel & Klein, 1969) and the loss of familiar friends and environment through moving. Chambless and Goldstein (1980) find that a considerable number of agoraphobics suffer from a blocked grief response. Such individuals have avoided going through the normal mourning process (see Kubler-Ross, 1969) and when reminded of their loss, experience what they label as anxiety, though to an observer they appear grief-stricken. Bowlby's (1973) work would suggest that people who react to loss with incapacitating fear have been traumatized in early childhood by separation.

In other cases, the precipitating event appears to be a more physical trauma, including surgery, childbirth, hypoglycemic attacks, endocrine fluctuations, and adverse reactions to prescribed or illegally obtained drugs. Analytical writers have tended to subsume these responses under castration anxiety or separation. For example, a woman experiencing postpartum onset of agoraphobia is presumed to be responding with anxiety to the separation of the child from her body. Such explanations ignore the physical stress of drastic hormonal changes after birth as well as the psychological stress of caring for a new infant. Agoraphobics reporting this type of onset appear to be different from those with intense separation anxiety. Klein describes them as essentially normal individuals premorbidly (Zitrin *et al.*, 1976). Those seen at Temple University Medical School, however, do seem to have a particular personality style in addition to responding hysterically. They appear to be highly perfectionistic individuals with strong obsessive traits. Generally, they report a history of having been hypochondriacal and having become very anxious if something was "not right" about their bodies or appearance. Whatever the source of stress, panic attacks occur in all of these cases, and a conditioned fear of fear takes hold. Thus, avoidance of entrapment based on fear of fear appears to be the most basic common denominator for agoraphobics.

Treatment

The most effective treatments established for agoraphobia are *in vivo* exposure (flooding) (reviewed by Marks, 1978) and drug treatment with antidepressants (Zitrin *et al.*, 1976; Ballenger, Sheehan, & Jacobson, Note 1). During *in vivo* exposure, an agoraphobic is asked to enter progressively more anxiety-evoking situations and to remain there, despite anxiety, until she finds that she has conquered her fear. The therapist may suggest the use of particular coping mechanisms to deal with the anxiety thus elicited. Clients may be treated in this fashion individually or in groups. Self-help groups to facilitate *in vivo* exposure are becoming more common. In addition, spouses may be trained to carry out the treatment (Mathews, Teasdale, Munby, Johnston, & Shaw, 1977). A review of the literature on this approach, substantiates the claim that statistically significant improvement may be reliably obtained. It is erroneous, however, to assume that this means that most clients are cured, that is, become asymptomatic. Given the relative novelty of this approach and the fluctuating course of agoraphobia, the stability of change effected in this manner is even more tenuously established.

In our own experience with this approach, a minority of clients are cured. Though most improve moderately to substantially, a considerable number relapse. Recent research by Hafner (Hafner, 1977; Milton & Hafner, 1979) has corroborated our clinical impression that these relapses are due to marital conflicts which reemerge when the agoraphobic partner improves.

Research by Ballenger *et al.* (Note 1) and by Klein and his colleagues (Klein *et al.*, 1978) has demonstrated the value of antidepressant medication in the treatment of agoraphobia. The controlled studies to date have employed phenelzine (Nardil) and imipramine (Tofranil), but it is likely that chemically related drugs would have similar effects. These so-called antidepressants appear to help, not so much by lifting depression, but by interfering with the onset of panic attacks. Once free from the fear of attacks, agoraphobics are less reluctant to venture forth. Anxiety and avoidance typically remain high, however, and some type of systematic intervention such as *in vivo* exposure is generally required.

Though decidedly helpful, drug treatment does not seem to be a panacea. In our population, 25% of clients refuse to take the medication because of hypochondriacal concerns. Of those who do attempt a serious trial of medication, relapse is common after the drug is withdrawn if the precipitating conflict and resulting panic attacks are still present. This is to be expected, since clients treated with drugs have not learned to cope with panic attacks. Yet another group of clients fail to budge despite their reports that panic attacks are, indeed, less severe when they are required to enter avoided situations.

Thus, while more agoraphobics are being helped than ever before, we cannot concur with some workers in the field that the answers have been found. Among those who improve, relapse continues to be a significant problem. Our clinical experience and Hafner's data point strongly to interpersonal conflict as one neglected factor. Hence, the treatment program we have devised emphasizes marital therapy and conflict resolution (Chambless & Goldstein, 1980). A controlled trial is needed to verify the significance of interpersonal conflict in therapeutic change.

The remaining factor in the etiology and maintenance of agoraphobia has been completely ignored in studies on therapy outcome. This is the agoraphobic's excessive reliance on having a stable attachment figure in her environment. This separation anxiety blocks progress in conflict resolution, in that agoraphobics will remain in decidedly unhappy relationships rather than face a separation that is, to them, terrifying. In addition, their improvement is frequently precarious and threatens to crumble in the face of the inevitable losses that occur in one's life. Resolution of this core fear thus seems essential for stable change. Consistently effective methods for reducing this terror elude us to date, and we target this problem as the most urgent question to address in the treatment of agoraphobia.

Summary

Agoraphobia and conversion hysteria are related syndromes, in that both frequently emerge in women of a hysterical personality type. Women are particularly vulnerable to these problems, as the sick or fearful role is an acceptable one for females in our culture. Both syndromes begin in the context of stress and may be construed as maladaptive solutions to conflict. Thus, the woman who feels trapped by her marriage but afraid to leave is relieved of the decision by a fear which prohibits her going out alone. The woman who is "sick and tired" of nursing an infirm parent[3] can go off duty when she develops her own illness. Once developed, the symptoms are usually reinforced by family members who feel inconvenienced but not threatened by these sex-role-appropriate behaviors.

It seems possible that as we are undergoing a cultural shift in expectations for women, more women may find themselves in conflict, having to choose between the safer, though limited, role of the dependent, helpless woman and a more challenging, and hence more immediately stressful, life as a truly independent being. Should this be the case, we may find symptoms of agoraphobia and conversion hysteria on the increase as women struggle with the decision to stand on their own two feet and walk out of their traps.

Reference Note

1. Ballenger, J., Sheehan, D., & Jacobson, G. *Antidepressant treatment of severe phobic anxiety.* Paper presented at the meeting of the American Psychiatric Association, Toronto, May 1977.

[3]Krohn (1978) has noted that most of Freud's patients with hysterical symptoms were young women who had been obliged to give up their own pursuits in order to nurse an ailing relative.

References

Agras, S., Sylvester, D., & Oliveau, D. The epidemiology of common fears and phobias. *Comprehensive Psychiatry*, 1969, *10*, 151–156.

Andrews, J. D. W. Psychotherapy of phobias. *Psychological Bulletin*, 1966, *66*, 455–480.

Arkonac, O., & Guze, S. B. A family study of hysteria. *New England Journal of Medicine*, 1963, *268*, 239–242.

Beck, A. T. *Cognitive therapy and the emotional disorders*. New York: International Universities Press, 1976.

Bendefeldt, F., Miller, L. L., & Ludwig, A. M. Cognitive performance in conversion hysteria. *Archives of General Psychiatry*, 1976, *33*, 1250–1254.

Berg, I. School phobia in the children of agoraphobic women. *British Journal of Psychiatry*, 1976, *128*, 86–89.

Berg, I., Marks, I., McGuire, R., & Lipsedge, M. School phobia and agoraphobia. *Psychological Medicine*, 1974, *4*, 428–434.

Blinder, M. G. The hysterical personality. *Psychiatry*, 1966, *29*, 227–235.

Bowlby, J. *Separation: Anxiety and anger*. New York: Basic Books, 1973.

Brady, J. P., & Lind, D. L. Experimental analysis of hysterical blindness. *Archives of General Psychiatry*, 1961, *4*, 331–339.

Buss, A. *Psychopathology*. New York: Wiley, 1966.

Chambless, D. L., Foa, E. B., Groves, G. A., & Goldstein, A. J. Brevital in flooding with agoraphobics. *Behaviour Research and Therapy*, 1979, *17*, 243–251.

Chambless, D. L., & Goldstein, A. J. Agoraphobia. In A. J. Goldstein & E. B. Foa (Eds.), *Handbook of behavioral interventions: A clinical guide*. New York: Wiley–Interscience, 1980.

Emmelkamp, P. M. G., & Cohen-Kettenis, P. T. Relationship of locus of control to phobic anxiety and depression. *Psychological Reports*, 1975, *36*, 390.

Engel, G. L. Conversion symptoms. In C. M. MacBryde (Ed.), *Signs and symptoms: Applied physiology and clinical interpretation*. Philadelphia: J. B. Lippincott, 1970.

Fodor, I. G. The phobic syndrome in women. In V. Franks & V. Burtle (Eds.), *Women in therapy*. New York: Bruner/Mazel, 1974.

Freud, S. [*The standard edition of the complete psychological works of Sigmund Freud*] (J. Strachey, Ed. and trans.) (24 vols.). London: Hogarth Press, 1953–1966.

Freud, S. *Dora: An analysis of a case of hysteria*. New York: Collier, 1963. (Originally published, 1905).

Freud, S. *The problem of anxiety*. New York: Norton, 1964. (Originally published, 1936).

Goldstein, A. J. Learning theory insufficiency in understanding agoraphobia—a plea for empiricism. In *Proceedings of the first meeting of the European Association for Behaviour Therapy and Behaviour Modification*. Munich: Urban and Schwarzenberg, 1973.

Goldstein, A. J., & Chambless, D. A. A reanalysis of agoraphobia. *Behaior Therapy*, 1978, *9*, 47–59.

Hafner, R. J. The husbands of agoraphobic women and their influence on treatment outcome. *British Journal of Psychiatry*, 1977, *131*, 289–294.

Hafner, R. J., & Milton, F. The influence of propranolol on the exposure *in vivo* of agoraphobics. *Psychological Medicine*, 1977, *7*, 419–425.

Hallam, R. S., & Hafner, R. J. Fears of phobic patients: Factor analyses of self report data. *Behaviour Research and Therapy*, 1978, *16*, 1–6.

Halleck, S. L. Hysterical personality traits. *Archives of General Psychiatry*, 1967, *16*, 750–757.

Hersen, M., & Barlow, D. H. *Single case experimental designs*. New York: Pergamon, 1976.

Klein, D. F., Zitrin, C. M., & Woerner, M. Antidepressants, anxiety, panic, and phobia. In M. A. Lipton, A. DiMascio, & K. F. Killam (Eds.), *Psychopharmacology: A generation of progress*. New York: Raven Press, 1978.

Krohn, A. *Hysteria: The elusive neurosis*. New York: International Universities Press, 1978.

Kubler-Ross, E. *On death and dying*. New York: Macmillan, 1969.

Lazare, A., & Klerman, G. L. Hysteria and depression: The frequency and significance of hysterical personality features in hospitalized depressed women. *American Journal of Psychiatry*, 1968, *124*, 48–56.

Maccoby, E. E., & Jacklin, C. N. *The psychology of sex differences*. Stanford, Calif.: Stanford University Press, 1974.

Marks, I. M. Components and correlates of psychiatric questionnaires. *British Journal of Medical Psychology*, 1967, *40*, 261–272.

Marks, I. M. Agoraphobic syndrome (phobic anxiety state). *Archives of General Psychiatry*, 1970, *23*, 538–553. (a)

Marks, I. M. The classification of phobic disorders. *British Journal of Psychiatry*, 1970, *116*, 377–386. (b)

Marks, I. M. The origins of phobic states. *American Journal of Psychotherapy*, 1970, *24*, 652–657. (c)

Marks, I. M. Exposure treatments: Clinical studies in phobic, obsessive compulsive and allied disorders. In W. S. Agras (Ed.), *Behavior therapy in clinical psychiatry* (2nd ed.). New York: Little, Brown, 1978.

Marks, I. M., & Herst, E. R. A survey of 1,200 agoraphobics in Britain. *Social Psychiatry*, 1970, *5*, 16–24.

Mathews, A. M., Teasdale, J., Munby, M., Johnston, D., & Shaw, P. A home-based treatment program for agoraphobia. *Behavior Therapy*, 1977, *8*, 915–924.

McCutcheon, B. A., & Adams, H. E. The physiological basis of implosive therapy. *Behaviour Research and Therapy*, 1975, *13*, 93–100.

Meichenbaum, D. H. Sequential strategies in two cases of hysteria. *Behaviour Research and Therapy*, 1966, *4*, 89–94.

Mendel, J. G. C., & Klein, D. F. Anxiety attacks with subsequent agoraphobia. *Comprehensive Psychiatry*, 1969, *10*, 190–195.

Milton, F., & Hafner, J. The outcome of behaviour therapy for agoraphobia in relation to marital adjustment. *Archives of General Psychiatry*, 1979, *36*, 807–811.

Money, J., & Erhardt, A. A. *Man and woman: Boy and girl*. Baltimore: Johns Hopkins Press, 1972.

Munford, P. R., Reardon, D., Liberman, R. P., & Allen, L. Behavioral treatment of hysterical coughing and mutism: A case study. *Journal of Consulting and Clinical Psychology*, 1976, *44*, 1008–1014.

Prochaska, J. O. Symptom and dynamic cues in the implosive treatment of test anxiety. *Journal of Abnormal Psychology*, 1971, *77*, 133–142.

Rapaport, D., Gill, M. M., & Schafer, R. *Diagnostic psychological testing* (Rev. ed.) (R. Holt, Ed.). New York: International Universities Press, 1968.

Roberts, A. H. Housebound-housewives: A follow-up study of phobic anxiety states. *British Journal of Psychiatry*, 1964, *110*, 191–197.

Snaith, R. P. A clinical investigation of phobias. *British Journal of Psychiatry*, 1968, *114*, 673–697.

Solyom, L., Silberfeld, M., & Solyom, C. Maternal overprotection in the etiology of agoraphobia. *Canadian Psychiatric Association Journal*, 1976, *21*, 109–113.

Stefanis, C., Markidis, M., & Christodoulou, G. Observations on the evolution of the hysterical symptomatology. *British Journal of Psychiatry*, 1976, *128*, 269–275.

Stefansson, J. G., Messina, J. A., & Meyerowitz, S. Hysterical neurosis, conversion type: Clinical and epidemiological considerations. *Acta Psychiatrica Scandinavica*, 1976, *53*, 119–138.

Stephens, J. H., & Kamp, M. On some aspects of hysteria: A clinical study. *Journal of Nervous and Mental Disease*, 1962, *134*, 305–315.

Terhune, W. B. The phobic syndrome, *Archives of Neurology and Psychiatry*, 1949, *62*, 162–172.

Veith, I. *Hysteria: The history of a disease*. Chicago: University of Chicago Press, 1965.

Watson, J. P., & Marks, I. M. Relevant and irrelevant fear in flooding: A crossover study of phobic patients. *Behavior Therapy*, 1971, *2*, 275–293.

Weekes, C. *Simple, effective treatment of agoraphobia.* New York: Hawthorn, 1976.

Winokur, G., & Leonard, C. Sexual life in patients with hysteria. *Diseases of the Nervous System,* 1963, *24,* 337–343.

Wolowitz, H. M. Hysterical character and feminine identity. In J. Bardwick (Ed.), *Readings on the psychology of women.* New York: Harper and Row, 1971.

Wolpe, J., & Lang, P. A fear survey schedule for use in behavior therapy. *Behaviour Research and Therapy,* 1964, *2,* 27–30.

Ziegler, F. J., Imboden, J. B., & Meyer, E. Contemporary conversion reactions: A clinical study. *American Journal of Psychiatry,* 1960, *116,* 901–910.

Zitrin, C. M., Klein, D. F., Lindeman, C., Tobak, P., Rock, M., Kaplan, J., & Ganz, V. H. Comparison of short-term treatment regimens in phobic patients: A preliminary report. In R. L. Spitzer & D. F. Klein (Eds.), *Evaluation of psychological therapies.* Baltimore: Johns Hopkins Press, 1976.

Zitrin, C. M., Klein, D. F., & Woerner, M. G. Behavior therapy, supportive psychotherapy, imipramine and phobias. *Archives of General Psychiatry,* 1978, *35,* 307–316.

CHAPTER 6

Eating Disorders: Obesity and Anorexia

SUSAN C. WOOLEY

ORLAND W. WOOLEY

The treatment of obesity and eating disorders presents a number of dilemmas, stemming from the fact that the definition of problems and of acceptable solutions is heavily influenced by the cultural value placed on slenderness in women. It is the purpose of this chapter to highlight the practical, theoretical, and philosophical problems inherent in this field and to raise questions requiring further analysis and research.

The population which this chapter concerns is women who want to or who are intentionally losing weight. Many are in some form of treatment, but even those who are not are influenced by the trends and current customs of treatment. The very existence of treatments participates in the cultural designation and definition of physical and emotional disorders, thereby shaping the way people feel about themselves and what they do.

Psychological Dimensions of Weight Problems

It is customary to define obesity in terms of pounds above ideal weight, that is, in strictly physical terms. Anorexia nervosa, on the other hand, is defined jointly by deviation from normal weight, physical abnormalities (e.g., amenorrhea and bradycardia), and psychological features (e.g., obsessive preoccupation with weight loss, distorted body image, and a "morbid fear of becoming fat") (see Bruch, 1973). These definitions have the result that anorexia nervosa is recognized as a "nervous and

Susan C. Wooley and Orland W. Wooley. Department of Psychiatry, University of Cincinnati College of Medicine, Cincinnati, Ohio.

mental disorder," with eligibility for third-party payments, while obesity is not, however severe the accompanying psychological problems. This has tended to obscure or trivialize the disturbances experienced by some obese patients, usually women, which may be comparable in form and intensity to those seen in anorexia.

Psychological functioning in the obese has generally been a matter of concern only to the extent that it helps to explain, or suggest strategies to modify, assumed "overeating." The search for personality features which can explain all or most cases of obesity has proven virtually futile. At the same time, there appears to be a definable "psychology of obesity" which has as its subject matter the impact of obesity on the individual. This topic encompasses the relationships of the obese to significant others and to society, the effects of repeated failure to achieve weight-loss goals, and the interrelationship between eating behavior and the degree of desperation to achieve slenderness. Understanding requires a historical view of the interplay of these factors over time. It is clear that some women achieve more or less satisfactory but stable resolutions, while others show progressive degrees of preoccupation with a problem they cannot solve.

In recognition of this fact, it would seem advantageous to categorize weight and eating disorders along two separate and partially independent dimensions. The first of these is the extent to which body weight deviates from population norms. The second dimension is the extent to which the desire to lose weight becomes a chronic focus of effort and worry, with adverse effects on well-being and overall functioning. This dimension represents a little-acknowledged continuum marked at one end by satisfaction with one's body or, more commonly, occasional desires to lose weight which are easily realized or forgotten. At the other extreme is anorexia nervosa, in which the drive to be thin becomes so all-consuming, with such severe distortions of body image, that the desire to achieve the distorted ideal may lead to death. In between lie a number of syndromes which appear to be increasingly common in women.

Although the pattern of binge eating and vomiting is a recognized variant of anorexia nervosa, if enough food is kept down or if the binges are sufficiently frequent and the vomiting postponed long enough, enough food can be absorbed to prevent the extreme weight losses which are a criterion for the diagnosis of anorexia nervosa. There is reason to suspect that a new syndrome is emerging in which binge vomiting is used as a means of maintaining an approximately "normal" weight without the severe distortion of body image or the progression to emaciation seen in classic anorexia. Such patients may appear physically normal and escape diagnosis and treatment. Frequently, the behavior pattern has been adopted in imitation of peers, so that this might be one of the few psychological disorders which could be regarded as "contagious" and in which something akin to "epidemics" may appear. In a report of an experimental treatment of this syndrome, which they dubbed "bulimarexia," Boskind-Lodahl and her colleagues reported that their outreach effort to locate sufficient numbers of patients to form groups produced responses from over 100 women at Cornell University (Boskind-Lodahl, 1976; Boskind-Lodahl & Sirlin, 1977).

Though not so severe as classic anorexia, this syndrome probably should not be assumed to be a passing phase. We have seen several patients in whom the syndrome, begun in adolescence, had persisted in secrecy for 10 to 15 years, with progressive dysfunction. One professional woman had gradually reached a level of 30 or more binge-vomiting episodes daily. In a supportive group of patients with the same problem, she confided that she was resorting to illegal—and, in her own eyes, immoral—activities to support the high cost of her "food habit." Every effort to quit vomiting resulted in an intolerable weight gain with rapid reinstatement of the pattern. Another patient, whose physician father had recognized that something was wrong, had permitted herself to be treated for alcoholism for 6 years rather than admit she was a binge vomiter. There may, indeed, be spontaneous cures, but clearly the potential exists for protracted and debilitating problems for which treatment is long delayed.

Also on this continuum are chronic dieters. Their problems seem less dramatic— probably because the behaviors in which they engage are familiar and common ones. But extended over periods of years, the effects of chronic dieting and preoccupation with weight can take a serious toll. The dieting efforts of such patients may number in the dozens, over spans of from 10 to 40 years, and include repeated hospitalizations, stays at reducing spas, and multiple forms of outpatient treatment by physicians, psychologists, nutritionists, hypnotherapists, and self-help groups. In its most extreme form, the effort to be slender becomes so central to self-acceptance that all other life activities are relegated to relative unimportance. If weight is too high, the patient will avoid seeing friends, refuse to attend social events, avoid sex, and post-pone or drop out of training or careers. The plan is always to begin or resume these activities once weight is lost, but for many that day never comes, or, if it does, it is short-lived.

There is tremendous variability among patients on this dimension of weight obsession, but it appears to bear little relationship to actual body weight. Hall (Note 1) reported that half of the applicants to a weight-loss program were within normal weight limits (i.e., within 10% of average weight), an experience informally validated by many who treat obesity. Among applicants for treatment, the intensity of disturbance often seems greatest in those who are minimally overweight. This clinical impression requires validation, but it is not hard to speculate on reasons why this might be so. The women who care the most may be the most successful in warding off frank obesity, despite the cost. Conversely, the more obese women may be more accepting of their condition as a result of initial differences in aspiration or greater acceptance by significant others, or because weight reduction has proven so futile that they have given up. Thus, to summarize, there is a continuum of psychological disturbance related to inability to achieve or maintain what the individual regards as an acceptable weight. Severe distress is by no means limited to anorexic patients. The development of an appropriate diagnostic category would increase detection and permit quantification of an aspect of weight disorders which, at present, is probably often ignored or left to chance improvement.

Cultural Pressures to Reduce

Much of the intensity of affect surrounding weight control must be blamed on cultural standards which clearly have a greater impact on women than on men. Research data suggest that, regardless of gender, obese children are heavily stigmatized for their weight. These data, reviewed by O. W. Wooley, Wooley, and Dyrenforth (1979), include the findings of Staffieri (1967, 1972) that male children (6-10 years) describe endomorphic silhouettes in a uniformly negative way, for example, "cheats, dirty, argues, forgets, gets teased, lazy, sloppy, lies, mean, ugly, stupid." Females use similar adjectives but add, "worries, fights, naughty, sad and lonely," suggesting an even greater emphasis on the social alienation of obese children. Lerner (1969) found that males (10-20 years) believed endomorphic adult males to be inferior to mesomorphic ones on nearly all dimensions tested, and Lerner and Gelbert (1969) found that kindergarten children showed a consistent aversion to headless photographs of chubby children. Lerner and Korn (1972) found that chubby as well as average 5-, 15-, and 20-year-old males assigned to drawings of endomorphs descriptive phrases they themselves judges to be "bad." Using a method for measuring preferred personal distance, Lerner (1973) found that (6-, 7-, and 8-year-old) children sought greatest distance from endomorphs. Matthews and Westie (1966) found similar results in the preferred social distance of high school students from obese children when contrasted with handicapped ones. Lower rankings of obese than handicapped children were also obtained in studies by Richardson, Goodman, Hastorf, and Dornbusch (1961) and by Goodman, Dornbusch, Richardson, and Hastorf (1963), using samples of children and adults. These studies document the dislike and ostracism of obese children by other children and by adults and point to the likely origins of self-hatred.

Beginning with adolescence, females appear to be much more concerned than males about their weight. Clifford (1971) reported that females 11–19 years of age were more critical of their bodies than were male peers. Jourard and Secord (1955) found that women have a shared "ideal female figure" which, as a group, they fail to achieve. This ideal was summarized as being "smaller than you are in all dimensions except bust." Douty, Moore, and Hartford (1974) found that 59% of college females rated themselves low on "satisfaction with figure," and Beck, Ward-Hull, and McLear (1976) found that college women and women oriented toward achievement prefer smallness. Most women not only value smallness, but as shown by Halmi, Goldberg, and Cunningham (1977), overestimate their own size.

There are also data to suggest that women are more harshly penalized for failure to achieve slenderness, as, in general, women are more often denied or granted access to social privilege on the basis of physical appearance (e.g., see Elder's, 1969, demonstration of the importance of attractiveness in upward social mobility of women through marriage). Thus, Canning and Mayer (1966) showed that obese high school girls were less likely than slender peers to be accepted to colleges, despite comparable qualifications. The Midtown Manhattan study showed obese women, but not men, to be downwardly socially mobile (Goldblatt, Moore, & Stunkard, 1965). Also, the inverse relationship between weight and social class was far stronger for women than for men. Explicit weight criteria for admission to training are relatively common in the female-dominated profession of nursing, but rare or nonexistent in medical training. Although hard data are lacking, one strongly suspects that job discrimination on the basis of weight is more common for women.

Media insults to the obese seem more often to have women than men as their targets, for example, the featuring of ("Mama") Cass Elliott's weight as the most prominent piece of biographic information at the time of her death, or *Time's* printing of a letter to the editor which stated of Boston Symphony conductor Sarah Caldwell, "I am proud to see women take their place in music. However, one cannot regard Sarah Caldwell as anything but a big blob of blubber." A recent *New York Times Magazine* article on treatment of loss of sexual desire in marriage states:

"As important as what is being treated is what is *not* being treated—
specifically, Dr. Kaplan emphasizes, impossible situations. These might
include a husband whose wife is obese and crippled by arthritis . . . 'the
husband's lack of attraction *has a basis in reality*' [emphasis added], Dr.
Kaplan says."

It is curious how we come to regard changing fashions as aesthetic
absolutes. In speaking of the preferences of past generations for heavy
women, Gubner (1974) states, "Obesity, with all its dismal connotations,
is a 20th century word" (p. 7). It is worth noting, in passing, that men are
indirectly affected by the culture's restrictive definitions of female
beauty, experiencing ridicule or shame if the women they love do not
meet the standard or if, worse yet, they *prefer* women who do not meet
the standard. Social pressure to conform in choosing mates was a major
topic of a discussion group for men at the September 1979 convention of
the National Association to Aid Fat Americans.

Men, too, of course, suffer from failure to meet cultural preferences
in body build, probably most commonly with regard to height. The fact
that there is nothing that can be done to change this characteristic may,
however, be more of a blessing than a curse. For it is in large part the
constant effort of women to change their bodies—and their constant
failure—that seems to create emotional problems. Obesity is unfortunately—and incorrectly—considered a voluntary condition, even in the
eyes of some state laws in which it has been upheld as a basis for refusing
employment on the grounds that, like hair length, it is not a protected
right.

Medical Pressures to Reduce

Cultural prejudice against obesity gains strong support from medical
evidence that overweight is associated with increased health risks. This
fact, as stated, is beyond dispute. But that it justifies repetitive dieting is
open to question, and especially in the case of women.

Gubner (1974) writes:

> Weight is of greatest concern to and weight loss is pursued most avidly by
> women, who are actually least affected in terms of health and survival.
> Among women, the actual/expected mortality ratio rises negligibly from
> underweight women to women who are markedly obese. . . . Among women
> with marked overweight (average heights 5' 3" to 5'6" and weights 195 to
> 254 lb.) the mortality rates are still lower than among men in the most
> favorable build category, i.e., underweight (Tables 25, 28, Build and Blood
> Pressure Study). Dublin and Marks . . . at Metropolitan Life Insurance

Company likewise found no progressive rise in mortality among obese women up to the range of 60–74% above average weight. (p. 9)

These marked differences in the impact of obesity on mortality rates in men and women receive surprisingly little mention in discussions on health risks; in all likelihood, they are not known by many people who treat obesity. Moreover, the vast majority of women who seek treatment for obesity fall in the mild-to-moderate ranges of overweight in which the increased risk to health is minimal or nonexistent for both sexes. Recent data from the National Institute on Aging suggest that the current standards for ideal weight are probably set too low for both sexes and that longevity is increased by somewhat higher body weights.

Even if a decreased weight would be advantageous to health, the procedures for attaining it entail health risks. Since weight is usually regained and diets repeated, these risks are not altogether insignificant. Hall and Havassy (in press) cite a United States Public Health Service report that indicates that repeated gains and losses put stress on the cardiovascular system and lead to increased deposition of cholesterol. There are also risks associated with the use of drugs to aid in weight loss. Prior to their more stringent regulation in 1972, 85% of amphetamine prescriptions were issued to women (Balter, 1974). A 1974 survey of physicians specializing in weight loss found that 65% used amphetamines most or all of the time in treating overweight patients (Asher, 1974). Occasional deaths occur during fasting and modified fasting. The risks associated with intestinal bypass are so great that·the psychological rather than the health benefits of weight loss are often invoked to justify their use.

Finally, as Aldebaran (1977) notes, it is not necessarily true that a person who has lost weight attains the same desirable prognosis for obesity-related disorders as a person who is naturally slim. There is sufficient evidence that obese people differ constitutionally from lean ones to require that actual tests of the long-term benefits of weight loss be conducted. Aldebaran (1977) cites the finding of excellent health among the obese inhabitants of an Italian-American community in which overweight was socially accepted as evidence that the stress associated with overweight in modern society may contribute importantly to health problems.

These considerations are sufficient to cast doubt on what have become nearly universal pressures to reduce for reasons of improved health. The benefits to mildly and moderately obese women are certainly questionable. At the very least, recommendations should be based on individual assessment of risk factors, taking into account family history and past and current health status. A reexamination of the entire question of when to recommend weight loss for women probably is in order.

Outcome of Weight-Reduction Programs

Of course, if obesity could be readily reversed or controlled, there would be little problem. But despite enormous efforts to develop effective treatments, obesity has proved to be among the most refractory of disorders. In a classic paper, Stunkard and McLaren-Hume (1959) reported that based on the few follow-up studies available, only 5% of patients treated in medical outpatient clinics had lost 40 or more pounds and maintained the loss for a year. Their pleas for more study of long-term maintenance went largely unheeded, and in a later review of outcome of behavioral treatment, Stunkard and Penick (1979) wrote:

> Even behavior therapists who document their results with particular care, have reported six month (or longer) follow-up evaluation in only 12% of the studies in which follow-up was appropriate ... and with good reason: Weight losses have been so modest that their fate has been a matter of little consequence. Nevertheless, enough follow-up studies have been conducted to permit a disturbing conclusion: Most obese people regain most of the weight they have lost in most treatments for obesity. (p. 801)

Their review concludes that clinically significant losses are least well maintained and that, based on the careful work of Wilson and colleagues (Ashby & Wilson, 1977), "there is no current method which will improve these results." Even a program which had shown excellent maintenance at 1 year showed high relapse rates at 5-year follow-up, supporting the bleak but probably realistic view that if one waits long enough, the results of even the best programs will wash out.

The failure of other programs to produce clinically significant levels of weight loss even during the period of active treatment has spurred the development and use of more rigorous techniques, especially hospital fasts, followed in recent years by "modified protein-sparing fasts," often in combination with behavioral treatment. Long-term follow-up data on these techniques are rare, but, in general, the maintenance of results is poor even at 6–18 months (Hoffman, 1978). These failures have, in turn, led to the use of even more drastic procedures, including jaw wiring, intestinal bypass, and gastric resection, all of which produce weight loss primarily by reducing food intake (S. C. Wooley, Wooley, & Dyrenforth, 1980).

From the standpoint of research on treatment of obesity, even small differences in outcome among various modalities are of paramount importance. However, for the purpose of understanding the overall impact of weight problems on women's lives, it is sufficient to note that the overall prognosis for the population represented in treatment studies is poor. Even researchers who remain optimistic about the prospects of eventually developing techniques to ensure long-term compliance with dietary restrictions sufficient to maintain losses usually concede that to stay slender, patients may have to adapt to a lifetime of chronic hunger.

Understanding Poor Outcome

Research findings of the past two decades have helped to explain why weight loss is so difficult to achieve and maintain. More than 20 studies have demonstrated that, on the average, the obese eat no more than the lean. Nor has it been possible to isolate distinctive features of an obese eating style. (For review of these findings, see S. C. Wooley, Wooley, & Dyrenforth, 1979a.) Thus, to produce weight loss, it is often necessary to produce marked reductions in an essentially normal intake level.

Caloric restriction, in turn, produces decreases in metabolic rate, so that to continue losing weight, patients must usually make further reductions (e.g., Apfelbaum, Bostsarron, & Lacatis, 1971; Bray, 1969; Drenick & Dennin, 1973; Kleiber, 1961). Several studies suggest that, in contrast to lean subjects in whom overfeeding leads to lessened efficiency and less than predicted weight gain (e.g., Miller & Mumford, 1967; Miller, Mumford, & Stock, 1967; Sims & Horton, 1968), the obese show no such tendency (Mahler, 1972; Passmore, Strong, Swindells, & El Din, 1963). In other words, the obese, as a group, gain weight more readily when they overeat. Animal studies have shown that following periods of restriction, increased metabolic efficiency may lead to exceptionally rapid weight gain (Boyle, Storlien, & Keesey, 1978).

It has been suggested that the physiologic threat of starvation may permanently alter the body's tendency to waste excess calories (Keston, 1978; S. C. Wooley *et al.*, 1979a). Clearly, certain profound metabolic adjustments are made, for in animals and humans, weight regained after loss contains greatly higher percentages of adipose tissue (Keys, Brozek, Henschel, Mickelson, & Taylor, 1950; Szepesi, 1978). Similarly, under conditions of severely restricted intake, genetically obese animal strains develop adipose tissue at the expense of lean tissue (Powley, 1977).

The contribution of genetic factors in human obesity remains controversial, but it is likely that the well-documented tendency for obesity to run in families is due in part to hereditary forces. The alternative view—that learning of deviant eating patterns accounts for the high

correlations in parent–child weights—is weakened by the recurrent finding that obese children do not eat more than their peers, but rather, tend
to eat less. This phenomenon has been observed in infants showing high
growth rates (Rose & Mayer, 1968), in obese adolescents (Johnson,
Burke, & Mayer, 1956), and, most persuasively, in meticulous studies of
the food intake and energy expenditure of "preobese" offspring of two
obese parents, 80% of whom are destined to become obese (Griffiths &
Payne, 1976).

Although inactivity may contribute to the etiology and/or maintenance of obesity, it would be a mistake to assume that this points to a
panacea. Spontaneous activity level may itself be a regulated variable,
influenced by genetic predisposition (Griffiths & Payne, 1976). Size-
matched individuals with comparable activity levels may still vary greatly
in net energy expenditure (Rose & Williams, 1961). And alteration of
activity level may prove to be as difficult as alteration of habitual diet,
although it is too early to draw firm conclusions (for review, see Brownell
& Stunkard, in press).

There is, of course, great variability in the ease with which overweight individuals can lose weight and in the tendency to regain lost
weight. Unfortunately, there has been little progress in predicting who
will be successful. Prediction is a common problem in situations with
extremely disparate base rates for the relevant outcomes but one which
makes the question of whom to treat very problematic. For reasons that
are only beginning to be understood, failure is virtually inevitable in a
substantial percentage of patients seeking treatment.

Weight Loss and Self-Control

The inability to predict outcome is, from the standpoint of the therapist,
an inability to control it. And yet, for the individual patient there is an
illusion of control which, for understandable reasons, the therapist tends
to encourage. Referring to this paradox, the feminist writer Aldebaran
(1977) states: "The failure of reducing diets is fat peoples' collective
experience. Therapy tells us to ignore this experience. *You* can lose
weight if *you* try hard enough. If *you* failed *you* were not motivated
enough" (p. 5).

It is true that with prolonged starvation, anyone can lose weight.
And it is true that eating and activity are "voluntary" behaviors, but the
ability to control them in the face of powerful drives falls outside the
capability of most people. Keys *et al.* (1950) report that starved men may
be unable to curb the impulse to eat, even knowing that the conse-

quences may be fatal. Small wonder that anorexics experience their success in renouncing food as an immense personal accomplishment. They often experience an almost exultant sense of power. This sensation, and the visible evidence of accomplishment in the form of an emaciated body, are consistently described by anorexics as the motivation for their behavior. And yet, the disorder is a tragic parody of control (Bruch, 1973).

The same may be said, though to a somewhat lesser degree, of many chronic dieters who at times show almost superhuman efforts of will accompanied by great euphoria. And yet, the overall picture is more one of a person controlled by food than the reverse. Diet breaking is experienced as a complete loss of control, and the continuous alternation of periods of starvation with periods of indulgence may result in a breakdown of the normal patterning and regularity of food ingestion which are the essence—or at least the major tool—of durable control.

It seems to be a reasonable hypothesis that for many women, the ability to control food intake and body weight becomes a symbol or index of the ability to control life in general, with the result that successes are experienced with a pleasure disproportionate to the tangible social or physical benefits of reduced body weight, while failure is experienced as profoundly demoralizing. This phenomenon is widely recognized as a central feature of anorexia nervosa, but it is rarely discussed in connection with overweight. We have observed that women often seem to seek psychological treatment for overweight when the sense of ineffectiveness produced by diet failures has generalized to other areas of living or, the converse, when they attempt to counteract a sense of helplessness in areas unrelated to eating by reinstating control over food. The control over food produces an almost "artificial" sense of power. Although weight loss per se may be irrelevant to the real source of difficulty, the feeling of control may "spill over" with good results. This effect is apt to be temporary, however, since weight is usually regained.

It is interesting to consider some of the reasons why weight control should have become such an important metaphor in so many women's lives. It offers a challenge of sufficient difficulty that nearly everyone respects success. The results are visible. The culture places a high value on the end product of slenderness, because it represents not only beauty, but also health and a disciplined lifestyle. Yet even these considerations do not seem a fully adequate explanation. It may be the very fact that failure *is* so common and is attributed to personal shortcomings that produces preservation. Once having failed, it is not easy to leave the arena with self-esteem intact.

Other possibilities could be mentioned. Weight control may be one of the few arenas in which frank competition among women has been sanctioned and even fostered. Greater external demands on women to achieve may, in some, force a retreat and a narrowing of the sphere in which accomplishment is attempted. Probably the most universal psychological characteristic of anorexics is their conformity to social demands for high achievement, coupled with a profound distrust of their real abilities which causes them to feel that nothing they do is ever good enough. The attainment of control over eating permits—and ultimately forces—escape from other pressures.

Avoidance of stress associated with mature functioning, in particular, fear of sexuality and intimacy, has often been cited as a cause of both anorexia (Bemis, 1978) and obesity (e.g., Hamburger, 1951). In these formulations, the emphasis has usually been on the inappropriate use of food as an immediate response to stress and on motivation to achieve the obese or emaciated state as a means of deterring social advances. There is little doubt that both these processes may occur in some instances. The point made here, however, is that dieting may also be a common and maladaptive response to stress. This may go entirely unrecognized in obese patients and may be recognized relatively late in the development of anorexia, which often begins as a seemingly normal and appropriate attempt to lose weight. Further study of precipitants to dieting and of the conditions under which dieting becomes compulsive could provide useful information about the relationship between control of food and sense of control in women.

Outcome of Treatment of Anorexia Nervosa

An appreciation of the interrelationship between weight loss and sense of control is helpful in understanding the difficulty in maintaining positive outcome in the treatment of anorexia nervosa. In a comprehensive review, Bemis (1978) stresses the importance of distinguishing between short- and long-term outcome. Many programs, including a variety of behavioral and family therapies, have been found to be highly successful in producing weight gain. However, long-term follow-up studies reveal the frequency with which relapse occurs. Bemis reports that less than one-half of patients studied have shown a satisfactory long-term adjustment. Not surprisingly, among patients who gain during hospitalization, one-third to one-fourth begin to eat compulsively, some becoming obese.

Programs relying heavily on the application of external contingencies may fail to engender a sense of self-control in patients and may fail to alleviate anxiety over eating and weight gain. As noted earlier, the period of refeeding following weight losses is apt to be accompanied by unusually rapid gain and exaggerated hunger. It is easy to see how these experiences might serve to reinstate or even intensify earlier concerns about eating. At the same time, Bemis (1978) states that "psychoanalytic therapy has proven singularly ineffective in altering anorexic behavior" (p. 600), suggesting that explicit attention to modification of eating patterns may be essential. It can be concluded, in agreement with Bemis (1978), that effective treatment of anorexia is likely to require attention to all facets of the problem, including eating behavior, family interaction, developing autonomy, and issues in social adjustment. Difficulties in achieving a stable control of food intake and in achieving a sense of competency should be expected to occur and anticipated in therapy. Long-term treatment in support groups consisting of patients at varying levels of recovery might prove a beneficial addition to current programs.

Treatment and Autonomy

To what extent do current treatment methods for obesity and eating disorders address the relationship between control of food intake and sense of effectiveness in women? To what extent do they promote autonomy, both in the selection of treatment goals and in the choice of methods for achieving them? Since these issues are psychological ones, it is not surprising that they are most often overlooked in predominantly medical treatments. Although it is not the purpose of this chapter to analyze medical treatment techniques, the attitudes imparted by physicians are of interest to psychotherapists because most patients have been, and continue to be, exposed to them. The medical view comprises an important aspect of the cultural milieu.

Medical Treatments

The physician's overriding sense of responsibility to do something is well exemplified in the following quote:

> Office counseling, the keystone of treatment, requires time, patience and understanding for *total restructuring of the patient's thinking concerning his problem* [emphasis added]. Obese persons may deny the presence of excess poundage and increased calorie intake or if they admit their handicap, they will attribute weight gains to ill-defined causes beyond their control . . . not consult physicians. The physician cannot equivocate in stressing that their overweight is, indeed, present, is not inevitable, implies significant hazards, confers no benefits and will respond to creation of a negative calorie balance. (Cohen, 1974, pp. 31, 33)

For analysts of language usage, it is interesting how often the phrase "attack obesity" appears in the chapters of the volume edited by Lasagna (1974), along with calls for the physician to be "persistent," "aggressive," and so on. The same emphasis on persuading patients to accept the goal of weight loss is found in the program of the 1979 meeting of the American Society of Bariatric Physicians. Titles of talks include: "How to Talk the Obese Patient into Becoming Thin," "Hypnoanalysis for the Resistant Obese Patient," "Management of the Difficult Obese Patient Who Does Poorly on Weight-Loss Programs," and "How Obese Patients Talk Themselves into Resisting Becoming Thin." The effects of such pressures, and the female patient's interpretation of their meaning, offer an important area for further study.

Psychotherapy

What has been the attitude of psychotherapists toward obese women? Historically, there have been a number of viewpoints, but by far the major contributions have been made by the analyst Bruch, whose intensive work in the area of eating disorders spans several decades. Bruch's pioneering work with obese and anorexic patients made genuine autonomy the cornerstone of treatment, and she sought to repudiate earlier psychodynamic views of eating disorders:

> I feel that obese and anorexic patients appear singularly unresponsive to traditional psychoanalysis. This, however, does not render them untreatable, but psychotherapy must be modified to meet their personal problems. The aim of therapy is to assist them in developing a more competent, less painful and less ineffective way of handling problems.... Close collaborative work with the therapist is a new type of experience; his [sic] being *listened* to and not being told by someone else what he "really" feels or means is important because his own contributions are being regarded as worthwhile. (Bruch, 1973, pp. 336, 337)

This view, which for the first time pointed to similarities between the psychological problems of anorexic and obese patients, replaced a rather confusing array of dynamic hypotheses about the origins of obesity. As Stunkard (1967) noted, "Countless psychic impulses, symbolic meanings, conflicts and dynamics, particularly orality and pathological dependency have been proposed. The very diversity of these factors argues against the existence of any one which operates in all cases of obesity" (p. 1060).

Indeed, the lack of evidence for many early theories has led to a decline in their systematic application. It would be a mistake to assume, however, that interventions based loosely on these formulations are not still common in psychotherapy. Even when weight problems are not the major focus of treatment, overweight is apt to be attributed to developmental disorders, with a search for underlying and unconscious causes of overeating.

To the extent that such unsubstantiated concepts are still applied without careful regard to the particular characteristics of the patient, and without regard to important individual differences in eating habits and in constitution, women may be said to suffer from a regrettable stereotyping, including not only unproven assumptions about the meaning of overeating but also the more fundamental assumption that obesity implies overeating. The following entry is taken from the diary of a patient in psychotherapy whose food intake was later found to be well below average but who believed her eating to be deviant and unconsciously self-destructive.

> *I appear again*
> *and again*
> *at the cupboard*
> *at the refrigerator*
> *and do not soothe with food*
> *but rather torment myself*
> *I feel emotional*
> *and physical death*
> *Yet this very real fear is not enough*
> *to stop that subconscious drive.*
> *It is like the animals running each year*
> *to their death leap into the sea.*
> *I am propelled to my destruction*
> *by a self-created inner force*
> *that eludes me.*

If psychotherapy is to have as a major, or even subsidiary, goal changing weight or eating behavior, it seems imperative that therapists modify traditional techniques to require the collection of pertinent data. The risk of not doing so, illustrated in the case material presented above, is that the patient may become involved in a painful search for psychological explanations of behaviors which are better understood physiologically, or which may even be normal and require no explanation. This problem is a particularly critical one in the treatment of eating disorders, since there is such tremendous variability in the extent to which deviant eating patterns are associated with weight disorders. Although not inherently prescriptive, psychotherapy may become a vehicle for transmitting bias and misinformation which undermines women's sense of competency and lowers their aspirations.

Bruch (1973) has advocated the separation of psychotherapy and

management of weight loss or gain through referral to a physician for
the latter. It is not clear whether there is any real advantage to such a
division, in which the patient strives for autonomy via psychotherapy
and is "managed" by a physician for weight change. Fully acknowledging
the difficulties of weight loss, Bruch (1973) finds that it is difficult to
bring eating under the same autonomous control she seeks to produce in
other areas, stating:

> Most people find it easier to substitute the rational authority of another
> person for freedom of choice with continuous self-denial.... One might
> expect that people with a rational motive for reducing weight would do well
> if given a general understanding of nutrition and that they then would
> restrict the intake of high caloric foods.... I have rarely seen it to be suc-
> cessful in those who have permitted obesity to develop. (p. 312)

Despite the difficulties of controlling food intake and weight—or,
more precisely, because of them—an argument could be made that these
issues should be integrated with other aspects of therapy. If, indeed,
people with a rational motive for losing weight and a thorough understanding of the changes required rarely succeed, this suggests the existence of unidentified problems which may be only temporarily alleviated
by applying outside authority. Because of the intimate interplay between
sense of control over diet and sense of control over self, it might be
especially important that patients choose their own course, carefully
weighing the costs and benefits of dieting. It would be useful to compare
the long-term results of self- and other-directed weight-loss programs
both by the traditional criterion of weight loss and by additional criteria
reflecting sense of control and degree of continuing weight obsession.

Behavior Therapy

If reliance on outside authority seems problematic in the treatment of
weight disorders, the provision of concrete guidance is to be applauded.
Behavior therapy has generated many techniques which can be of substantial assistance to patients in gaining an objective understanding of
their own eating behavior and the immediate determinants of both controlled and uncontrolled episodes of eating (Stunkard & Penick, 1979).
Behavior therapy has helped to demystify obesity by substituting an
empirical analysis of behavior for a search for remote causes of (often
unspecified) behaviors. The careful investigation of the role of experienced hunger, mood shifts, and setting variables in the determination of
food intake provides the patient with practical information which can be
easily used to make decisions. In addition, some of the techniques which
have grown out of this field can be of use to individuals, although the

overall relationship between compliance with these suggestions and weight loss is dubious (Brownell & Stunkard, 1978).

However, taking into consideration the complex problems experienced by women with weight disorders, it is appropriate to question whether behavior therapy provides a sufficiently comprehensive point of view. There is a minimal emphasis on the important process of setting and periodically reappraising goals, and behavior therapists, like others, often see their role as enforcing an acceptance of treatment. This view is reflected in discussions of how to increase motivation and change negative outcome expectations. One recent paper speaks of "debunking" patients' "false beliefs" about causes of obesity, including personality or metabolic problems. It is not clear what is meant by "false beliefs," but given the current state of knowledge, therapists should be cautious in making such judgments. More importantly, behavioral treatments, which are typically quite short-term and limited in their goals, overlook many potentially important ways in which women with weight problems could be helped. Outstanding among these is to help women deal effectively with a society that places undue importance on meeting passing standards of physical beauty.

Feminist Treatment Paradigms

In a discussion of outcome measurement in treatment of obesity, Feinstein (1974) asks:

> Since so many tend to regain the weight they lose, why go through the charade over and over again? Why not demand that long-term efficacy be demonstrated for any drug, diet or other regimen proposed for use in weight reduction? To make that demand would lead us into the traps produced by the dehumanized science of our era. We would ignore the satisfaction of the lady who got into the size 12 dress for the wedding. (p. 87)

This comment well illustrates the current dilemma. As things now stand, most women do want to lose weight, and respect for their autonomy could be taken to mean that the therapist should cooperate unquestioningly in implementing the steps which might help them achieve their goal, even though the odds are poor. And yet, when the choice is so firmly rooted in sexist values of the culture, the therapist has an obligation to deal with this fact. The report of the American Psychological Association Task Force on Sex Bias and Sex-Role Stereotyping in Psychotherapeutic Practice (1975) states, "Psychologists should recognize the reality, variety, and implications of sex-discriminatory practice in society and should facilitate client examination of options in dealing with such practices" (p. 1122). The application of this guide-line to the treatment of obesity and eating disorders has barely begun.

Boskind-Lodahl (1976) has reported on the use of group treatment for bulimarexia with an explicitly feminist orientation. A major treat-ment strategy is an analysis of the ways in which the group members have allowed their sense of self-worth to be defined by the judgments of men. Flack and Grayer (1975) have described the use of consciousness-raising groups which "work toward illuminating what it is like to be fat in American society, with the additional goals of raising self-esteem and lessening self-punishment" (p. 484). If this program has any fault, it is an underestimation of the biologic barriers to weight loss and an insistence that obesity is "chosen"— for example, "obese women do not see being fat as a choice; the desire to overeat is so overpowering that the woman feels helpless and out of control" (Flack & Grayer, 1975, p. 485). On the other hand, there is an explicit statement that "the choice to remain fat or to become thin is your own business and does not affect our regard for you" (pp. 484-485).

Another welcome contribution is Loro, Fisher, and Levonkron's (1979) study of a behavioral treatment of obesity which "encouraged development of individuals' own application of a model of self-control . . . and was designed to be less directive than many behavioral treatment packages and . . . more realistic about the expectations of sub-jects and the actual eating habits of overweight and normalweight people" (p. 141). Although the study emphasized comparison of weight loss between the experimental and control treatments, it also included ratings of general improvement, judgment of the program, and attribu-tion of success. In all instances in which significant differences were found, the experimental group proved superior.

Behavioral treatment of obesity and eating disorders has been com-bined with analysis of cultural pressures and therapy designed to in-crease self-esteem and competency in women (S. C. Wooley, Wooley, & Dyrenforth, 1979b). The careful monitoring of eating behavior and its determinants allows patients to get a clearer picture of whether and to what extent their food intake is unusual, to recognize and quantify the extent to which hunger versus emotional and environmental factors lead to eating, and to specify the degree of restriction necessary for weight loss. When this program is integrated with an exploration of alternatives to dieting as a solution to social alienation and self-hate, the patient is in a better position to judge whether continued dieting is, indeed, justified.

It is worth noting that while all women are exposed in varying degrees to pressures to be thin, some career choices create additional pressures. Dancers, for example, have been exposed to increasingly stringent standards of slenderness whose negative effects on health have recently become a focus of study. Vincent (1979) cites evidence that clinical anorexia nervosa is disproportionately represented among ballet dancers, while dancers, as a group, display many anorexic characteristics. Their attitudes to food resemble those of anorexic patients, and one-third of those surveyed had not had a menstrual period for 3 or more months. Although ballet dancing is listed by the Department of Labor as the most physically strenuous occupation, the low caloric intakes of dancers provide compelling evidence of the capacity for metabolic adaptation.

Implicit and explicit weight quotas also create problems for models, entertainers, airline stewardesses, and many other women whose jobs involve "meeting the public." For example, an airline stewardess treated in our clinic had been forced over the years to fast for increasingly long periods of time in order to pass the monthly weight check. She sought treatment when the cumulative effects of fasting on energy expenditure were so severe that she was no longer able to meet the quotas even by remaining on an 800 calorie/day diet (on which she gained weight).

The threat of loss of livelihood as a result of weight gain presents a particularly frustrating problem. From a diagnostic standpoint, disentangling appropriate efforts to meet weight requirements from early phases of anorexia nervosa may be difficult. Treatment options are apt to be limited. If long-term dieting has created metabolic adaptation, there may be no solution which does not carry the risk of weight gain. As Vincent (1979) notes in speaking of the problems of dancers with long histories of food restriction, "the result may be a suboptimal diet, suboptimal energy reserves, and difficulty climbing out of this self-excavated metabolic rut" (p. 39).

Amelioration of these problems may require multiple avenues of assistance, including outreach efforts to locate those affected, the development of prevention programs, and public and employer education. In some instances, efforts to combat unduly restrictive weight requirements are clearly in order.

Mothers and Obesity Prevention

I usually tell the mother of a teenage child that mothers are my biggest problem. . . . The problem with mothers is that they rationalize for the child. They say that we're all out of carrots and green beans so you can have half as many peas, or they say, since you're sick today you should drink lots of juice. . . . The second thing they do wrong is that they don't keep the proper foods stocked at home. They run out of diet soda . . . or run out of carrots and celery. . . . The third thing they do is fail to bring the child back to see me. They're too busy that afternoon with the bowling or with the hairdresser or whatever. (Collipp, 1974, p. 65)

Leaving aside the assumptions that mothers alone should do the shopping and cooking, that carrots are better than peas, that women spend their afternoons in frivolous activities at the expense of their children's health, and leaving aside the discomfort engendered by this barrage of female stereotypes and arbitrary opinions, there remain fundamental questions about prevention of obesity which are of great concern to women.

There are no data to support the belief that obese children eat more than their peers, either before or after weight gain. Thus, it is unclear *how* obesity should be prevented. And, if the effort to control one's own food intake is often anguishing, the effort to control someone else's is probably more so. Although some obese patients report that their parents urged them to clean their plates, it has been our experience that many more describe an unending battle in which their mothers tried to keep them from eating and they rebelled—openly or in secret (S. C. Wooley & Wooley, 1979). The intensity of discord may have undermined family relationships or made eating a source of perpetual conflict.

The confusion in this area is great. Experts disagree on nearly every point: whether or not there are "critical periods"; the influence of infant feeding practices; the etiologic importance of food intake and activity level; and the extent of genetic predetermination of obesity. In the absence of real knowledge, mothers, most of whom do not want their children to suffer from fatness or from hunger and preoccupation with food, are taking much of the responsibility and much of the blame for their children's overweight. The custom that holds mothers accountable needs to be reexamined, with an equal sharing of effort between parents and a recognition of the possible limits to what can be accomplished and the multiple aspects of the problem. If efforts to "cure" his or her obesity fail, the fat child must be helped to cope with the negative attitudes of society. This may be hard to do once parents themselves have become overidentified with the cultural valuation of thinness, suggesting the need for reconsideration of approaches to prevention and treatment of childhood obesity.

Research Priorities

Basic research on obesity and anorexia nervosa is flourishing, and there is reason to hope that the next few decades will provide answers to some of the riddles and perhaps even solutions to some of the problems.

However, in the meanwhile, and independent of these efforts, there are important questions regarding women and weight disorders which should be explored.

1. Although we know that many women suffer from chronic dissatisfaction with their bodies and can point to some of the broad cultural pressures related to this fact, we know very little about the specific conditions that determine which women will be affected and which will not. In particular, we know very little about women who live comfortably with their bodies, and these might be a useful group to study, contrasting their backgrounds, current social environments, and personal characteristics with those of women who have marked problems in this area.

2. A related and unanswered question is the relationship between body image/weight obsession and overall functioning. To what extent, and in what ways, do insecurities over appearance affect the ability of women to assert themselves socially, professionally, and intellectually? Effects could be sought in global measures of accomplishments and level of functioning and in very specific behavioral observations which could point to the typical ways in which such insecurities are expressed in interpersonal or other behaviors (e.g., self-effacement, excessive compliance). Until these questions are answered, it remains unclear just how important a problem this is, though one can be fairly certain that it is responsible for considerable discontent.

3. The lack of treatment techniques to alleviate poor body image is somewhat surprising. One reason may be that early reports showing that even weight loss to a desired level did not correct poor body image suggested that poor body image was, in some sense, refractory to intervention or even immutable. However, this only demonstrates again that self-perceptions are poorly related to the "objective" reality of physical appearance and should not discourage efforts to develop ways to modify these perceptions. This would seem to be a particularly suitable area for the experimental application of cognitive-behavior-modification procedures. It seems likely that the knowledge gained in treatment of depression would have some applicability to treatment of body-image disorders. In a sense, the major difference between the two is the focus and specificity of self-dissatisfaction.

4. If the future is like the past, new variants of treatment for obesity and eating disorders are likely to spring up each year. Assuming that these continue to carry modest success rates, health professionals will continue to be confronted with the question of whether to encourage or discourage patients from "trying again." A relevant consideration is the long-term impact of chronic dieting (and frequent failure). The physiologic and metabolic effects are of great importance but fall outside

the scope of this chapter. However, it would be just as important to gain some objective information about psychological effects to replace the uncertain knowledge contained in clinical impressions. To do this may require longitudinal studies as well as cross-sectional comparisons between dieters and nondieters, since there are important selection factors involved. We need to know more about what happens to women who make weight and eating a central feature of their lives and whether the problems warrant more serious attention than they have received in the past.

Reference Note

1. Hall, S. Personal communication, October 1, 1979.

References

Aldebaran. Fat liberation—A luxury? An open letter to radical (and other) therapists. (Quotes taken from an unpublished manuscript supplied by the author; this article subsequently appeared in *State and Mind*, 1977, *5*, 34.)

American Psychological Association Task Force. Report of the Task Force on Sex Bias and Sex-Role Stereotyping in Psychotherapeutic Practice. *American Psychologist*, 1975, *30*, 1169–1175.

Apfelbaum, M., Bostsarron, J., & Lacatis, D. Effect of caloric restriction and excessive caloric intake on energy expenditure. *American Journal of Clinical Nutrition*, 1971, *24*, 1405–1409.

Asher, W. L. Appetite supressants as an aid in obesity control. In L. Lasagna (Ed.), *Obesity: Causes, consequences, and treatment*. New York: Medcom, 1974.

Ashby, W. A., & Wilson, G. T. Behavior therapy for obesity: Booster sessions and long term maintenance of weight loss. *Behaviour Research and Therapy*, 1977, *15*, 451–464.

Balter, M. Extent and character of amphetamine use. In L. Lasagna (Ed.), *Obesity: Causes, consequences, and treatment*. New York: Medcom, 1974.

Beck, S. B., Ward-Hull, C. I., & McLear, P. M. Variables related to women's somatic preferences of the male and female body. *Journal of Personality and Social Psychology*, 1976, *34*, 1200–1210.

Bemis, K. M. Current approaches to the etiology and treatment of anorexia nervosa. *Psychological Bulletin*, 1978, *85*, 593–617.

Boskind-Lodahl, M. Cinderella's stepsisters: A feminist perspective on anorexia nervosa and bulimia. *Signs: Journal of Women in Culture and Society*, 1976, *2*, 341–356.

Boskind-Lodahl, M., & Sirlin, J. The gorging–purging syndrome. *Psychology Today*, 1977, *10*, 50–52.

Boyle, P. C., Storlien, H., & Keesey, R. E. Increased efficiency of food utilization following weight loss. *Physiology and Behavior*, 1978, *21*, 261–264.

Bray, G. Effect of caloric restriction on energy expenditure in obese patients. *Lancet*, 1969, *2*, 397–398.

Brownell, K. D., & Stunkard, A. J. Behavior therapy and behavior change: Uncertainties in programs for weight control. *Behaviour Research and Therapy*, 1978, *16*, 301.

Brownell, K. D., & Stunkard, A. J. Physical activity in the development and control of obesity. In A. J. Stunkard (Ed.), *Obesity*. Philadelphia: Saunders, in press.

Bruch, H. *Eating disorders: Obesity, anorexia, and the person within.* New York: Basic Books, 1973.

Canning, H., & Mayer, J. Obesity—Its possible effect on college acceptance. *New England Journal of Medicine,* 1966, *275,* 1172–1174.

Clifford, E. Body satisfaction in adolescence. *Perceptual and Motor Skills,* 1971, *33,* 119–125.

Cohen, B. M. The internist's approach. In L. Lasagna (Ed.), *Obesity: Causes, consequences, and treatment.* New York: Medcom, 1974.

Collipp, P. J. Open discussion. In L. Lasagna (Ed.), *Obesity: Causes, consequences, and treatment.* New York: Medcom, 1974.

Douty, H. I., Moore, J. B., & Hartford, D. Body characteristics in relation to life adjustment, body image and attitudes of college females. *Perceptual and Motor Skills,* 1974, *39,* 499–521.

Drenick, E. J., & Dennin, H. F. Energy expenditure in fasting men. *Journal of Laboratory and Clinical Medicine,* 1973, *81,* 421–430.

Elder, G. H. Appearance and education in marriage mobility. *American Sociological Review,* 1969, *34,* 519–533.

Feinstein, A. R. How do we measure accomplishment in weight reduction? In L. Lasagna (Ed.), *Obesity: Causes, consequences, and treatment.* New York: Medcom, 1974.

Flack, R., & Grayer, E. D. A consciousness raising group for obese women. *Social Work,* 1975, *20,* 484–486.

Goldblatt, P. B., Moore, M. E., & Stunkard, A. J. Social factors in obesity. *Journal of the American Medical Association,* 1965, *192,* 1039–1044.

Goodman, N., Dornbusch, S. M., Richardson, S. A., & Hastorf, A. H. Variant reactions to physical disabilities. *American Sociological Review,* 1963, *28,* 429–435.

Griffiths, M., & Payne, P. R. Energy expenditure in small children of obese and nonobese parents. *Nature,* 1976, *26,* 698–700.

Gubner, R. Overweight and health: Prognostic realities and therapeutic possibilities. In L. Lasagna (Ed.), *Obesity: Causes, consequences, and treatment.* New York: Medcom, 1974.

Hall, S. M., & Havassy, B. The obese woman: Causes, correlates, and treatment. *Professional Psychology,* in press.

Halmi, K. A., Goldberg, S. C., & Cunningham, S. Perceptual distortion of body image in adolescent girls: Distortion of body image in adolescence. *Psychology and Medicine,* 1977, *7,* 253–257.

Hamburger, W. W. Emotional aspects of obesity. *Medical Clinics of North America,* 1951, *35,* 483–499.

Hoffman, R. Starvation diets in the treatment of obesity. *Obesity and Bariatric Medicine,* 1978, *7,* 10–16.

Johnson, M. L., Burke, B. S., & Mayer, J. Relative importance of inactivity and over-eating in the energy balance of obese high school girls. *American Journal of Clinical Nutrition,* 1956, *4,* 37–44.

Jourard, S. M., & Secord, P. R. Body-cathexis and the ideal female figure. *Journal of Abnormal and Social Psychology,* 1955, *50,* 243–246.

Keston, R. H. The famine syndrome. The protection of endogenous protein through metabolic inhibition. *International Journal of Obesity,* 1978, *2,* 483. (Abstract)

Keys, A., Brozek, J., Henschel, A., Mickelson, O., & Taylor, H. *The biology of human starvation.* Minneapolis: University of Minnesota Press, 1950.

Kleiber, J. *The fire of life: An introduction to animal energetics.* New York: Wiley, 1961.

Lasagna, L. (Ed.). *Obesity: Causes, consequences, and treatment.* New York: Medcom, 1974.

Lerner, R. M. The development of stereotyped expectancies of body build–behavior relations. *Child Development,* 1969, *40,* 137–141.

Lerner, R. M. The development of personal space schemata toward body build. *The Journal of Psychology,* 1973, *84,* 229–235.

Lerner, R. M. & Gelbert, E. Body build identification, preference, and aversion in children. *Developmental Psychology,* 1969, *1,* 456–462.

Lerner, R. M., & Korn, S. J. The development of body-build stereotypes in males. *Child Development*, 1972, *43*, 908–920.

Loro, A. D., Fisher, E. B., & Levonkron, J. C. Comparison of established and innovative weight-reduction treatment procedures. *Journal of Applied Behavior Analysis*, 1979, *12*, 141–155.

Mahler, R. The relationship between eating and obesity. *Acta Diabetologica Latina*, 1972, *8* (Suppl. 1), 449–468.

Mathews, V., & Westie, C. A preferred method for obtaining rankings: Reactions to physical handicaps. *American Sociological Review*, 1966, *31*, 851–854.

Miller, D. S., & Mumford, P. Gluttony: An experimental study of overeating on low or high protein diets. *American Journal of Clinical Nutrition*, 1967, *20*, 1212–1222.

Miller, D. S., Mumford, P., & Stock, M. Gluttony: Thermogenesis in overeating man. *American Journal of Clinical Nutrition*, 1967, *20*, 1223–1229.

Passmore, R., Strong, J., Swindells, Y. E., & El Din, N. The effect of overfeeding on two fat young women. *British Journal of Nutrition*, 1963, *17*, 373–383.

Powley, T. The ventromedial hypothalamic syndrome, satiety, and a cephalic phase hypothesis. *Psychological Review*, 1977, *84*, 89–106.

Richardson, S. A., Goodman, N., Hastorf, A. H., & Dornbusch, S. M. Cultural uniformity in reaction to physical disabilities. *American Sociological Review*, 1961, *26*, 241–247.

Rose, G. A., & Williams, R. T. Metabolic studies on large and small eaters. *British Journal of Nutrition*, 1961, *15*, 1–9.

Rose, H. E., & Mayer, J. Activity, caloric intake, and the energy balance of infants. *Pediatrics*, 1968, *41*, 18–29.

Sims, E. A. H., & Horton, E. S. Endocrine and metabolic adaptation to obesity and starvation. *American Journal of Clinical Nutrition*, 1968, *21*, 1455–1470.

Staffieri, J. R. A study of social stereotype of body image in children. *Journal of Personality and Social Psychology*, 1967, *7*, 101–104.

Staffieri, J. R. Body build and behavior expectancies in young females. *Developmental Psychology*, 1972, *6*, 125–127.

Stunkard, A. J. Obesity. In A. M. Freedman & H. I. Kaplan (Eds.), *Comprehensive textbook of psychiatry*. Baltimore: Williams and Wilkins, 1967.

Stunkard, A. J., & McLaren-Hume, M. The results of treatment for obesity. *Archives of Internal Medicine*, 1959, *103*, 79–85.

Stunkard, A. J., & Penick, S. B. Behavior modification in the treatment of obesity: The problem of maintaining weight loss. *Archives of General Psychiatry*, 1979, *36*, 801–806.

Szepesi, B. A model of nutritionally induced overweight: Weight "rebound" following caloric restriction. *International Journal of Obesity*, 1978, *2*, 390. (Abstract)

Vincent, L. M. *competing with the sylph*. New York: Andrews and McMeel, 1979.

Wooley, O. W., Wooley, S. C., & Dyrenforth, S. R. Obesity and women: II. A neglected feminist topic. *Women's Studies International Quarterly*, 1979, *2*, 81–92.

Wooley, S. C., & Wooley, O. W. Obesity and women: I. A closer look at the facts. *Women's Studies International Quarterly*, 1979, *2*, 69–79.

Wooley, S. C., Wooley, O. W., & Dyrenforth, S. R. Theoretical, practical and social issues in behavioral treatments of obesity. *Journal of Applied Behavior Analysis*, 1979, *12*, 3–25. (a)

Wooley, S. C., Wooley, O. W., & Dyrenforth, S. R. Obesity treatment re-examined: The case for a more tentative and experimental approach. In N. Krasnegor (Ed.), *Behavioral analysis and treatment of substance abuse* (NIDA Research Monograph No. 25). Washington, D. C.: U.S. Government Printing Office, 1979. (b)

Wooley, S. C., Wooley, O. W., & Dyrenforth, S. R. The case against radical interventions (from NIH Consensus Development Conference on Surgical Treatments of Obesity, December 1978). *American Journal of Clinical Nutrition*, 1980, *33*, 465–471.

CHAPTER 7

Marital and Family Conflicts

ALAN S. GURMAN

MARJORIE H. KLEIN

Marriage today is viewed with trepidation. Many people in their 20s see the risks. They fear the decision for themselves and increasingly postpone it. They find that their friends and parents are divorcing. Some have experienced their parents' marital conflicts firsthand. Women especially are worried that marriage may restrict and even stifle their personhood. Yet, they also know that alternate lifestyles may not meet their long-range needs for security and companionship. Divorces are occurring at record rates, and the impact of these divorces is felt personally and socially even by couples whose marriages remain intact. Increasing numbers of couples struggle to apply new values and principles in their marriages, sometimes with mixed results. Thus, raised to see marriage as "happily ever after," we find insecurity and confusion on all sides. Indeed, the popular question, "What is the problem with marriage?", may be restated, "What is not a problem with marriage?"

The Prevalence of Marital and Family Conflict and Its Impact on Women

The answer to a seemingly simple question about the prevalence of marital and family conflict becomes extremely complex, since there are many ways to define the phenomenon. Are we to look at the divorce rate? At the balance of satisfaction and open strife and tension in families? And what of other undocumented manifestations such as the silent symptomatic suffering of one partner, mutual long-term anger and bitterness, sexual dysfunction, alcoholism, acting out, or spouse or

Alan S. Gurman and Marjorie H. Klein. Department of Psychiatry, University of Wisconsin Medical School, Madison, Wisconsin.

child abuse? All these and more must be considered in any tabulation of marital risk rates. And this does not consider newer risks, that is, the stresses and strains involved in trying to have a liberated relationship, to live androgynously, to survive with a raised consciousness and with the awareness of pain and imperatives for personal change that must flow from that.

Because of these complexities, it is difficult to estimate the prevalence of marital conflict with any precision. The rates of some manifestations, such as divorce, are fairly well known, but the rates of other expressions of marital and family conflict are not yet clear, nor do we have any information about the overlap or independence among different aspects.

Rates of Divorce

Recent census surveys suggest that rates of marriage postponement, divorce, and remarriage are all on the increase. In the '70s, the rate of marriage for women in the age range of 20–24 was down from a previous peak of 67.2% to a new low of 54.4% (Glick & Norton, 1973; Sklar & Berkoff, 1975). Also, in the '70s, the rate of divorce was rising at a steady rate to a new high of 4.5% per 1000 persons (Prochaska & Prochaska, 1978). This translates into a lifetime divorce risk rate of about 30%.

Marital Conflict

Not all marital conflict ends in divorce, however. Unfortunately, the data in this area are more difficult to obtain. At the very least, one must combine clinic census data and the results of surveys of "normal" populations, recognizing that methods of sampling, definitions, and assessments of conflict and/or happiness and satisfaction vary widely. Thus, the data from the University of Wisconsin Psychiatry Outpatient Clinic, which we can present in some detail, tend to underestimate overall rates of marital conflict because patients come primarily from the university community. Nonetheless, even in this clinic we find among new patients 22 years of age or older that 25% of their primary and 42% of their secondary complaints are about marital conflict, family problems, or sexual problems. When the same patients were asked to rate "relationship with spouse," 29% gave a negative rating, 18% a neutral rating, and 53% a positive rating. It is not surprising that the intake team designated couple or family therapy as a desirable therapy in 26% of these intakes and that 22% actually received couple or family therapy as their primary modality, with another 10% receiving this treatment as a secondary modality.

Higher rates of marital and family conflict are found in surveys of other clinic populations. In a survey by Gurin, Veroff, and Feld (1960), it was found that 42% of mental health service consumers saw their problems as marital, with another 17% mentioning other family members. Overall, Henry, and Woodward (1974) reported that 58% of 2000 outpatient visits were for marriage-related problems. In another survey of family service clients (Parad & Parad, 1968), a much higher rate of family conflict (75%) was reported. Weiss and Aved (1978) found that "overuse" of family practice services was associated with marital conflict and that marital satisfaction (low) and depression (high) were both predictors of physical complaints. In addition, it can be noted that 40% of children born in the present decade spent at least some of their early years in single-parent homes and that roughly 17% of American children presently live in single-parent homes (Martin, 1979).

Rates of marital and family conflict among non-help-seeking populations are more difficult to estimate. One problem is that many surveys have focused on estimates of satisfaction and happiness, which have been criticized rightly for being invalid or biased indicators of marital stability (Hicks & Platt, 1970; Laws, 1971). Results of surveys have also indicated qualitatively different kinds of conflict and issues depending upon the values and expectations of the couples (e.g., companionship vs. institutional marriage; Hicks & Platt, 1970). What is clear, in any case, is that marital stability and reports of marital happiness are not necessarily related. It has also emerged from recent research that marital satisfaction changes over time, with some studies pointing to increasing strains and stresses during the active childrearing years (e.g., Blood & Wolfe, 1960; Bradburn & Caplovitz, 1965) and other showing long-range increases in conflict (e.g., Paris & Paris, 1966). This complexity has led Hicks and Platt (1970) to recommend that "perhaps it is time to discard the global concept of marital happiness altogether" (p. 63). They argue that it will be more important for researchers to look at indicators of marital relations which are not so heavily influenced by values and societal expectations. They also suggest the importance of stresses and life changes in understanding marital and family conflict.

Marital Status and Mental Disorder

Current studies of the relationship between marital status and mental disorders are also relevant in estimating the prevalence of marital conflict, for this research may indicate where marital conflict is primarily expressed or exacerbated by the symptomatic status of one marital partner, that is, disorder *in* marriage as contrasted with disorders *of* marriage. The general finding in this area is that while married people utilize mental health services less, higher rates of symptomatology occur among the divorced and separated and among married and widowed women. This has led Gove and Tudor (1973), Weissman and Klerman (1977), and Radloff (1975) to suggest that married women are at greater risk for depression, at a rate of two times that for men. Various community surveys suggest that about 25% of married women are depressed or symptomatic at some point in their lives (e.g., Bernard, 1973; Meile, Johnson, & Porter, 1976; Perlin & Johnson, 1977). Although the direction of causality is unclear, marital friction is characteristic of depressed women (Weissman & Paykel, 1974).

The focus on epidemiologic studies of depression should not divert our attention from other areas where psychological symptoms and marital conflict may also be associated. Agoraphobia, more common among women than men, has been noted recently to be on the increase (Goldstein & Chambless, 1978), and the cooccurrence of agoraphobia and marital conflict has been documented frequently (e.g., Hafner, 1977; Milton & Hafner, in press). Alcoholism is another example of a problem, now increasing among women, where marital conflict, if not contributing causally, must inevitably result (Paolino & McCrady, 1978a). Recent reports also suggest a high level of sexual dysfunction among married women Hite (1976) reports that 49% of women rarely or never reach orgasm during coitus and that another 19% require some form of manual stimulation. While some couples may develop comfortable sexual styles, it is difficult to believe that differences in sexual pace and needs for stimulation do not constitute important marital stresses. There are other aspects of marital conflict where prevalence figures are almost impossible to obtain at present. One example which we observe clinically, in a university community, is conflicts resulting from changing values, particularly with regard to women's liberation and the (sometimes unequal) desire for marital equality. Research on the relationship of sex-role issues to marital conflict is clearly indicated, as is research on the relationships of partners in alternative lifestyle arrangements, including alternative sexual lifestyles.

Since we have no basis for knowing how to combine rates of marital and family conflict from these different domains, it is extremely difficult to arrive at any meaningful estimate of the overall rate. We would be unrealistic, however, if we did not conclude that marital and family conflict is extremely prevalent in our culture. Perhaps it is a reflection of our own values to add that we would suspect unreliable reporting due to the presence of strong defense mechanisms or question the quality of relationship of any couple that appears to weather the stresses and strains of marriage and family life, over the whole of its life span, without experiencing some manifestations of conflict at one time or another.

Theoretical Explanations for Marital and Family Conflict

It is far more interesting to consider different explanations of marital and family conflict, for the array of theories that have been advanced tells us more about the complexity of the subject than do any of the prevalence figures. While fashions in research and theory may make different views of marital–family conflict and associated problems more or less popular at different times, we venture that all are relevant and valid. Certainly, the various factors interact. They also reflect different perspectives: Structural–cultural explanations are anchored in nonclinical, epidemiologic, personality, and social-psychological research. Clinical approaches are more responsible for interactional theories. What is lacking and needed are integrations that do justice to the complex interplay of culture, values, social structure, family process, and individual attributes to explain conflicts in marriage (see Brown & Harris, 1978, for an attempt at integration for the problem of depression). This is particularly important if women are to be freed from being defined in terms of marital roles and from bearing primary responsibility for maintaining family harmony.

Structural, Cultural, and Political Theories of Marital and Family Conflict

A long-standing debate over the relative contributions of social–structural versus individual personality factors to a range of problems has been joined in the '70s by feminists who have sharpened our awareness of ways that imbalances in power, status, and social–economic resources have contributed to women's status and to their personalities, self-images, and characteristic pathology (e.g., Bernard, 1973; Chesler, 1972; Firestone, 1970; Rich, 1976). Much of the debate has focused on marriage, particularly the "traditional" or "institutional" marriage, which epitomizes the negative consequences of sexism and sex-role stereotypes for women. Conceptions of the impact of economic variables on marriage illustrate the double jeopardy that has been inherent in the traditional female role. Economic conditions, employment, and economic benefits available to families are known to affect the harmony and stability of the family unit (Bachrach, 1978; Hicks & Platt, 1970; Meile *et al.*, 1976; Perlin & Johnson, 1977). Women are economically devalued and dependent; social status and economic rewards accrue to women through men but impact directly on women, especially in the case of divorce or separation. Other sources of stress are inherent in the traditional role. There is growing evidence that children impose a particular strain on women (e.g., Perlin & Johnson, 1977; Radloff, 1975) at the same time that we find that work outside the home can cause stressful role conflict and overload (Bernard, 1976).

Long-range cultural changes also threaten marriage. Increases in social mobility and decreases in social integration over the 20th century have broken down important support systems for families and for women. There was once a clear and secure place in the social order for married young people, with definite expectations for functioning within the extended family unit. Although this value system promulgated divisions according to sex roles and was often confining to women, it also accorded more status and social support for women in their domain than is true today. For example, Smith-Rosenberg (1975) has described powerful and supportive women's networks in the 19th century as important emotional and psychological resources. It is interesting that these networks, which probably were the victims of rapid social changes of the early decades of the 20th century, are now being rediscovered by women. This rediscovery is clearly reflected in women's interest in an responsiveness to consciousness-raising groups (Kravetz, 1978). The rediscovery of the woman's perspective is also reflected in recent attempts to explore the mother–daughter relationships in the popular and feminist literature (e.g., Friday, 1978; Rich, 1976). The development of feminism and the growth of the women's liberation movement has also contributed to marital conflict by making women more aware of their oppression and powerlessness. Women are in a time of transition when their consciousness, that is, their awareness of past oppression, present pain, and future possibilities, runs well ahead of their ability to transform themselves and to alter society.

The spectrum of structural, cultural, policital, and social variables are all related to marital conflict, as they affect the viability of the marital partners within the unit or exert disabling influences on one member, usually the wife. These variables tend to shade into one another. Economists and sociologists can present evidence for women's lower social and economic status. Considering cultural trends, we can talk of the changing role of the family in our culture, of changing values, and of the breakdown of support systems, both for women and for the nuclear family unit. From a feminist perspective, we can speak of the low status and self-esteem that women have experienced due to sexism and the negative effects of traditional sex roles. Analyses of marriage which focus on (1) women's relative lower status, (2) the limited satisfactions or rewards inherent in the traditionally defined wife role, (3) the psychological effects of lack of personal choice and individuality that women have experienced, or (4) the role conflict and strain imposed by specific stressors such as childrearing or social isolation exemplify structural–cultural contributions to marital and family conflict. These analyses especially highlight the conflicts women experience within marriages and families.

Life-Span Development and Crisis

The renewed interest in life-span development brings a most welcome perspective to our understanding of marital conflict. It allows us to see some conflicts and crises as part of a normal developmental process, especially in relation to abrupt transitions or "passages" which disrupt or perturb previous adaptations. In addition, it draws attention to the marital conflicts that arise when partners are at different life-cycle phases. Sheehey (1974), in particular, has described the implications of life-span development for women and for marriage. She has described ways that sex roles interact with life-cycle issues as marital stressors. The results of her interviews support the view, theoretically developed by Loevinger (1966), Block (1973), and others, that androgyny is a higher stage of adult development, in which individuals and couples transcend the barriers imposed by adherence to rigid sex roles.

Some implications of present life-span developmental theories must be taken with caution, as Barnett and Baruch (1978) note. Much of the research was done by males with male subjects (e.g., Levenson, Darrow, Klein, Levenson, & McKee, 1976; Valliant, 1975). The centrality of career development in the view of Levinson and others is an example. If women were to adhere to career-oriented developmental timetables, they would risk role conflict unless marital–family priorities were reordered. At the same time, the development of a life-cycle perspective appropriate to the female life span has been defined primarily in terms of a biologic timetable in which motherhood is the "main event." Views of feminine identity development have been women's self-image as centered on and completed by her relations with males (Erikson, 1964). Some of these myths, especially about the female biologic life cycle, are only now being dispelled. We have already mentioned recent evidence that childbearing, once thought of as a women's peak experience, is instead a significant stressor and cause of conflict. We can also look beyond the childbearing years (which, in many ways, have served as our model for marital relationships) to the possibility of different patterns of marital relations during the postparental years. Retirement and the empty nest may produce a transitional crisis in couples, but this may have been overestimated (Radloff & Rae, in press). The freedom from strains related to occupational and childbearing roles may free couples for a new period of growth, with freedom to develop more flexible and androgynous ways of relating (e.g., a transition from the instrumental to the companionship marriage). In general, life-span theories for both women and men have paid insufficient attention to adult needs to integrate work and family roles through all stages of development.

Interactional Theories of Marital and Family Conflict

Against this subtle, complex collage of structural, cultural, and political views of marital–family conflict, there exist numerous interactional theories (Gurman & Kniskern, 1980; Paolino & McCrady, 1978b) which usually occupy the conscious conceptual foreground of psychotherapists who are called upon to help the distressed marriage or family. They differ from the structural explanations in the greater degree of responsibility for conflict ascribed to individuals, a distinction that is of key importance in the contrast between traditional and feminist analyses (Klein, 1976). Here, we can offer but a flavor of the varying views of marital and family conflict that characterize the major conceptual models operative in the 1970s. These models are described in detail elsewhere (Gurman & Kniskern, 1980c).

Models of Marital Conflict

The three major competing perspectives on the nature and origins of marital conflict (Paolino & McCrady, 1978b) are the psychoanalytic, the behavioral, and the systems. Despite a good deal of commonality among treatment methods (Gurman, 1978), these perspectives offer quite different views of the sources of marital conflict and dissatisfaction. The *psychoanalytic–object relations* view emphasizes the intrusions on the marital relationship which derive from spouses' previous and current failures to differentiate themselves from their families of origin, thereby leading to bilateral transferences and unconscious collusion aimed at the reduction or avoidance of anxiety in personally "loaded" areas of psychological functioning. Such developmental deficiencies may lead to "the inevitable frustration of inappropriate needs" (Meissner, 1978, p. 44) which are based on unconscious expectations of the marital partner. Everyday challenges to normal idealization virtually guarantee conflict in the face of the nonfulfillment of unspoken (and unspeakable) needs of people with rigid, undifferentiated internal object relations schemata (representations). The fulfillment of conscious needs is further impaired by the operation of internally paradoxical, conflicting needs in each spouse (e.g., "I want you to treat me like a responsible adult, but I fear I am incapable of being an adult, so 'help' me by being my mother/father"). The ambivalent and double-binding style of the "dependent" personality in interpersonal conflict situations may be particularly relevant to many women raised in traditional sex roles (Symonds, 1976).

The *behavioral* perspective, in contrast, emphasizes the current, overt origins of marital disharmony (Jacobson, 1980). Couples who are especially at risk are those who have failed to learn, develop, or implement effective communication and problem-solving skills. Such skill deficits predictably lead to patterns of interaction, that is, attempts at mutual influence, that are characterized by high rates of coercion, that is, efforts to change the spouse's behavior through aversive control (e.g., nagging, blaming, attacking) rather than positive control, that is, positive reinforcement of desired behaviors. Principles from a cognitive-behavioral framework (e.g., Beck, 1967) are also particularly relevant to women in light of the growing research evidence of their tendency to make external and helplessness-oriented attributions (e.g., Frieze, 1976). To date, cognitive therapy strategies have had only minimal impact on behavioral marriage and family therapy (Gurman, 1978; Gurman & Knudson, 1978).

Approaches to the understanding of marital conflict from a *systems theory* view are many (Gurman, 1978). The most prominent and influential among these approaches is communication theory (e.g., Haley, 1963; Watzlawick, Beavin, & Jackson, 1967). Conflict derives, in part, from a discrepancy between the report (content) and command (relationship definition) aspects of behavior between spouses. Over time, patterns of communication emerge as implicit and covert "rules" governing the interactions of spouses. Since all interpersonal behavior has as its consequence, if not its purpose, the definition of the relationship between people, a fundamental process of struggling for power and control of the definition of the marital relationship is inevitable. Conflict is not inherent in such transactional patterns, but it is made more likely by a couple's simultaneous communication at multiple levels (e.g., wife verbally demands her husband's respect for her opinions, while doing so in only a quasi-assertive manner colored by frequent hesitation, averting of direct eye contact, soft voice, etc.).

Despite different levels and targets of focus among these three competing perspectives, there is the following commonality:

> Conflict is always the result of attempts to define the relationship (between husband and wife). . . . In all cases and despite language differences among the theories, the argument would be that the individual's felt needs were not being met in the relationship as it existed. (Gurman, 1978, p. 536)

Models of Family Conflict

Since behavioral (e.g., Gordon & Davidson, 1980), psychodynamic (e.g., Skynner, 1980), and communications (e.g., Bodin, 1980) views of the nature of *family* conflict greatly overlap those perspectives' notions of marital conflict, they will not be addressed here further. We will briefly outline the views of two other major models of family functioning and conflict, those of structural theory (Minuchin, 1974) and Bowen theory (Bowen, 1978).

Structural theory offers as a central notion that of boundaries between individuals and among family subsystems, for example, parent and child subsystems. These are said to exist on a continuum from disengaged, to clear, to enmeshed. Marital and family conflict is made likely when a family that functions toward either the enmeshed or disengaged ends of the continuum responds to stress, whether between individuals or between the family and the external world, or as a result of developmental transitions. Thus, for example, when a family with rigid role patterns confronts a common developmental issue such as the youngest child's departure from the home, it may be thrown into crisis when its traditional organization of patterned transactions is no longer effective.

Bowen theory, deriving from a general systems, biologic–evolutionary view, postulates that relationship conflict emerges from the relative operative power of two processes, the emotional and the intellectual. "Differentiation of self," the Bowenite construct most centrally implicated in articulating the appearance of psychopathology and of relationship conflict, relates to these two psychological processes directly. "Fusion," the opposite of differentiation, is the result of one's experience being dominated by the emotional system, and differentiation clearly implies behavior determined by the intellectual system. While it is a good deal oversimplified, it can be said, as a summary of the Bowen view, that marital and family conflict arises when the individual participants in a relationship are poorly (internally) differentiated.

Research on Marital Conflict

Although it is not our purpose to review this research in any detail, we feel compelled to make a few observations about this aspect of the issue. Research on marital conflict has reflected the dominant cultural conception of marriage: Traditional views of marriage have been apparent in the questions researchers have asked and in their definitions of variables chosen for measurement. The results of this research have also reflected the impact, particularly the impact on women, of this dominant value system (e.g., Hicks & Platt, 1970; Laws, 1971). More specifically, concepts of marital stability and happiness as the main criteria for marital success have clearly dominated the field. The pathways to stability and happiness have generally been defined by ideal conceptions of marriage as involving (1) a value system shared by the couple, often involving the wife's conformity to the husband's values and needs, and (2) a division of labor, with task specialization along sex-role lines. Discrepancies in perceptions between partners or deviance from roles are often interpreted as evidence of disruption and strain. Investigations of working wives, for example, focus on the disruptive impact on the family, without considering alternative interpretations of structural variables (such as economic stressors) that may be involved. Indeed, marriage has generally been viewed as a closed system: The functioning of the family unit is evaluated primarily in terms of the relationship among members. Relationships with the outside world, particularly for the wife, are not considered or, if considered, are seen as disruptive influences. The validity of this conception is clearly challenged by results of current epidemiologic studies which document the impact of outside variables such as social structure, economic conditions, and stressful life events on both individual and marital stability (e.g., Perlin & Johnson, 1977).

The results of research on marital conflict have also documented the lower power and status of women. The success of the family unit is more often judged by the husband's achievements than by the wife's. At the same time, the woman's work within the household is devalued or overlooked, so that the contributions of the instrumental aspects of her role are minimized (e.g., Blood & Wolfe, 1960; Laws, 1971). Husbands are also accorded more influence than wives: The finding that the wife's accurate perception of her husband's values is more important for marital happiness than the husband's accurate perception of his wife's values is an example (Stuckert, 1963). A second example comes from research on marital communication: While it is generally agreed that communication is a good thing, it becomes clear that communication of "good" feelings, particularly from the wife to the husband, is preferred (Cutler & Dyer, 1965).

The influence of alternative views of marriage, compatible with feminist principles, is only slowly beginning to be seen in marital research. A cursory review of the recent literature shows a smattering of studies dealing with "women's issues." Some researchers are looking at ways in which working women can resolve role conflicts by extensive sharing of household responsibilities with husbands (Bailyn, 1970). Other research is questioning the assumption that childrearing years are peak years for women and that the empty-nest years are depressing (e.g., Perlin & Johnson, 1977; Radloff & Rae, in press). In general, however, marital research from a feminist perspective is still in its infancy, and many issues still require investigation. We need to know a lot more about role sharing, paternal parenting, the effects of assertiveness as a mode of conflict resolution, etc. Perhaps more central would be analyses of the influence of changing values and expectations as facilitators of or constraints upon the capacity of families to develop androgynous lifestyles, and attention to processes of influence and resistance involved when one marital partner is more "liberated" than the other.

Marital and Family Therapies: Operative Models and Their Implications for Women in Treatment

In this section, we will attempt to note succinctly the most prominent routes by which influential clinical theories of marital–family interaction, pathology, and therapy may run the risk of implicitly endorsing, reinforcing, and perpetuating values about women as participants in marriages and families in ways that are harmful to their short- and long-term psychological welfare. We see little evidence in any of the currently dominant models of family therapy of *explicit* attitudes that are contrary to what we, at least, view as feminist life goals. In fact, one major survey (Fisher & Sprenkle, 1978) of marriage and family therapists' perceptions of healthy family functioning offers no evidence of systematic gender-role bias among such clinicians. Abramowitz (1977) studies the judgments of family-therapy-oriented clinicians regarding parents' contributions to their children's problems. She found that these practitioners' judgments of each parent's need for treatment was related to the traditionality of their sex-role attitudes; for example, more traditional therapists judges the mothers of disturbed girls to need more treatment than mothers of disturbed boys. It is interesting to note, however, that female respondents in the sample outnumbered male respondents 2 to 1.

The dangers that do inhere in these models are more likely, we think, to manifest themselves in the hands of therapists who, while technically sound in their clinical application, are victims of their own sex roles and may fail to see beyond their favorite conceptual schemes, or who may ignore the subtle metalevel implications and effects of their interventions. In another context, Alexander (Note 1) has spoken of the difference between taking a clinical method into the consulting room versus being *taken by* the method. What follows are some examples, within different family therapy models, of how family therapists may be "taken" in ways that fall far short of optimal for women. Some of these manifestations have been examined elsewhere (e.g., Hare-Mustin, 1978).

While the focus of this chapter is on marital and family therapy treatments of relationship conflict, it must be remembered that individual psychotherapy for the "identified patient," especially the symptomatic or dissatisfied spouse, is still a dominant treatment course preferred by many psychotherapists. As one of us (Gurman, 1978; Gurman & Kniskern, 1978a, 1978b) has emphasized elsewhere, individual treatment of marital problems is clearly both less effective and more deterioration-inducing than conjoint treatment methods. Moreover, offering individual therapy for marital problems to a woman is likely to go very far toward inappropriately reinforcing a woman's sense of socialized guilt for marital disharmony and toward implictly placing the responsibility for the major burden of change on her shoulders. Thus, there are salient reasons, on both empirical and political bases, to argue against the treatment of martial problems via individual therapy for the woman in relationship conflict.

Psychodynamic Models

Gurman (1978) has argued that perhaps the major deficiency in psychodynamic articulations of marital and family conflict lies in their potential for excessive clinical concern with the historical and unconscious origins of such conflict (often in one marital partner), such that the current interaction is insufficiently addressed as itself the source of salient relationship difficulties. Psychodynamicists' not uncommon penchants toward pathologizing human experience may further contribute to a misplaced focus in treating relationship struggles in ways that dilute the impact on women of concrete political and cultural events and forces.

Intergenerational Models

Each of the three prominent intergenerational models of family therapy (Gurman & Kniskern, 1980c) offers different treatment-relevant values that may operate against the psychological interests of women. Bowen Therapy (Bowen, 1978), as Hare-Mustin (1978) notes, is implicitly, yet profoundly, biased against women by its explicit valuing of intellectual processes over emotional processes. Hare-Mustin (1978) points out, "Bowen ignores the fact that women's socialization encourages them to be emotional and intuitive rather than rational" (p. 184). The influential experiential therapy model of Whitaker (Whitaker & Keith, 1980) offers the clinical notion that while couples may divorce legally, emotional divorce is essentially impossible to achieve. Left unchallenged by women patients, such a view, when translated into concrete therapeutic intervention strategies, holds out enormously self-defeating potential in terms of women's taking responsibility for such major life decisions. Finally, the contextual family therapy of Boszormenyi-Nagy (Boszormenyi-Nagy & Ulrich, 1980) has been indicted by Hare-Mustin (1978) for its explicit support of sex-stereotyped roles.

Behavioral Models

Consistent with their empirical clinical emphasis, behavioral models of marital and family therapy (e.g., Jacobson, 1980; Patterson, 1971) aspire to noninferential modes of intervention that hold out a promise of descriptive, functional, value-free treatment. In point of fact, however, behavioral therapies for marital–family discord are replete with metalevel assumptions and attitudes that may be dangerous to the psychological health of women. For example, the behavioral treatment of marital conflict (Jacobson, 1980) explicitly emphasizes the treatment goals of both improved communication skills and improved problem-solving skills. On the surface, such a dual emphasis would appear to respect both traditionally "feminine" (i.e., affective) and "masculine" (i.e., rational) relationship styles. Still, as Gurman and Knudson (1978) and Gurman, Knudson, and Kniskern (1978) have pointed out, in practice behavioral marriage therapists give far more weight to the power of rational processes in therapeutic change and, while teaching effective communication skills, clearly disavow any allegiance to the relationship-defining value of less controlled, metered expression of powerful affect, especially anger. Still, assertiveness-training procedures can be compatibly integrated with standard communication-skills-training methods and serve as useful antidotes to traditionally role-sanctioned feminine passivity and dependency. Numerous behavioral sex therapy strategies (Heiman, LoPiccolo, & LoPiccolo, 1980) also reinforce attitudes of shared overt mutual influence and the assumption of responsibility for one's own needs.

Systems Models

As Hare-Mustin (1978) has noted, in structural family therapy, Minuchin (1974) "sees himself as modeling the male executive functions, forming alliances, most typically with the father, and . . . demanding that the father resume control of the family" (p. 184). While there is often wise clinical *strategic* value to such an approach, since fathers are routinely the less involved of the parents in childrearing, and such maneuvers may strengthen the generational boundary, such modeling may also have unexamined, negative secondary effects. The "strategic" family therapies (Stanton, 1980) are characterized, in part, by an explicit disinterest in individual (unconscious) motivation and overt examination of the phenomenologic meaning of individual experience and by a highly directive–prescriptive style of therapist intervention. Such therapists run the risk of offering couples and families therapeutic directives that, while accurately and perceptively addressing family organizational–transactional dimensions, may fail entirely to grapply explicitly with the substantive details and sources of a women's suffering and dissatisfaction in her parental or marital role.

Evaluating the Outcomes of Marital and Family Therapy

The history of empirical assessment of the outcomes of marital–family therapy is a very brief one and, indeed, is almost entirely a phenomenon of the 1970s (Gurman & Kniskern, 1978a). The professional forces inhibiting the scope and impact of research activity in the field have been considered at length elsewhere (Gurman & Kniskern, 1978a, 1978b). Despite the abbreviated empirical heritage of marital–family therapy, there now have appeared over 300 relevant reports and studies (Gurman & Kniskern, 1978a). The rate of appearance of *reviews* of this literature has begun to outstrip the rate of generation of new investigations, and there now exist over two dozen analyses (Gurman & Kniskern, 1980a) of this sort, ranging from broad assessments of the status of family therapy as a science (e.g., DeWitt, 1978; Gurman & Kniskern, 1978a, 1980a, 1980b; Wells & Dezen, 1978) to more focal domains such as behavioral marriage therapy (Jacobson, 1979; Jacobson & Martin, 1976), marital communication skill training (Birchler, 1979), and group family therapy (Strelnick, 1977).

Elsewhere (Gurman & Kniskern, 1978a, 1980a), we have discussed in detail the complex issues that must be considered in the choice of outcome criteria in marital–family therapy research, especially those issues involving the vantage points from which change should be assessed and the levels of inference inhering in various classes of change measures. We have also proposed a comprehensive schema to guide the selection of appropriate family subunits for assessment (Gurman & Kniskern, 1978a). In this section, we will briefly review the nature of common outcome criteria used in previous research as they specifically relate to women's issues and will propose a number of guidelines and recommendations for the choice of marital–family therapy outcome criteria that are sensitive to women as the consumers of such therapies.

One of us (Klein, 1976) has already noted possible sources of gender bias in psychotherapy outcome research. To the extent that these same instruments (self-ideal correlations, some social adjustment scales, etc.) are used in marital or family therapy research, they will be subject to the same criticisms. Looking at change measures in marital–family outcome studies per se, it seems that there are few measures that explicitly reveal gender bias. On the other hand, careful scrutiny of the outcome indices appearing in the literature reveals several profound, though subtle, trends which may nonetheless serve to obscure significant issues in the delivery of family therapy services to women. The four themes around which such obfuscation occurs involve (1) the vantage point from which change is measured, (2) the use of normative behavior as a criterion for improvement, (3) the family units in which change is assessed, and (4) the degree of discrimination among various levels of treatment goals.

Vantage Points for Assessing Change

Conclusion 1. A large proportion of outcome studies have used therapists' global ratings as the sole criterion of therapeutic change. In addition to the obvious and severe limitations inherent in the use of any single perspective for assessing clinical change, there are difficulties, in the adoption of the therapist's perspective alone, that are specific to women's issues. Since most marital–family therapists, like most individual psychotherapists, are male, and since male therapists in particular have been revealed (APA Task Force, 1975; Rice & Rice, 1977) to be hardly free of sexist attitudes, the wisdom of relying on such therapists' formulations of the problem and views of change in family relationships is seriously questioned. For example, therapists historically have been guilty of blaming or scapegoating women by holding them responsible for marital or family conflict (e.g., the schizophrenogenic mother; Jackson, Block, Block, & Patterson, 1958). Although this may be changing (e.g., Abramowitz, 1977), we suspect that the process will be very gradual. Two clinical vignettes will serve to illustrate the inappropriateness of relying on therapists' views of change alone. The first exemplifies therapist bias involving sex roles.

> A family therapy case (juvenile delinquent daughter), father, a trained carpenter who had not sought employment for five years. Mother had gone out and gotten a job and had supported the family for most of that time.

Interpretation—girl was disturbed because of sex-role reversal of family—
father was exhorted to seek a job which he did and mother (was) then
described as hostile and castrating because she didn't quit her job. (APA
Task Force, 1975, p. 1172)

The second vignette, reported by Koch and Koch (1976), blatantly
illustrates how a male therapist's blind adherence to a specific therapeutic technology may mask the implicit endorsement of the view of women
as sex objects.

The husband was more interested in sex than his wife. The husband wanted
to have fellatio. The wife's interests ran in the direction of having an ideally
furnished apartment; French Provincial furniture was more to her taste. A
contract was then negotiated whereby the husband got fellatio five times a
week and the wife . . . got her French Provincial furniture. (p. 40)

Recommendation 1.   The outcomes of marital–family therapy must
be assessed from multiple vantage points. Since the use of global ratings
of outcome by therapists is suspect due to unspoken gender bias that
may influence such ratings, behaviorally and situationally specific
criteria are required in addition to the use of highly inferential judgments (e.g., assessment of family dynamics) that may be sought from
therapists. Some of the same cautions may apply to husbands' assessments. Moreover, we agree with Fiske (1975) that agreement among
rating perspectives should not be routinely expected or aimed for, but
that investigation of the unique components of perceptions of therapeutic change is necessary. This is especially important because use of indices of interspouse agreement or convergence, without attention to specific consent or direction of change, may perpetuate the assumption that
convergence and conformity between spouses are a sine qua non of a
happy marriage. This assumption is dangerous, because wives have
heretofore been expected to do more converging and conforming, and
also because it places conflict in a peculiar perspective. It is not the
presence of conflict per se (which is well-neigh inevitable) but the integ-
rity with which conflict is expressed and the equity of its resolution that
should be important in assessing outcome.

Normative Behavior as the Criterion of Change

Beyond traditional concerns with statistically significant change, several
leading workers (e.g., Kazdin & Wilson, 1978; Garfield, Note 2) have
begun to emphasize the need for researchers to demonstrate the clinical
significance of treatment effects. Kazdin and Wilson (1978) have argued
that a major criterion on which the importance of therapeutic effects can

be based is a patient's achievement of "normative levels of behavior after treatment" (p. 408). While acknowledging that for certain populations (e.g., the mentally retarded), normative standards may not be an appropriate criterion, Kazdin and Wilson (1978) assert that "the limitations of normative data as a universal criterion need not detract from the problem areas where individuals can be *returned to normative levels* of functioning" (p. 408, emphasis added). It is clear that the use of such normative criteria of change is a risky strategy in attempting to assess marital-family therapy outcome in ways that are sensitive to women's roles. This is especially dangerous in cases where changes in one spouse's attitudes and expectations (e.g., a women becoming more liberated) are a source of the conflict. The implicit endorsement of change criteria that are likely to be biased against the psychological welfare of women has occurred frequently through the use of four particular types of outcome measures: (1) modified verbal behavior, (2) married versus divorced status, (3) global marital satisfaction, and (4) level of family functioning.

Conclusion 2A.   The common use of "positive" and "negative" verbal behaviors as criteria for the outcome of marital therapy, especially in behavioral studies (e.g., Harrell & Guerney, 1976; Jacobson, 1977; Margolin & Weiss, 1978), has the potential for reinforcing stereotypical feminine passivity and nonassertiveness. The clearest illustration of this danger involves the well-known Marital Interaction Coding System (MICS) (Hops, Wills, Patterson, & Weiss, Note 3), in which verbal behaviors such as Agreement and Compromise are coded as positive, while those involving, for example, Disagreement, Interruption, and Criticism, are coded as negative. While there is evidence (e.g., Jacobson, 1979) that the relative rates of positive and negative verbal behaviors discriminate between distressed and nondistressed couples, the failure of researchers to attend to the idiosyncratic meaning of such behaviors in particular dyads may often obscure both the positive value of "negative" verbal behavior and the negative value of "positive" verbal behavior (cf. Gurman & Knudson, 1978; Gurman *et al.*, 1978). For example, a formerly nonassertive wife may show increased autonomy and the use of overt power through marital therapy and greatly increase her frequency of verbal disagreement, criticism, and complaints. Such an acceleration of negative behaviors may, indeed, betoken her profound efforts to redefine the marital relationship as egalitarian and as one in which accommodation to her husband's needs and desires has been replaced by a willingness to engage in conflict openly. Nonetheless, failure to attach the clinically appropriate meaning to the appearance of these new behaviors may result in ultimate coding of her behavior as a "poor" outcome. Conversely, the precipitous drop-off of such behaviors when they occur at high rates early in therapy *may* imply the wife's regression to passive, dependent means of obtaining "reinforcement" from her husband.

Recommendation 2A. Since the use of normative rates and patterns of positive and negative verbal behaviors between spouses may allow for faulty conclusions about the outcomes of therapy for specific cases, the use of available interaction coding systems must be modified to reflect accurately the clinically and interpersonally idiosyncratic meaning of changes in such behaviors.

Conclusion 2B. Despite the increasing rate of divorce, documented earlier, the fact remains that most married couples do not divorce. On the other hand, engaging in the normative behavior of "remaining married" obviously does not in itself necessarily imply a positive outcome of therapy for husbands or for wives. As Gurman and Kniskern (1978a) have pointed out, "the fact of divorce does not serve as a useful criterion of the effectiveness of marital therapy without taking into account the goals tailored to a given couple's needs" (p. 881). Nonetheless, several studies (e.g., Hickman & Baldwin, 1970; Hixenbaugh, 1931; Matanovich, 1970) have explicitly used reconciliation as the primary index of therapeutic effectiveness. To our knowledge, only one study to date Cookerly, 1973, 1976) has individualized posttreatment marital status, such that the investigator could identify both "good" and "poor" divorces and "good" and "poor" non-divorces.

For women, there are risks and dangers involved both in divorcing and in not divorcing. Examples of the risks that are frequently inherent in divorcing include social stigmatization, loss or fragmentation of peer social support networks (e.g., friendship relations developed via the marriage relationship), and difficulties in entering or returning to the work force because of undeveloped, underdeveloped, or unused job or career skills. *Not* divorcing carries with it risks as well. These risks are often more subtle and, therefore, perhaps more insidious. The personal psychological cost of not divorcing has been described well by Klein (1976): "Bearing the responsibility for the harmonious functioning of husband and children, for whose emotional health she is often held accountable, almost inevitably requires a personally painful deference, vigilance and often acquiescence to others' demands and needs" (p. 91). Even more concretely, as we have documented earlier, remaining in a marriage that is stunting of an individual's growth may have serious sequelae in the form of severe psychiatric disturbance.

Recommendation 2B. The *categorical* use of married versus divorced status as a criterion for treatment outcome is likely in many cases to obscure the personal meaning of such a status for women and is, therefore, worthy of total abandonment in future research. On the other hand, a more discriminating use of marital status as an outcome measure when tailored to an understanding of its meaning for specific individuals (e.g., Cookerly, 1976) is strongly endorsed.

Conclusion 2C. Global measures (e.g., Locke & Wallace, 1959) of marital satisfaction and adjustment, while reliably able to discriminate between distressed and nondistressed relationships, obscure a host of issues pertinent to women in marriage. Most profoundly, scores on such paper-and-pencil inventories reveal nothing about the *sources* of satisfaction and dissatisfaction in the relationship. Since women, far more than men, are expected to accommodate to their mates' needs (cf. Barry, 1970) in order to insure marital stability, such inventories are highly problematic from a feminist view. That is, the implicit value judgments (cf. Croake & Lyon, 1978; Laws, 1971) inherent in the item composition of such inventories often define "successful" marriages in ways that reinforce and perpetuate stereotyped standards of marriage that are quite inconsistent with relationship goals of egalitarianism, shared overt power, independence and autonomy, and role flexibility. Thus, the sources of marital satisfaction accounting for high (i.e., "satisfied") scores on such inventories run the risk of measuring, in essence, a woman's capitulation to culturally prescribed relationship standards that are destructive of her personal growth.

Recommendation 2C. Since some inventories of marital adjustment (e.g., Locke & Wallace, 1959) do have discriminant validity and allow for across-study comparisons of treatment effects, they are worthy of continued use. Still, their use needs to be supplemented by independent evidence that, for women, high posttherapy "adjustment" scores are not the result of excessive, personally stultifying accommodation to societally sanctioned relationship styles.

Conclusion 2D. One of the most commonly used outcome criteria in studies of family therapy (cf. Gurman & Kniskern, 1978a) has been that of "family functioning" (e.g., Coughlin & Wimberger, 1968; Kaffman, 1963; Laqueur, Laburt, & Morong, 1964; Sigal, Rackoff, & Epstein, 1967). The *concept* of family functioning is certainly important and of central interest to family clinicians, and its measurements is necessary in assessing the outcomes of family therapy. But, like the global measurement of intelligence, it tells us very little about the operative components in a family's transactional style and even less about the way costs and benefits are allocated in the family. Indeed, families can manage their transactions in ways that are *functional* by many routes. Clear communication, role flexibility, and open negotiation of differences can characterize functional families, but so can rigid generational and gender boundaries, as long as external and internal threats to such an organization are absent or avoided. The critical issue here, then, is a temporal one—what is functional at one point in time may be quite dysfunctional at another point. Also, what is functional for one family member may be dysfunctional for another. Thus, measures of family functioning per se are of limited usefulness without an assessment of the *adaptive* potential and impact of a given functional style. Families which are functional (e.g., can provide nurtuance, companionship, and socialization for children and can assure internal harmony) by conventional standards may run into great difficulty when confronted with women's emerging demands for alternative family structures, which include altered role responsibilities in areas such as child care, health maintenance, and job involvement.

Moreover, as much as family therapists may speak of the growth potential of their treatments, it is clear that a good deal of family therapy is oriented toward crisis intervention and the reestablishment of precrisis functionality of the family unit. Thus, the frequent use (Gurman & Kniskern, 1978a) of therapist ratings of family functioning may be biased *against* the induction of family transactional patterns that are in the long-range, adaptive interests of women.

Recommendation 2D. With these considerations in mind, we recommend the development of measurement strategies that address both the present level of family functioning *and* an assessment of the relative costs and benefits of such functioning for women. In a word, what is functional for the family may be deleterious for women.

Selecting the Appropriate Unit for Assessing Change

Elsewhere (Gurman & Kniskern, 1978a, 1978b), we have proposed a comprehensive schema to guide the selection of appropriate family subunits in evaluating the outcomes of marital–family therapy. Here, we will focus on one particular consideration in such a decision-making process, the meaning of the posttreatment symptomatic status of the identified patient (IP).

Conclusion 3. Approximately one-half of the existing studies of family therapy outcome and approximately one-quarter of marital therapy studies have limited the assessment of change to that occurring in the IP (Gurman & Kniskern, 1978a). The importance of retaining IP status as an outcome measure is obvious: (1) IP symptoms are often straightforwardly defined and measured, allowing for rather high levels of reliability and validity; (2) since there needs to be some consensus for family members, therapists, and researchers as to what should constitute relevant treatment dimensions, IP status at least offers a common denominator; (3) families, couples, and individuals, as the consumers of family treatments, expect symptomatic IP improvement.

Still, there are two important conditions under which assessment of IP status alone may fail to address issues of real significance to women. The first condition involves clinical situations in which the IP is not a woman, for example, alcoholic husband, acting-out adolescent, or depressed child. The sole use of IP change as the index of clinical outcome in such cases has the potential of failing to document the negative effects of IP improvement on women. For example, the behavioral treatment of childhood behavior problems within the family (e.g., Patterson, 1971) frequently is carried out with minimal child involvement in the treatment process (Gurman & Kniskern, 1978a). Since fathers are much less likely than mothers to initiate treatment (Hare-Mustin, 1978), even the most "successful" operant modification of undesirable child behaviors runs the risk of inadvertently reinforcing the stereotypical view of mothers as carrying the major burden of child care and responsibility for internal family harmony.

The second condition under which sole focus on IP status may be insensitive to women's issues is when the IP *is* a woman. This is especially likely in cases of marital discord. Here, positive IP change, in symptomatic terms, may mask negative change at a metalevel. The reduction of presenting symptoms, for example, a married woman's depression, assumes a conceptual model in which suffering is equivalent to pathology. Given this premise, a reduction of symptomatology is defined as therapeutic improvement. Such a model of symptom removal may, however, reinforce oppressive social stereotypes. Thus, Klein (1976) has noted that "pain in response to a bad situation is adaptive, not pathological. . . . The depression, and later the anger, of the woman trapped in an unsatisfying role [e.g., marital] . . . may be healthy steps in recognizing and doing something about a dehumanizing situation" (p. 90).

Recommendation 3. Rosman (Note 4) has argued that symptom improvement may be "instrumental in facilitating other outcome possibilities" in family therapy (p. 6). Still, it is rare to find empirical demonstrations of positive facilitations of this sort and likely that symptomatic improvement of either the woman IP or non-woman IP may conceal more profound negative outcomes for women in marital–family therapy. Therefore, we believe that it is essential that researchers address the "functional significance of pain as well as the qualitative and quantitative" nature of symptoms (Klein, 1976, p. 90) involving marital or family distress. When a woman is not the IP in a family therapy situation, the effects of changes in other family members and units must be evaluated in the light of the secondary effects of such changes on the woman. When a woman *is* the IP in marital or family therapy, her symptomatic change is not in itself a sufficient index of a genuinely positive therapeutic outcome.

Levels and Sequences of Treatment Goals

Two other domains must be considered briefly in this discussion of issues relevant to the outcomes of marital–family therapy from a woman's perspective. These are *initial versus emergent* treatment goals and *mediating versus ultimate* goals.

Initial goals are those which reflect the changes explicitly desired by couples, families, or individual members of couples or families early in treatment. While assessment of the achievement of such goals is valuable in its own right, it must be remembered that many, perhaps even most, courses of marital–family therapy also involve patient goals that are not explicitly stated at the outset but which emerge during the process of therapy. Such emergent goals may arise as a direct result of therapeutic intervention geared toward the clarification of patient aims and expectations or may have been in the patient's awareness at the outset of treatment, yet remained initially unspoken for a variety of reasons.

Conclusion 4. There are three major processes that may occur in marital–family therapy as a result of which women's emergent goals may assume primary phenomenologic importance. First, initial goals may reflect traditional "feminine" modes of self-presentation, for example, self-disparagement and undue assumption of responsibility for relationship difficulties or expressing the pain for the marriage or family as a whole. A "nonsexist" therapist (Rice & Rice, 1977) may help such a woman redefine her relationship difficulties in interactional terms, so that the nature of her relationship dysfunction attribution shifts markedly. Second, a woman may enter treatment with perceptible skill deficits, for example, low assertiveness, that initially preclude direct expression of desired relationship changes. Appropriate coping skills may be taught either directly through skill training or indirectly through therapist modeling, for example, via cotherapy, resulting in the woman's increased ability to confront the sources of her marital or family dissatisfaction. Finally, a woman may enter therapy quite aware of her requirements for relationship change, yet be apprehensive about "rocking the boat" too much or too quickly. Therapist support for the expression of already-in-awareness relationship change desires may facilitate their expression after the early stages of treatment.

In any case, assessment of marital–family therapy outcome is made both clinically more relevant and more congruent with the actual evolution of the therapeutic change process when the levels of achievement of both initial goals and emergent goals are incorporated into the research protocol (Gurman & Kniskern, 1980a).

A related issue in the determination of treatment goals that are sensitive to women's needs in marital–family therapy involves the distinction between *mediating* and *ultimate* goals:

> Mediating goals are those which reflect the clinician's assumptions regarding the necessary steps and stages through which a patient must progress if the treatment is to be effective. These goals represent the postulated enabling or intermedidate conditions which will permit the attainment of the ultimate goals. The ultimate goals of psychotherapy must, however, go beyond such hypothesized mediating variables as inferences regarding the resolution of neurotic conflicts, growth, . . . etc. (Parloff, 1976, p. 317)

Mediating and ultimate goals in marital–family therapy are often confused by both clinicians and researchers: Improved communication skill may be taken as equivalent to increased intimacy when it really represents only an efficient and cautious new style of verbal expression; a redistributed division of household labor may be confused with role flexibility when it actually reflects only a serious avoidance of coming to grips with fundamental matters of gender self-definition; etc.

In this context, the danger for women is that they, and their therapists, may settle for outcomes that reflect only intermediate levels of change, such that only a surface level of alteration of the basic self-definition and relationship definitions is achieved. A husband may now share equally in washing the dishes, changing the diapers, etc., yet retain a privately held attitude of how he "helps out" his wife that belies the apparent meaning of his new behavior. The wife of this man may, herself, foster the collusive delusion that her husband has changed his behavior by having come to empathize genuinely with his wife's former [sic] dehumanizing position in the family.

Recommendation 4.   Given these considerations, it is necessary in future research on the outcomes of marital–family therapy that such confusion between the achievement of mediating and ultimate goals be precluded by the inclusion of measures designed to explicitly assess change at both levels.

Finally, there is a special need for long-term follow-up. There is good reason to predict that for a clinically significant proportion of women in marital–family therapy, both social and familial pressures to "regress to the mean" of stereotypical styles of relating may, over time, overwhelm the therapeutic improvement achieved. Documentation of such a phenomenon, as well as investigation of its causes, would be quite valuable in attempting to redesign treatment interventions to lower the probability of its future occurrence.

Conclusion

In the foregoing discussion, we have been concerned primarily with criteria that characterize events within the marital of family unit. It is important, however, to conclude with a brief discussion that puts marriage in the broader perspective of individual partners' ties with the outside world and their awareness of cultural-political issues. To the extent that we look for outcome criteria *solely within* the marital or family unit, we tacitly endorse the view that married people must derive their primary identities and satisfactions within this unit. While this may, indeed, have been true of traditional marriage and family life, even there, there have been differential expectations for men and women. This is, of course, changing rapidly. More and more women work and are working at careers which are salient to their identities and very important to their lives. Thus, it becomes essential to integrate this perspective into our view of marital and family functioning. If we view "healthy" family functioning as that in which each individual can comfortably integrate roles inside and outside the family, then outcome criteria that touch upon individuation, autonomy, and comfortable anchorage with the outside world become increasingly important. We believe that this perspective is particularly important for women. We are concerned that those women who have developed and invested their identities in caring for others, who have lived for and through others, may have failed to develop levels of individuation, autonomy, and authenticity that are necessary to carry them through periods of living alone. Considering the divorce rate, and the fact that women tend to outlive men, we see this as crucially important.

Finally, we would like to close with a note about the place of political awareness and feminist consciousness in marital and family therapy. While not all families or partners within families accept women's liberation as a legitimate goal for couples, it is difficult to imagine an individual or a couple who is not aware of or touched in some way by the rapid political and cultural changes of the '60s and '70s. Thus, while we are not suggesting that all couples accept our values of sexual equality, we would argue that it is important to consider different levels of awareness and different needs for change within families and how value discrepancies are resolved during treatment. Some issues, such as endorsement of a liberated ideology or demands for shared parenthood, may take on a special importance in family therapy outcome. They may not only symbolize crucial changes in "set" or political awareness, but also may be pivotal changes on which a host of other steps toward attitudinal and behavior change may depend.

Reference Notes

1. Alexander, J. Technical, conceptual and relationship skills in behavioral family therapy. In A. Gurman (Chair), *Limitations of behavior-exchange procedures in marital and family therapy*. Symposium presented at the meeting of the Association for the Advancement of Behavior Therapy, San Francisco, December 1975.
2. Garfield, S. L. *Some reflections on the nature of psychotherapy*. Presidential Address presented at the meeting of the Society for Psychotherapy Research, Madison, Wis., June 1977.
3. Hops, H., Wills, T. A., Patterson, G. R., & Weiss, R. L. *Marital interaction coding system*. Unpublished manuscript, University of Oregon, 1971.
4. Rosman, B. *Outcome and other criteria in the evaluation of family therapy*. Paper presented at the meeting of the American Orthopsychiatric Association, New York, October 1977.

References

Abramowitz, C. V. Blaming the mother: An experimental investigation of sex-role bias in countertransference. *Psychology of Women Quarterly,* 1977, *2,* 24–34.

American Psychological Association Task Force. Report of the Task Force on Sex Bias and Sex-Role Stereotyping in Psychotherapeutic Practice. *American Psychologist,* 1975, *30,* 1169–1175.

Bachrach, L. L. *Marital status and mental disorder: An analytical review.* (DHEW Publication No. [ADM] 78–217). Rockville, Md.: Alcohol, Drug Abuse and Mental Health Administration, 1978.

Bailyn, L. Career and family orientations of husbands and wives in relation to marital happiness. *Human Relations,* 1970, *23,* 97–114.

Barnett, R. C., & Baruch, G. K. Women in the middle years: A critique of research and theory. *Psychology of Women Quarterly,* 1978, *3,* 187–197.

Barry, W. A. Marriage research and conflict: An integrative review. *Psychological Bulletin,* 1970, *73,* 41–54.

Beck, A. T. *Depression: Clinical, experimental and theoretical aspects.* New York: Hoeber, 1967.

Bernard, J. *The future of marriage.* New York: Bantam, 1973.

Bernard, J. Change and stability in sex-role norms and behavior. *Journal of Social Issues,* 1976, *32*(3), 2078–223.

Birchler, G. R. Communication skills in married couples. In A. S. Bellack & M. Hersen (Eds.), *Research and practice in social skills training.* New York: Plenum Press, 1979.

Block, J. H. Conceptions of sex role: Some cross-cultural and longitudinal perspectives. *American Psychologist,* 1973, *28,* 512–526.

Blood, R. O., & Wolfe, D. M. *Husbands and wives: The dynamics of married living.* Glencoe, Ill.: The Free Press, 1960.

Bodin, A. The family therapy approach of the Mental Research Institute. In A. S. Gurman & D. P. Kniskern (Eds.), *Handbook of family therapy.* New York: Brunner/Mazel, 1980.

Boszormenyi-Nagy, I., & Ulrich, D. Contextual family therapy. In A. S. Gurman & D. P. Kniskern (Eds.), *Handbook of family therapy.* New York: Brunner/Mazel, 1980.

Bowen, M. *Family therapy in clinical practice*. New York: Aronson, 1978.

Bradburn, N. M.,& Caplovitz, D. *Reports on happiness*. Chicago: Aldine Press, 1965.

Brown, G. W., & Harris, T. *Social origins of depression. A study of psychiatric disorder in women*. London: Tavistock, 1978.

Chesler, P. *Women and madness*. Garden City, N.Y.: Doubleday, 1972.

Cookerly, J. R. The outcome of the six major forms of marriage counseling: A pilot study. *Journal of Marriage and the Family*, 1973, *35*, 608–611.

Cookerly, J. R. Evaluating different approaches to marriage counseling. In D. H. L. Olson (Ed.), *Treating relationships*. Lake Mills, Ia.: Graphic, 1976.

Coughlin, F., & Wimberger, H. Group family therapy. *Family Process*, 1968, 7, 37–50.

Croake, J. W., & Lyon, R. S. Research design in marital adjustment studies. *International Journal of Family Counseling*, 1978, *6*, 32–35.

Cutler, B. R., & Dyer, W. G. Initial adjustment processes in young married couples. *Social Forces*, 1965, *44*, 195–201.

De Witt, K. N. The effectiveness of family therapy: A review of outcome research. *Archives of General Psychiatry*, 1978, *35*, 549–561.

Erikson, E. H. The inner and outer self: Reflections on womanhood. *Daedelus*, 1964, *93*, 582–606.

Firestone, S. The dialectic of sex: The case for feminist revoluation. New York: Morrow, 1970.

Fisher, B. L., & Sprenkle, D. H. Therapists' perceptions of healthy family functioning. *International Journal of Family Counseling*, 1978, *6*, 9–18.

Fiske, D. A source of data is not a measuring instrument. *Journal of Abnormal Psychology*, 1975, *84*, 20–23.

Friday, N. *My mother, myself*. New York: Knopf, 1978.

Frieze, I. H. Causal attributions and information seeking to explain success and failure. *Journal of Research in Personality*, 1976, *10*, 293–305.

Glick, P. C., & Norton, A. J. Perspectives on the recent upturn in divorce and remarriage. *Demography*, 1973, *10*, 301–314.

Goldstein, A. J., & Chambless, D. L. A reanalysis of agoraphobia. *Behavior Therapy*, 1978, *9*, 47–59.

Gordon, S., & Davidson, N. Parent training and the behavioral treatment of families. In A. S. Gurman & D. P. Kniskern (Eds.), *Handbook of family therapy*. New York: Brunner/Mazel, 1980.

Gove, W., & Tudor, J. Adult sex roles and mental illness. *American Journal of Sociology*, 1973, *78*, 812–835.

Gurin, E., Veroff, J., & Feld, S. *Americans view their mental health*. New York: Basic Books, 1960.

Gurman, A. S. Contemporary marital therapies: A critique and comparative analysis of psychoanalytic, behavioral and systems theory approaches. In T. J. Paolino & B. S. McCrady (Eds.), *Marriage and marital therapy*. New York: Brunner/Mazel, 1978.

Gurman, A. S., & Kniskern, D. P. Research on marital and family therapy: Progress, perspective and prospect. In S. Garfield & A. Bergin (Eds.), *Handbook of psychotherapy and behavior change* (2nd ed.). New York: Wiley, 1978. (a)

Gurman, A. S., & Kniskern, D. P. Deterioration in marital and family therapy: Empirical, clinical and conceptual issues. *Family Process*, 1978, *17*, 3–20. (b)

Gurman, A. S., & Kniskern, D. P. Family therapy outcome research: Knowns and unknowns. In A. S. Gurman & D. P. Kniskern (Eds.), *Handbook of family therapy*. New York: Brunner/Mazel, 1980. (a)

Gurman, A. S., & Kniskern, D. P. The outcomes of family therapy: Implications for training and practice. In G. Berenson & H. White (Eds.), *Annual review of family therapy, 1978*. New York: Human Sciences Press, 1980. (b)

Gurman, A. S., & Kniskern, D. P. (Eds.). *Handbook of family therapy*. New York: Brunner/Mazel, 1980. (c)

Gurman, A. S., & Knudson, R. M. Behavioral marriage therapy: I. A psychodynamic–systems analysis and critique. *Family Process*, 1978, *17*, 121–138.

Gurman, A. S., Knudson, R. M., & Kniskern, D. P. Behavioral marriage therapy: IV. Take two aspirin and call us in the morning. *Family Process*, 1978, *17*, 165–180.

Hafner, R. J. The husbands of agoraphobic women and their influence on treatment outcome. *British Journal of Psychiatry*, 1977, *131*, 419–425.

Haley, J. Marriage therapy. *Archives of General Psychiatry*, 1963, *8*, 213–234.

Hare-Mustin, R. T. A feminist approach to family therapy. *Family Process*, 1978, *17*, 181–194.

Harrell, J., & Guerney, B. Training married couples in conflict negotation skills. In D. H. L. Olson (Ed.), *Treating relationships*. Lake Mills, Ia.: Graphic, 1976.

Heiman, J., LoPiccolo, J., & LoPiccolo, L. The treatment of sexual dysfunction. In A. S. Gurman & D. P. Kniskern (Eds.), *Handbook of family therapy*. New York: Brunner/Mazel, 1980.

Hickman, M. E., & Baldwin, B. Use of programmed instruction to improve communication in marriage. *Family Coordinator*, 1970, *20*, 121–125.

Hicks, M. W., & Platt, M. Marital happiness and stability: A review of the research in the sixties. *Journal of Marriage and the Family*, 1970, *32*, 59–78b.

Hite, S. *The Hite report: A nationwide study of female sexuality*. New York: Macmillan, 1976.

Hixenbaugh, E. R. Reconciliation of marital maladjustment: An analysis of 101 cases. *Social Forces*, 1931, *10*, 230–236.

Jackson, D. D., Block, J., Block, J., & Patterson, V. Psychiatric conceptions of the schizophrenic parent. *AMA Archives of Neurology and Psychiatry*, 1958, *79*, 448–459.

Jacobson, N. S. Problem-solving and contingency contracting in the treatment of marital discord. *Journal of Consulting and Clinical Psychology*, 1977, *45*, 92–100.

Jacobson, N. S. Behavioral treatments for marital discord: A critical appraisal. In M. Hersen, R. M. Eisler, & P. M. Miller (Eds.), *Progress in behavior modification* (Vol. 7). New York: Academic Press, 1979.

Jacobson, N. S. Behavioral marital therapy. In A. S. Gurman & D. P. Kniskern (Eds.), *Handbook of family therapy*. New York: Brunner/Mazel, 1980.

Jacobson, N. S., & Martin, B. Behavioral marriage therapy: Current status. *Psychological Bulletin*, 1976, *83*, 540–556.

Kaffman, M. Short-term family therapy. *Family Process*, 1963, *2*, 216–234.

Kazdin, A. E., & Wilson, G. T. Criteria for evaluating psychotherapy. *Archives of General Psychiatry*, 1978, *35*, 407–416.

Klein, M. H. Feminist concepts of therapy outcome. *Psychotherapy: Theory, Research, and Practice*, 1976, *13*, 89–95.

Koch, J., & Koch, L. *The marriage savers*. New York: Coward, McCann, and Geoghegan, 1976.

Kravetz, D. Consciousness-raising groups in the 1970s. *Psychology of Women Quarterly*, 1978, *3*, 168–186.

Laqueur, H., Lubert, H., & Morong, E. Multiple family therapy: Further developments. *International Journal of Social Psychiatry*, 1964, Congress Issue, 70–80.

Laws, J. A feminist review of marital adjustment literature: The rape of the Locke. *Journal of Marriage and the Family*, 1971, *33*, 483–516.

Levenson, D. J., Darrow, C. N., Klein, E. B., Levenson, M. H., & McKee, B. *The seasons of a man's life*. New York: Knopf, 1978.

Locke, H. J., & Wallace, K. M. Short marital adjustment and prediction tests: Their reliability and validity. *Marriage and Family Living*, 1959, *21*, 251–255.

Loevinger, J. The meaning and measurement of ego development. *American Psychologist*, 1966, *21*, 195–206.

Margolin, G., & Weiss, R. L. Comparative evaluation of therapeutic components associated with behavioral marital treatments. *Journal of Consulting and Clinical Psychology*, 1978, *46*, 1476–1486.

Martin, P. A. Dynamics of family interactions. *Journal of Continuing Education in Psychiatry,* 1979, *40*(1), 23-36.

Matanovich, J. P. The effects of short-term group counseling upon positive perceptions of mate in marital counseling. *Dissertation Abstracts International,* 1970, *31,* 2688A.

Meile, R. L., Johnson, D. R., & Porter, St. L. Marital role, education and mental disorder among women: Test of an interaction hypothesis. *Journal of Health and Social Behavior,* 1976, *17,* 295-230.

Meissner, W. The conceptualization of marriage and family dynamics from a psychoanalytic perspective. In T. J. Paolino & B. S. McCrady (Eds.), *Marriage and marital therapy.* New York: Brunner/Mazel, 1978.

Milton, F., & Hafner, R. J. The outcome of behaviour therapy for agoraphobia in relation to marital adjustment. *Archives of General Psychiatry,* in press.

Minuchin, S. *Families and family therapy.* Cambridge, Mass. Harvard University Press, 1974.

Overall, J. E., Henry, B. W., & Woodward, A. Dependence of marital problems on parental family history. *Journal of Abnormal Psychology,* 1974, *83,* 446-450.

Paolino, T. J. & McCrady, B. S. *The alcoholic marriage.* New York: Grune and Stratton, 1978. (a)

Paolino, T. J., & McCrady, B. S. (Eds). *Marriage and marital therapy: Psychoanalytic, behavioral and systems theory perspectives.* New York; Brunner/Mazel, 1978. (b)

Parad, L. G., & Parad, H. J. A study of crisis-oriented planned short-term treatment: Part II. *Social Casework,* 1968, *49,* 418-426.

Paris, B. L. & Paris, E. B. A longitudinal study in marital satisfaction. *Sociological and Social Research,* 1966, *50,* 212-222.

Parloff, M. B. The narcissism of small differences—and some big ones. *International Journal of Group Psychotherapy,* 1976, *26,* 311-319.

Patterson, G. R. Behavioral intervention procedures in the classroom and in the home. In A. Bergin & S. Garfield (Eds.), *Handbook of psychotherapy and behavior change.* New York: Wiley, 1971.

Perlin, L. I., & Johnson, J. S. Marital status, life-strains and depression. *American Sociological Review,* 1977, *42,* 704-715.

Prochaska, J., & Prochaska, J. Twentieth century trends in marriage and marital therapy. In T. J. Paolino & B. S. McCrady (Eds.), *Marriage and marital therapy.* New York: Brunner/Mazel, 1978.

Radloff, L. S. Sex differences in depression: The effects of occupation and marital status. *Sex Roles,* 1975, *1,* 249-265.

Radloff, L. S., & Rae, D. S. Susceptibility and precipitating factors in depression: Sex differences and similarities. *Journal of Abnormal Psychology,* in press.

Rice, D. G., & Rice, J. K. Non-sexist "marital" therapy. *Journal of Marriage and Family Counseling,* 1977, *3,* 3-9.

Rich, A. *Of woman born.* New York: Norton, 1976.

Sheehey, G. *Passages: Predictable crises of adult life.* New York: Dutton, 1974.

Sigal, J., Rakoff, V., & Epstein, N. Indications of therapeutic outcome in conjoint family therapy. *Family Process,* 1967, *6,* 215-226.

Sklar, J., & Berkoff, B. The American birth rate: Evidences of a coming rise. *Science,* 1975, *189*(4204), 693-700.

Skynner, A. C. R. The group-analytic approach to family therapy. In A. S. Gurman & D. P. Kniskern (Eds.), *Handbook of family therapy.* New York: Brunner/Mazel, 1980.

Smith-Rosenberg, C. The female world of love and ritual: Relations between women in nineteenth century America. *Signs,* 1975, *1,* 1-30.

Stanton, M. D. Strategic approaches to family therapy. In A. S. Gurman & D. P. Kniskern (Eds.), *Handbook of family therapy.* New York: Brunner/Mazel, 1980.

Strelnick, A. H. Multiple family group therapy: A review of the literature. *Family Process,* 1977, *16,* 307-326.

Stuckert, R. P. Role perception and marital satisfactions: A configurational approach. *Marriage and Family Living*, 1963, *26*, 415–419.

Symonds, M. The psychodynamics of aggression in women. *American Journal of Psychoanalysis*, 1976, *36*, 195–203.

Valliant, G. E. Natural history of male psychological health: III. Empirical dimensions of mental health. *Archives of General Psychiatry*, 1975, *32*, 420–426.

Watzlawick, P., Beavin, J. H., & Jackson, D. D. *Pragmatics of human communication.* New York: Norton, 1967.

Weiss, R. L., & Aved, B. M. Marital satisfaction and depression as predictors of physical health status. *Journal of Consulting and Clinical Psychology*, 1978, *46*, 1379–1384.

Weissman, M. M., & Klerman, G. L. Sex differences and the epidemiology of depression. *Archives of General Psychiatry*, 1977, *34*, 98–111.

Weissman, M. M., & Paykel, E. S. *The depressed woman: A study of social relationships.* Chicago: University of Chicago Press, 1974.

Wells, R. A., & Dezen, A. E. The results of family therapy revisited: The nonbehavioral methods. *Family Process*, 1978, *17*, 251–274.

Whitaker, C. A., & Keith, D. V. Symbolic–experiential family therapy. In A. S. Gurman & D. P. Kniskern (Eds.), *Handbook of family therapy.* New York: Brunner/Mazel, 1980.

PART THREE

Traditional and Alternative Approaches

CHAPTER 8

Psychodynamic Perspectives

ALEXANDRA G. KAPLAN

LORRAINE YASINSKI

Introduction

There has been considerable interest during the past decade in investigating gender differences across a wide variety of situations (cf. Maccoby & Jacklin, 1974). This interest has extended to studies of women and mental health and, more specifically, women and psychotherapy (e.g., Chesler, 1971, 1972). Whether gender has a random or systematic influence in therapy has become a major point of contention between those who believe that cultural beliefs and attitudes about women influence therapists, clients, and what transpires in therapy and those who do not.

Considered together, most of the empirical investigations on women and psychotherapy undertaken during this period have resulted in inconsistent and oftentimes contradictory data (see, e.g., Bergin & Lampert, 1978; Parloff, Waskow, & Wolfe, 1978; Stricker, 1977; Zeldow, 1978). Garfield, in an article reviewing research on client variables in psychotherapy, goes so far as to conclude that "one cannot make much of a case for sex being a significant variable in psychotherapy" (1978, p. 214). This assertion, while warranted by the inconclusive data, contrasts sharply with the findings of researchers in other areas of psychology (e.g., Eagly, 1978; Henley, 1977) and in other social sciences such as sociology (e.g., Chodorow, 1978; Wilson, 1978) and criminology (e.g., Shacklady Smith, 1978; Stang Dahl & Snare, 1978). Eagly's findings, in fact, suggest that in studies of gender differences, something like researcher countertransference may influence the observation and interpretation of differences.

Failure to observe gender differences in psychotherapy research may also be due to the positivistic paradigm which guides much

Alexandra G. Kaplan and Lorraine Yasinski. Department of Psychology, University of Massachusetts, Amherst, Massachusetts.

psychological research. Within this framework, there is a presupposition of random or nonsignificant relationships between independent and dependent variables unless proven otherwise. In the case of most research on psychotherapy, the gender of the participants is not of hypothetical importance, and when it *is* specifically of interest, it is presumed initially to exert random effects within the psychotherapeutic situation, unless demonstrated otherwise. However, information on where, when, how, and with whom a gender effect emerges is generally lacking. It appears that many researchers in this area may be more interested in trying to "prove" the hypothesis of no differences, although this is theoretically impossible. (For an exception, see Orlinsky & Howard, 1975, 1976.)

The presumption that women and men are not viewed, evaluated, and treated in systematically different ways also underlies (and is a necessary condition for) traditional modes of treatment for psychological and emotional problems. In this instance, the situational determinants of difficulties that women and men bring to therapy are not expected to vary systematically with gender. For both women and men, the source of the symptoms is thought to be located intrapsychically (i.e., a product of each person's idiosyncratic history). If situational factors prove to outweigh psychological factors in determining an individual's problems, then a necessary condition for psychotherapy is absent. In fact, if the client is not convinced of the psychological nature of her or his symptoms, therapy is assumed to be of no benefit (Malan, 1976; Sifneos, 1972).

The social-situational factors common to women in this culture (e.g., economic dependence), then, are not implicated in the "etiology" of their personal disorders and, as such, are not seen as salient factors in the treatment. By extension, a woman client's ability to contextualize her feelings of dis-ease within the environment will not be a factor in determining outcome. We would question here the increasingly accepted notion that changes in inner experience constitute a positive outcome for women in therapy. Given the cultural and institutional prejudices against women, it is not enough that a woman client leave therapy with an increase in self-esteem, regardless of the extent or nature of behavior change. We question whether it can be considered a "successful" therapy when the client "adjusts" to the cultural, societal, and familial contexts in which she lives without an awareness and understanding of their impact on her.

While disregarding the sociopolitical conditions affecting women, most traditional therapies are, nonetheless, informed by theories and notions of practice which reflect cultural beliefs about and societal attitudes toward women. While theoretical orientation per se is thought to reveal little of what actually transpires in therapy and does not seem to significantly affect outcome (Bergin & Lampert, 1978; Luborsky, Singer, & Luborsky, 1975; Meltzoff & Kornreich, 1970), it has been suggested that therapists who are most committed to their orientation are more effective than those who are not (Frank, 1973). Thus, the impact of therapists' conceptual frameworks on women in therapy may be masked by varying levels of therapist commitment and effectiveness. Given this, it seems timely and reasonable to investigate the theories and technical considerations of traditional therapies for evidence of a systematic gender bias, including attitudes toward both women and men. That this may be a crucial area of investigation is further indicated by evidence suggesting that the client's identification with the therapist (and his or her explanations and conceptualizations) is a critical therapeutic variable (Fairbairn, 1952; Guntrip, 1971; Kernberg, 1976; Strupp, 1969, 1973, 1978; Winnicott, 1978).

To the extent that therapists are committed to and enthusiastic about their theoretical orientations, we would assume that they are influenced by the theory of psychological development, the implicit or explicit models of mental health, and the methods of clinical practice advanced in their orientations. These sources can impact on the content of therapy—the distinction between problematic and nonproblematic issues and the areas chosen for intense exploration—as well as on the nature of the client–therapist relationship. Both content and relationship can, in turn, affect outcome measures, which vary widely and may include both participants' estimates of the value of therapy, improvements in the clients' self-esteem, and evidence of psychological and/or behavioral change following termination.

We have chosen to explore the implications for women in therapy of the three most prevalent traditional theoretical orientations: Freudian (psychoanalytic), Rogerian (client-centered or nondirective), and Sullivanian (interpersonal). At Frank's (1979) suggestion, each orientation is reviewed separately for evidence of explicit and/or implicit attitudes toward women. We have found, with few exceptions (e.g., Kronsky, 1971; Menaker, 1974), virtually no research which focuses specifically on the application of each theory to women in therapy.

We do not attempt to answer the "Grand Prix" question of which orientation is most "effective" for women, then, because of unavailability of relevant data and the currently inadequate conceptualizations of positive outcome for women. Instead, the two major aspects of each theoretical orientation—developmental theory and therapeutic techniques and goals—will be assessed in the following manner. First, do the theories of psychological development promote an image of women as conforming to stereotypical sex-role expectations? This might include equating mental health with a heterosexual orientation, placing primacy on the roles of wife and mother, or valuing stereotypical feminine qualities such as passivity or submissiveness. Is it implied that female development parallels that of males? Are there indications that the standard is male and substandard female? We believe that a developmental theory which equates female development with the development of femininity may serve to foster a primary emphasis on the intrapsychic sources of conflict, to the exclusion of the sociopolitical conditions which shape women's development.

Second, do the methods and goals of traditional therapy serve to constrict women's growth and/or scope of their self-knowledge? Is there evidence that certain therapeutic techniques foster traditional sex roles in women, encourage dependency, or advocate conventional forms of female sexuality (cf. APA Task Force, 1975)? In other words, are traditional therapeutic techniques used to manipulate female clients in the direction of biased expectations? We will discuss the extent to which each orientation restricts women's self-knowledge by focusing on individualistic factors rather than on the interface between the person and society. The assessment of each theoretical orientation concludes with suggestions for research.

Freudian Psychoanalysis

Developmental Theory

Freud's basic position on psychosexual development can be found in "Three Contributions to the Theory of Sexuality" (1905/1938). He focuses on the first five years of life and, in particular, on the progressive attachment of sexual or libidinal energy to bodily zones as crucial for normal development. Initially, the infant's sexual energies are not localized; that is, the infant is polymorphously perverse. Within the first year, concerns with hunger and feeding focus sexual pleasure on the mouth, or oral zone. During the second and third years, control over bodily functions, namely, retention and expulsion of feces, becomes of primary concern and the source of pleasure. The anal zone thus becomes eroticized, and the infant moves out of the oral phase. Around the fourth and fifth years, the child discovers the pleasures of masturbation and moves into the phallic state of psychosexual development. It is here that Oedipal concerns, discussed below, become salient. Following the phallic stage, the child ceases to display overt sexuality and enters into the latency stage. This stage is terminated with the resurgence of sexual urges at puberty, which propels the child into the last, genital, stage of development. Libidinal energies, which have been directed toward self-induced pleasure, now become directed toward members of the other sex.

Because Freud provides a great deal of speculation about sex differences that occur as a result of girls' and boys' differential negotiation of the Oedipal stage, we will describe Freud's theory of female Oedipal development in some detail, including conflicting evidence and critiques of this theory. We have drawn from three major papers: "Some Psychical Consequences of the Anatomical Distinction between the Sexes" (Freud, 1925/1953), "Female Sexuality" (Freud, 1931/1974a), and "Femininity" (Freud, 1933/1974b). In general, Freud places the beginning of gender identity development in the Oedipal stage. For girls, this stage is initiated by their discovery of the male penis and their realization that it is superior to their own inconspicuous organ. This momentous discovery of the "fact" of her castration and its resultant penis envy leads the girl to relinquish her previous libidinal ties to her mother, in that mother is also missing a penis and is held responsible for this loss. Although she maintains a primary identification with her mother, she manages to transfer her libidinal strivings to her father. Freud and those who have followed him have described a number of emotional and behavioral consequences that are associated with the Oedipal stage in women. These can be summarized as follows:

1. Because of her envy of the penis, the girl relinquishes her clitoral masturbation out of a sense of shame. This prepares her for the subsequent shift to vaginal sexuality which is seen as necessary for mature, adult heterosexual functioning.
2. Because the clitoris has been the source of both sexual pleasure and pain (shame), the female becomes characterized by an excessive concern with her own body (narcissism) and a tendency to masochism, or pleasure derived from pain (Bonaparte, 1953; Deutsch, 1944).
3. The transition from clitoral to vaginal sexuality occurs at adolescence and is equated with a transition from activity to passivity. Although Freud denies that he is equating passivity with femininity, he does suggest that femininity may be linked with "giving preference to passive aims" (1933/1974b, p. 94).
4. Girls are never able fully to compensate for their penis envy, although they partially do so by replacing a wish for the penis by a wish for a baby. However, remnants of penis envy remain, leaving women with exaggerated feelings of shame and envy.

5. Because the Oedipus complex is never fully resolved in women, they are characterized by a less fully developed superego and, hence, by weaker moral development than men.
6. Three possible lines of development can occur, depending on how girls negotiate the Oedipal stage: neurosis (sexual inhibition), a masculinity complex, and normal femininity.

IMPLICATIONS FOR WOMEN

At a global level, criticisms of Freud's theory of female psychosexual development relate to the facts that the subordinate status and submissive characteristics of women which Freud observed are presented as natural and grounded in biology and that the meanings attributed to female characteristics emerge in comparison to male characteristics which are seen as standard. Within this framework, general criticisms of Freud's theory on women focus on its origins in the cultural norms of Victorian Vienna (Chesler, 1972; Figes, 1970; Salzman, 1967; Tennov, 1975), his notion of sexual phallic monism, of phallocentrism (Horney, 1926; Jones, 1933; Lewis, 1976; Menaker, 1974; Rawlings & Carter, 1977), and the undue generalizations that were made from female patients to women in general (Janeway, 1971). It has also been noted that Freud's writings concerning women are inconsistent and contradictory (Chassequet-Smirgel, 1970; Marmor, 1973).

Freuds conception of female psychosexual development met with an immediate round of challenges (Horney, 1926, 1935; Jones, 1927, 1933, 1935; Klein, 1960; Muller, 1932; Payne, 1936). These focused primarily on the inadequacy of the concept of penis envy and insufficient evidence for the switch from clitoral to vaginal masturbation. Both Horney (1926, 1935) and Thompson (1942, 1950) emphasized that while women may indeed envy men, it is an envy of their privileged status in society rather than their penis per se. Horney (1926) pointed out that Freud's view of penis envy is at base none other than a restatement of little boys' view of females.

In addition, Horney underscored Freud's neglect of "womb envy" in men and males' dread of women. Horney (1926, 1930/1967) found it "remarkable" that so little attention is placed on men's secret dread of women. She saw male dread of women as more deeply seated and even more energetically repressed than the boy's fear of his castrating father.

The themes raised by these earlier critics continue to be echoed by more recent writers commenting on Freud's position on women. The confusion of penis envy with envy of men's power and status in society is a frequently raised criticism (Chodoff, 1966; Cohen, 1966; Janeway,

1971; Marmor, 1973; Mead, 1974; Menaker, 1974; Salzman, 1967). In addition, Janeway (1971) makes the obvious point that females have not, in fact, been castrated, while Lerner (1977) associates penis envy with the fact that young girls are not taught about the clitoris at an early age. Moulton (1970) suggests three additional sources of penis envy in women: sibling rivalry with a brother, deep dependency needs for the mother which promote a wish for the penis so as to win mother back, and experience with a rejecting father, implying that if the daughter had a penis, he would be less rejecting.

Earlier speculations on inadequacies in Freud's distinction between clitoral and vaginal sexuality have been supported by studies of the female sexual response (Masters & Johnson, 1966). As Masters and Johnson have demonstrated in extensive research, there is only one orgasmic response, not two, and it is most readily elicited by clitoral stimulation. Vaginal orgasm, as distinct from clitoral orgasm, simply does not exist. While sexual stimulation leading to orgasm can occur vaginally or clitorally, the existence of only one orgasmic response creates strong disconfirmation of Freud's association of mature female sexuality with vaginal orgasm.

Recent studies of masturbatory patterns in young, pre-Oedipal girls have also provided evidence, contrary to the Freudian position, of early vaginal stimulation in young girls (Fraiberg, 1952; Kleeman, 1975, 1977; Roiphe, 1968; Sperling, Note 1).

Also falling under recent criticism is the identification of passivity, masochism, and narcissism as characteristic of the adult female personality. Freud associated passivity in women with the role that women play in sexual intercourse. However, as Marmor (1973) and Moulton (1970) have stressed, the female plays a receptive, but not a passive, role in sexuality. Moulton (1970) states explicit that "*receptive aims do not imply inertness:* the truly receptive vagina is grasping, secreting, and pleasure giving through its own functions" (p. 91). Additionally, Moulton (1970), Blum (1977), and Schafer (1977) question the association between femininity and masochism, distinguishing between females' more stoical stance and clinical masochism—"a pattern of accepting pain as a prerequisite to being loved or taken care of" (Moulton, 1970, p. 91).

Critiques of Freudian theory extend to his claim of women's lesser capacity for judgment and moral reasoning. Both Marmor (1973) and Schafer (1977) argue that rather than evidencing lesser morality, women seem to embody a higher level of moral development that men. Schafer (1977) identifies the superego as a "fierce, irrational, mostly unconscious vindictiveness against oneself" (p. 338) and as a "demonic aspect of mind" (p. 338). With this definition in mind, precisely because (according to Freudian theory) girls have weaker superegos, they should be "better suited than a boy to develop a moral code that is enlightened, realistic, and consistently committed to some conventional form of civilized interaction among people" (Schafer, 1977, p. 338). Freud also linked women's lesser morality to their need to be loved and willingness to bend their morality to fulfill this craving. However, as Schafer (1977) points out, male castration anxiety is so unresolved and so persistent that it logically should continuously lead men to violate conventional morality.

Disconfirmation of the Oedipal stage as the initial period for the development of gender identity has come from a series of studies (Money & Ehrhardt, 1972) that were not conducted in relation to Freudian theory but have been used to critique it (Galenson & Roiphe, 1977; Kleeman, 1977; Stoller, 1964, 1968, 1972, 1977). Money and Ehrhardt's (1972) work has demonstrated that "core gender identity" (a basic sense of the self as male or female; Stoller, 1977) is sufficiently developed by 18 months of age that changes of sex of assignment after that time cannot be made without risk of severe psychic damage. The basis for this development of core gender identity, furthermore, is neither anatomy nor hormones, but rather sex of assignment and rearing. Individuals born with abnormal sex hormone distributions and/or genitals discordant with their genetic sex have been found to be unimpaired in their development of core gender identity if their parents are clear and consistent in their sex of assignment and rearing. Thus, the psychosexual differentiation between males and females occurs at a much earlier period than the Oedipal years and is not rooted in the anatomical distinction between the sexes.

Parens (Note 2) and Parens, Pollock, Stern, and Kramer (1977) have systematically observed early mother–daughter relationships to determine whether or not there is evidence for the sequence of events proposed in Freud's theory of female Oedipal development: (1) evidence of a castration complex, (2) wish for a baby, and (3) rivalry with mother. From their observations, Parens and his colleagues determined that contrary to Freud's position, there are a variety of routes through which girls enter the Oedipal stage. For some, castration anxiety did appear initially, while for others, a wish for a baby or a heterosexual attachment to the father formed the initial stage. In that the wish for a baby can precede the emergence of penis envy, this wish cannot be seen as a defensive reaction to the absence of a penis. Thus, while not discounting the existence of an Oedipal stage for girls, Parens and his associates raise questions about Freud's description of its sequential development.

Other writers (Abelin, 1971; Kleeman, 1971) have observed girls' turning to the father far before the Oedipal years. Observations of father–daughter interactions have revealed that many infants have a specific relationship with their father before their first birthday. Also, girls show a tendency to demonstrate attachment to the father earlier than boys do.

Finally, based in part on the inadequacies of Freudian theory for explaining women's psychosexual development, a number of writers are turning to an exploration of the pre-Oedipal stage for an understanding of the formative roots of personality development in general and female personality development in particular (Balint, 1968; Brunswick, 1940/ 1969; Chodoff, 1966; Chodorow, 1978; Kernberg, 1976; Kleeman, 1977; Lampl-de Groot, 1927/1969; Masterson, 1976; Schafer, 1977; Winnicott, 1953). Freud himself acknowledged the possible importance of the pre-Oedipal stage for female development (1931/1974a, 1933/ 1974b), but he left it for others to develop this line of inquiry.

Psychotherapy

Freud's basic goal in psychoanalysis was that of making the unconscious conscious, of correcting the original process of repression (Freud, 1937/1963f). This was accomplished in his early work through cathartic methods and hypnosis and, later, by the patient's use of free associations to which the therapist offered interpretations (Freud, 1904/1963a). Patient and analyst each had a clearly defined role in this process. The task for the patient was to speak about whatever entered the mind, regardless of how meaningless or embarrassing such thoughts seemed. To facilitate the availability of such material, the patient was expected to undergo analysis in a state of abstinence, making no major relational changes during the course of treatment. The analyst, in turn, was to listen to the patient with "evenly hovering attention ... [bending] his own unconscious like a receptive organ to the emerging unconscious of the patient" (Freud, 1912/1963c, p. 122). The analyst was further warned to be "impenetrable" to the patient, reflecting to the patient what she or he had said but putting aside her or his own feelings.

Free association, as Freud soon discovered, was disrupted by resistances, patients' tendencies to avoid awareness of painful material by repeating them in behavior rather than remembering them (Freud, 1914/1963d). Frequently, this posture of repeating rather than remembering was enacted in the patient's relationship with the therapist, the transference. That is, unresolved, unconscious conflicts experienced in childhood would appear in excessive reactions to the therapist over what would be rational and justifiable (Freud, 1912/1963b). By 1914, Freud was advocating the development of a "transference neurosis," in which the full scope of the client's unconscious conflicts come into play in her or his relationship with the therapist and thus become amenable to analysis.

One of the specific aspects of the transference which Freud singled out for scrutiny, partly because, in his experience, it occurred so often, was that of transference love—the client (female) falling in love with the therapist (male) (Freud, 1915/1963e). Freud is clear in his warning to analysts that the patients' love for them is induced by the analytic situation and not by their personal charm. Furthermore, the expression of such love can be seen as a form of resistance, an impediment to the analytic work. Specifically, by declaring her love for the therapist, the patient may be attempting to reassure herself of her irrisistibility, make inroads into her therapist's authority by reducing him to the status of lover, and gain those advantages which accrue from the gratification of her love.

Freud is equally clear in his statements to analysts as to how such transference love should be handled. Essentially, he exhorts analysts to neither give in to these expressions of affection nor try to suppress them: "He must face the transference love boldly, but treat it like something unreal, as a condition which must be gone through during the treatment and traced back to its unconscious origins" (Freud, 1915/1963e, p. 174). Consistent with his focus on the heterosexual triangle as the formative stage for women, then, Freud identifies women's erotic transference as a potentially major part of their therapeutic work. The development of transference love would permit the analyst to explore the conflicts inherent in the earlier, heterosexual strivings that lay behind the patient's reactions to him.

IMPLICATIONS FOR RESEARCH ON WOMEN IN THERAPY

The central aspects of Freudian theory and therapy that have direct bearing on women in therapy include the developmental goal of genital heterosexuality, the focus on eroticized transference, and the impenetrable, objective stance of the analyst.

One possible line of research, then, would be to document the extent to which successful analytic therapy for women is equated (especially in therapists' ratings) with the attainment of an unambivalently heterosexual orientation. That successful treatment and heterosexuality are considered synonymous is suggested in the developmental theory and by outcome research on homosexual males (Bieber, 1962), in which success is clearly equated with a shift to a heterosexual orientation.

Patients' ratings of success of their therapy could also be studied in this regard. Are those patients who feel most validated by their therapists and most pleased with their progress those who are heterosexual and who did not question their sexual orientation?

Research might also focus on the extent to which this heterosexual orientation in analytic therapy fosters life choices of marriage and motherhood following therapy, at the expense of a broader range of options. Is there any evidence, for example, that women who had been pursuing careers become less inclined to do so and more inclined to focus their energies on home and family following treatment? Do women clients feel that they have gained in their capacity for integrating home and career roles? Of interest in this regard would be both the patterns of choice evidenced by women following termination and changes in life direction before and after treatment.

Research studies might also investigate women's feelings about their own sexuality following therapy. Based on Freudian theory, one would expect that after therapy, women would equate sexual satisfaction with heterosexual intercourse, at the expense of other forms of sexual gratification. The prevalence of such restricted forms of sexual expression could be investigated, as well as the extent to which women, following termination, feel comfortable with their sexuality and in control of their means of sexual expression.

Freud's emphasis on transference love suggests a need to research both the incidence and effects on outcome of a patient's experience of an eroticized transference. Several process variables are at issue here. First, are there specific demographic factors such as age and sex of patient and therapist that are most closely associated with the existence of an eroticized transference? For example, is transference love most likely to occur with a young, attractive, single female patient and an older male therapist? Second, are there certain sequences of events within the course of treatment that are likely to occur when the patient's sexual experiences have been a primary focus of exploration and, in particular, when it has been the therapist, more than the patient, who has determined this focus? Third, in line with Freud's suggestion that an eroticized relationship seems intended to reduce the authority of the therapist, are such relationships more likely to occur when patient and therapist have been struggling with issues of authority? For example, are eroticized relationships more likely to occur when the therapist strictly follows Freud's prescription of coldness and inscrutability, which the client has been challenging? To approach these questions from the other direction, are eroticized relationships less likely to evolve when the analyst permits a genuine, mutual relationship to develop and makes clear her or his own humanness (Colm, 1973)?

The impact of an eroticized transference on outcome measures stands as another subject for investigation. Are patients who developed eroticized transferences which were then analyzed more likely to be unconflicted in their later intimate relationships, as Freudian theory would predict? Or might the arousal of such feelings impede the patients' later capacity for intimacy? Eroticized transferences might also affect patients' feelings about themselves during and following treatment. How do sexualized therapeutic relationships, for example, affect patients' posttermination feelings of self-worth, of confidence in themselves?

The extent to which analytic therapists succeed in maintaining an objective, mirror-like stance with their patients should be subjected to research scrutiny. Is there evidence that outcome factors (in terms of both behavioral measures and patients' feelings about themselves) are affected by their therapists' attitudes toward women or the degree of the therapists' commitment to Freudian developmental theory? Do women, after analytic psychotherapy, seem more prone to accepting a passive orientation to life or do they seem equally able to adopt a more active, outgoing stance? In other words, do either the therapist's own attitudes toward women or the notion of femininity embedded in psychoanalytic theory influence the work toward specific goals in therapy, irrespective of the patient's own inclinations? Is psychoanalytic therapy, in the long run, a form of conformist influence on women, in which their own needs and strivings become subordinated to their adjustment to current social conditions? While there has been some work describing modifications of psychoanalytically oriented therapy for application to the specific problems of women (Kronsky, 1971; Menaker, 1974), to what extent have these modifications become part of the work and training of therapists? And do these modifications make a difference in the posttermination behavior of women?

Rogerian Therapy

Developmental Theory

Rogers proposes that there is a natural course of human development which will result in a healthy, well-adjusted person, unless this course is interfered with by faulty learnings. It is the dynamics of this process, rather than a sequence of stages, which is the focus of Rogers' developmental theory. The driving force behind individual development, the "actualizing tendency," is the need to "actualize, maintain and enhance the experiencing organism" (Rogers, 1951, p. 487). Rogers assumes that the healthy person is aware of all of her or his behavior and in any given situation will consciously choose response patterns that are most instrumental in effectively achieving this goal.

Rogers' developmental theory is concerned with those subjectively observable responses which are the crucial antecedents to overt behavior. The individual might be motivated to act on the basis of need or tension reduction, the wish for expansion through growth, or the desire for development toward autonomy (Rogers, 1957). Whether or not the individual's actions succeed in their desired intentions of maintaining and enhancing the self, however, depends on the external response to them. Rogers discusses these external responses not in terms of actual reactions, but rather in terms of the individual's perception and evaluation of these responses. If these responses are judged to be negative in terms of maintaining or enhancing the self, then these behaviors are likely not to recur. If the responses are judged to be positive, however, then it is likely that these behaviors will recur or become habitual.

In the ideal developmental pattern of a fully functioning person, those behaviors initiated by the actualizing tendency would invariably lead to positive subjective evaluations based on environmental responses. This would permit the person to remain attentive to all of her or his affective responses as they occur and to choose a course of action consistent with her or his own judgments of what is desirable. However, consistently positive responses to one's behavior seldom occur. Instead, incongruities develop between those behaviors motivated by the actualizing tendency and those behaviors positively responded to by others. This creates a state of anxiety or tension which results in perceptions of reality becoming circumscribed through denial or distortion. These inappropriate habits of attending and habitual self-evaluative thoughts which reject "organically satisfying experiences" (Rogers, 1957) impede the normal developmental process.

IMPLICATIONS FOR WOMEN

On the surface, Rogers' developmental schema seems to provide at least the beginnings of a useful model for understanding female development. Within his model, one can recognize the tensions that can result when women behave in ways that are innately satisfying, only to find these behaviors thwarted by their environment. However, by focusing so heavily on subjective evaluations, Rogers fails to identify those sociopolitical or interpersonal forces which may impact differentially on men and women and which serve to constrict women's self-enhancement and available options. Because the absence of gender differences is embedded in Rogerian theory, he has little to say about how the consistent developmental patterns that characterize women as a class have come to evolve. By taking a phenomenologic or subjectivistic point of view, Rogers does not identify the objectively observable aspects of the environment and their potential impact on development. While Rogers' developmental theory does not seem distorted in its application to women, neither does it elucidate much in the way of developmental processes specific to women.

Psychotherapy

Rogers' approach to psychotherapy, alternatively called client-centered therapy or nondirective therapy, centers on three primary hypotheses (Rogers & Dymond, 1954):

1. The client contains, within herself or himself, the capacity to understand those forces which are causing pain and to reorganize her or his life in the direction of greater self-enhancement.
2. This capacity will best be facilitated when the therapist creates a climate characterized by (a) a genuine acceptance of the unconditional worth of the client, (b) an attempt to understand the client's feelings as she or he experiences them, without any attempt to diagnose, alter, or interpret these feelings, and (c) a continuing attempt to convey something of this empathic understanding to the client.
3. Within such an accepting atmosphere, the client will reorganize herself or himself at both conscious and unconscious levels so as to cope with life in a more constructive and satisfying manner.

For Rogers, a client's behavior can be understood only from the client's observational vantage point. Thus, the focus of therapy is on the client's subjectively observable responses. The therapist has two primary tasks in working with the client on these responses. The first is to create the conditions in which such responses will be verbalized and explored, so that the client can essentially change herself or himself. Specifically, the three therapist factors of genuineness, unconditional positive regard, and empathy, combined with the client's awareness of these factors, are seen as both necessary and sufficient for producing constructive personality change in the client (Rogers, 1957, 1975). Any inner barriers that keep the therapist from understanding what it feels like to be the client at any point in time will impede the therapeutic work.

The therapist's second primary task is to bring about changes in the way the client attends to, thinks about, and evaluates herself or himself. In this way, the client can be freed of faulty learnings and become what she or he was *innately* built to be. The therapist does not directly work to change such thoughts by interpreting or explaining them, but rather simply directs the client's attention to them. It is assumed that once the client learns to think in an undistorted manner, behavioral change will inevitably follow. Because the direction of change is squarely within the client's hands, the client does not develop a dependency on the therapist, nor does she or he see the therapist as wiser or more knowing than herself or himself. The therapist influences the direction of the work but refrains from influencing the content. Based on this approach, it is thought that the therapist's values, biases, and countertransferential attitudes do *not* interfere with the therapy.

IMPLICATIONS FOR RESEARCH ON WOMEN IN THERAPY

Despite the "formidable number of studies" (Parloff, Waskow, & Wolfe, 1978) that have been undertaken to test Rogers' hypotheses about the nature of therapy, the impact of the sex of client or therapist on either process or outcome variables has not emerged as a major area of investigation. Early studies of client-centered therapy (e.g., Dymond, 1954; Seeman, 1954) found that females showed a significantly larger change in favor of increased adjustment (as measured by Q-sorts, TAT responses, and therapists' ratings) than did males. However, neither researcher offered an explanation for this finding, save Dymond's comment that "something in the therapy situation itself was responsible for this difference" (1954, p. 81).

We would assume that this "something" would go beyond the necessary conditions for effective treatment posited by Rogers, in that the effectiveness of these conditions has not been clearly demonstrated by research (Meltzoff & Kornreich, 1970; Rachman, 1971). Instead, it seems likely that women's enhanced self-image following therapy might be affected by such variables as sex of therapist, consistency between clients' and therapists' values, and/or the nature of the problems that women bring to therapy. On this last point, it would be instructive to investigate whether women who are seeking nontraditional options show as much improvement as do women seeking more conformist solutions.

The impact of consistency between client and therapist values also merits investigation. It is assumed that, in client-centered therapy, the stance of the therapist prevents her or his values and beliefs from impacting on the therapeutic work. Validation of this lack of impact needs to be tested as it applies to women in therapy, given Truax's (1966) finding that, in general, client-centered therapists tend to reinforce certain types of responses more than others. For example, Broverman, Broverman, Clarkson, Rosenkrantz, and Vogel (1970) found that therapists from a variety of theoretical orientations held a less socially valued standard of mental health for women than for men. However, it remains to be seen whether therapists' conceptions of mental health for women are related to women clients' changes in self-image. In other words, protestations of client-centered therapists notwithstanding, is there evidence that therapists' attitudes toward women might interfere with their capacity to validate growth for all of their women clients?

Finally, although changes in self-image are of interest, it is in the area of behavioral outcome measures that the most significant effects of psychotherapy can be sought, although these have generally been neglected in outcome research on client-centered therapy. Do women who have been treated within a client-centered orientation reveal greater independence in their interpersonal relationships following therapy than they did before therapy? Do women, at the end of therapy, seem to have accepted their right to make conscious choices about the direction of their life, and do they, in fact, evidence a variety of lifestyles? In other words, are the independence and freedom of choice that client-centered therapy claims to foster demonstrated in the clients' behavior within the real world?

Sullivanian Therapy

Developmental Theory

Sullivan has been considered the originator of what is called the "interpersonal theory of psychiatry." According to Sullivan (1953), personality consists of a relatively enduring pattern of recurring interpersonal relationships which characterize human life. As such, an individual's personality cannot be studied apart from her or his relationships with others.

Sullivan understood individual development in terms of "interpersonal relations, as defined and structured by the individual's culture, along with the gradually unfolding maturational pattern of the growing child" (Mullahy, 1970, p. 122). In his stage theory of development, interpersonal events mark the majority of transitions from one stage to the other.

Sullivan's developmental model is portrayed in *The Interpersonal Theory of Psychiatry* (1953), *Personal Psychopathology* (Note 4), and, to a lesser extent, *The Psychiatric Interview* (1954). Very briefly, the first stage, infancy, is shaped by the infant's relationship to the mothering one. The mothering one is experienced by the infant as an all-powerful being who can communicate warmth and support or anxiety to the infant. This early relationship is seen as crucial in initiating patterns that will be reflected in later developmental stages. The next stage, childhood, is initiated by the onset of speech. Speech develops by means of rewards given to the infant by significant others for associating certain sounds with certain objects or experiences. The transition to the third stage, the juvenile era, is marked by the beginning of contact with playmates. Within this stage, the child begins to develop her or his social self and to look not only to the family but also to teachers and peers for learning the standards and expectations of her or his culture.

The fourth stage, preadolescence, is characterized by the formation of friendships with peers of the same sex, the "chum." These chumship years mark the beginning of genuine human relationships that are not characterized by the child's dependence on an older person. The fifth stage, early adolescence, is characterized by early attempts at forming heterosexual relationships, learning to deal with sexual urges, and separating erotic needs from needs for intimacy. In the sixth stage, late adolescence, comfort with one's sexual needs is consolidated, permitting the individual to explore and utilize vocational and educational opportunities. This prepares the individual for movement into the last stage, adulthood, which is marked by the formation of a durably satisfying relationship with another person, in which the sexual drive is the inducing motive.

IMPLICATIONS FOR WOMEN

Sullivan's theory is one in which sexuality in general and heterosexuality in particular play a major role, especially in the last few stages. However, although sexual maturation is a developmental factor for both males and females, Sullivan's model is based on specifics that derive almost exclusively from the male experience. For example, in discussing early adolescence, Sullivan (1953) asserts that the commonly held distinction between the "good girl" and the "bad girl" impairs boys' ability to simultaneously satisfy their needs for sexuality and self-esteem. The meaning for girls of the good girl/bad girl dichotomy, however, remains unexplored. Similarly, Sullivan (1953) suggests that males with sexual problems in adulthood might well have benefited from adolescent initiation into heterosexuality by a prostitute or an "experienced women." However, female initiation into sexuality and its impact on adult sexual functioning are not addressed.

In his discussion of the earlier years, Sullivan by and large does not attend to gender differences in progression through the various stages. Although extremely sensitive to the importance of early parent–infant interactions, he fails to note aspects of those interactions which might be linked to the sex of the infant (cf. Chodorow, 1978). Gender differences are mentioned as an issue in the childhood years, mainly that each parent is more favorably disposed to the child of the same sex. This is related, in Sullivanian theory, to the process by which children of each sex learn the cultural prescriptions of appropriate behavior for boys and girls. However, the *content* of these prescriptions and their specific implications for women's later development are unexplored.

Psychotherapy

Sullivan defines psychotherapy as "a situation of primarily *vocal* communication in a *two-group*, more or less *voluntarily integrated* on a progressively unfolding *expert–client* basis for the purpose of elucidating *characteristic patterns of living*. . . of the client. . . in the revealing of which he expects to derive benefit" (1954, p. 4). Central to this process is the role of the therapist as "participant observer," in which the therapist's principal instrument of observation is the self. Thus, therapy is marked by a process of reciprocal emotions, with client and therapist continually reflecting the feelings of the other.

The therapist, in Sullivan's model, is also an active participant, using her or his role as expert in a number of specific ways. Therapy is begun, for example, with an examination of why the client has sought therapy, followed by the obtaining of a detailed history, throughout which the therapist is ever attuned to nuances of verbal and especially vocal expressions of conflict. This information-gathering is concluded, in the reconnaissance stage, by a summary statement by the therapist, in which a justification for the therapeutic work is established.

The bulk of therapy consists of a detailed inquiry, in which the hypotheses of the earlier stages are tested. The therapist, while trying not to arouse anxiety in the client, seeks to identify those interpersonal factors which produce anxiety in the client. Anxiety, according to Sullivan, is the "chief handicap to communication" (1954, p. 107). Thus,

Sullivan feels that "this dealing with anxiety in relation to others is a work of exquisite refinement and crucial importance" (1954, p. 107). Throughout this inquiry, the therapist is continually attending to the possibility that the client is reflecting feelings put forth by the therapist, especially feelings of anxiety.

At the point of termination, the expert role of the therapist figures prominently. She or he makes a final summary statement to the client about what has been learned during the course of the interviews, gives the client a prescription of action in which the client is to engage, and makes a final assessment of expected life consequences of the prescription (Sullivan, 1954). Finally, client and therapist take formal leave of one another.

IMPLICATIONS FOR RESEARCH ON WOMEN IN THERAPY

From Sullivan's approach to therapy two major variables emerge which merit study as to their relationship to process and outcome variables for women in therapy. The first of these concerns the prominent role of anxiety. If Sullivan is correct that a major task of therapy is the alleviation of anxiety, then it would be useful for research to document those aspects of therapy which are associated with higher anxiety levels for women, especially if, in turn, such higher anxiety levels are indeed associated with less favorable outcomes. Some conditions that might foster anxiety in women clients could come from combinations of client/ therapist *demographic* variables. If, for example, social class, race, and/or sex of client and therapist differ, is this more conducive to higher anxiety levels than if client and therapist are similar on some or all of these variables? Also, discrepancies between the *values* of client and therapist might be conducive to higher anxiety levels. If anxiety is associated with discrepancies in values, how does this affect clients' perception of the therapy as fostering their self-esteem and their feelings of being understood by the therapists?

The second major relevant aspect of Sullivan's approach deals with his portrayal of the therapist as "expert." As noted above, this includes a diagnostic history-taking, a formulation of the client's problems, and a summary of progress and prescription for further action at the end of the therapy work. It would be useful to document whether this level of the therapist dictating to the client what her problems are and what life changes would be recommended impacts on the client's feelings of self-confidence, pride in her own abilities, sense of mastery, etc. It would also be useful to document the extent to which therapists' prescriptions are influenced by the importance placed on long-term heterosexual relationships in Sullivan's developmental theory. Do therapists working within a Sullivanian framework suggest a range of options for women at the termination of therapy, or are those suggestions generally limited to the roles of wife and mother? If their prescriptions are restricted in this manner, how does this affect life changes in their female clients following termination? Given the extent of formalized input the therapist makes into structuring the therapeutic work and suggesting the direction for posttherapeutic adjustment, it seems possible that Sullivanian therapists are vulnerable to using therapy as a form of social control (cf. Hurvitz, 1974), directly translating societal expectations about women into prescriptions for women's behavior.

Conclusion

This chapter has gone "back to the basics" of traditional therapies, that is, to the theoretical notions and clinical techniques espoused by three of the most popular traditions. In both of these areas, gender bias is ubiquitous, reflected in a masculinist orientation to theory and technique. Although this bias is more explicit in some orientations than in others, it appears in each of them in the form of prescriptions for "adjustment" to prevailing cultural conditions and imperatives and in developmental theories in which the male is the norm. Specific aspects of the female experience, as viewed from the female's own perspective, are systematically excluded. Thus, female, in all of these traditions, is confounded with dependent or subordinate.

It seems probable, given this confusion, that the practice of psychotherapy by therapists trained in and committed to any of these orientations will be (nonconsciously) sexist and heterosexist. This is not to say that all traditional therapy as practiced by any clinician will necessarily serve the purpose of the status quo. What it does mean, though, is that the practice of and research on individual psychotherapy must take into account the systematic biases inherent in its particular theoretical base and technical suggestions. Not only do researchers need to rethink the values underlying the intended goals of therapy, but also (and perhaps more importantly) there is a need to begin searching for and documenting the *unintended consequences*. One of the goals of this research, to paraphrase Freud, should be to render the nonconscious, conscious.

The psychotherapeutic situation is not a world unto itself, as is implied in most of the existing empirical research. Therapists, clients, and the institutions in which therapy is conducted have a place in and are affected by the cultural context. Despite differences, all three traditional orientations reviewed herein hold in common basic assumptions which deny, distort, or devalue the female experience in a male-dominated culture. This cultural order is not only a system of power relations but also a system of meanings in which maleness is standard (which is perhaps the most important interpretation of the Broverman *et al.*, 1970, findings) and where certain elements of femininity, notably, its association with strength or homosexuality, are excluded (Lipshitz, 1978).

The major recommendation for research on psychotherapy and women with which we conclude this chapter, a broad and radical one, we admit, is to reject the assumption of random gender effects in *any* social interaction until proven otherwise. It is clear that innovations in research must precede further development in this area of inquiry. While Sullivan's belief that we are all much more simply human than otherwise emphasizes, rightly, the continuity of human experience, it also serves to mask the crucial differences, within this culture, of gender, ethnic, racial, and class variables.

Reference Notes

1. Sperling, E. *Research in early genital arousal, an overview of theory and method.* Paper presented at the meeting of the American Psychoanalytic Association, December 1970.
2. Parens, H. *A preliminary report from the project, "Correlations of the libidinal availability of the mother with the development of psychic structure in the child."* Unpublished manuscript, 1971.
3. Kleeman, J., *Who needs a father?* Unpublished manuscript, 1971.
4. Sullivan, H. S. *Personal psychopathology.* Unpublished manuscript, copyright W. A. White Foundation, 1965.

References

Abelin, E. The role of the father in the separation–individuation process. In J. B. McRevitt & C. F. Settlage (Eds.), *Separation–individuation.* New York: International Universities Press, 1971.

American Psychological Association Task Force. Report of the Task Force on Sex Bias and Sex-Role Stereotyping in Psychotherapeutic Practice. *American Psychologist,* 1975, *30,* 1169–1175.

Balint, M. *The basic fault.* London: Tavistock, 1968.

Bergin, A. E., & Lampert, M. J. The evaluation of therapeutic outcomes. In S. Garfield & A. Bergin (Eds.), *Handbook of psychotherapy and behavior change.* New York: Wiley, 1978.

Bieber, I. (Ed.). *Homosexuality: A psychoanalytic study.* New York: Basic Books, 1962.

Blum, H. P. Masochism, the ego ideal, and the psychology of women. In H. P. Blum (Ed.), *Female psychology: Contemporary psychoanalytic views.* New York: International Universities Press, 1977.

Bonaparte, M. *Female sexuality.* New York: International Universities Press, 1953.

Broverman, I. K., Broverman, D. M., Clarkson, F. E., Rosenkrantz, P., & Vogel, S. R. Sex role stereotypes and clinical judgments of mental health. *Journal of Clinical and Consulting Psychology*, 1970, *34*, 1–7.

Brunswick, R. M. The pre-oedipal phase of libido development. In R. Fleiss (Ed.), *The psychoanalytic reader*. New York: International Universities Press, 1969. (Originally published, 1940.)

Chassequet-Smirgel, J. *Female sexuality*. Ann Arbor: University of Michigan Press, 1970.

Chesler, P. Women as psychiatric and psychotherapeutic patients. *Journal of Marriage and the Family*, 1971, *33*, 746–759.

Chesler, P. *Women and madness*. Garden City, N.Y.: Doubleday, 1972.

Chodoff, P. Feminine psychology and infantile sexuality. In J. Masserman (Ed.), *Science and psychoanalysis* (Vol. 10). New York: Grune and Stratton, 1966.

Chodorow, N. *The reproduction of mothering*. Berkeley: University of California Press, 1978.

Cohen, M. B. Personal identity and sexual identity. *Psychiatry*, 1966, *29*, 1–14.

Colm, H. The therapeutic encounter. In H. Ruitenbeek (Ed.), *The analytic situation*. Chicago: Aldene Press, 1973.

Deutsch, H. *The psychology of women: A psychoanalytic perspective*. New York: Grune and Stratton, 1944.

Dymond, R. F. Adjustment changes over therapy from self-sorts. In C. R. Rogers & R. F. Dymond (Eds.), *Psychotherapy and personality change*. Chicago: Univeristy of Chicago Press, 1954.

Eagly, A. H. Sex differences in influencibility. *Psychological Bulletin*, 1978, *85*, 86–116.

Fairbairn, R. *Object relations theory of the personality*. New York: Basic Books, 1952.

Figes, E. *Patriarchal attitudes*. Greenwich, Conn.: Fawcett, 1970.

Fraiberg, S. A critical neurosis in a two-and-a-half year old girl. In R. S. Eissler (Ed.), *The psychoanalytic study of the child* (Vol. 7). New York: International Universities Press, 1952.

Frank, J. D. *Persuasion and healing* (2nd ed.). Baltimore: Johns Hopkins University Press, 1973.

Frank, J. D. The present status of outcome studies. *Journal of Consulting and Clinical Psychology*, 1979, *47*, 310–316.

Freud, S. Three contributions to the theory of sexuality. In A. A. Brill (Ed.), *The basic writings of Sigmund Freud*. New York: Modern Library, 1938. (Originally published, 1905.)

Freud, S. Some psychical consequences of the anatomical distinction between the sexes. In J. Strachey (Ed.), *The standard edition of the complete psychological works of Sigmund Freud* (Vol. 19). London: Hogarth Press, 1953. (Originally published, 1925.)

Freud, S. On psychotherapy. In P. Reiff (Ed.), *Freud: Therapy and technique*. New York: Collier Books, 1963. (a) (Originally published, 1904.)

Freud, S. The dynamics of the transference. In P. Reiff (Ed.), *Freud: Therapy and technique*. New York: Collier Books, 1963. (b) (Originally published, 1912.)

Freud, S. Recommendations for physicians on the psychoanalytic method of treatment. In P. Reiff (Ed.), *Freud: Therapy and technique*. New York: Collier Books, 1963. (c) (Originally published, 1912.)

Freud, S. Further recommendations in the technique of psychoanalysis: Recollection, repetition, and working through. In P. Reiff (Ed.), *Freud: Therapy and technique*. New York: Collier Books, 1963. (d) (Originally published, 1914.)

Freud, S. Further recommendations in technique of psychoanalysis: Observations on transference love. In P. Reiff (Ed.), *Freud: Therapy and technique*. New York: Collier Books, 1963. (e) (Originally published, 1915.)

Freud, S. Analysis terminable and interminable. In P. Reiff (Ed.), *Freud: Therapy and technique*. New York: Collier Books, 1963. (f) (Originally published, 1937.)

Freud, S. Female sexuality. In J. Strouse (Ed.), *Women in analysis*. New York: Dell, 1974. (a) (Originally published, 1931.)

Freud, S. Femininity. In J. Strouse (Ed.), *Women in analysis.* New York: Dell, 1974. (b) (Originally published, 1933.)

Galenson, E., & Roiphe, H. Some suggested revisions concerning early female development. In H. P. Blum (Ed.), *Female psychology: Contemporary psychoanalytic views.* New York: International Universities Press, 1977.

Garfield, S. L. Research on client variables in psychotherapy. In S. Garfield & A. Bergin (Eds.), *Handbook of psychotherapy and behavior change.* New York: Wiley, 1978.

Guntrip, H. *Psychoanalytic theory, therapy, and the self.* New York: Basic Books, 1971.

Henley, N. M. *Body politics: Power, sex and nonverbal communication.* Englewood Cliffs, N.J.: Prentice-Hall, 1977.

Horney, K. The flight from womanhood. *International Journal of Psychoanalysis,* 1926, *1,* 324-39.

Horney, K. The dread of women. *International Journal of Psychoanalysis,* 1932, *13,* 348-60.

Horney, K. The problem of feminine masochism. *The Psychoanalytic Review,* 1935, *22,* 241-257.

Horney, K. The distrust between the sexes. In H. Kelman (Ed.), *Feminine psychology.* New York: Norton, 1967. (Originally published, 1930.)

Hurvitz, N. Manifest and latent functions in psychotherapy. *Journal of Consulting and Clinical Psychology,* 1974, *42,* 301-302.

Janeway, E. *Man's world, woman's place: A study in social mythology.* New York: Delta, 1971.

Jones, E. The early development of female sexuality. *International Journal of Psychoanalysis,* 1927, *8,* 459-472.

Jones, E. The phallic phase. *International Journal of Psychoanalysis,* 1933, *14,* 1-33.

Jones, E. Early female sexuality. *International Journal of Psychoanalysis,* 1935, *16,* 263-273.

Kernberg, O. F. Some methodological and strategic issues in psychotherapy research: Research implications of the Menninger Foundation's Psychotherapy Research Project. In R. L. Spitzer & D. F. Klein (Eds.), *Evaluation of psychological therapies.* Baltimore: Johns Hopkins University Press, 1976.

Kleeman, J. Genital self-stimulation in infant and toddler girls. In A. Marcus & J. Francis (Eds.), *Masturbation: From infancy to senescence.* New York: International Universities Press, 1975.

Kleeman, J. Freud's views on early female sexuality in the light of direct child observation. In H. P. Blum (Ed.), *Female psychology: Contemporary psychoanalytic views.* New York: International Universities Press, 1977.

Klein, M. *The psychoanalysis of children.* New York: Grove Press, 1960.

Kronsky, B. J. Feminism and psychotherapy. *Journal of Contemporary Psychotherapy,* 1971, *3,* 89-98.

Lampl-de Groot, J. The evolution of the oedipus complex in women. In R. Fleiss (Ed.), *The psychoanalytic reader.* New York: International Universities Press, 1969. (Originally published, 1927.)

Lerner, H. Parental mislabeling of female genitals as a determinant of penis envy and learning inhibitions in women. In H. P. Blum (Ed.), *Female psychology: Contemporary psychoanalytic views.* New York: International Universities Press, 1977.

Lewis, H. B. *Psychic war in men and women.* New York: New York University Press, 1976.

Lipshitz, S. (Ed.). *Tearing the veil: Essays on femininity.* Boston: Routledge and Kegan Paul, 1978.

Luborsky, L., Singer, B., & Luborsky, L. Comparative studies of psychotherapies: Is it true that "Everybody has won and all must have prizes"? *Archives of General Psychiatry,* 1975, *32,* 995-1008.

Maccoby, E., & Jacklin, C. *The psychology of sex differences.* Stanford, Calif.: Stanford University Press, 1974.

Malan, D. H. *Toward the validation of dynamic psychotherapy: A replication.* New York: Plenum Press, 1976.

Marmor, J. Changing patterns of femininity: Psychoanalytic interpretations. In J. B. Miller (Ed.), *Psychoanalysis and women*. Baltimore: Penguin Books, 1973.

Masters, W., & Johnson, V. *Human sexual response*. Boston: Little, Brown, 1966.

Masterson, J. F. *Psychotherapy of the borderline adult: A developmental approach*. New York: Brunner/Mazel, 1976.

Mead, M. On Freud's view of female psychology. In J. Strouse (Ed.), *Women in analysis*. New York: Dell, 1974.

Meltzoff, J., & Kornreich, M. *Research in psychotherapy*. New York: Atherton Press, 1970.

Menaker, E. The therapy of women in light of psychoanalytic theory and the emergence of a new view. In V. Franks & V. Burtle (Eds.), *Women in therapy*. New York: Brunner/Mazel, 1974.

Money, J., & Ehrhardt, A. A. *Man and woman, boy and girl*. Baltimore: Johns Hopkins University Press, 1972.

Moulton, R. A survey and re-evaluation of the concept of penis envy. *Contemporary Psychoanalysis*, 1970, *7*, 84–104.

Mullahy, P. *Psychoanalysis and interpersonal psychiatry*. New York: Science House, 1970.

Muller, J. A contribution to the problem of libidinal development of the genital phase of girls. *International Journal of Psychoanalysis*, 1932, *13*, 361–368.

Orlinsky, D. E., & Howard, K. I. *Varieties of psychotherapeutic experience*. New York: Teachers College Press, 1975.

Orlinsky, D. E., & Howard, K. I. The effect of sex of therapist on the therapeutic experiences of women. *Psychotherapy: Theory, Research, and Practice*, 1976, *13*, 82–88.

Parens, H., Pollock, L., Stern, J., & Kramer, S. On the girl's entry into the Oedipus Complex. In H. P. Blum (Ed.), *Female psychology: Contemporary psychoanalytic views*. New York: International Universities Press, 1977.

Parloff, M. B., Waskow, I. E., & Wolfe, B. E. Research on therapist variables in relation to process and outcome. In S. Garfield & A. Bergin (Eds.), *Handbook of psychotherapy and behavior change*. New York: Wiley, 1978.

Payne, S. A conception of femininity. *British Journal of Medical Psychology*, 1936, *15*, 18–33.

Rachman, S. *The effects of psychotherapy*. New York: Pergamon Press, 1971.

Rawlings, E. I., & Carter, D. K. *Psychotherapy for women: Treatment toward equality*. Springfield, Ill.: Charles C. Thomas, 1977.

Rogers, C. R. *Client-centered therapy*. Boston: Houghton Mifflin, 1951.

Rogers, C. R. The necessary and sufficient conditions of therapeutic personality change. *Journal of Consulting Psychology*, 1957, *21*, 95–103.

Rogers, C. R. Empathic: An appreciated way of being. *Counseling Psychologist*, 1975, *5*, 2–10.

Rogers, C. R., & Dymond, R. F. (Eds.). *Psychotherapy and personality change*. Chicago: University of Chicago Press, 1954.

Roiphe, H. On an early genital phase; with an addendum on genesis. In R. S. Eissler (Ed.), *The psychoanalytic study of the child* (Vol. 10). New York: International Universities Press, 1968.

Salzman, L. Psychology of the female: A new look. *Archives of General Psychiatry*, 1967, *17*, 195–203.

Schafer, R. Problems in Freud's psychology of women. In H. P. Blum (Ed.), *Female psychology: Contemporary psychoanalytic views*. New York: International Universities Press, 1977.

Seeman, J. Counselor judgments of therapeutic process and outcome. In C. R. Rogers & R. F. Dymond (Eds.), *Psychotherapy and personality change*. Chicago: University of Chicago Press, 1954.

Shacklady Smith, L. Sexist assumptions and female delinquency: An empirical investigation. In C. Smart & B. Smart (Eds.), *Women, sexuality and social control*. Boston: Routledge and Kegan Paul, 1978.

Sifneos, D. *Short-term psychotherapy and emotional crisis.* Cambridge, Mass.: Harvard University Press, 1972.

Stang Dahl, T., & Snare, A. The coercion of privacy: A feminist perspective. In C. Smart & B. Smart (Eds.), *Women, sexuality and social control.* Boston: Routledge and Kegan Paul, 1978.

Stoller, R. A contribution to the study of gender identity. *International Journal of Psychoanalysis,* 1964, *45,* 220–226.

Stoller, R. *Sex and gender.* New York: Science House, 1968.

Stoller, R. The "bedrock" of masculinity and femininity: Bisexuality. *Archives of General Psychiatry,* 1972, *26,* 207–212.

Stoller, R. Primary femininity. In H. P. Blum (Ed.), *Female psychology: Contemporary psychoanalytic views.* New York: International Universities Press, 1977.

Stricker, G. Implications of research for psychotherapeutic treatment of women. *American Psychologist,* 1977, *32,* 14–22.

Strupp, H. H. Towards a specification of teaching and learning in psychotherapy. *Archives of General Psychiatry,* 1969, *21,* 203–212.

Strupp, H. H. Toward a reformulation of the psychotherapeutic influence. *International Journal of Psychiatry,* 1973, *11,* 263–327.

Strupp, H. H. Psychotherapy research and practice: An overview. In S. Garfield & A. Bergin (Eds.), *Handbook of psychotherapy and behavior change.* New York: Wiley, 1978.

Sullivan, H. S. *The interpersonal theory of psychiatry.* New York: Norton, 1953.

Sullivan, H. S. *The psychiatric interview.* New York: Norton, 1954.

Tennov, D. *The hazardous cure.* New York: Anchor Books, 1975.

Thompson, C. Cultural pressures in the psychology of women. *Psychiatry,* 1942, *5,* 331–339.

Thompson, C. Some effects of the derogatory attitude toward female sexuality. *Psychiatry,* 1950, *13,* 349–354.

Truax, C. B. Reinforcement and non-reinforcement in Rogerian psychotherapy. *Journal of Abnormal Psychology,* 1966, *71,* 1–9.

Wilson, D. Sexual codes and conduct: A study of teenage girls. In C. Smart & B. Smart (Eds.), *Woman, sexuality and social control.* Boston: Routledge and Kegan Paul, 1978.

Winnicott, D. W. Transitional objects and transitional phenomena. *International Journal of Psychoanalysis,* 1953, *34,* 89–97.

Winnicott, D. W. *The family and individual development.* London: Tavistock, 1978.

Zeldow, P. B. Sex differences in psychiatric evaluation and treatment. *Archives of General Psychiatry,* 1978, *35,* 89–93.

CHAPTER 9

Behavior Therapies

ELAINE A. BLECHMAN

The aim of this chapter is to suggest researchable directions for behavior modification with women, directions that will avoid sex-role stereotyping, help individual women clients, and promote equity between men and women. The mental health, social science, and medical professions all contributed to restriction of women. A consideration of how this took place suggests directions, which, if taken by the behavior modification discipline, might benefit modern women.

Because behavior modification is applied to human problems, many of which are created by the prevailing social system, it can become, as can any psychotherapy, a technological fix that dampens individual complaints while perpetuating social inequity. Rather than enlarge upon real and potential misuses of behavior modification, I suggest in this chapter basic overriding principles for behavioral intervention with women. Hopefully, these principles will guide the discipline away from technological fix and toward social system change.

Historical Notes on Behavior Modification with Women

In the 1890s, the variability hypothesis was a common scientific justification for the unequal status of women: "Because variation from the norm was already accepted as the mechanism of evolutionary progress . . . and because it seemed that the male was the more variable sex, it soon was universally concluded that the male is the progressive element in the species" (Shields, 1975, p. 743). Freud's concept of instinctually based masculine and feminine personality types was of this zeitgeist. His words bear repetition, since they were restated with agreement by a leading psychologist (Bronfenbrenner, 1960):

Elaine A. Blechman. Department of Psychology, Wesleyan University, Middletown, Connecticut.

For women what is ethically normal is different from what it is in men. Their superego is never so inexorable, so independent of its emotional origins as we require it to be in men. . . . We must not allow ourselves to be deflected from such concessions by the denials of feminists, who are anxious to force us to regard the two sexes as completely equal in position and worth; but we shall, of course, willingly agree that the majority of men are also far behind the masculine ideal. (Freud, 1925/1961b, p. 257)

In Freud's writings, homosexuality, paranoia, and depression are all attributed to excessively masculine identifications by women and feminine identifications by men (Freud, 1921/1955, 1923/1961a, 1925/1961b, 1915/1962). Normal psychosexual development and·the survival of modern civilization depend upon the adoption by men and women of sex roles that suit their anatomies and society's demands (Fenichel, 1953; Freud, 1923/1961a, Jahoda, 1977). Freudian sex-typed identification was incorporated by the foremost anthropological, sociological and psychological theories of child development and personality of this century, including early social-learning theory (Bandura & Walters, 1963; Burton & Whiting, 1961; Gewirtz & Stingle, 1968; Kagan, 1958; Miller & Dollard, 1941; Parsons & Bales, 1955; Sears, 1957). In early social-learning theory, the concept of identification lost its instinctual origins and was often called a generalized imitative tendency. But it retained the idealization of conventional sex roles.

Sex-typed identification was thoroughly rejected by social-learning-theory revisionists (Bandura, 1969, 1977a, 1977b; Gewirtz, 1969; Maccoby, 1966; Maccoby & Jacklin, 1974; Mischel, 1966, 1970, 1973). In this new view of social learning, sex-typed identification with parents is no longer a central regulator of moral, intellectual, social, and affective development. And so the nuclear family in which anatomy determines the allocation of roles to parents is not a prerequisite for healthy child development. Replacing identification as an explanatory concept is social learning of specific competencies and general problem-solving skills. As children mature, they abstract from their experiences rules about the relationships between behavior and consequence, and they acquire a facility for solving unfamiliar problems and responding to the demands of novel situations. One of the rules that children often learn concerns conventional social expectations about the typical behavior of men and women. Better-adjusted and more intelligent children are most likely to learn this rule and to know how to follow it when necessary, just as they are most likely to learn many other useful social rules and behavior repertoires. Better-adjusted and more intelligent children are also most likely not to be restricted by conventional sex-role expectations when these expectations hinder progress toward important goals. Sex typing may be a product, but it is not a cause of advanced social and intellectual development.

Behavior modification as it is now practiced is a product of both the early and the revised social-learning positions. The two incompatible views crystallized recently when Rekers and Lovaas (1974) reported on the behavioral treatment of "deviant" sex-role behaviors in young boys. Kindergarten-aged boys who preferred toys and activities that girls typically choose were trained to avoid these and choose more conventionally masculine pursuits by a combination of positive reinforcement and punishment. Proponents of the treatment drew upon early social-learning theory and argued that the boys' unconventional behavior predicted later-life adjustment problems (Rekers, Bentler, Rosen, & Lovaas, 1978). Behaviorally oriented critics of the treatment drew upon revised social-learning theory (Nordyke, Baer, Etzel, & LeBlanc, 1977; Winkler, 1977) and questioned whether practitioners should accede to parents' demands for more conventionally behaved sons. They suggested that if treatment is necessary, the goal should be androgynous and not stereotypically masculine behavior.

Cognitive-behavior modification (Mahoney, 1974; Meichenbaum, 1973) is a new specialty within behavior modification. Its focus on the cognitive and symbolic processes, which many behaviorists purposefully ignore, and its kinship with social psychology suggest that cognitive-behavior modification may encourage sensitivity to sex-role bias. The revised social-learning position is the foundation for the recommendations of this chapter which are directed at the behavior modification and cognitive-behavior modification disciplines.

What is behavior modification with women? Behavior modification as it is now practiced is not a straightforward application of laws of learning to human behavior. A current and widely accepted definition states that behavior modification consists of "procedures based on explicit and systematic application of principles and technology derived from research in experimental psychology, procedures that involve some change in the social and environmental context of a person's behavior" (Stolz, Wienckowski, & Brown, 1975, p. 1029). Anatomical sex is a crude summary variable that does not reliably predict behavior (Gewirtz, 1969). For this good reason, there is no women's behavior modification with distinctive methods and goals. But women are major consumers of behavior modification treatments for depression, obesity, and phobias, and of parent training and social-skills (assertiveness) training. For this chapter, illustrations of behavior modification with women are drawn from empirical research published primarily in 1977 and 1978, in which the sample exhibited problems of clinical severity and women were represented proportionately or overrepresented.[1]

Many treatments that are applied to women and called behavior modification differ markedly from the definition of behavior modification provided above. A critic of "the perils of behavior modification in the treatment of anorexia nervosa," Bruch (1974) forced tube feedings on hospitalized anorexic women who failed to eat. She found no post-hospital maintenance of weight gain and concluded (and Bemis, 1978, concurred) that behavior modification does not work with anorexics since their families promote their condition. Bruch attributed this failure to punishment, which she equated with behavior modification. It is a fallacy to reason that because behavior modification sometimes involves punishment, every use of punishment is behavior modification (Goldiamond, 1978).

Bruch correctly pointed out that the family of the anorexic woman is a substantial portion of her environment. In the words of one woman, eating is the only thing "my family can't make me do" (Hauserman & Lavin, 1977). When family members were taught how to respond to the eating behavior of their anorexic relatives, patients maintained at home the weight they gained in the hospital (Hauserman & Lavin, 1977; Monti, McCrady, & Barlow, 1977). The latter two studies correctly identified and effectively altered environmental events controlling eating behavior. Thus, they satisfy the definition of behavior modification provided earlier.

Behavior Modification with Women and Social Change

A paradox confronts mental health and medical professionals when individual women request help with legitimate problems. Radical social critics argue that when professionals alleviate women's suffering, pressure evaporates that might otherwise force society to grant women equality and eliminate root causes of their mental and physical suffering (Chesler, 1972).

Radical feminist criticism assumes that the psychotherapeutic treatment of the individual woman (e.g., Chesler, 1971, 1972; Rossi, 1964; Williams, 1977) (1) does not change the environmental conditions which damage all women; (2) convinces the woman that there is some-

---

[1]The research cited appeared primarily in *Behavior Modification, Behaviour Research and Therapy, Behavior Therapy, Journal of Applied Behavior Analysis, Journal of Behavior Therapy and Experimental Psychiatry,* and *Journal of Consulting and Clinical Psychology.*

thing wrong with her body or mind and that this enduring deficiency, uncontrollable by her, causes her problem; (3) convinces the woman that her deficiency is shared by all women because of their anatomical similarity; (4) provides a standard treatment that ignores individual differences between women; and (5) produces changes in the presenting problem that are at best short-lived and superficial. Radical feminists further charge that narrow improvements in the presenting problem require that the woman be everlastingly dependent upon the therapist or physician, who is a substitute for the husband (Williams, 1977). No change is brought about in skills or beliefs that would allow the woman to fare well in an adverse environment after treatment ends. No change is brought about in the home, work, and school settings that cause similar problems for many women (Rossi, 1964).

The feminist critique echoes the sentiments of the revised social-learning position regarding early behavior modification practices (Holland, 1978). The technology of behavior modification is neutral with respect to social values. It can be used to keep women as members of an underclass, or it can be used to promote equality between men and women.

Recommended Procedures for Behavior Modification with Women

An ideal match of behavior modification technology and the treatment of women requires a thorough functional analysis of behavior to determine what current condition promotes the behavior summarized in the presenting problem or diagnosis: prevailing environmental contingencies, general problem-solving inadequacies, or specific skill deficiencies (Bandura, 1977a). One woman may be unassertive only at work with male supervisors; all women who work with her may have similar difficulties. A second woman may be generally maladroit in her social behavior. A third woman, in other respects socially adept, may rarely state her preferences strongly.

Objective evidence about the conditions which control the problem behavior should dictate the remedy: environmental restructuring in the first case, training to solve a general set of social problems in the second case, and specific skill training in the third. When the conditions which maintain a woman's problems are accurately identified, and this information dictates the remedy applied, intervention is most likely to be effective in the short and long run, to generalize over settings and response classes, to produce few negative side effects for the individual woman, and to produce favorable ecological change for other women and men. Thus, the formerly unassertive woman would become more assertive at work, resulting in her promotion; she would continue to assert herself at work with good results for many years; she would assert herself with friends and family members, although she had not been trained to do so; her self-esteem and sense of personal power would increase, although training focused only on assertive behavior; her nurturant behavior would not diminish as her assertiveness grew; and other people at work would become more assertive following her example. In short, an accurate identification of the conditions maintaining problem behavior contributes to treatment for the total woman and to social change.

Behavior Measurement in the Selection of an Intervention and Its Evaluation

Objective measurement of behavior in either natural or analogue settings has great advantages for women, both in the selection of an appropriate intervention and in its evaluation.

Quantitative observational ratings reduce the chance of observer bias so common in qualitative ratings of women (Kent, O'Leary, Diament, & Dietz, 1974; Shuller & McNamara, 1976). When men formed global ratings, they judged depressed women as far more impaired than depressed men, while women made no such distinction (Hammen & Peters, 1977). Objective quantitative ratings might have prevented this sex bias. Heterogeneity among women with similar global problems is less likely to be obscured when behavior is directly observed rather than indirectly inferred from interviews or tests. Variability among women affecting the course of treatment has been described for obesity (Ashby & Wilson, 1977; Coates, 1977; Jeffery, Wing, & Stunkard, 1978; Wilson, 1978), agoraphobia (Goldstein & Chambless, 1978), unassertiveness (Galassi, 1978), and depression (Depue & Monroe, 1978).

Repeated measurement of behavior over different settings suggests specific interventions far better than global diagnostic labels (Kanfer & Grimm, 1978). It inhibits the tendency of practitioners to form stable early judgments of women clients that persist despite discrepant information (Meehl, 1960). Perhaps it is for this reason that behaviorally trained clinicians were less influenced in their judgments of interview behavior when the interviewee was identified as a patient than were psychodynamically trained clinicians (Snyder, 1977).

During intervention, measurement of behavior or of the permanent products of behavior may provide a better index of progress than client self-report. Women's reports of their adherence to a weight-loss program did not account for their successful weight reduction (Stalonas, Johnson, & Christ, 1978). Self-reports of cigarettes smoked were discrepant from serum thiocynate levels (Brockway, Kleinmann, Edelsen, & Grunewald, 1977). As Nisbett and Wilson (1977) have pointed out, there may be no true introspection of the sort needed for accurate self-reports of behavior. People may be unaware of much of their behavior and of external antecedents and consequences.

Despite its apparent advantages to women, objective behavior measurement is not common before or during intervention. Psychological tests, structured and unstructured interviews, and rating scales often substitute for direct behavior measurement even among behaviorally oriented practitioners. There are economic and logistic reasons for this substitution. Many institutions and agencies customarily rely upon test batteries for diagnosis and treatment planning and are unfamiliar with behavior measurement. Insurance companies and state governments reimburse practitioners for diagnostic interviews and tests but not for measurement of behavior in its natural environs. Because of federal regulations administrators are reluctant to sanction direct behavior measurement.

Direct measurement of behavior in natural settings is rare. Interviews and inferences drawn from behavior sampled in unusual settings are more common methods of data collection. As a result, women's problems are often regarded as deficiencies in the individual woman, while the contribution of settings to deficient behavior is ignored. Women themselves are likely to promote this misattribution in an interview. Depressed women, who are likely to seek help, take far more personal responsibility for their difficulties than do men (Zigler & Phillips, 1960). A lack of information about the effects of home, work, and community settings on women's behavior, combined with women's tendency to self-blame, may accout for American women's disproportionate reliance upon individual psychotherapy (Rossi, 1964) and for the absence of efforts to change settings that handicap women.

The psychiatric hospital provides good examples of how a setting can induce dysfunctional behavior and promote the belief that the origin of the deficit is within the residents. A group of elderly women with chronic brain syndrome were more incontinent and behaved more bizarrely on an unadorned hospital ward than on a token economy ward (Mishara, 1978). Explosive chronic female psychiatric patients argued and fought less when behavior observers regularly visited their ward (Matson & Stephens, 1978). Such women are typically observed in only one setting, and it is assumed that their behavior is a product of individual deficits. Systematic observation in two different settings revealed that some of the women's behavior was produced by a noxious environment.

Compared to direct observation of behavior in natural settings, psychological tests, interviews, and informal observations of behavior in deficient and artificial settings are less likely to yield information about general setting deficits or about deficient setting × person interactions. They are more likely to result in the prescription of remedies that do not change the woman's environment. They are also cheaper and easier to administer. For these reasons, there is a need for development of methods of measuring women's behavior before, during, and after intervention. To gain wide acceptance, these methods would have to be no more costly over the course of treatment than a standard psychological test battery. They would sample excess and deficit behaviors in natural and analogue settings in a manner acceptable to women clients, and they would incorporate sophisticated reliability checks. Assessment of social skills is moving in this direction (Barlow, Abel, Blanchard, Bristow, & Young, 1977; Hollandsworth, Glazeski, & Dressel, 1978). With a few exceptions (e.g., Hersen, Bellack, & Turner, 1978; Williams & Ciminero, 1978), women have not been included in this research.

Skill Training: Choosing Goals and Evaluating Effectiveness

As a discipline, behavior modification emphasizes the controlling effects of external social and physical events on human behavior. Such widely disseminated interventions as the token economy and the programmed classroom represent feats of environmental restructuring. There is considerable evidence that the settings in which most women live, work, and study exercise unfavorable, even noxious, effects. Nevertheless, only a few behavioral interventions with women focus on engineering environments that promote competent behavior. Two utopian novels portray the benefits of social engineering for women: *Herland,* first serialized in the magazine *Forerunner* at the turn of the century (Gilman, 1979), and *Walden II* (Skinner, 1948).

Most behavioral interventions with women fall in the skill-training category. Judging by the methods sections of recent research reports, women are the major voluntary consumers of training aimed at modifying smoking, overeating, anorexia, parenting, anxiety, unassertiveness, depression, and migraine and tension headaches. In some cases, such as parent training, male clients are rarely involved. Only in the behavioral treatment of alcoholism and in the teaching of social skills to psychiatric patients do women appear underrepresented. The focus on skill training is understandable. It is consistent with the American appreciation of individual accomplishment and with the American health care system which encourages practitioners to change individuals rather than settings. A shift of emphasis toward environmental change and primary prevention of women's mental health problems requires social and economic incentives now unavailable.

If skill training is to embody the ideal match between behavior modification technology and women's treatment needs, the goals for skill training must be selected after the client's current skill repertoire has been assessed. Target skills should be selected which, when acquired, will remediate the woman's presenting problem and increase the woman's control over her behavior and environment. For example, socially isolated elderly women were trained as foster grandparents for severely retarded children (Fabry & Reid, 1978). Delinquent girls were taught to call adults' attention to their good work (Seymour & Stokes, 1976). Systematic desensitization and negative practice allowed a rape victim to decrease the fear and compulsive door checking that had prevented her from "living her life in the manner of her choosing" (Wolff, 1977). Two child-abusing young single mothers were tangibly rewarded for successfully using positive reinforcement with their children; abuse by mothers declined, and the children were not removed from their homes (Sandler, VanDercar, & Milhoon, 1978). The depression, anger, and fear of these women could have been suppressed with systematic desensitization or drugs. Instead, these women were taught skills that increased their chances of personal success and interfered with the unpleasant emotions and deficient behaviors described by their initial presenting problems.

In skill training, a woman learns a repertoire of behavior likely to produce desirable consequences in specific situations. Construction of repertoires of competent behavior for women is hard, because adult women have traditionally been expected to be ineffective at some major adult pursuits. Target repertoires for skill training cannot be chosen by social consensus of peers or mental health experts, as some have suggested (Bellack, Hersen, & Turner, 1978; Wolf, 1978), because even experts' judgments are influenced by clients' sex. Expert and peer men and women judges identified comparable noncoercive behaviors as assertive when enacted by men but aggressive when enacted by women (Rich & Schroeder, 1976); rated assertive behavior as healthy but suitable only for men (Broverman, Broverman, Clarkson, Rosenkrantz, & Vogel, 1970); approved of successful men but not of successful women

(Monahan, Kuhn, & Shaver, 1974); and judged men as more skillful than women (Etaugh & Brown, 1975).

In skill training, "normal" or "happy" or "positive" behaviors often make up the standard repertoire. Unfortunately, none of these adjectives describes good criteria for the construction of skill-training repertoires for women. Much behavior that is now statistically typical of women is well regarded neither by men nor by women. Both college men and women reported wanting to be more masculine (Jones, Chernovetz, & Hansson, 1978). Normals and recently hospitalized schizophrenics agreed that the ideal psychiatric patient is a woman (LaTorre & Piper, 1979). Statistically normal behavior is not necessarily effective. Normal parents and teachers do not appear to be good contingency managers (Forehand & Wells, 1977), and people of normal weight appear to eat no differently from the obese (Adams, Ferguson, Stunkard, & Agras, 1978).

Women who say they are happily married may describe fewer unresolved problems in their marriages than women who say they are unhappy (Birchler & Webb, 1977), but it would be risky to use the behavior of self-reported happily married women as the target repertoire for skill training. The women who are openly least happy with their marriages may have more outside interests, depend less on their marriages for satisfaction, and strive less to describe their marriages in socially desirable terms, yet they may be equally effective as marital partners. Observer judgment of behaviors as positive or negative is also an inadequate method of selecting a repertoire for skill training. The frequency of communication behaviors judged positive or negative by observers did not predict husbands' and wives' global ratings of marital satisfaction (Margolin, 1978).

Androgynous people who score high on both masculine and feminine dimensions of sex-role inventories appear more psychologically healthy and higher in self-esteem than those whose interests, attitudes, and skills are sex-typed (Block, 1973; O'Connor, Mann, & Bardwick, 1978; Spence, Helmreich, & Stapp, 1975). Therefore, some behaviorists have recommended that the ideal target repertoires for skill training comprise androgynous behaviors (Nordyke *et al.*, 1977; Winkler, 1977). This is consistent with Kessler and Albee's proposal (1975) to make the behavior of resistant, immune, or socially competent people the goal of primary prevention. There is disagreement about the comparability of findings across sex-role inventories (Gaudreau, 1977; Kelly, Furman, & Young, 1978). It is unclear what behavior distinguishes those who describe themselves as androgynous from those who describe themselves as sex-typed (Worrel, 1978). Do ordinarily intelligent people describe themselves as androgynous when this is what the situation demands? More information is needed before androgyny can be accepted as a criterion for construction of skill-training repertoires.

The best criterion for construction of skill-training repertoires for women may be effectiveness. Women tennis stars are closely observed on television, their gestures mimicked by avid players, simply because the stars' behavior has proved effective. To employ an effectiveness criterion, applied researchers must isolate the behavior that distinguishes women with specific skills and general competencies. There are 38.8 million women in the labor force in the United States (Hoffman, 1977); the population of single-mother households is rising; 62% of single mothers of preschool children work (Hoffman & Nye, 1974); and, by all accounts, working married women will continue to have the major responsibility for childrearing. So it is imperative that we learn how it is that some women succeed at rearing children alone, rise in male-dominated occupations, or succeed in childrearing, marriage, and an occupation.

A skill-training repertoire, no matter how it has been constructed, cannot ensure that all women exposed to it will derive equal benefit. Two types of evidence must be routinely collected about the specific short-term effects of skill training: that the woman has mastered the repertoire she was taught and, more important, that the woman's control over important consequences has increased. It is no success for a woman to be trained in a standard repertoire of assertive behavior and then lose her job rather than be promoted; to be trained in eating behavior but not lose weight or keep it off; or to be trained in smoking self-control but not quit smoking. Skill training should result in demonstrable competence in specific areas of deficiency (DeGiovanni & Epstein, 1978; Galassi, 1978; Heimberg, Montgomery, Madsen, & Heimberg, 1977).

Many popular applications of skill training neglect behavior measurement during and after intervention and rely entirely upon a standard training repertoire uniformly administered to all women. Assertiveness training is a case in point (Galassi, 1978; Phillips, 1978). One widely marketed assertiveness-training program for women, when evaluated, was found thoroughly ineffective (Kwiterovich & Horan, 1977). At some point during the dissemination of skill training, the training repertoire and procedures may be adopted while the measurement procedures are abandoned. But without objective behavior measurement during intervention, neither the practitioner nor the client knows what progress has been made and what component of intervention was responsible for progress. Without objective measurement, a procedure directly contributing to the success of intervention may be missing.

When applied researchers develop and evaluate skill-training procedures, they should strive to make measurement as attractive to practitioners as the skill-training repertoire. When public health officials communicate to potential women consumers of skill training, they should inform them of the importance of objective measurement and encourage them to inquire how outcome will be evaluated and how intervention will be fine tuned to accomodate objective data. More than most women realize, the technology of behavior measurement can reduce their reliance upon the mystifying advice of experts.

The Single-Case Design

Single-case designs have considerable scientific value (Baer, 1977), since they provide information about the effectiveness of treatment procedures with small numbers of subjects. Intervention with rare disorders can be studied, since each case is treated as a complete experiment. Standard treatment procedures can be evaluated with allowance for the differing rates of progress of individual clients. Long-term follow-up can then focus on the vicissitudes of maintenance in a group of clients who were equally improved at the end of treatment. Because of this flexibility, a shift away from group-comparison designs toward single-case designs has been advocated for the evaluation of treatment of obesity (Jeffery *et al.*, 1978; Wilson, 1978), smoking (DeRicco, Brigham, & Garlington, 1977), and family conflict (Humphreys, Forehand, McMahon, & Roberts, 1978).

Traditional treatment approaches have been criticized for offering standard remedies that ignore individual differences between women and for producing change that is short-lived and superficial. The technology of single-case designs (Hersen & Barlow, 1976) provides a way to adjust skill training to suit the progress of the individual woman and to ensure short-term effectiveness. These designs also provide an "implicit technology of generalization" (Stokes & Baer, 1977), allowing intervention to simultaneously aim for specific short-term results and their generalization over time, settings, and response classes.

A modified-reversal design guided the treatment of a bulimic anorexic woman who frequently overate, induced vomiting, and took large doses of laxatives (Monti *et al.*, 1977). Caloric intake, weight, and vomiting were continuously monitored. In the hospital, an intervention phase of reinforcement for caloric intake and weight gain alternated with a phase of reinforcement plus feedback about intake until it was clear that information and reinforcement together increased appropriate intake. Later phases added contingency contracting and systematic desensitization to thoughts that she was a "bad person." There was successful maintenance over a 6-month follow-up period. The methods employed in this case could be employed by the practitioner who wants to improve service to women clients. Visual inspection of continuous data was used to compare the effectiveness of each intervention phase with others. Phases were alternated to ensure that reinforcement plus information (rather than some adventitious event) caused improvement.

Unfortunately, single-case designs are not always used to further the effective treatment of the individual woman. In one study, three psychiatric patients were trained in social skills (Marzillier & Winter, 1978). The two male patients improved but not the female, who "found the sessions very stressful particularly as they involved role playing, videotaped recording, and contact with two male therapists" and declined further treatment. A phase which lacked these noxious ingredients could have been added, withdrawn, and then reinstated. Such a design might have provided generally useful information about social-skills training and contributed to successful treatment of the woman client.

Single-case designs are not widely used by practitioners, nor are they familiar to most women consumers of mental health services. Before dissemination of this empirically based approach to treatment can be urged, more information about side effects is needed. Women's self-esteem and sense of personal control may increase when objective data about their own behavior, rather than abstract theories of human functioning, are used to plan treatment. Practitioners may experience similar attitudinal benefits. But these by-products of clinical use of single-case designs remain to be documented.

Training for Generalization over Time, Settings, and Responses

With increasing evidence of the short-term specific effectiveness of skill-training procedures for women, attention has turned to generalization. Maintenance of effects over time, generalization of specific effects over settings and response classes, and the spread of effects over people within the same social ecology are being evaluated. There is encouraging evidence of 6–12 months' maintenance of weight gain by anorexic women (Hauserman & Lavin, 1977; Kellerman, 1977), weight loss by obese women (Ashby & Wilson, 1977), cessation of smoking (Lando, 1977; Lichtenstein & Rodrigues, 1977), reduction in women's migraine headaches (Gainer, 1978), reduction in female sexual dysfunction (Nemetz, Craig, & Reith, 1978), subsiding of a woman's ulcerative colitis (Susen, 1978), and increase in marital adjustment (Jacobson, 1977). Still, the concern for maintenance in women's skill training is not as widespread as it should be. Once again, assertiveness training provides an example. A review of assertiveness-training research reported that 55% of the studies collected no follow-up data and 26% had followed clients for only 1 month (Heimberg *et al.,* 1977). Popular applications of skill training to women probably collect equally little or even fewer follow-up data.

Train and hope (Stokes & Baer, 1977) is surely the most popular approach to maintenance. The collection of follow-up data 6 months or 1 year after treatment ends is little solace to the clients whose improved functioning does not persist. A more cautious approach to maintenance is the booster treatment—small doses of training administered after successful treatment ends. Boosters have not contributed to maintenance of weight loss by obese women (Ashby & Wilson, 1977; Kingsley & Wilson, 1977), smoking cessation (Elliott & Denney, 1978; Relinger, Bornstein, Bugge, Carmody, & Zohn, 1977), or women's fear reduction (Lineham, Rosenthal, Kelley, & Theobald, 1977).

What seem to be needed are methods of programming maintenance during treatment. One way to do this is by gradually withdrawing cues unique to the training process. When follow-up begins, the new skill has already been rehearsed in the natural setting away from all training cues. Elderly socially isolated women were first trained as foster grandmother–tutors for severely handicapped children (Fabry & Reid, 1978). Over the next 11 weeks, the teacher gradually diminished the time she spent with the women. But the women's tutoring behavior did not change for the 11 weeks and for 4 follow-up weeks. Had there been some deterioration, the teacher might have reappeared briefly. In this approach to maintenance, helpers plan their own obsolescence. This method of reducing women's dependence upon experts deserves wider application and evaluation.

Maintenance can also be programmed by tapping dormant natural contingencies (Seymour & Stokes, 1976; Stokes & Baer, 1977). For women, this is often accomplished by training husbands to prompt and reinforce desirable behavior in their wives. This solution works best for women with cooperative husbands. Agoraphobic women were treated with a program carried out by the woman and her husband at home; the program worked least well for couples most dissatisfied with their marriages (Mathews, Teasdale, Munby, Johnston, & Shaw, 1977). Obese men and women with cooperative spouses were randomly assigned to couples' weight-loss training or solo training. Those with uncooperative spouses received solo training (Brownell, Heckerman, Westlake, Hayes, & Monti, 1978). At 3- and 6-month follow-up, dieters with cooperative spouses had lost the most weight, 30% during the follow-up period.

Agoraphobic women tend to be helpless and stereotypically feminine, relying for guidance first upon parents and later upon husbands (Fodor, 1974). Following successful treatment of agoraphobic behavior, women's tendency to depend upon others for help might increase if maintenance of their newly found freedom requires their husbands' intervention. Husbands could be involved right after successful treatment to ensure early maintenance of the new skills; later, their involvement could taper off as their wives show increasing success at being on their own away from home. Although this approach to maintenance has obvious advantages for the agoraphobic woman, it still might damage the marital relationship. Negative effects on the woman's other skill repertoires and on the family ecology might be anticipated whenever a husband is involved in programming the maintenance of his wife's newly acquired skills.

Generalization over Settings and Response Classes

Cultural stereotypes prompt women to act inconsistently across settings and people: to be efficient and assertive at work, maternal and subdued at home, and outgoing and attractive at social gatherings. Pressures toward inconsistency affect women more than men. Consider the number of advertisements promoting the virture of products such as perfume and dual-purpose clothing which ostensibly ease the woman's transition from home to office to evening entertainment.

The compartmentalization to which women are acculturated has unfortunate yet rarely considered implications. Maintenance of a newly learned skill over time—the hallmark of successful treatment—often depends upon generalization of the skill over settings and response classes. But for women, the latter two types of generalization are unlikely to be automatic products of successful treatment.

Generalization of a skill over settings is often measured by analogue tests designed to duplicate natural settings. Because analogue tests of fearfulness and social skills may be less representative of women's social environment than is usually assumed (Bellack *et al.*, 1978; Lick & Unger, 1977), external validity checks should be as routine as interrater reliability checks. Regional differences in women's lifestyles and shifts in attitudes toward women over time restrict the external validity of the most carefully developed analogue test. It may be less costly to sample women's behavior in several natural settings than to constantly recalibrate analogue behavior tests.

Since the culture may limit women's free generalization of new skills across settings, and since maintenance over time after therapy is probably a function of generalization over settings during therapy (Koegel & Rincover, 1977), more effort should be directed at evaluating and programming setting generalization during treatment. The result may be resolution of the dilemma of maintenance which confronts most areas of behavior change with women.

An obvious but logistically difficult way to promote setting generalization is by exposing the client to a generous sample of natural situations during training (Stokes & Baer, 1977). If the therapist is able to reproduce salient features of critical situations, the client can be exposed to imagined rather than real situations, and major logistic problems can be avoided. A procedure called flooding relief (Hayes & Barlow, 1977) used imagined scenes to reduce fears and teach assertive interpersonal behavior to a facially disfigured woman hospitalized for depression. Because of strangers' shocked reactions to her appearance, she had avoided public transportation and was housebound for 7 years. The therapist described aversive encounters with strangers to the client; she could sometimes escape and sometimes avoid hearing these descriptions by making forthright statements that fit the situation. The woman was soon riding buses and maintained her progress to a 6-month follow-up.

In the wake of the cognitive revolution, behaviorists are freely exploring the practical implications of links between thought, speech, and motor behavior. During World War II, social psychologists attempted to change citizenship behavior by influencing patriotic attitudes. Now, cognitively oriented behavior therapists aim to change maladaptive behavior by influencing irrational attitudes, assuming that attitude change will heighten generalization across settings and response classes. The feminist movement emphasizes the unconscious irrational ideologies which many women harbor and which restrict them. Attempts to change women clients' attitudes and the hope that attitude change will lead to general behavior change are consistent with the feminist analysis.

Attempts to influence women's attitudes do not always lead to behavior change or generalization. Unassertive women outpatients were assigned to either modeling plus behavior rehearsal, modeling plus behavior rehearsal plus rational therapy, consciousness-raising, or an untreated waiting list (Wolfe & Fodor, 1977). Women in the first condition observed and rehearsed assertive behavior in intimidating situations; those in the second condition did this and discussed irrational beliefs about assertiveness. The first two groups of women improved equally and significantly more than the others in their performance in familiar and novel situations. Agoraphobic women appear to have prototypically feminine attitudes (Fodor, 1974). Yet agoraphobic clients' behavior and attitudes benefited more from *in vivo* exposure to frightening situations than from cognitive restructuring (Emmelkamp, Kuipers, & Eggeraat, 1978). Mothers in a workshop for child-behavior-modification training received either didactic pretraining, placebo pretraining, or no pretraining (O'Dell, Flynn, & Benlolo, 1977). Mothers who received no pretraining improved most in skills and attitudes.

New attitudes can be expected to lead to new behavior when the woman knows how to perform the desired behavior but does not do so because of inhibiting circumstances (Bandura, 1977b). O'Dell and his colleagues (1977) reasoned that the mothers they trained did not know how to respond to children. Those who received no pretraining did best because they spent all their time at home rehearsing their new skills; mothers who received pretraining improved less because they divided their time between theorizing about what to do and rehearsal.

When a woman behaves confidently at home and timidly elsewhere, it may seem reasonable to conclude that she knows how to act assertively everywhere but does not do so because of some irrational self-defeating attitude. The best way to help her would appear to be through attitude change. In fact, conditions unique to women's experience prevent them from learning how to act competently in some critical adult-life situations. Rape and assault by strangers, acquaintances, and kin are real threats to women of all ages and social strata. As a result, many otherwise adequate women fear being alone and with strangers, rely upon men for physical guardianship, and generally act helpless. The inconsistency of their behavior is not a product of irrational attitudes; it is a genuine skill deficiency. Attempts at attitude change might have two unfortunate results: The women might enter dangerous situations unprepared, or they might proclaim their fearlessness but continue to act timidly. In theory, changes in women's attitudes should change their behavior in familiar and novel situations. In practice, attitude change may have none of these desired effects, possibly because of the many external pressures on women to act inconsistently across situations. Admittedly, neither new attitudes nor new skills help women exposed to situations which are physically dangerous to enter and psychologically costly to avoid.

Those who stress the need to treat "the whole woman" indirectly suggest the importance of response generalization. Women who seek treatment for phobias, obesity, or family problems probably want general rather than specific improvement. Systematic desensitization of phobic imagery does not appear to produce general changes in physiology, behavior, and attitudes. Mathews (1971) concluded that systematic desensitization's most frequent result is lessened physiologic reactivity to phobic stimuli, followed somewhat later by less fearful self-reported attitudes to those stimuli. This conclusion is corroborated by a recent investigation which found that neither systematic desensitization nor its components changed socially anxious women's interpersonal behavior or self-reports, but imaginal exposure of any kind significantly decreased their observable anxiety (O'Brien & Borkovec, 1977). Wilson (1978) has called for an evaluation of the effects of obese women's weight loss on self-esteem and interpersonal relationships. To date, no one seems to have questioned the general effects for women of successful parent training.

Response generalization is equally important in the treatment of men and women: Its general principles undoubtedly do not differ between the sexes. Even so, sex influences the prevailing social environment. For example, the relationship between physical prowess and heterosexual behavior is different for women and men. Magazine ads tell us that a man's success at dating and mating will grow when he learns to defend himself against bullies who kick sand in his face at the beach. How is a woman's popularity with men affected when she becomes expert at self-defense? It is conceivable that her relationships with men might suffer. Skill training aimed at increasing a woman's physical self-confidence and eliminating her irrational fears of assault must anticipate some negative side effects. It is advisable to measure changes in the woman's heterosexual behavior and to plan what to do if deficits emerge as training progresses. With male clients, such precautions, although admirable, seem less necessary.

Because of sex differences in social customs, some interventions may have better specific and general effects on one sex than on another. Some cultural differences give women an advantage in treatment. Anorgasmic women were randomly assigned to individual or group treatment or to an untreated control group (Nemetz et al., 1978). Treatment combined relaxation training, filmed vignettes depicting female sexual approach behavior, and homework assignments with a male partner. Whether treated individually or in groups, clients showed specific and general improvement in sexual anxiety, behavior, and attitudes after treatment and 1 year later; but women treated in groups improved somewhat more than those treated individually. The treatment used in this study appears suitable for men with sexual dysfunction, and the group treatment has the advantage of being economical. Still, it would be unwise to ignore the possible interaction between sex and treatment outcome. Men might benefit less from group than from individual treatment because they tend to embellish accounts of their sexual activities to other men and to fear sexual arousal in the presence of other men.

Skill Training as a Replacement for Drug Treatment of Women

Women receive a disproportionate amount of drug prescriptions for emotional and physical complaints (Fidell, Note 1). Depressed women outpatients received more psychotherapy sessions and higher doses of medication than otherwise indistinguishable male counterparts (Stein, DelGaudio, & Ansley, 1976). The drugs in question have documented tolerance, carryover, and rebound effects (Morris & Beck, 1974; Ribordy & Denney, 1977; Sharpless, 1965). A good number of women may be caught in a vicious cycle: The initial course of medication interferes with general functioning, the woman and her physician attribute this to the original complaint, and the dosage is increased. The woman is now convinced that she can function only with the help of medication.

In fact, medication usually is superior to nonspecific therapy. A casework approach was compared to amitriptyline; the latter alone was as potent as the two together (Klerman, DeMascio, Weissman, Prusoff, & Paykel, 1974). No advantage was found for group psychotherapy over imipramine plus brief psychiatric contact (Covi, Lipman, Derogatis, Smith, & Pattison, 1974). Amitriptyline was superior to marital therapy for the relief of symtoms in depressed women (Friedman, 1975). These studies are considered by many physicians and drug companies to be evidence of the superiority of drugs to any form of psychotherapy and of the biologic basis of such disorders as depression.

Examined more closely, studies finding medication superior to therapy have these attributes. The medication is known from previous empirical evidence to affect relevant symptoms; there is no similarly strong empirical evidence of the effectiveness of the comparison therapy. And so the study is a straw-man test of unequal contestants. Although the circumstances under which the medication is administered are highly standardized, the circumstances under which the therapy is administered are highly variable. The rules governing therapy's variability from patient to patient, or session to session, are not explicitly set out in a deskside reference manual. Thus, the study builds greater heterogeneity into the therapy group than into the drug group, increasing the likelihood that the latter will prove superior. Finally, the drug treatment proves superior in symptom relief, but no evidence is provided of persistence of change over time or of generalization over settings and responses. No evidence is provided that the woman has learned new skills and attitudes that reduce her dependence upon experts and immunize her from relapse.

Recent challenges of skill training to drug treatment of women have yielded encouraging findings. Prospective endoscopy patients were randomly assigned to view a videotape of the endoscopy procedure zero, one, or three times; those who viewed the tape three times showed less distress in heart rate, observer ratings, and self-report and required less diazepam prior to the procedure than the other two groups (Shipley, Butt, Horwitz, & Farbry, 1978). Obese women, 15% overweight or more, were randomly assigned to behavioral treatment (Stuart & Davis, 1972), the drug Fenfluramine, or a waiting-list control; at a 12-month follow-up, only the women in the first group weighed significantly less than they had at the start of treatment (Öst & Götestam, 1976). Severe adult insomniacs were randomly assigned to progressive relaxation training plus relaxation tape, placebo control, or no treatment. The first two groups significantly reduced their consumption of sleep-inducing medication (Lick & Heffler, 1977).

Hospitalized chronic organic and nonorganic low-back-pain patients who would not participate in physical therapy received contingent verbal reinforcement from a physical therapist for increases in measured activity, publicly displayed graphs of activity level, or contingent verbal reinforcement plus a graph; they demonstrated changes in pain-related behavior as a function of verbal reinforcement and feedback, alone and together (Cairns & Pasino, 1977). Training in the control of blood volume, pulse, and frontalis muscle action potential reduced combined migraine–muscle tension headaches (Sturgis, Tollison, & Adams, 1978).

Case studies have described the reduction of pain medication dependence in a migraine headache sufferer given temperature discrimination training (Gainer, 1978), a pregnant woman with essential hypertension given anxiety management training (Bloom & Cantrell, 1978), and an elderly woman with chronic eczematous dermatitis given hand-warming training (Manuso, 1977). In a related example, a woman with ulcerative colitis recovered after conditioned relaxation training for the abdominal area (Susen, 1978).

Drug/skill training comparisions could well be undertaken for the many problems women have that are routinely treated with drugs. Wilson (1978) suggested such a comparison for obesity. It seems needed as well for depression, anxiety, and the affective changes that may accompany childbirth, menstruation, and menopause. Such drug/skill training comparisons should administer both treatments under optimal conditions, with an expert in each field validating the procedure during its administration. Multiple-baseline designs with small numbers of subjects can tease out response-specific and situation-specific drug effects and skill-training effects (Shafts & Sulzbacher, 1977; Wulbert & Dries, 1977), as can group-comparison designs with larger samples.

When such comparisons reveal that the best regimen is both drugs and skill training, the opportunity should be seized to refine the skill-training intervention rather than resort to a biochemical explanation of skill training's partial success.

Recommendations

Behavioral interventions with women can produce social systems change, equitable treatment of women and men, and effective mental health services for individual women clients. To promote these aims, I have recommended principles for the conduct of behavior modification with women.

To avoid the sex bias that permeates popular methods of assessing women's behavior, the following recommendations were made for behavioral assessment.

1. A thorough functional analysis of behavior should be conducted to determine what conditions control problem behavior and to select an intervention strategy.
2. Quantitative observational ratings and repeated measurement of behavior in different natural settings should be used for the initial assessment of client needs and for subsequent evaluation of intervention.
3. The decision that a problem is caused by deficits in the woman rather than in the environment must be made cautiously, since environmental defects are frequently ignored.

Although these recommendations are consistent with recent developments in behavior assessment technology, neither social nor economic incentives encourage practitioners to comply with these recommendations. Objective sex-fair methods of assessing women's behavior and social policy changes leading to adoption of the resulting technology are both needed.

To avoid treatment which merely suppresses the woman's complaint and perpetuates environments harmful to women, the following recommendations were made for skill training.

1. Goals for skill training should be chosen which are likely to remediate the presenting problem and increase the woman's control over her behavior and environment.

2. Target behaviors should be selected for skill training which help women achieve desired consequences. More information is needed about the behavior of successful women and about the characteristics of work, home, and school settings which promote competent female behavior.

3. The success of skill training depends upon its specific and general effects. The specific target skill must be mastered, and it must survive for a considerable time after training ends. At the least, the newly acquired skill should not harm the client's functioning or disrupt her interpersonal relationships. At best, the newly acquired skill should generalize to novel settings and response classes and improve the client's social ecology. The technology of single-case designs could be used by practitioners to assess specific and general effects and to anticipate the need for generalization during training. Information about the attitudinal by-products of clinical use of single-case technology and social and economic incentives leading to use of this technology are both needed.

4. Maintenance of new skills over time, a characteristic of successful intervention, often requires generalization over novel settings and responses. Efforts to program maintenance during training cannot ignore the need for generalization. Inferences about generalization cannot be drawn from clinical research with men, since social conditions encourage women to behave inconsistently across settings and interfere with generalization and maintenance. The attribution of inconsistency across situations to irrational attitudes must be made cautiously; social conditions promote inconsistency in women and mask genuine skill deficits. Some skill deficits result from conditions which are insurmountable by the individual woman and require widespread social change rather than skill training of individual women. To design skill-training procedures which yield specific and general benefits, more information is needed about the relationship between different classes of women's behavior and about the effects of sex-linked social customs on treatment outcomes.

The guidelines for behavior modification with women recommended in this chapter are intended to move the discipline away from technological fix and toward social systems change. For their emotional and behavioral complaints, most women receive drug treatment, the prototypic technological fix. To treat these complaints, skill-training procedures which are as economical and easily disseminated as drugs must be developed.

ACKNOWLEDGMENT

Preparation of this chapter was supported in part by NIMH grant 31403 to the author.

Reference Note

1. Fidell, L. S. *Put her down on drugs: Prescribed drug usage in women.* Paper presented at the meeting of the Western Psychological Association, Anaheim, Cal., May 1973.

References

Adams, M., Ferguson, J., Stunkard, A. J., & Agras, S. The eating behavior of obese and nonobese women. *Behaviour Research and Therapy*, 1978, *16*, 225-232.

Ashby, W. A., & Wilson, G. T. Behavior therapy for obesity: Booster sessions and long-term maintenance of weight loss. *Behaviour Research and Therapy*, 1977, *15*, 451-463.

Baer, D. M. "Perhaps it would be better not to know everything." *Journal of Applied Behavior Analysis*, 1977, *10*, 167-172.

Bandura, A. Social-learning theory of identificatory processes. In D. A. Goslin (Ed.), *Handbook of socialization theory and research.* Chicago: Rand McNally, 1969.

Bandura, A. *Social-learning theory.* Englewood Cliffs, N.J.: Prentice-Hall, 1977. (a)

Bandura, A. Self-efficacy: Toward a unifying theory of behavioral change. *Psychological Review*, 1977,*84*, 191-215. (b)

Bandura, A., & Walters, R. H. *Social learning and personality development.* New York: Holt, Rinehart, and Winston, 1963.

Barlow, D. H., Abel, G. G., Blanchard, E. B., Bristow, A. R., & Young, L. D. A heterosocial skills behavior checklist for males. *Behavior Therapy*, 1977, *8*, 229-239.

Bellack, A. S., Hersen, M., & Turner, S. M. Role-play tests for assessing social skills: Are they valid? *Behavior Therapy*, 1978, *9*, 448-461.

Bemis, K. M. Current approaches to the etiology and treatment of anorexia nervosa. *Psychological Bulletin*, 1978, *85*, 593-617.

Birchler, G. R., & Webb, L. M. Discriminating interaction behaviors in happy and unhappy marriages. *Journal of Consulting and Clinical Psychology*, 1977, *45*, 494-495.

Block, J. H. Conceptions of sex roles. *American Psychologist*, 1973, *28*, 512-526.

Bloom, L. J., & Cantrell, D. Anxiety management training for essential hypertension in pregnancy. *Behavior Therapy*, 1978, *9*, 377-382.

Brockway, B. S., Kleinmann, G., Edelsen, J., & Grunewald, K. Non-aversive procedures and their effect on cigarette smoking. *Addictive Behaviors*, 1977, *2*, 121-128.

Bronfenbrenner, U. Freudian theories of identification and their derivatives. *Child Development*, 1960, *31*, 15-40.

Broverman, I. K., Broverman, D. M., Clarkson, F. E., Rosenkrantz, P., & Vogel, S. R. Sex-role stereotypes and clinical judgments of mental health. *Journal of Consulting and Clinical Psychology*, 1970,*34*, 1-7.

Brownell, K. D., Heckerman, C. L., Westlake, R. J., Hayes, S. C., & Monti, P. M. *Behaviour Research and Therapy*, 1978, *16*, 323-334.

Bruch, H. Perils of behavior modification in the treatment of anorexia nervosa. *Journal of the American Medical Association,* 1974, *230,* 1419–1422.

Burton, R., & Whiting, J. M. The absent father and cross-sex identity. *Merrill-Palmer Quarterly,* 1961, *7,* 85–97.

Cairns, D., & Pasino, J. A. Comparison of verbal reinforcement and feedback in the operant treatment of disability due to chronic low back pain. *Behavior Therapy,* 1977, *8,* 621–631.

Chesler, P. Women as psychiatric patients and psychotherapeutic patients. *Journal of Marriage and the Family,* 1971, *33,* 746–759.

Chesler, P. *Women and madness.* New York: Avon, 1972.

Coates, T. J. Theory, research, and practice in treating obesity: Are they really all the same? *Addictive Behaviors,* 1977, *2,* 95–103.

Covi, L., Lipman, R. S., Derogatis, L. R., Smith, J. E., & Pattison, J. H. Drugs and group psychotherapy in neurotic depression. *American Journal of Psychiatry,* 1974, *131,* 191–197.

DeGiovanni, I. S., & Epstein, N. Unbinding assertion and aggression in research and clinical practice. *Behavior Modification,* 1978, *2,* 173–192.

Depue, R. A., & Monroe, S. M. Learned helplessness in the perspective of the depressive disorders: Conceptual and definitional issues. *Journal of Abnormal Psychology,* 1978, *87,* 3–20.

DeRicco, D. A., Brigham, T. A., & Garlington, W. K. Development and evaluation of treatment paradigms for the suppression of smoking. *Journal of Applied Behavior Analysis,* 1977, *10,* 173–181.

Elliott, C. H., & Denney, D. R. A multiple component treatment approach to smoking reduction. *Journal of Consulting and Clinical Psychology,* 1978, *46,* 1330–1339.

Emmelkamp, P. M. G., Kuipers, A. C. M., & Eggeraat, J. B. Cognitive modification versus prolonged exposure *in vivo:* A comparison with agoraphobics as subjects. *Behaviour Research and Therapy,* 1978, *16,* 33–42.

Etaugh, C., & Brown, B. Perceiving the causes of success and failure of male and female performances. *Developmental Psychology,* 1975, *11,* 103.

Fabry, P. L., & Reid, D. H. Teaching foster grandparents to train severely handicapped persons. *Journal of Applied Behavior Analysis,* 1978, *11,* 111–123.

Fenichel, O. *The collected papers of Otto Fenichel.* New York: Norton, 1953.

Fodor, I. G. The phobic syndrome in women. In V. Franks & V. Burtle (Eds.), *Women in therapy.* New York: Brunner/Mazel, 1974.

Forehand, R. E., & Wells, K. C. Teachers and parents: Where have all the "good" contingency managers gone? *Behavior Therapy,* 1977, *8,* 1010.

Friedman, A. S. Interaction of drug therapy with marital therapy in depressed patients. *Archives of General Psychiatry,* 1975, *32,* 619–637.

Freud, S. Group psychology and the analysis of the ego. In J. Strachey (Ed.), *Standard edition of the complete psychological works of Sigmund Freud* (Vol 18). London: Hogarth, 1955. (Orginally published, 1921.)

Freud, S. The ego and the id. In J. Strachey (Ed.), *Standard edition of the complete psychological works of Sigmund Freud* (Vol. 19). London: Hogarth, 1961.(a) (Originally published, 1923.)

Freud, S. Some psychical consequences of the anatomical distinction between the sexes. In J. Strachey (Ed.), *Standard edition of the complete psychological works of Sigmund Freud* (Vol. 19). London: Hogarth, 1961(b). (Originally published, 1925.)

Freud, S. A case of paranoia running counter to the psychoanalytic theory of the disease. In J. Strachey (Ed.), *Standard edition of the complete psychological works of Sigmund Freud* (Vol. 14). London: Hogarth, 1962. (Orignally published, 1915.)

Gainer, J. C. Temperature discrimination training in the biofeedback treatment of migraine headache. *Journal of Behavior Therapy and Experimental Psychiatry,* 1978, *9,* 185–188.

Galassi, J. P. Review of *Achieving assertive behavior: A guide to assertive training* by H. H. Dawley, Jr. & W. W. Weinrich. *Behavior Therapy,* 1978, *9,* 132–133.

Gaudreau, P. Factor analysis of the Bem sex-role inventory. *Journal of Consulting and Clinical Psychology,* 1977, *45,* 299–302.

Gewirtz, J. L. Mechanisms of social learning: Some roles of stimulation and behavior in early development. In D. A. Goslin (Ed.), *Handbook of socialization theory and research.* Chicago: Rand McNally, 1969.

Gewirtz, J. L., & Stingle, K. G. Learning of generalized imitation as the basis for identification. *Psychological Review,* 1968, *75,* 374–397.

Gilman, C. P. *Herland.* New York: Pantheon Books, 1979.

Goldiamond, I. The professional as double agent. *Journal of Applied Behavior Analysis,* 1978, *11,* 178–184.

Goldstein, A. J., & Chambless, D. L. A reanalysis of agoraphobia. *Behavior Therapy,* 1978, *9,* 47–59.

Hammen, C. L., & Peters, S. D. Differential responses to male and female depressive reactions. *Journal of Consulting and Clinical Psychology,* 1977, *45,* 994–1001.

Hauserman, N., & Lavin, P. Post-hospitalization continuation treatment of anorexia nervosa. *Journal of Behavior Therapy and Experimental Psychiatry,* 1977, *8,* 309–314.

Hayes, S. C., & Barlow, D. H. Flooding relief in a case of public transportation phobia. *Behavior Therapy,* 1977, *8,* 742–746.

Heimberg, R. G., Montgomery, D., Madsen, C. H., Jr., & Heimberg, J. S. Assertion training: A review of the literature. *Behavior Therapy,* 1977, *8,* 953–971.

Hersen, M., & Barlow, D. H. *Single-case experimental designs: Strategies for studying experimental change.* New York: Pergamon, 1976.

Hersen, M., Bellack, A. S., & Turner, S. M. Assessment of assertiveness in female psychiatric patients: Motor and autonomic measures. *Journal of Behavior Therapy and Experimental Psychiatry,* 1978, *9,* 11–16.

Hoffman, L. W. Changes in family roles, socialization and sex differences. *American Psychologist,* 1977, *32,* 644–657.

Hoffman, L. W., & Nye, F. I. *Working mothers.* San Francisco: Jossey Bass, 1974.

Holland, J. G. Behaviorism: Part of the problem or part of the solution? *Journal of Applied Behavior Analysis,* 1978, *11,* 163–174.

Hollandsworth, J. G., Jr., Glazeski, R. C., & Dressel, M. E. Use of social-skills training in the treatment of extreme anxiety and deficient verbal skills in the job-interview setting. *Journal of Applied Behavior Analysis,* 1978, *11,* 259–269.

Humphreys, L., Forehand, R., McMahon, R., & Roberts, M. Parent behavioral training to modify child non-compliance: Effects on untreated siblings. *Journal of Behavior Therapy and Experimental Psychiatry,* 1978, *9,* 235–238.

Jacobson, N. S. Problem solving and contingency contracting in the treatment of marital discord. *Journal of Consulting and Clinical Psychology,* 1977, *45,* 92–100.

Jahoda, M. *Freud and the dilemmas of psychology.* New York: Basic Books, 1977.

Jeffery, R. W., Wing, R. R., & Stunkard, A. J. Behavioral treatment of obesity: The state of the art 1976. *Behavior Therapy,* 1978, *9,* 189–199.

Jones, W. H., Chernovetz, M. E. O'C., & Hansson, R. O. The enigma of androgyny: Differential implications for male and female? *Journal of Consulting and Clinical Psychology,* 1978, *46,* 298–313.

Kagan, J. The concept of identification. *Psychological Review,* 1958, *65,* 296–305.

Kanfer, F. H., & Grimm, L. G. Freedom of choice and behavioral change. *Journal of Consulting and Clinical Psychology,* 1978, *46,* 873–878.

Kellerman, J. Anorexia nervosa: The efficacy of behavior therapy. *Journal of Behavior Therapy and Experimental Psychiatry,* 1977, *8,* 387–390.

Kelly, J. A., Furman, W., & Young, V. Problems associated with the typological measurement of sex roles and androgyny. *Journal of Consulting and Clinical Psychology,* 1978, *46,* 1574–1576.

Kent, R. M., O'Leary, K. D., Diament, C., & Dietz, A. Expectation biases in observational evaluation of therapeutic change. *Journal of Consulting and Clinical Psychology,* 1974, *42,* 774–780.

Kessler, M., & Albee, G. W. Primary prevention. In M. R. Rosenzweig & L. W. Porter (Eds.), *Annual review of psychology* (Vol. 26). Palo Alto, Cal.: Annual Reviews, 1975.

Kingsley, R. G., & Wilson, G. T. Behavior therapy for obesity: A comparative investigation of long-term efficacy. *Journal of Consulting and Clinical Psychology,* 1977, *45,* 288–298.

Klerman, G., DiMascio, A., Weissman, M., Prusoff, B., & Paykel, E. Treatment of depression by drugs and psychotherapy. *American Journal of Psychiatry,* 1974, *131,* 186–191.

Koegel, R. L., & Rincover, A. Research on the difference between generalization and maintenance in extra-therapy responding. *Journal of Applied Behavior Analysis,* 1977, *10,* 1–12.

Kwiterovich, D. K., & Horan, J. J. Solomon evaluation of a commercial assertiveness program for women. *Behavior Therapy,* 1977, *8,* 501–502.

Lando, H. A. Successful treatment of smokers with a broad-spectrum behavioral approach. *Journal of Consulting and Clinical Psychology,* 1977, *45,* 361–366.

LaTorre, R. A., & Piper, W. E. Gender identity and gender role in schizophrenia. *Journal of Abnormal Psychology,* 1979, *88,* 68–72.

Lichtenstein, E., & Rodrigues, M. P. Long-term effects of rapid smoking treatment for dependent cigarette smokers. *Addictive Behaviors,* 1977, *2,* 109–112.

Lick, J. R., & Heffler, D. Relaxation training and attention placebo in the treatment of severe insomnia. *Journal of Consulting and Clinical Psychology,* 1977, *45,* 153–161.

Lick, J. R., & Unger, T. E. The external validity of behavioral fear assessment. *Behavior Modification,* 1977, *1,* 283–306.

Lineham, K. S., Rosenthal, T. L., Kelley, J. E., & Theobald, D. E. E. Homogeneity and heterogeneity of problem class in modeling treatment of fears. *Behaviour Research and Therapy,* 1977, *15,* 211–216.

Maccoby, E. Sex differences in intellectual functioning. In E. Maccoby (Ed.), *The development of sex differences.* Stanford, Cal.: Stanford University Press, 1966.

Maccoby, E. E., & Jacklin, C. N. *The psychology of sex differences.* Stanford, Cal.: Stanford University Press, 1974.

Mahoney, M. J. *Cognition and behavior modification.* Cambridge: Ballinger, 1974.

Manuso, J. S. J. The use of biofeedback-assisted hand-warming training in the treatment of chronic eczematous dermatitis: A case study. *Journal of Behavior Therapy and Experimental Psychiatry,* 1977, *8,* 445–446.

Margolin, G. Relationship among marital assessment procedures. *Journal of Consulting and Cinical Psychology,* 1978, *46,* 1556–1558.

Marzillier, J. S., & Winter, R. Success and failure in social skills training: Individual differences. *Behaviour Research and Therapy,* 1978, *16,* 67–84.

Matson, J. L., & Stephens, R. M. Increasing appropriate behavior of explosive chronic psychiatric patients with a social-skills training package. *Behavior Modification,* 1978, *2,* 61–76.

Mathews, A. M. Psychophysiological responses to the investigations of desensitization and related procedures. *Psychological Bulletin,* 1971, *76,* 73–91.

Mathews, A., Teasdale, J., Munby, M., Johnston, D., & Shaw, P. A home treatment program for agoraphobia. *Behavior Therapy,* 1977, *8,* 915–924.

Meehl, P. E. The cognitive activity of the clinician. *American Psychologist,* 1960, *15,* 19–27.

Meichenbaum, D. Cognitive factors in behavior modification: Modifying what clients say to themselves. In C. M. Franks & G. T. Wilson (Eds.), *Annual review of behavior therapy theory and practice* (Vol. 1). New York: Brunner/Mazel, 1973.

Miller, N. E., & Dollard, J. *Social learning and imitation.* New Haven: Yale University, 1941.

Mischel, W. A social-learning view of sex differences in behavior. In E. Maccoby (Ed.), *The development of sex differences.* Stanford, Cal.: Stanford University Press, 1966.

Mischel, W. Sex-typing and socialization. In P. H. Mussen (Ed.), *Carmichael's manual of child psychology* (Vol. 2). New York: Wiley, 1970.

Mischel, W. Toward a cognitive social learning reconceptualization of personality. *Psychological Review,* 1973, *80,* 252–283.

Mishara, B. L. Geriatric patients who improve in token economy and general milieu treatment programs: A multivariate analysis. *Journal of Consulting and Clinical Psychology,* 1978, *46,* 1340–1348.

Monahan, L., Kuhn, D., & Shaver, P. Intrapsychic versus cultural explanations of the "fear of success" motive. *Journal of Personality and Social Psychology,* 1974, *29,* 60–64.

Monti, P. M., McCrady, B. S., & Barlow, D. H. Effect of positive reinforcement, informational feedback, and contingency contracting on a bulimic anorexic female. *Behavior Therapy,* 1977, *8,* 258–263.

Morris, J. B., & Beck, A. T. The efficacy of anti-depressant drugs: A review of research (1958–1972). *Archives of General Psychiatry,* 1974, *30,* 667–674.

Nemetz, G. H., Craig, K. D., & Reith, G. Treatment of female sexual dysfunction through symbolic modeling. *Journal of Consulting and Clinical Psychology,* 1978, *46,* 62–73.

Nisbett, R. E., & Wilson, T. D. Telling more than we can know: Verbal reports on mental processes. *Psychological Review,* 1977, *84,* 231–259.

Nordyke, N. S., Baer, D. M., Etzel, B. C., & LeBlanc, J. Implications of the stereotyping and modification of sex role. *Journal of Applied Behavior Analysis,* 1977, *10,* 553–557.

O'Brien, G. T., & Borkovec, T. D. The role of relaxation in systematic desensitization: Revisiting an unresolved issue. *Journal of Behavior Therapy and Experimental Psychiatry,* 1977, *8,* 359–364.

O'Connor, K. O., Mann, D. W., & Bardwick, J. M. Androgyny and self-esteem in the upper-middle class: A replication of Spence. *Journal of Consulting and Clinical Psychology,* 1978, *46,* 1168–1169.

O'Dell, S., Flynn, J., & Benlolo, L. A comparison of parent training techniques in child behavior modification. *Journal of Behavior Therapy and Experimental Psychiatry,* 1977, *8,* 261–268.

Öst, L., & Götestam, K. G. Behavioral and pharmacological treatments for obesity: An experimental comparison. *Addictive Behaviors,* 1976, *1,* 331–338.

Parsons, T., & Bales, R. F. *Family socialization and interaction process.* New York: The Free Press, 1955.

Phillips, L. W. The soft underbelly of behavior therapy: Pop behavior mod. *Journal of Behavior Therapy and Experimental Psychiatry,* 1978, *9,* 139–140.

Rekers, G. A., Bentler, P. M., Rosen, A. C., & Lovaas, O. I. Child gender disturbances: A clinical rationale for intervention. *Psychotherapy: Theory, Research, and Practice,* 1978, *14,* 2–11.

Rekers, G. A., & Lovaas, O. I. Behavioral treatment of deviant sex-role behaviors in a male child. *Journal of Applied Behavior Analysis,* 1974, *7,* 173–190.

Relinger, H., Bornstein, P. H., Bugge, I. D., Carmody, T. P., & Zohn, C. J. Utilization of adverse rapid smoking in groups: Efficacy of treatment and maintenance procedures. *Journal of Consulting and Clinical Psychology,* 1977, *45,* 245–249.

Ribordy, S. C., & Denney, D. R. The behavioral treatment of insomnia: An alternative to drug therapy. *Behaviour Research and Therapy,* 1977, *15,* 39–50.

Rich, A. R., & Schroeder, H. E. Research issues in assertiveness training. *Psychological Bulletin,* 1976, *83,* 1081–1096.

Rossi, A. S. Equality between the sexes: An immodest proposal. In R. J. Lifton (Ed.), *The woman in America.* Boston: Beacon Press, 1964.

Sandler, J., VanDercar, C., & Milhoon, M. Training child abusers in the use of positive reinforcement practices. *Behaviour Research and Therapy,* 1978, *16,* 169–176.

Sears, R. R. Identification as a form of behavior development. In D. B. Harris (Ed.), *The concept of development.* Minneapolis: University of Minnesota, 1957.

Seymour, F. W., & Stokes, T. F. Self-reporting in training girls to increase work and evoke staff praise in an institution for offenders. *Journal of Applied Behavior Analysis,* 1976, *9,* 41–54.

Shafts, F., & Sulzbacher, S. Comparing treatment tactics with a hyperactive preschool child: Stimulant medication and programmed teacher intervention. *Journal of Applied Behavior Analysis*, 1977, *10*, 13–20.

Sharpless, S. K. Hypnotics and sedatives. In L. S. Goodman & A. Gilman (Eds.), *The pharmacological basis of therapeutics*. New York: Macmillan, 1965.

Shields, S. A. Functionalism, Darwinism, and the psychology of women: A study of social myth. *American Psychologist*, 1975, *30*, 739–754.

Shipley, R. H., Butt, J. H., Horwitz, B., and Farbry, J. E. Preparation for a stressful medical procedure: Effect of amount of stimulus preexposure and coping style. *Journal of Consulting and Clinical Psychology*, 1978, *46*, 499–507.

Shuller, D., & McNamara, J. R. Expectancy factors in behavioral observation. *Behavior Therapy*, 1976, *7*, 519–527.

Skinner, B. F. *Walden II*. New York: Macmillan, 1948.

Snyder, C. R. "A patient by any other name" revisited: Maladjustment or attributional locus of problems? *Journal of Consulting and Clinical Psychology*, 1977, *45*, 101–103.

Spence, J. T., Helmreich, R., & Stapp, J. Ratings of self and peers on sex-role attributes and their relation to self-esteem and conceptions of masculinity and femininity. *Journal of Personality and Social Psychology*, 1975, *32*, 29–39.

Stalonas, P. M., Johnson, W. G., & Christ, M. Behavior modification for obesity: The evaluation of exercise, contingency management and program adherence. *Journal of Consulting and Clinical Psychology*, 1978, *46*, 463–469.

Stein, L. S., DelGaudio, A. C., & Ansley, M. Y. A comparison of male and female neurotic depressives. *Journal of Clinical Psychology*, 1976, *32*, 19–21.

Stokes, T. F., & Baer, D. M. An implicit technology of generalization. *Journal of Applied Behavior Analysis*, 1977, *10*, 349.

Stolz, S. B., Wienckowski, L. A., & Brown, B. S. Behavior modification: A perspective on critical issues. *American Psychologist*, 1975, *30*, 1027–1048.

Stuart, R. B., & Davis, B. *Slim chance in a fat world*. Champaign, Ill.: Research Press, 1972.

Sturgis, E. T., Tollison, C. D., & Adams, H. E. Modification of combined migraine–muscle contraction headaches using BVP and EMG feedback. *Journal of Applied Behavior Analysis*, 1978, *11*, 215–223.

Susen, G. R. Conditioned relaxation in a case of ulcerative colitis. *Journal of Behavior Therapy and Experimental Psychiatry*, 1978, *9*, 3.

Williams, C. L., & Ciminero, A. R. Development and validation of a heterosexual skills inventory: The survey of heterosexual interactions for females. *Journal of Consulting and Clinical Psychology*, 1978, *46*, 1547–1548.

Williams, J. H. *Psychology of women*. New York: Norton, 1977.

Wilson, G. T. Methodological considerations in treatment outcome research on obesity. *Journal of Consulting and Clinical Psychology*, 1978, *46*, 687–702.

Winkler, R. C. What types of sex-role behavior should behavior modifiers promote? *Journal of Applied Behavior Analysis*, 1977, *10*, 549–552.

Wolf, M. M. Social validity: The case for subjective measurement *or* How applied behavior analysis is finding its heart. *Journal of Applied Behavior Analysis*, 1978, *11*, 203–214.

Wolfe, J. L., & Fodor, I. G. Modifying assertive behavior in women: A comparison of three approaches. *Behavior Therapy*, 1977, *8*, 567–574.

Wolff, R. Systematic desensitization and negative practice to alter the aftereffects of a rape attempt. *Journal of Behavior Therapy and Experimental Psychiatry*, 1977, *8*, 423–426.

Worrel, J. Sex roles and psychological well-being: Perspectives on methodology. *Journal of Consulting and Clinical Psychology*, 1978, *46*, 777–791.

Wulbert, M., & Dries, R. The relative efficacy of methylphenidate (Ritalin) and behavior modification techniques in the treatment of a hyperactive child. *Journal of Applied Behavior Analysis*, 1977, *10*, 21–31.

Zigler, E., & Phillips, L. Social effectiveness of symptomatic behavior. *Journal of Abnormal Psychology*, 1960, *61*, 231–238.

CHAPTER 10

Feminist Therapy

LUCIA ALBINO GILBERT

A monk ran into a party of handmaids of the lord on a certain journey. Seeing them he left the road and gave them a wide berth. But the Abbess said to him: "If you were a perfect monk, you would not even have looked close enough to see that we were women."

Desert fathers of the fourth century

Introduction

The focus of this chapter is feminist therapy. Its specific objectives are to describe the process and goals of feminist therapy, to show how this approach to therapy differs from more traditional approaches, and to recommend those areas of research that would be most heuristic at the present time.

Before turning to these three topics, several problems encountered in this area of research will be briefly addressed. Although much has been written about feminist therapy, very few empirical data are available. Hence, where appropriate, data from related areas of research will be included. An additional complication is how to identify a feminist therapist (Liss-Levinson, Note 1). Self-identification is the most direct approach to determining who is a feminist therapist. Alternatively, identification could be based on therapists' attitudes toward the roles, attributes, and behavior of women and men; membership in feminist organizations or consciousness-raising groups; and awareness and/or participation in feminist issues.

However, because attitudes and behavior often differ (Wicker, 1969), more comprehensive procedures may be necessary to identify feminist therapists. For example, a group of expert judges could rate random excerpts from several therapy interviews with the same client, a

Lucia Albino Gilbert. Department of Educational Psychology, The University of Texas at Austin, Austin, Texas.

cross section of clients, or a constant role-played client. Initial research efforts might best be directed toward comparing self-definitions of feminist therapists or criteria-based classification procedures (e.g., Feminist Therapy Roster of the Association of Women in Psychology) with therapists' behavior in analogue or actual psychotherapeutic interactions with female clients. In this way, the validity of therapists' self-definitions or procedures based on specific criteria for identifying feminist therapists could be assessed.

Two additional points need to be made. The first concerns the value and feasibility of comparing feminist and traditional approaches to psychotherapy; the second, the relationship of the psychology of women to feminist therapy.

Feminist therapy arose out of a discontent with more traditional therapies. A great deal of this dissatisfaction stemmed from sexist assumptions in existing theories and measures of therapeutic outcome. Among these assumptions were presumed differences between the genders that perpetuated a patriarchal system in which prestige and power rightfully belonged to the male gender. Because of certain basic premises in feminist therapy, which are to be discussed later, and its implicit long-term goals, meaningful comparisons between feminist therapy and other approaches to psychotherapy may not be possible and may take the form of trying to compare apples with oranges. Moreover, since the ultimate goal of feminist therapy is to change the traditional system, spending considerable energy in comparing feminist and traditional approaches to psychotherapy appears contradictory. In addition, there is considerable evidence that investigations of specific interventions leading to specific changes (Gomes-Schwartz, Hadley, & Strupp, 1978; Meltzoff & Kornreich, 1970) and of particular therapist and client variables (Orlinsky & Howard, 1978) are far more useful than comparisons of the effects of general types of therapy. For these reasons, this chapter does not include recommendations on comparing feminist therapy with other treatment modalitites. Instead, it is argued that research efforts should focus on *what happens in feminist therapy,* what client and therapist variables are important to what does or does not happen, and what positive and enduring effects result from feminist therapy.

Related to this problem of differences in philosophy, treatment goals, and outcome criteria are common assumptions regarding the level of analysis: Whom does one ask when inquiring about the "adjustment of clients" and on what basis are these judgments made? Past research has focused almost exclusively on the characteristics of the individual, with little reference to context (Bronfenbrenner, 1977). Moreover, most psychologists tend to view "an individual's functioning within the framework of some theory of personality structure which *transcends* so-cial adaptation and subjective well-being" (Strupp & Hadley, 1977, p. 189, emphasis added). As a consequence, therapists, in their roles as interpreters of society and of individual behaviors within a particular theroretical framework, should be "enlightened" concerning the effects of both sociological and cultural factors on the behavior and status of women and, perhaps more important to the present argument, the growing body of knowledge on the psychology of women. Without this enlightenment, the theories which underlie approaches to psycho-therapy will remain inadequate. Herein, then, lies the importance of the psychology of women to feminist therapy.

What Is Feminist Therapy?

Definitions of Feminist and Feminist Therapy

The term "feminist" is defined as "a person who advocates political, social, and economic equality between women and men" (*Webster's New Collegiate Dictionary*, 1979, p. 418). Feminist therapy, unfortunately, is more difficult to define. The basic assumption underlying feminist therapy is that ideology, social structure, and behavior are inextricably interwoven. Our society's ideology of egalitarianism interacts with the norms of our social institutions such that women are expected to ac-commodate without strain to a set of discriminatory role behaviors and sex-typed personality characteristics. To counter the consistently harm-ful effects on the development of women of this contradiction between ideology and social reality, an alternative to existing psychotherapies emerged. This approach, now called feminist therapy, not only incorpo-rates an awareness of the effects of ideology and social structure on the behavior of women but also contains several principles considered essen-tial to the development of autonomous and self-actualized women and to the eventual establishment of a social structure consistent with the feminist ideology of egalitarianism (Barrett, Berg, Easton, & Pomeroy, 1974; Kirsh, 1974; Lerman, 1974; Mander & Rush, 1974; Marecek & Kravetz, 1977; Rawlings & Carter, 1977; Brodsky, Note 2).

As already noted, several recent writers (Bronfenbrenner, 1977; Strupp & Hadley, 1977) question the usefulness of traditional psycholog-ical approaches that focus exclusively on how individuals learn and carry cultural values and social roles and on how they adjust to society. Bron-fenbrenner (1977), for example, proposes a broad approach to research in human development that focuses on the progressive accomodation, throughout the life span, between individuals and their changing environments. The environment includes not only immediate settings containing the developing person but also the "larger social contexts, both formal and informal, in which the settings are embedded" (Bronfenbrenner, 1977, p. 514). Similarly, the tripartite model recommended by Strupp and Hadley (1977) includes evaluations of psychotherapeutic outcomes from the individual client, representatives of society, and the mental health professional. Strupp and Hadley (1977) believe that therapists must increase their awareness of the social repercussions of changes sought by clients and use their awareness to facilitate clients' ability to deal with societal reactions to their individual behavior. They also emphasize the importance of demonstrating the relevance (or lack thereof) of one's theory of personality to measurable changes that occur in client's self-reports and in their perceptions of social reality.

A perusal of the literature on feminist therapy (Holroyd, 1976; Kirsh, 1974; Lerman, 1974; Marecek & Kravetz, 1977; Rawlings & Carter, 1977; Brodsky, Note 2; Earnhart, Note 3; Marshall, Note 4; Sprei-Ott, Note 5; Whittaker-Leidig, Note 6) makes apparent two important principles: (1) "the personal is political," and (2) the therapist–client relationship is viewed as egalitarian. The most common ways of incorporating these two basic principles into practice are outlined below. Compared with more traditional therapies, feminist therapy also views certain content areas as particularly important to therapy with women. These include rape, pregnancy, menopause, childbirth, body image, menstruation, issues of physical power, and sexual preference.

What Happens in Feminist Therapy?
PRINCIPLE ONE: THE PERSONAL IS POLITICAL

Separating the Internal from the External. The client learns to differentiate between what she has been taught and has accepted as socially appropriate for her from what might actually be appropriate. Thus, therapists encourage clients to evaluate the influence of social roles and norms on their personal experience and to see the relationship between sociological and psychological factors.

Validation of the Female Experience. Through therapy, the client comes to understand the role of society in shaping all individuals and, in particular, its role in shaping the behavior of women. The client learns that she is not crazy.

Exploration of Values and Attitudes by Therapists. Therapists constantly explore their own values and attitudes concerning women and confront tendencies within themselves toward maintaining things as they are.

An Emphasis on Change Rather than "Adjustment." Given the way that women have been socialized and their present status and role in society, societal changes are necessary for significant improvement to occur in women's lives.

PRINCIPLE TWO: THE THERAPIST–CLIENT RELATIONSHIP IS VIEWED AS EGALITARIAN

Shopping Around for a Therapist. The client is encouraged to take a consumer attitude in seeking out psychological services and in asking questions. This attitude keeps her informed and "demystifies" the therapist as a person of unique power and knowledge.

Enhancement of a Sense of Personal Power. Throughout therapy, the client is encouraged to experience greater self-confidence and to be more self-directed and autonomous. Contracting with the therapist for specific therapeutic goals may also occur.

Encouraging of Self-Nurturance. Rather than always nurturing others first, women are made aware that they, too, have rights and can nurture themselves. Related to self-nurturing is learning to value oneself as a woman, learning to value other women as women, and receiving mutual support and nurturance from other women.

Modeling by the Therapist. Modeling by the therapist, which often includes self-disclosure of the therapist's experiences as a woman in our society, is thought to help the client validate her experience as well as to widen her options and goals.

> The therapist by being who she is can serve as a model for the kind of woman who knows herself and her psychological boundaries, who relates in a human female way and can express her own gentleness along with her own definiteness. Not least, she can share with the client in a very important way about what it means to be a women in this society. There is a potential bond arising out of a communality of experiences. (Lerman, 1974, pp. 8–9)

Expression of Anger. The process of assuming power in one's life may bring up feelings of anger, and dealing with anger is essential to feminist therapy. Like the assumption in Gestalt therapy, it is thought that once a woman understands the broad implications of her traditional role and place in society, she cannot act as she did before. Wherever she looks, she will be aware of how she has been oppressed, how everything is defined in terms of "he," etc. When this occurs, the client may feel disoriented, and normal interactions with significant others may be disrupted. Typically, she will experience a great deal of anger about expected societal roles, the way she relates to various people, and so on. This anger, and working through it, are part of the feminist therapy.

Theoretical Underpinnings of Feminist Therapy

According to recent writers, no one theory underlies the practice of feminist therapy. Holroyd (1976), for example, feels that feminist therapists can take any number of different orientations, including the psychoanalytic. She views feminist therapy as a combination of a radical therapy philosophy with humanistic therapy techniques. Sherman (Note 7), however, suggests that the ideological differences between psychoanalysis and feminist therapy may be too great for a feminist therapist to hold a psychoanalytic orientation. Feminist therapy is also thought to be heavily influenced by Rogers' self-theory, which emphasizes the importance of a congruence between self-perceptions and societal expectations. Although traditional therapies have focused on realigning the self to society and hence on "teaching women to know their place," feminist therapy considers self-perceptions as valid and the lack of congruence as the result of inequities in society that need to be changed. Other writers consider feminist therapy not as a separate system parallel to existing therapies but as an approach that will change and be incorporated within other therapies (Marecek & Kravetz, 1977).

Although issues regarding the theoretical underpinnings of feminist therapy are still unclear, considerable agreement exists regarding the two basic principles discussed earlier, the goals of feminist therapy, and the differences between feminist and traditional psychotherapies. Feminist therapy (1) "invariably requires adoption of *new attitudes*, not just *new techniques*" (Johnson, 1976, p. 76); (2) advocates the political, social, and economic equality of women and men; and (3) brings society into the therapy with individuals. Although the therapist can work directly only with clients and cannot change the reality of their world, helping clients gain a more accurate understanding and assessment of their environment may permit/encourage/foster plans of action that, in turn, will change others or the clients' own adverse environmental conditions (Sherman, Note 7). Feminist therapists also agree that, regardless of socialization, women need to know how to cope with their lives: "In spite of how her environment leans on her, a woman, nevertheless, has to know how to engage with it in ways which will be nourishing and zestful, not just successful acts of self-betrayal. She is creating her own life, bit by bit" (Polster, 1974, pp. 249–250).

The tenets of feminist therapy do not preclude considering men as feminist therapists. At the same time, Chesler (1972) and others believe that a woman client can be understood and helped best by a *woman* therapist who is herself a feminist. Present research evidence on the effect of the therapist's gender on outcome (Parloff, Waskow, & Wolfe,

1978; Tanney & Birk, 1976), however, indicates that investigations of therapist gender effects would be far less heuristic than investigations of what happens in feminist therapy, of methods to provide more effective treatment for women, and of procedures to foster feminist attitudes and knowledge of the psychology of women among mental health professionals and the consumers of their services. Data that indicated the importance of validating the female experience and modeling by the therapist would, of course, modify this conclusion.

Nonsexist and Feminist Psychotherapy: A Comparison

Nonsexist psychotherapy usually refers to appropriately equal treatment for women and men. Although feminist therapy embraces the need for nonsexist treatment, it also incorporates the political values and philosophy of feminism in its therapeutic values and strategies. The underlying assumption in feminist therapy that the personal and political cannot be separated makes awareness of the social system essential to effective therapy with women.

Jesse Bernard (1975) helps make the basic distinction between non-sexist and feminist therapy more clear:

> The feminist critique of the socialization paradigm does not deny that children are socialized for different roles, but it argues that even if socialization no longer emphasized the differences between the pink-clad and blue-clad infants, the infants would still grow up in a world that retains an institutional set of biases ... so long as the institutional structures of our society favor men, the feminist critics say, the question arises as to can women, no matter how well prepared psychologically and intellectually, expect to be dealt with on the basis of their merits rather than on the basis of their sex? Emphasis on socialization merely offers an easy out, it does not open doors. (pp. 17–18)

Opening doors, according to the tenets of feminist therapy and to Bernard, calls for "an attack on the institutional structure that embalms these differences in the form of discrimination against women" (Bernard, 1975, p. 18).

Relevant Empirical Data

This section reviews recent empirical data in psychotherapy that directly bear on research concerning feminist therapy. Certain client and therapist variables related to the therapeutic process and effective outcome are summarized, and then findings on the relationship of process to outcome are discussed. Because research on feminist therapy is limited, empirical evidence on those variables thought to be important to feminist therapy will help greatly in identifying promising areas for future research efforts.

Client Variables

In a recent paper, Bergin and Lambert (1978) concluded: "We believe the hypothesis is supportable that the largest proportion of variation in therapy outcome is accounted for by preexisting client factors, such as motivation for change, and the like. Therapist personal factors account for the second largest proportion of change, with technique variables coming in a distant third" (p. 180). Procedures that match or pair clients and therapists on particular characteristics are viewed as particularly promising to understanding the degree to which therapeutic outcome is positive for clients. At the same time, they note that the numerous conceptual and methodological problems in reported research prevent any firm conclusions about the relationship between specific client variables and therapeutic outcome.

A further problem, and one alluded to earlier in this chapter, is the criteria used to assess outcome. Traditional therapies focus on how individuals learn and carry cultural values and social roles and how they adjust to society. The measures developed, different as they may be, assess "adjustment" according to societal expectations for individual behavior (e.g., Long-Laws, 1971). The detrimental effect of traditional outcome criteria on positive female development is apparent in areas of symptom removal, self-esteem, quality of interpersonal relationships, and role performance, where the "adjusted" woman learned and accepted her place (Klein, 1976). This problem presents a challenge to researchers of feminist therapy, since measures based on the normative adjustment of women to current society are inappropriate for assessing outcomes resulting from feminist therapy. In addition to sex-fair personality instruments, examples of appropriate measures of individual adjustment from the perspective of feminist therapy might include the degree to which clients differentiate between the internal and the external, endorse androgynous self-descriptions, feel unrestricted by societal values and roles, value themselves as women, and value other women.

CLIENT CHARACTERISTICS

The relationships of age, race, social class, ethnic origin, and psychotherapeutic settings to feminist therapy will not be discussed in detail, because little research literature has accumulated to date in these areas. The scanty data available indicate that women entering feminist and traditional therapies do not differ in age, education, employment status, occupational level, place of residence (urban, suburban, or rural), marital status (Marecek, Kravetz, & Finn, 1979), level of pretherapy stress, or target complaints (Johnson, 1976; Marecek *et al.*, 1979). As with traditional therapy, feminist therapy typically has been used with a rather homogeneous group of educated middle-class white females in outpatient facilities. Those women entering feminist therapy are more likely to be child-free and to hold more radical political views than are those in traditional therapies (Marecek *et al.*, 1979). Because of the restriced samples employed in these studies, however, these data should be interpreted with considerable caution.

RELATIONSHIP OF CLIENT CHARACTERISTICS TO THERAPEUTIC OUTCOME

The one study available on the relationship of client characteristics to therapeutic outcome indicates that clients' attitudes toward feminism are important to effective therapeutic outcome. Marecek *et al.* (1979) found that the retrospective self-report of clients who identified themselves as members of the women's movement evaluated feminist therapy as more helpful than traditional therapies, whereas both kinds of therapies were rated as equally effective by nonmembers. (Clients indicated whether their therapists were feminist or traditional in orientation.)

Therapist Variables
THERAPIST CHARACTERISTICS

The characteristics of feminist therapists remain relatively unexplored, although characteristics of feminists have received considerable attention by researchers. These studies indicate that feminists, as defined by membership in a feminist organization or high scores on a feminism scale, generally view themselves as more politically liberal (Fowler, Fowler, & Van de Riet, 1973; Pawlicki & Almquist, 1973) and active (Stoloff, 1973), actively achieving (Cherniss, 1972; Joesting, 1971), dominant and self-confident (Doyle, 1975; Fowler & Van de Riet, 1972), autonomous and independent (Cherniss, 1972; Dempewolff, 1974; Fowler & Van de Riet, 1972), aggressive and potent (Fowler & Van de Riet, 1972; Tipton, Bailey, & Obenchain, 1975), self-actualizing (Hjelle & Butterfield, 1974), and higher in self-esteem (Cherniss, 1972) than do nonfeminists (those scoring lower or nonmembers). Feminists also showed greater behavioral flexibility in a sex-typed situation (help-seeking) than did more traditional subjects (Wallston, 1976). The few studies including both male and female feminists found no differences due to gender on the particular characteristics investigated.

Kitchener, Corazzini, and Huebner (1975) found that female counselors who considered themselves feminists were rated higher by counseling center directors on their ability to deal with a wide range of problems and to develop outreach programs than those who did not consider themselves feminists. Finally, female therapists and female community mental health center therapists rated mothers as more mentally healthy than did male community mental health center therapists (Aslin, 1977). These male therapists also perceived healthy adults in more "male-valued terms" than they did healthy females, wives, and mothers. Ratings of the four groups did not differ for the female therapists, however (Aslin, 1977).

RELATIONSHIP OF THERAPIST CHARACTERISTICS TO THERAPEUTIC OUTCOME

Two characteristics of therapists, independent of the treatment setting or the clients treated, have emerged as particularly important to feminist therapy: therapist values and therapist knowledge of women. In reviewing research on therapist variables in relation to process and outcome, Parloff _et al._ (1978) conclude that therapist values appear to have far greater importance than demographic variables such as sex and ethnicity or therapist personality variables.

> Values seem to be an inherent part of the therapy process and therefore appear to be necessarily affected by the outcome of therapy. Understanding the particular relationships that link the values of therapist and patient seems to us a priority area of research. (p. 271)

The modicum of empirical evidence available lends support to the influence of therapist attitudes on their perceptions of clients. Bosma (1975), for example, found that among 50 women therapists, feminists rated clients shown in videotaped vignettes as stronger and less ill than did nonfeminists. Similarly, Gilbert (Note 8) found that sutdent counselors holding liberal and moderate attitudes toward the roles of women and men differed along traditional sex-role lines in their attributions regarding the role behavior of a male and female client presented as a written case study. In a study designed to instill more feminist attitudes in student counselors, Gilbert and Waldroop (1978) found a strong positive correlation between students' profeminist attitudes and ratings of effective student counselor performance. Johnson (1976), on the other hand, found no differences in retrospectively self-reported posttherapy improvement and client satisfaction between women seen in a feminist therapy collective and women seen in a more traditional clinic or private practice setting. However, clients in the Johnson study were seen in groups by female therapists for an average of 4 months; whereas clients in the traditional setting were seen individually by male therapists for an average of 10 months.

A related area of high importance and promise to research is the degree of similarity between the values of therapists and clients. The study of Marecek *et al.* (1979) indicates that feminist therapy is equally effective for feminist and nonfeminist clients, whereas traditional therapy is less effective for feminist clients than for nonfeminist clients. Similarly, the 20% of the feminist therapy clients in the Johnson study (1976) who did not consider themselves feminist showed improvement with therapy, although to a lesser extent than the feminist clients. These findings support the importance of value similarity for female clients seeking therapy as well as the positive consequence of the "conversion-of-values" phenomenon reported in the psychotherapeutic outcome literature. Beutler, Pollack, and Jobe (1978), for example, found a strong relationship between patients' acquisition of their therapists' values and their ratings of improvement. Thus, improvement in psychotherapy may be related to the extent to which the therapist and client share the same attitudes initially or to the adoption by female clients of their therapist's feminist values. Gomes-Schwartz, *et al.* (1978) also note the importance of patient similarity and complementarity in values and attitudes. Although the findings are mixed, they believe that both shared value systems and shared beliefs about how therapy should be conducted are associated with more positive therapeutic outcomes.

Therapists' knowledge about the lifestyles, values, and beliefs of their clients (Parloff, *et al.*, 1978) may also influence therapeutic outcome. Understanding the psychology of women and keeping abreast of research findings in this area are underscored in the report of the American Psychological Association Task Force on Sex Bias and Sex-Role Stereotyping in Psychotherapeutic Practice (1975). However, since very few relevant data are available (Kenworthy, Koufacos, & Sherman, 1976; Sherman, Koufacos, & Kenworthy, 1978), this area seems particularly fruitful for future research. Comparing feminist therapists with varying levels of knowledge on the psychology of women with regard to particular process and outcome variables is one possible first step.

Technique and Process Variables Related to Therapeutic Outcome

In addition to indicating what appear to be the most important findings concerning the relationship of process to effective therapeutic outcome, this section summarizes data pertinent to the components of feminist therapy set forth above.

THE PERSONAL IS POLITICAL

The ability of clients to differentiate social prescriptions from personal needs and goals and to evaluate the influence of social roles and norms on their personal experience (separating the internal from the external) as well as on the behavior of other women (validation of the female experience) is crucial to this aspect of feminist therapy. Also important are the emphasis on change rather than adjustment and the active questioning by therapists of their value systems and attitudes regarding the personality characteristics and roles of women in our society. Apart from the two studies cited earlier (Johnson, 1976; Marecek *et al.*, 1979) and the positive findings obtained from consciousness-raising groups (Brodsky, 1973; Kravetz, 1976, 1978; Nassi & Abramowitz, 1978), few data are available regarding the client's ability to separate the internal from the external. Considerable anecdotal data, however, support the importance of this process to effective therapeutic outcome (cf. Franks & Burtle, 1974; Lerman, 1974; Marecek & Kravetz, 1977; Rawlings & Carter, 1977).

Similarly, there is very little literature demonstrating the effect on therapeutic outcome of emphasizing change rather than adjustment. But the considerable evidence provided by Chesler (1972) and others well documents the negative effects resulting from the past emphasis on adjustment. Research on assertion training for women (Jakubowski, 1977) and on active approaches to helping women change their roles (Hansen & Rapoza, 1978) lend some support to the positive effects of emphasizing change rather than adjustment.

THE THERAPIST-CLIENT RELATIONSHIP IS VIEWED AS EGALITARIAN

In contrast to the first principle, this key component of feminist therapy is more clearly related to data in the existing psychotherapy literature. The relevant studies are divided into five areas: (1) disclaiming the position that therapists are experts about their clients; (2) informing clients of their rights and privileges and of the nature of psychotherapy and encouraging them to shop around for a therapist; (3) using techniques which enhance clients' self-confidence, self-direction, autonomy, and sense of personal power; (4) facilitating the expression of anger; and (5) modeling by the therapist, including appropriate self-disclosure. The literature summarized here is not intended to be comprehensive, but rather to provide an indication of the importance of pursuing research in each area.

Therapist Not Taking the Position of Expert. The relationship of outcome to clients' perceptions or therapists' self-perceptions of expertness has received little attention by researchers. Lorr (1965), however, did report that clients who viewed their therapists as authoritarian had significantly poorer outcomes than did other clients.

Informing Clients. Both Orlinsky and Howard (1978) and Parloff *et al.* (1978) note the importance of "role induction" to positive therapeutic outcome. The studies reviewed by these authors, although employing several methodologies, strongly suggest that some orientation of clients to the nature of therapy encourages them to remain in therapy and enhances the process and outcome of psychotherapy. The studies reviewed by Parloff *et al.* (1978) included induction procedures such as interviews, tape recordings, or films. In view of these findings, similar positive effects would be anticipated from the orienting techniques typically used in feminist therapy: interviewing clients on the telephone or in person, providing clients with a consumer's guide to nonsexist therapy (National Organization for Women, 1978), and/or encouraging clients to ask questions regarding therapist attitudes and values, fees, and time schedules (Hare-Mustin, Marecek, Kaplan, & Liss-Levinson, 1979).

Enhancing Autonomy. Several types of evidence suggest that enhancing autonomy in clients is important to successful therapeutic outcomes. Saltzman, Luetgert, Roth, Creaser, and Howard (1976) report that clients who felt a greater sense of responsibility for solving their own problems rated the outcome of therapy more highly than did clients who placed the responsibility more on their therapists. Tovian (1977) found two clusters of feelings significantly associated with improvement in clients—feeling "relieved" and "confident." In their review of therapist variables, Orlinsky and Howard (1978) note a convergence of findings indicating that the "patient's perceptions of the therapist's manner as affirming the patient's value is positively and significantly associated with good therapeutic outcome" (p. 298). There is also evidence that better outcomes occur with therapists who are viewed as encouraging independence than with those who are not (Lorr, 1965; Martin & Sterne, 1976).

The Therapist as Role Model. Providing models of desired behavior can be a powerful way to change expectations and behavior (Bandura, 1969; Rosenthal & Bandura, 1978). Effective female models may provide a form of social sanction for certain roles, behaviors, personal attributes, and attitudes and may help clients not only in validating their experience but also in broadening their self-perceived options and goals. There is considerable evidence that female models in nontraditional occupational roles significantly affect the career interests of women (e.g., Lockheed, 1975; Plost, 1974; Tangri, 1972). O'Leary's (1977) review of the research on nontraditional role models underscores both the impact of these models on female career development *and* the few role models available. Because of the scarcity of effective role models, female therapists may take on added importance as examples of women who have "made it" (Tanney & Birk, 1976).

Attributes of models pertaining to therapists as effective role models are their relevance and credibility for clients. Determinants of their impact as models, however, would be a function of context, the clients' inferences and standards of comparison, and model–client similarity (Rosenthal & Bandura, 1978).

The influence of the therapist as a role model has received little research attention. Sapolsky (1965) reported that female clients who saw therapists as similar to themselves in self-image were judged as significantly more improved. Confirmatory evidence also comes from Johnson's (1976) pilot study on feminist therapy. Three of the top ten items clients found to be most helpful were "seeing therapists as competent women; knowing that, as women, therapists have shared the female experience; and discovering that other women are central and helpful" (p. 75). In addition, considerable anecdotal data support the importance of the feminist therapist as a positive role model for female clients (Lerman, 1974; Marecek & Kravetz, 1977).

Another aspect of role modeling often mentioned in the feminist therapy literature is *self-disclosure*. The influence of therapist self-disclosure on therapeutic outcome has been widely investigated. Modeling has been shown repeatedly to have a positive effect on client self-disclosure (Krumboltz, Becker-Haven, & Burnett, 1979).

Self-disclosures in the therapeutic situation can take several forms (McCarthy & Betz, 1978; Waldroop, Note 9). The most common forms are self-involving "here-and-now" disclosures, in which therapist's experience of the client in the dyadic interaction is shared; "there-and-now" disclosures, in which present information about the therapist not related to feelings arising from the dyadic interaction is shared (e.g., "I am currently reading a new book on the psychology of women"; and "there-and-then" disclosures, in which past information about the therapist not related to feeling arising from the dyadic interaction is shared (e.g., "I received my degree from Yale").

Disclosures of the here-and-now type take the form of confrontation, nurturance, feedback, and so on, and they are usually classified under therapist genuineness. Genuineness or self-congruence generally is associated with positive therapeutic outcome (Orlinsky & Howard, 1978).

Since self-disclosure in the feminist therapy situation might often take the form of there-and-now and there-and-then disclosures, the literature in this area should be particularly useful. The relationship of these types of self-disclosures to effective therapeutic outcomes, however, is less clear (Krumboltz *et al.*, 1979). Factors of varying degrees of importance include the number, timing, count, and content of disclosures; therapist's status, warmth, and supportiveness; and client's gender, trait level of self-disclosure, and experience with and expectations of psychotherapy and psychotherapists.

Lerman (1974) sees modeling and self-disclosure as essential in feminist therapy (cf. p. 8). The importance of identification and the communality of experience women share with other women are also pointed out by Krause (1971) and Mander and Rush (1974). Empirical evidence for the importance of a common experience comes from Jeske (1973), who reported that patients in group psychotherapy who identified more often with the experiences reported by other clients tended to have more favorable outcomes in comparison to those who felt less identified. In addition, Hoffman-Graff (1975) found counselor self-disclosures (there-and-then) to affect positively student self-ratings of procrastination. Considerable support also comes from the literature on the effect of consciousness-raising groups (cf. Kravetz, 1978).

Facilitating the Expression of Anger. A number of feminist writers view the expression of anger as essential to the establishment of women's personal power (Bernardez-Bonesatti, 1978; Lerman, 1974; Mueller & Whittaker-Leidig, Note 10). Cline-Naffziger (1974), writing on frustration, oppression, and anger in women's lives from an environmental stress perspective, emphasizes the importance of resolving anger as opposed to reserving it:

> If the woman can learn to express her anger and accept that the other will not necessarily change, she has grown. She then knows that avoiding anger can mean avoiding the "response-ability" of managing her own life. The other "response-ability" of angry women is to seek, demand, and initiate change ... women must be encouraged to put their anger energy on the sources of power. Anger energy is more potent when focused on those above rather than those around or those below. (pp. 55–56)

Nichols' (1974) findings support the effectiveness of emotive techniques in brief individual psychotherapy with clients from a university population. There is additional evidence that affect expressed in the form of anger and hostility is positively related to therapeutic outcome (Crowder, 1972; Mintz, Luborsky, & Auerbach, 1971). Therapist perceptions also support the facilitative effect of clients' experience of strong feelings (e.g., Gendlin, Jenney, & Shlien, 1960; Roether & Peters, 1972).

Conclusion

Psychotherapy has been viewed as an interpersonal process characterized by a positive cohesive bond between the participants. An effective
investment of energy, good personal contact, and a sense of affirmation
communicate an acceptance and encouragement of independence "that
can be challenging as well as supportive out of concern and respect for
the other person's basic interest and autonomy" (Orlinsky & Howard,
1978, p. 317). Orlinsky and Howard believe that more research is
needed on therapy as experience, that is, "the occurring involvement in
the therapeutic experience as it is viewed internally from the perspective
of the participant-observer" (p. 296) (e.g., feeling a greater sense of
responsibility, affirming clients' values, encouraging independence,
holding similar perceptions). This focus is in contrast to a continued
emphasis on therapy as activity (e.g., vocal style, number of minutes
spoken per session), as association (e.g., session length, time payment),
or as dramatic interpretation (e.g., therapist and client messages). Orlinsky and Howard's views of effective psychotherapy and the direction
of future research efforts agree quite well with what feminist therapists
report to be effective for clients and with what happens in feminist
therapy.

Research Priorities

Future research in the area of feminist therapy should focus on providing empirical evidence that feminist therapy does, in fact, help women,
gaining a greater understanding of its basic components, and delineat-
ing more clearly "which of its specific procedures obtains which results
with which clients in what amount of time and how enduring the effects
are" (Meltzoff & Kornreich, 1970, p. 200).

   Although the research literature on variables relevant to what is
postulated to happen in feminist therapy provides confirmatory evidence for all the areas reviewed, three areas emerge as particularly
promising:

   1. therapists as role models
   2. shared values regarding how therapy should be conducted, in-
      cluding role induction
   3. shared attitude and belief systems

The first area is far more complex to investigate than the other two, with
such variables as client–therapist similarity, attitudinal and personality
characteristics of the therapist, and content and timing of self-

disclosures being highly relevant. (Greater detail on these variables was provided earlier in this chapter.)

Other high-priority areas are the following:

4. establishing the validity of procedures for classifying mental health professionals as feminist therapists
5. developing appropriate measures of therapeutic outcome, both short-term (e.g., increased self-esteem) and long-term (e.g., increased social activism)
6. developing effective methods of training in feminist therapy
7. documenting the relationship between a client's ability to differentiate the internal from the external and therapeutic outcome
8. facilitating the process of working through anger
9. investigating the relationships between knowledge of the psychology of women, therapist effectiveness, and therapeutic outcome

The ideal method for investigating feminist therapy would be to observe the therapy, describe it in a systematic way, and then draw conclusions. As Stricker (1977) points out, however, the problems with sampling clients, therapists, etc., are enormous, and whether one could even reach definitive conclusions is not insured. In addition, investigating the client–therapist interaction requires collaboration and trust between the therapist and the researcher, an alliance which might not be obtained easily, even among feminist therapists and feminist researchers. One also needs to take into acount the disruption of the natural therapeutic treatment and to strike a balance between high ethical standards and rigorous experimental control. For these reasons, the direct observation and systematic description of ongoing feminist therapy may be difficult. Researchers may want to consider alternative investigative approaches such as retrospective reports by clients and analogue studies. Although there are problems with these kinds of methodologies (cf. Stricker, 1977), they can be valuable if the experimenter takes adequate care in planning the study and in interpreting the results (Kazdin, 1978a). Single-case experimental designs also are useful (Kazdin, 1978b). For example, the process of working through anger using techniques such as desensitization, psychodrama, and assertion training could be explored and assessed by this method.

ACKNOWLEDGMENTS

The author acknowledges with genuine gratitude the assistance of Linda Manning in the preparation of this chapter. Scott Coahran provided the quote from the desert fathers.

Reference Notes

1. Liss-Levinson, N. *Criteria of feminist therapy.* Paper and discussion presented at the Mid-Winter Research Conference of the Association for Women in Psychology, Knoxville, Tenn., February 1976.
2. Brodsky, A. M. *Is there a feminist therapy?* Paper presented at the meeting of the Southeastern Psychological Association, Atlanta, March 1975.
3. Earnhart, B. *A conceptual framework for the process of feminist therapy.* Unpublished manuscript, 1976.
4. Marshall, P. S. *Self-nurturance and feminist therapy.* Unpublished manuscript, Colorado State University, 1976.
5. Sprei-Ott, J. *Feminist therapy: A review of the issues.* Unpublished manuscript, University of Maryland, 1976.
6. Whittaker-Leidig, M. *Feminist therapy.* Unpublished manuscript, University of Colorado, 1976.
7. Sherman, J. A. *Freud's theory and feminism: A reply to Juliet Mitchell.* Paper presented at the annual meeting of the American Psychological Association, San Francisco, August 1977.
8. Gilbert, L. A. *Counselors-in-training attributions about sex-role behavior: The influence of gender and attitudes.* Unpublished manuscript, University of Texas at Austin, 1979.
9. Waldroop, J. *Therapist genuineness and self-disclosure: An empirical comparison.* Unpublished manuscript, University of Texas at Austin, 1977.
10. Mueller, K., & Whittaker-Leidig, M. *Women's anger and feminist therapy.* Unpublished manuscript, Boulder Mental Health Center and University of Colorado, 1976.

References

American Psychological Association Task Force. Report of the Task Force on Sex Bias and Sex-Role Stereotyping in Psychotherapeutic Practice. *American Psychologist,* 1975, *30,* 1169–1175.

Aslin, A. L. Feminist and community mental health center psychotherapists' expectations of mental health for women. *Sex Roles,* 1977, *3,* 537–544.

Bandura, A. *Principles of behavior modification.* New York: Holt, Rinehart, and Winston, 1969.

Barrett, C., Berg, P., Easton, E., & Pomeroy, E. Implcations of women's liberation and the future of psychotherapy. *Psychotherapy: Theory, Research, and Practice,* 1974, *2,* 1–16.

Bergin, A. E., & Lambert, M. J. The evaluation of therapeutic outcome. In S. L. Garfield & A. E. Bergin (Eds.), *Handbook of psychotherapy and behavior change.* New York: Wiley, 1978.

Bernard, J. S. *Women, wives, and mothers: Values and options.* Chicago: Aldine, 1975.

Bernardez-Bonesatti, T. Women and anger: Conflicts with aggression in contemporary women. *Journal of the American Medical Women's Association,* 1978, *33,* 215–219.

Beutler, L. E., Pollack, S., & Jobe, A. "Acceptance," values and therapeutic change. *Journal of Consulting and Clinical Psychology,* 1978, *46,* 198–199.

Bosma, B. J. Attitudes of women therapists toward women clients, or a comparative study of feminist therapy. *Smith College Studies in Social Work,* 1975, *46,* 53–54.

Brodsky, A. M. The consciousness-raising group as a model for therapy with women. *Psychotherapy: Theory, Research, and Practice,* 1973, *10,* 24–29.

Bronfenbrenner, U. Toward an experimental ecology of human development. *American Psychologist,* 1977, *32,* 513–531.

Cherniss, C. Personality and ideology: A personological study of women's liberation. *Psychiatry,* 1972, *35,* 109–125.

Chesler, P. *Women and madness.* Garden City, N.Y.: Doubleday, 1972.

Cline-Naffziger, C. Women's lives and frustration, oppression and anger. *Journal of Counseling Psychology,* 1974, *21,* 51–56.

Crowder, J. E. Relationship between therapist and client interpersonal behaviors and psychotherapy outcome. *Journal of Counseling Psychology,* 1972, *19,* 68–75.

Dempewolff, J. A. Some correlates of feminism. *Psychological Reports,* 1974, *34,* 671–676.

Doyle, J. A. Self-actualization and attitudes toward women. *Psychological Reports,* 1975, *37,* 899–902.

Fowler, M. G., Fowler, R. L., & Van de Riet, H. Feminism and political radicalism. *Journal of Psychology,* 1973, *83,* 237–242.

Fowler, M. G., & Van de Riet, H. K. Women today and yesterday: An examination of the feminist personality. *Journal of Psychology,* 1972, *82,* 269–276.

Franks, V., & Burtle, V. (Eds.). *Women in therapy.* New York: Brunner/Mazel, 1974.

Gendlin, E. T., Jenney, R., & Shlien, J. Counselor ratings of process and outcome in client-centered therapy. *Journal of Clinical Psychology,* 1960, *16,* 210–213.

Gilbert, L. A., & Waldroop, J. Evaluation of a procedure for increasing sex-fair counseling. *Journal of Counseling Psychology,* 1978, *25,* 410–418.

Gomes-Schwartz, B., Hadley, S. W., & Strupp, H. H. Individual psychotherapy and behavior therapy. *Annual Review of Psychology,* 1978, *29,* 455–471.

Hansen, L. S., & Rapoza, A. S. *Career development and counseling of women.* Springfield, Ill.: Charles C. Thomas, 1978.

Hare-Mustin, R. T., Marecek, J., Kaplan, A. G., & Liss-Levinson, N. Rights of clients, responsibilities of therapists. *American Psychologist,* 1979, *34,* 3–16.

Hjelle, L. A., & Butterfield, R. Self-actualization and women's attitudes toward their roles in contemporary society. *Journal of Psychology,* 1974, *87,* 225–230.

Hoffman-Graff, M. A. Sex pairing and self-disclosure in counseling (Doctoral dissertation, University of Minnesota, 1975). *Dissertation Abstracts International,* 1976, *37,* 460B–461B. (University Microfilms No. 76-14, 894)

Holroyd, J. Psychotherapy and women's liberation. *Counseling Psychologist,* 1976, *6,* 22–28.

Jakubowski, P. A. Self-assertion training procedures for women. In E. I. Rawlings & D. K. Carter (Eds.), *Psychotherapy for women: Treatment towards equality.* Springfield, Ill.: Charles C. Thomas, 1977.

Jeske, J. O. Identification and therapeutic effectiveness in group therapy. *Journal of Counseling Psychology,* 1973, *20,* 528–530.

Joesting, J. Comparison of women's liberation members with their non-member peers. *Psychological Reports,* 1971, *29,* 1291–1294.

Johnson, M. An approach to feminist therapy. *Psychotherapy: Theory, Research, and Practice,* 1976, *13,* 72–76.

Kazdin, A. E., Evaluating the generality of findings in analogue therapy research. *Journal of Consulting and Clinical Psychology,* 1978, *46,* 673–686. (a)

Kazdin, A. E. Methodological and interpretive problems of single-case experimental designs. *Journal of Consulting and Clinical Psychology,* 1978, *46,* 629–642. (b)

Kenworthy, J. A., Koufacos, C., & Sherman, J. Women and therapy: A survey of internship programs. *Psychology of Women Quarterly,* 1976, *1,* 125–137.

Kirsh, B. Consciousness-raising groups as therapy for women. In V. Franks & V. Burtle (Eds.), *Women in therapy.* New York: Brunner/Mazel, 1974.

Kitchener, K. S., Corazzini, J. G., & Huebner, L. A. A study of counseling center hiring practices: What does it take for a woman to be hired? *Journal of Counseling Psychology,* 1975, *22,* 440–445.

Klein, M. H. Feminist concepts of therapy outcome. *Psychotherapy: Theory, Research, and Practice,* 1976, *13,* 89–95.

Krause, C. The femininity complex and women therapists. *Journal of Marriage and the Family,* 1971, *33,* 476–482.

Kravetz, D. Consciousness-raising groups and group psychotherapy: Alternative mental health resources for women. *Psychotherapy: Theory, Research, and Practice,* 1976, *13,* 72–76.

Kravetz, D. Consciousness-raising groups in the 1970's. *Psychology of Women Quarterly.* 1978, *3,* 168–186.

Krumboltz, J. D., Becker-Haven, J. F., & Burnett, K. F. Counseling psychology. *Annual Review of Psychology,* 1979, *30,* 555–602.

Lerman, H. *What happens in feminist therapy.* Paper presented at the meeting of the American Psychological Association, New Orleans, September 1974. (Also in S. Cox [Ed.], *Female psychology: The emerging self.* Chicago: Science Research Associates, 1976.)

Lockheed, M. Female motive to avoid success: A psychological barrier or a response to deviancy? *Sex Roles,* 1975, *1,* 41–50.

Long-Laws, J. A feminist review of marital adjustment literature: The rape of the locke. *Journal of Marriage and the Family,* 1971, *33,* 483–515.

Lorr, M. Client perceptions of therapists: A study of the therapeutic relation. *Journal of Consulting Psychology,* 1965, *29,* 146–149.

Mander, A. V., & Rush, A. K. *Feminism as therapy.* New York: Random House, 1974.

Marecek, J., & Kravetz, D. Women and mental health: A review of feminist change efforts. *Psychiatry,* 1977, *40,* 323–329.

Marecek, J., Kravetz, D., & Finn, S. A comparison of women who enter feminist therapy and women who enter traditional therapy. *Journal of Consulting and Clinical Psychology,* 1979, *47,* 734–742.

Martin, R. J., & Sterne, A. L. Post hospital adjustment as related to therapists' in-therapy behavior. *Psychotherapy: Theory, Research, and Practice,* 1976, *13,* 267–273.

McCarthy, P. R., & Betz, N. E. Differential effects of self-disclosing versus self-involving counselor statements. *Journal of Counseling Psychology,* 1978, *25,* 251–256.

Meltzoff, J., & Kornreich, M. *Research in psychotherapy.* New York: Atherton Press, 1970.

Mintz, J., Luborsky, L., & Auerbach, A. Dimensions of psychotherapy: A factor-analytic study of ratings of psychotherapy sessions. *Journal of Consulting and Clinical Psychology,* 1971, *39,* 106–120.

Nassi, A. J., & Abramowitz, S. P. Raising consciousness about women's groups: Process and outcome research. *Psychology of Women Quarterly,* 1978, *3,* 139–156.

National Organization for Women. *A consumers' guide to nonsexist therapy.* New York Chapter of the National Organization for Women, 1978.

Nichols, M. P. Outcome of brief cathartic psychotherapy. *Journal of Consulting and Clinical Psychology,* 1974, *42,* 403–410.

O'Leary, V. *Toward understanding women.* Monterey, Calif.: Brooks/Cole, 1977.

Orlinsky, D. E., & Howard, K. I. The relation of process to outcome in psychotherapy. In S. L. Garfield & A. E. Bergin (Eds.), *Handbook of psychotherapy and behavior change.* New York: Wiley, 1978.

Parloff, M. B., Waskow, P. E., & Wolfe, B. E. Research on therapist variables in relation to process and outcome. In S. L. Garfield & A. E. Bergin (Eds.), *Handbook of psychotherapy and behavior change.* New York: Wiley, 1978.

Pawlicki, R. E., & Almquist, C. Authoritarianism, locus of control and tolerance of ambiguity as reflected in membership and non-membership in a women's liberation group. *Psychological Reports,* 1973, *32,* 1331–1337.

Plost, M. Effect of sex of career models on occupational preferences of adolescents. *Audio Visual Communication Review,* 1974, *22,* 41–50.

Polster, M. Women in therapy—a Gestalt therapist's view. In V. Franks & V. Burtle (Eds.), *Women in therapy.* New York: Brunner/Mazel, 1974.

Rawlings, E. I., & Carter, D. K. (Eds.). *Psychotherapy for women: Treatment towards equality.* Springfield, Ill.: Charles C. Thomas, 1977.

Roether, H. A., & Peters, J. J. Cohesiveness and hostility in group psychotherapy. *American Journal of Psychiatry,* 1972, *128,* 1014–1017.

Rosenthal, T., & Bandura, A. Psychological modeling: Theory and practice. In S. L.

Garfield & A. E. Bergin (Eds.), *Handbook of psychotherapy and behavior change.* New York: Wiley, 1978.

Saltzman, C., Luetgert, M. J., Roth, C. H., Creaser, J., & Howard, L. Formation of a therapeutic relationship: Experiences during the initial phase of psychotherapy as predictors of treatment duration and outcome. *Journal of Consulting and Clinical Psychology,* 1976, *44,* 546–555.

Sapolsky, A. Relationship between patient–doctor compatibility, mutual perceptions, and outcome of treatment. *Journal of Abnormal Psychology,* 1965, *70,* 70–76.

Sherman, J., Koufacos, C., & Kenworthy, J. A. Therapists: Their attitudes and information about women. *Psychology of Women Quarterly,* 1978, *2,* 299–313.

Stoloff, C. Who joins women's liberation? *Psychiatry,* 1973, *36,* 325–340.

Stricker, G. Implications of research for psychotherapeutic treatment of women. *American Psychologist,* 1977, *32,* 14–22.

Strupp, H. H., & Hadley, S. W. A tripartite model of mental health and therapeutic outcomes: With special reference to negative effects in psychotherapy. *American Psychologist,* 1977, *32,* 187–196.

Tangri, S. S. Determinants of occupational role innovation among college women. *Journal of Social Issues,* 1972, *28,* 177–199.

Tanney, M. F., & Birk, J. M. Women counselors for women clients? A review of the research. *Counseling Psychologist,* 1976, *6,* 28–32.

Tipton, R. M., Bailey, K. G., & Obenchain, J. P. Invasion of male's personal space by feminists and nonfeminists. *Psychological Reports,* 1975, *37,* 99–102.

Tovian, S. M. Patient experiences and psychotherapy outcome (Doctoral dissertation, Northwestern University, 1977). *Dissertation Abstracts International,* 1978, *38,* 4487B–4488B. (University Microfilms No. 7800758)

Wallston, B. S. The effects of sex role, self-esteem, and expected future interaction with an audience on help-seeking. *Sex Roles,* 1976, *2,* 353–366.

Webster's new collegiate dictionary. Springfield, Mass.: Merriam, 1979.

Wicker, A. Attitudes vs. actions: The relationship of verbal and overt behavioral responses to attitude objects. *Journal of Social Issues,* 1969, *25,* 41–78.

CHAPTER 11

Consciousness-Raising and Self-Help

DIANE KRAVETZ

One of the most impressive features of the second wave of the feminist movement has been the emergence of a myriad of self-help activities and organizations. These self-help groups serve multifaceted purposes and are directed in diverse ways toward changing the psychological, social, legal, economic, political, and cultural circumstances of women. These groups do not have uniform structures or philosophies and only in some instances are there formal (or informal) linkages among them. Included among these groups are the large, national women's rights organizations; a multitude of women's caucuses within academia, business, labor, and the professions; and many independent organizations and groups such as women's centers, women's music and theater groups, women's bookstores, and women's presses.

One important aspect of many of the self-help activities in the women's movement is the provision of alternatives to established health, mental health, and social services, which are seen as oppressive and unresponsive to the needs of women. Numerous alternative feminist service agencies have evolved, including women's counseling centers, abortion referral services, rape crisis centers, shelters for battered women, feminist therapy collectives, and women's health centers. Feminists have developed new models of mental health and new approaches to psychotherapy with women, which have been incorporated into the services of women's self-help agencies and in the self-help literature for women.

In all of these self-help activities, consciousness-raising (CR) has been a central feature. Understanding the nature of female oppression in a sexist society has been essential for assessing needs, establishing goals, and providing alternative programs and services. The primary mechanism for CR in the women's movement has been the CR group.

Diane Kravetz. School of Social Work, University of Wisconsin, Madison, Wisconsin.

Through CR groups, women come to understand the intricate relationships between public, systemic conditions and the individual aspects of their experiences; that is, "the personal becomes political." This chapter will review the research literature on CR in the women's movement, focusing on the therapeutic benefits of CR groups for women.

History of CR Groups

In their early stages, mid-1960s to early 1970s, CR groups consisted primarily of radical feminists, and group discussions focused on political analyses and the development of feminist ideology. Also, these early CR group members educated themselves and others through projects such as writing pamphlets and newsletters, serving as a "speakers' bureau," planning demonstrations and protests, and organizing other women's CR groups. As noted by Carden (1974) and Freeman (1975), the proliferation of CR groups during this period and public awareness of feminist thought can be largely attributed to their efforts. These early groups served as mechanisms for educating and radicalizing women and for creating a broad-based social concern with women's issues.

By the mid-1970s, the political education functions of social activists in these groups became less salient. The presence of sex bias and discrimination and the principles and goals of the women's movement had become increasingly discussed in the society at large. At the same time, the appeal of the personal growth and support aspects of CR groups became prevalent. CR groups became widely identified as a way for women to examine issues in their own lives in terms of their social conditioning. By altering women's perceptions of themselves and of society at large, CR groups were seen as mechanisms for both personal and social change. It is the personal change aspects of CR groups in the 1970s that are of most relevance to this chapter.

Differences between CR Groups and Psychotherapy

Although CR groups are viewed throughout the feminist literature as having significant personal change consequences for women, feminists have consistently asserted that CR groups are not therapy (Hanisch, 1971; Morgan, 1970; Susan, 1970; Zweig, 1971). Further, they discouraged women in CR groups from incorporating the theories and techniques they may have learned in therapy, or even in encounter groups (Dreifus, 1973; Tennov, 1973; Perl & Abarbanell, Note 1). The primary differences between CR groups and psychotherapy concern ideology, social context, structure, and process (Brodsky, 1973, 1977; Kirsh, 1974; Kravetz, 1976; Tennov, 1973; Warren, 1976).

The goals of traditional psychotherapy include changing individual attitudes, behaviors, and emotional states which are assumed to be deviant, sick, or maladaptive. Whether treatment is focused on recovery from illness, modifying problematic behaviors and emotional states, gaining insight, or discovering the underlying causes of symptoms, traditional psychotherapy is adjustment-oriented and focuses on the individual. Individual therapy assumes that the individual is the object of change, that the individual is responsible for the solutions, and that individual solutions are possible. Diagnosis and intervention in therapy are based on clinical theories and research as well as on the clinical experience of the therapist.

In contrast, in CR groups, institutional structures and social norms, as well as individual attitudes and behaviors, provide the framework for analysis. Through sharing, CR groups help women understand and deal with personal problems as they are related to their sex-role conditioning and experiences with sex bias and discrimination. Through this process, personal attitudes, behaviors, roles, and relationships, as well as social policies and practices, become targets for change. Although literature may be used to provide additional information, personal experiences of group members are considered the central ingredients for understanding problems and for devising solutions, both private and public.

The structure of the therapist–client (or therapist–patient) relationship is hierarchical and relies on the expertise of a trained professional, who is generally male. Typically, it is assumed that the therapist does not share the problems of the client and will not reveal personal material. The therapist professes to be morally neutral and nonjudgmental. Authority and control are maintained by the therapist, who establishes therapy goals and treatments. Conversely, CR groups are based on equal sharing of resources, power, and responsibility. They are generally leaderless and stress principles of sisterhood and the authority of personal experience. The structure of these groups inherently assumes and promotes women's abilities to be autonomous, self-directing, and competent. There is an assumption of shared experience and shared difficulties. CR groups emphasize being supportive and nonjudgmental toward group members' behaviors and attitudes but critically examine social values and political beliefs.

Some of the processes which occur in CR groups also occur in group psychotherapy, including provision of role models, sharing of personal experience, imparting of information, peer support, identifying commonalities, instillation of hope, and cohesiveness (Warren, 1976). However, group therapy is designed to be a corrective experience, based on exploration of individual factors and emphasizing the interpersonal relationships within the group as a major factor in the change process. CR groups are not viewed as a corrective experience but rather as a process of personal growth. CR groups also minimize the importance of interpersonal learning in the group; change occurs through women's increasing understanding of themselves as part of a larger social group and through viewing personal problems within the context of common social roles and social conditions.

Finally, therapy is conducted within conventional mental health institutions and social service agencies and in professional offices. CR groups are organized through a wide range of formal and informal networks and organizations, most of which are identified with the women's movement. Many of the small, multiservice alternative feminist agencies through which CR groups are formed share many of the characteristics of the CR groups themselves: (1) Their authority structure is collegial or collective; (2) emphasis is placed on personal growth and includes advocacy and social change as a focus of activity and analysis; (3) relationships with women are conducted in a personal, humanistic fashion; (4) they are located in a range of settings, including private homes, churches, libraries, schools, and community centers; and (5) they are grass-roots groups, working outside established institutions (Bayes, Whisnant, & Wilk, 1977; Galper & Washburne, 1976; McShane & Oliver, 1978; The Women and Mental Health Project, 1976).

These significant distinctions between CR groups and psychotherapy are unnecessarily blurred when CR groups are referred to as a form of therapy or of treatment. Nevertheless, based on personal accounts and research investigations of CR groups, there is a widespread belief among feminists that CR groups have served as effective mechanisms for resocialization and personal change for many women. In the professional literature, CR groups have been discussed as an alternative mental health resource for women (Brodsky, 1973, 1977; Kirsh, 1974; Kravetz, 1976; Warren, 1976). Numerous writers have also discussed the value of incorporating CR group principles and techniques in encounter groups (Meador, Solomon, & Bowen, 1972), in assertiveness training (Lange & Jakubowski, 1976; Phelps & Austin, 1975), and in education (Gerson, 1974; Grady, 1972; Moreland, 1976).

Studies of CR Groups

Studies of CR groups primarily include women who are white, middle-class adults with at least some college education, who live in urban/

suburban areas, a majority of whom are or have been married. Based on the characteristics of women in the women's movement during the late 1960s to the mid-1970s, it is likely that these studies accurately represent women in CR groups during this time.

Most studies of CR groups have been based on participant observation and personal interviews. In her field study, 1971–1973, Cassell (1977) used participant observation of a range of movement activities, interviews, a written questionnaire, measures of interaction in a women's liberation group, and analysis of feminist publications. In one case study of the first 5 months of a CR group, Cassell found that, through CR, women began to question the "automatic female assumption of domestic responsibility" and to explore ways to change their roles. Also, women developed a sense of closeness to each other and to other women, and they began to perceive themselves as a member of a larger group composed of women. Some women became increasingly dissatisfied or angry, and often their new consciousness and new demands placed a range of pressures on existing female–male relationships. Although the women shared a commitment to personal change, not all women actually made major changes in their lives. For some, the group seemed to function as a safety valve and helped them to maintain the status quo. For these women, generally married women with young children, the alternatives to their current situation were often perceived as worse, and/or they were waiting until their children were in school before making major changes in their lives.

Carden's (1974) study of the women's movement, 1969–1971, included interviews with movement members in seven major cities in the United States as well as participant observation of movement activities and analysis of movement publications. Like Cassell, Carden also observed cognitive restructuring, that is, a conscious change in group members' perspectives on their roles and on what it is to be a woman. Also, she found that among CR group participants, many women changed jobs, returned to school, or went back to paid employment; some (5–15%) became (or remained) involved in feminist social action projects. Carden concludes that "the degree of reconceptualization reached does not depend upon the group's life span but upon its members' openness to radical ideas and their prior commitment to a traditional or nontraditional lifestyle" (Carden, 1974, pp. 71–72).

Based on interviews with 17 women in CR groups, Newton and Walton (Note 2) found five types of CR group outcomes: (1) an altered world view: understanding the political and social aspects of women's experience and seeing women as a definitive group and society as divided into females and males; (2) changes in identity, including changes in body image and feelings about sexuality; (3) an enhanced sense of self-acceptance and a lessening of guilt and self-doubt; (4) change in reference groups and interpersonal relationships: seeing women as their primary reference group, having more women friends, and having more egalitarian relationships with men; and (5) changes in job/career orientation: an ambivalence toward careerism and a tendency to change their main area of interest to be directly related to movement activities.

Eastman (1973) observed one CR group of 14 women for 9 months during 1971–1972 (25 sessions) and conducted interviews with 11 members of the group. Toward the end of the group, group members reported that the impact of their group experience included increased autonomy, greater self-confidence and self-knowledge, changes in their negotiation of interpersonal relationships, and a growing sense of identity with other women. Some women became "starters" for other CR groups and worked on the creation of a women's center as an outgrowth of their CR group experience.

In the other participant observation and interview studies, CR group outcomes included similar findings: improved self-image; higher self-esteem; greater self-respect; increased feelings of competence and confidence; increased self-awareness and self-acceptance; increased awareness and expression of anger; improved attitudes toward and relationships with other women; the development of new understandings concerning sex roles; the development of a feminist identity; and a range of behavioral changes, including organized efforts to change women's circumstances at work and in the community (Kirkpatrick, 1975; Micossi, 1970; Whiteley, 1973; Acker & Howard, Note 3; Krug, Note 4; White, Note 5).

There have been comparatively few quantitative studies of CR groups. In a national survey of 1669 women in CR groups, Kravetz (1978) found that women's most important goals for the CR group experience were (1) to share thoughts and feelings about being a woman, (2) to increase self-awareness, (3) to learn about other women and their experiences, (4) to receive and give emotional support, and (5) to examine problems women have with their traditional roles. In this study, 71% of the women indicated that they had met their goals, 89% felt that they had had a constructive experience, and 89% enjoyed the experience. The majority of women in this survey actively encouraged other women to participate in a CR group and thought that many (or all) of the women they knew would benefit from being in a CR group. However, this study did not measure the nature or extent of personal change in these groups.[1]

[1]Results from this survey have also been described by Lieberman and Bond (1976).

Although women join CR groups to examine women's experiences and roles, Kravetz, Marecek, and Finn (Note 6) found that this common theme has different meanings for different women. More detailed analyses of data from the national survey revealed two central and separate motives for joining CR groups: (1) to solve personal problems and (2) to develop a more feminist perspective. The women entering CR groups for personal problem-solving tended to be housewives wtih children who were experiencing high levels of distress. Women who enter CR groups to develop (or strengthen) their feminism tended to be identified with the movement prior to joining a CR group, to be employed or students, to be "symptom-free," and not to have children. The results of this study suggested that for women who identified with the women's movement prior to joining a CR group, participation in CR groups reflected a desire to explore the linkages between feminist ideology and their own lives. For women who were not otherwise involved in the movement, CR groups were primarily a means for personal growth through shared understandings of problems common to women.

Riger (Note 7) compared 43 women who had been in a CR group for a least 6 months with 38 women who were beginning CR and 41 noninvolved women. Each woman completed a questionnaire consisting of a locus-of-control scale and measures of political attitudes and experiences. Riger found that those women who were already participants in the movement and the new recruits scored in the direction of external control on the "Feminist Ideology" and "System Blame" factors of the locus-of-control scale as compared with the noninvolved women. The changes most often reported by the experienced CR group members were (1) an increase in self-esteem, (2) and increase in primary relationships with women, and (3) an increased awareness of sex discrimination. Changes in political attitudes were least frequently mentioned. Riger concluded that participation in CR groups primarily leads to changes in the self and in interpersonal relationships and less so to changes in political attitudes and beliefs.

Follingstad, Robinson, and Pugh (1977) compared 22 women in two CR groups with differing time formats (both totaling 16 hours) with a control group, using group facilitators and structured group experiences. Measures of change included the Attitudes toward Women Scale, the Feminism Behavior Scale, the Expressed Acceptance of Self Scale, and the Marlowe–Crowne Social Desirability Scale. This study found significantly more self-reported profeminist attitudes and behaviors among the women in CR groups than among the controls. However, there were no significant differences on the personality measures.

Barrett (1978) compared the effectiveness for widows of three types of leader-led discussion groups focusing on "specific problems of widowhood" (self-help group), "the development of friendships" (confidant group), and "the roles of women in society" (CR group). The groups met over a 7-week period and were compared with a waiting-list control group. She found that in all three types of discussion groups, women showed more positive change in their health predictions and became less other-oriented than the controls. On items concerning the extent of help from the group and extent of learning in the group, the highest ratings occurred in the CR groups, the lowest in the self-help groups. The most frequently reported positive changes in this study were reduced feelings of unique experience, increased self-confidence, a more positive future outlook, the incorporation of help from the group, increased social contacts, and return to school. The most positive life changes occurred in the CR groups, the least in the self-help groups.

To summarize, the CR group outcomes most frequently reported in the research are (1) increased self-awareness, self-respect, and self-esteem; (2) increased awareness of the effects of traditional sex roles and sexism; (3) increased awareness of a commonality with other women; (4) improved relationships and a sense of solidarity with other women; (5) development of a sociopolitical analysis of female experience and the nature of female oppression; (6) change in interpersonal relationships and roles; and (7) participation in work and/or community activities to change the options and opportunities of women. The most prevalent findings across all studies concern changed perceptions and attitudes toward self, others, and society; there is a reorganization of attitudes and beliefs in a profeminist direction. The behavioral components or ramifications of these cognitive/emotional changes are less specifically documented but are frequently cited. Personality change is frequently noted, primarily based on self-report and observation.

Although quantitative studies are notably sparse, their results confirm the highly positive regard held toward these groups by the women in them. Given the ever-present questions concerning sampling problems, biased reporting, social desirability factors, and the possible lack of "objectivity" among many of the investigators, one must still be impressed with the consistency of findings, particularly those concerning increases or changes in women's awareness. The reported outcomes are very consistent with the stated purpose of these groups, that is, consciousness-raising.

Additional Research

There is some additional research that should be considered in assessing the therapeutic benefits and potential of CR groups. Some of the reported outcomes of CR groups may be related to the positive effects of all-women groups (Aries, 1976; Carlock & Martin, 1977; Halas, 1973; Jakubowski, 1977; Meador *et al.*, 1972; Wyckoff, 1971). Also, effective socioemotional behaviors continue to characterize women's performance in groups (Eskilson & Wiley, 1976; Piliavin & Martin, 1978), an example of one of the more positive aspects of traditional female conditioning. Finally, the processes which operate in these groups have been identified as important in promoting positive growth and change in counseling, psychotherapy, and growth groups (Frank, 1961, 1971; Lieberman, Yalom, & Miles, 1973; Rogers, 1957; Truax & Carkhuff, 1967; Yalom, 1975). The empathy and support emphasized in CR groups, combined with an explicit group purpose that focuses on cognitive restructuring through sharing of common experiences and feelings, may contribute to the overall positive evaluation and effectiveness of these groups.

In addition, some of the perceived benefits of these groups may be attributable to the informational/educational aspects of the CR group experience. In studies of CR in course settings, instructors incorporate various combinations of CR techniques, including lectures, films, structured exercises, readings, and group discussion. These CR activities were found (1) to help women adopt new roles, become aware of common oppression, gain strength from others' confrontations, develop self-awareness, and increase personal worth (Rose, McHugh, & DeLuco, Note 8); (2) to change women's attitudes toward women in a profeminist direction and to achieve change on some personal growth factors such as increased inner-directedness, acceptance of aggression, and capacity for intimate contact (Abernathy, Abramowitz, Roback, Weitz, Abramowitz, & Tittler, 1977); and (3) to increase women's viewing their own role and that of their ideal woman as more extrafamilial (Kincaid, 1977).

Outcomes of a CR group experience may also be affected by the fact that these groups are part of a growing social movement. Participation in a CR group may be accompanied by reading feminist literature and by involvement in other feminist activities. In Cherniss' (1972) study, for example, participation in women's liberation involved a weekly CR group and some time in political activity and in classes or workshops. In Kravetz's (1978) study, before joining a CR group, 25% of the women had been in a women's political group, 65% considered themselves to be members of the movement before joining a CR group, and 55% joined a CR group that was started by a women's organization. Therefore, feminists outside of the CR group may serve as a reference group and provide additional role models and support for some members of CR groups. For those women who participate in other movement activities, or who are in a group with such women, it may be impossible to isolate the effects of the CR group from the effects of participation in the movement.

For some women, the positive outcomes of CR groups may stem from CR being an integral part of their development as feminists. Some research indicates that, as compared with nonfeminists, feminists (1) have a high degree of achievement striving, a strong valuation of autonomy and independence, higher self-esteem, and more self-acceptance (Cherniss, 1972); (2) are more creative, original, and willing to take risks (Joesting, 1971); (3) are more internal in their sense of personal control (Sanger & Alker, 1972); (4) have a more positive perception of women (Nielsen & Doyle, 1975); (5) conform less (Goldberg, 1974); and (6) are more self-actualized (Hjelle & Butterfield, 1974). Such studies support the contention that feminism is therapeutic for women: "It is precisely because feminism includes the political that it is therapeutic. It is therapeutic to integrate the personal and the political. It is also especially important for women to see themselves as connected to and influential in public as well as private systems" (Mander & Rush, 1977, p. 49). Although it is beyond the scope of this chapter to speculate as to the multitude of factors which may have contributed to the results of these studies, it appears that women's mental helath may be positively affected by that constellation of factors that constitute being a feminist.

Recommendations for Future Research

In reviewing the research on women's CR groups, it becomes evident that specification of the nature, extent, and maintenance of change related to participation in these groups has not received adequate attention. In general, women join CR groups with the overall purpose of exploring women's experiences, roles, and social conditions. However, "being a member of a CR group" no longer sufficiently defines the sample of women in these groups. Women in CR groups have different psychological needs, personal circumstances, roles, political perspectives, and social–political involvements. Also, women enter CR groups with differing expectations and goals. Some women, for example, join to discuss issues that are of particular concern to their subgroup, for example, welfare mothers, professional women, lesbians, widows, and women from ethnic and racial minorities. Future research should (1) document the extent to which CR groups are used by different populations of women and (2) investigate the relationships among the various factors that motivate women to join CR groups and the nature and extent of change which occurs in these groups.

Differences in outcome may also be related to the nature of the group itself. Identification of women's circumstances, expectations, and goals may reveal differences among women who join leaderless groups, who, in turn, may differ from women who join structured, time-limited groups with leaders or group facilitators. Further, differences may be attributable to the specific processes and tasks which distinguish various types of groups. Finally, group composition factors may affect the nature of information imparted, the types of issues discussed, the variety of role models presented, and the range of alternatives considered. To substantiate and detail the therapeutic aspects of CR groups, longitudinal studies of different types of women and different types of groups would provide the most meaningful results.

In addition, attention must be given to the process of change for women over time. As noted by Kelman (1974), attitude "is not an index of action, but a determinant, component, and consequent of it.... Attitude and action are linked in a continuing reciprocal process, each generating the other in an endless chain" (p. 316). Understanding the relationships between attitude change and behavioral change for women, and the various contexts in which change does (or does not) occur, will provide the basis for meaningful research on the nature of women's therapeutic self-help. Some questions to be pursued include the following:

1. What specific behavioral and personality changes most consistently occur as a result of CR activities, especially CR groups? How do these outcomes differ for different types of women and in different types of groups?
2. To what extent do women incorporate their new insights and awareness into ongoing roles and relationships? How does this differ for different types of women?
3. What is the impact of women's CR group experience on their significant others—for example, partner, child(ren), close friends—and on their role performance at home, at work, and in their community?
4. In what ways do women find sources of support and direction as they attempt change? Do they use other, more problem-focused systems to achieve specific changes during or following their CR group; that is, do they enter therapy, assertiveness training, vocational counseling, political action groups, etc.? Do they join another type of CR or women's support group?
5. What are the relationships between women's participation in CR groups, their evolution as feminists, and their personal develop-

ment and psychological well-being? In what ways is the development of feminist ideology and participation in feminist political activity related to women's mental health?

Research should also be directed toward establishing the utility of CR groups through use of control groups and comparisons with other change-induction systems. In natural settings, control groups can be drawn from waiting lists, early dropouts, and those who attend informational meetings but do not join. Also, it is important to include women who leave their CR group before achieving their goals or whose entire group disbanded prior to its being a successful experience for its members. Useful comparison groups include leaderless, unstructured groups; structured groups with leaders; and CR classes and workshops. The therapeutic value of CR groups should also be evaluated through outcome studies that compare women in these groups with women in traditional therapy groups. It should be recognized, however, that meaningful comparisons with forms of therapy may be difficult, since women may be entering therapy and CR groups with different needs, levels of distress, and goals. Also, as discussed earlier, traditional therapies and CR groups significantly differ in ideology, structure, process, and goals; therefore, many outcome measures are not equally appropriate or relevant to both systems (Klein, 1976; Kravetz, 1976).

Since, to some extent, feminist ideology, political activity, and social change are primary ingredients in CR groups, the relative therapeutic value of CR groups may be best determined in studies that compare the effects of CR groups with various nonsexist and feminist approaches to therapy for women. Many established forms of therapy have been reexamined and modified to incorporate nonsexist values, goals, and interventions (for examples, see Franks & Burtle, 1974; Rawlings & Carter, 1977a). Also, feminists have developed approaches to therapy which explicitly incorporate feminist principles and values (Lerman, 1976; Marecek & Kravetz, 1977; Rawlings & Carter, 1977b; Brodsky, Note 9, Note 10). To varying degrees, these nonsexist and feminist approaches include various aspects of CR groups. Studies of these approaches as compared with traditional models of therapy also help identify the benefits of incorporating components of CR groups into mental health treatments for women.

Researchers may concentrate their efforts on isolating the components of CR groups and on measuring the effects of structured CR group experiences using student populations. Conducting research in the natural environment of these groups presents numerous problems. First, it may be difficult to gain access to those groups of women who are distrustful of social science researchers and professionals. Also, in grass-roots self-help groups, there may be no established context for distribution of forms and questionnaires as in conventional agencies. It remains a challenge to employ quantitative measures without modifying the nature of the groups in the process. Nevertheless, it is important to find ways to pursue such work, since most of the therapeutic benefits of CR groups have been observed in the small, grass-roots, leaderless CR groups. It is in their natural setting that the most meaningful and generalizable research on CR groups can occur.

It should be noted that, unlike in adjustment-oriented systems, change from CR groups may not produce more rewarding or more successful behaviors. Presenting a self-image and behaviors that deviate from the accepted norms of society may incur increasing difficulties for women. Some relationships may become more satisfying, but others are likely to become stressful. Parents, spouse, children, friends, relatives, and co-workers may be ambivalent, if not hostile, toward a woman's desire to make nontraditional changes in her life. Further, due to sexism in education and occupational realms, as well as in other social institutions, women may not be able to achieve the changes they desire. Assessment, then, must focus on whether or not women are behaving in a self-directing, autonomous manner and whether or not their behavior is the result of a conscious understanding of available options and a deliberate weighing of costs and benefits. As noted by Klein (1976), assessment of successful therapeutic outcomes for women must take into account changing roles and norms, as well as distinguish between soluble and insoluble issues. For assessing mental health, feminist models "are more likely to look at the processes that the individual uses to internalize and personalize values and roles, rather than at the specific content," although concerns with process "have always been much more difficult to formulate and translate into workable measurement systems" (Klein, 1976, p. 94).

There are other therapeutic self-help efforts by and for women which are designed specifically to provide alternatives to traditional therapy. Popular self-help books on assertiveness (e.g., Alberti & Emmons, 1970, 1975; Fensterheim & Baer, 1975; Galassi & Galassi, 1977; Gambrill & Richey, 1976; Jakubowski & Lange, 1978; Phelps & Austin, 1975), transactional analysis (Jongeward & Scott, 1978), and problem-solving groups (Wyckoff, 1977) have flooded the market. It appears that this literature on self-help treatments is being widely read by individual women and used in women's groups, programs, and classes, as well as in therapy. Although there is a broad literature on bibliotherapy and some research, particularly on self-instructional applications of behavior therapies, there has been little discussion or empirical evaluation of this aspect of women's self-help. Also, professionals and nonprofessionals in women's centers and alternative feminist agencies offer a wide range of services, including many forms of counseling and therapy, assertiveness training, women's awareness classes, etc. However, the nature and effects of these services have not been formally assessed.

It is important that research programs on alternatives to traditional mental health services for women include the full range of therapeutic self-help efforts for women. The results of such investigations would provide the basis for appropriate linkages and referrals between professionals and nonprofessionals serving women. Once the relative utility of various help-giving systems is established, women will be able to choose among systems and approaches, using them separately or in conjunction with one another, depending on their particular problems, goals, and personal preferences. The ultimate goal of many feminist self-help efforts is for women to have the power to control their own lives. Successful research investigations of these activities will depend on the development and application of research strategies that acknowledge, respect, and support this goal. Hopefully, the skills and resources of mental health researchers will contribute to the survival and growth of self-help activities that enhance women's personal growth and promote meaningful social change.

Reference Notes

1. Perl, H., & Abarbanell, G. *Guidelines to feminist consciousness raising,* 1976. (Available from G. Abarbanell and H. Perl, 1835 South Bentley, Los Angeles, Cal.)
2. Newton, E., & Walton, S. *The personal is political: Consciousness raising and personal change in the women's liberation movement.* Paper presented at the meeting of the American Anthropological Association, November 1971.
3. Acker, J., & Howard, M. *On becoming a feminist.* Paper presented at the meeting of the American Sociological Association, New Orleans, 1972.
4. Krug, T. *Women's lib: Consciousness raising in Montreal.* On file at the Montreal Ethnographic Data Bank, Sir George Williams University, Montreal, 1972.
5. White, H. R. *Becoming a feminist.* Unpublished honors paper, Douglass College, 1971.
6. Kravetz, D., Marecek, J., & Finn, S. *Factors influencing women's participation in consciousness-raising groups.* Manuscript submitted for publication, 1979.
7. Riger, S. *Locus of control beliefs and women's consciousness raising group participation.* Paper presented at the meeting of the American Psychological Association, San Francisco, 1977.
8. Rose, S., McHugh, M. C., & DeLuco, L. *Consciousness-raising in college curriculum.* Paper presented at the meeting of the Association for Women in Psychology, St. Louis, Mo., February 1977.
9. Brodsky, A. M. *Feminist therapy: In search of a theory.* Symposium presented at the meeting of the American Psychological Association, New Orleans, 1974.
10. Brodsky, A. M. *Is there a feminist therapy?* Paper presented at the meeting of the Southeastern Psychological Association, Atlanta, March 1975.

References

Abernathy, R. W., Abramowitz, S. I., Roback, H. B., Weitz, L. J., Abramowitz, C. V., & Tittler, B. The impact of an intensive consciousness-raising curriculum on adolescent women. *Psychology of Women Quarterly,* 1977, *2,* 138–148.

Alberti, R. E., & Emmons, M. L. *Your perfect right: A guide to assertive behavior.* San Luis Obispo, Cal.: Impact, 1970.

Alberti, R. E., & Emmons, M. L. *Stand up, speak out, talk back.* New York: Pocket Books, 1975.

Aries, E. Interaction patterns and themes of male, female, and mixed groups. *Small Group Behavior,* 1976, *7,* 7–18.

Barrett, C. J. Effectiveness of widows' groups in facilitating change. *Journal of Consulting and Clinical Psychology,* 1978, *46,* 20–31.

Bayes, M., Whisnant, L., & Wilk, L. A. The mental health center and the women's liberation group: An intergroup encounter. *Psychiatry,* 1977, *40,* 66–78.

Brodsky, A. The consciousness-raising group as a model for therapy with women. *Psychotherapy: Theory, Research, and Practice,* 1973, *10,* 24–29.

Brodsky, A. Therapeutic aspect of consciousness-raising groups. In E. I. Rawlings & D. K. Carter (Eds.), *Psychotherapy for women: Treatment toward equality.* Springfield, Ill.: Charles C. Thomas, 1977.

Carden, M. L. *The new feminist movement.* New York: Russell Sage Foundation, 1974.

Carlock, C. J., & Martin, P. Y. Sex composition and the intensive group experience. *Social Work,* 1977, *22,* 27–33.

Cassell, J. *A group called women: Sisterhood and symbolism in the feminist movement.* New York: David McKay, 1977.

Cherniss, C. Personality and ideology: A personological study of women's liberation. *Psychiatry,* 1972, *35,* 109–125.

Dreifus, C. *Woman's fate: Raps from a feminist consciousness-raising group.* New York: Bantam Books, 1973.

Eastman, P. C. Consciousness-raising as a resocialization process for women. *Smith College Studies in Social Work,* 1973, *43,* 153–183.

Eskilson, A., & Wiley, M. G. Sex composition and leadership in small groups. *Sociometry,* 1976, *39,* 183–193.

Fensterheim, H., & Baer, J. L. *Don't say yes when you want to say no: How assertiveness training can change your life.* New York: Dell, 1975.

Follingstad, D. R., Robinson, E. A., & Pugh, M. Effects of consciousness-raising groups on measures of feminism, self-esteem, and social desirability. *Journal of Counseling Psychology,* 1977, *24,* 223–230.

Frank, J. D. *Persuasion and healing: A comparative study of psychotherapy.* Baltimore: Johns Hopkins University Press, 1961.

Frank, J. D. Therapeutic factors in psychotherapy. *American Journal of Psychotherapy,* 1971, *25,* 350–361.

Franks, V., & Burtle, V. (Eds.). *Women in therapy.* New York: Brunner/Mazel, 1974.

Freeman, J. *The politics of women's liberation.* New York: David McKay, 1975.

Galassi, M. D., & Galassi, J. *Assert yourself: How to be your own person.* New York: Human Sciences Press, 1977.

Galper, M., & Washburne, C. K. A women's self-help program in action. *Social Policy,* 1976, *6,* 46–52.

Gambrill, E. D., & Richey, C. A. *It's up to you: The development of assertive social skills.* Millbrae, Cal.: Les Femmes, 1976.

Gerson, B. Consciousness-raising groups with elementary school girls: A case study. *Psychotherapy: Theory, Research, and Practice,* 1974, *11,* 30–35.

Goldberg, C. Sex roles, task competence, and conformity. *Journal of Psychology,* 1974, *86,* 157–164.

Grady, K. A proposal for consciousness-raising in the public schools. In *National Organization for Women Report on Sex Bias in the Public Schools.* New York: National Organization for Women, 1972.

Halas, C. All-women's groups: A view from inside. *Personnel and Guidance Journal,* 1973, *52,* 91-95.

Hanisch, C. The personal is political. In J. Agel (Ed.), *The radical therapist.* New York: Ballantine, 1971.

Hjelle, L. A., & Butterfield, R. Self-actualization and women's attitudes toward their role in contemporary society. *Journal of Psychology,* 1974, *87,* 225-230.

Jakubowski, P. Self-assertion training procedures for women. In E. I. Rawlings & D. K. Carter (Eds.), *Psychotherapy for women: Treatment toward equality.* Springfield, Ill.: Charles C. Thomas, 1977.

Jakubowski, P., & Lange, A. *The assertive option: Your rights and responsibilities.* Champaign, Ill.: Research Press, 1978.

Joesting, J. Comparison of women's liberation members with their nonmember peers. *Psychological Reports,* 1971, *29,* 1291-1294.

Jongeward, D., & Scott, D. *Women as winners.* Reading, Mass.: Addison-Wesley, 1978.

Kelman, H. C. Attitudes are alive and well and gainfully employed in the sphere of action. *American Psychologist,* 1974, *29,* 310-324.

Kincaid, M. B. Changes in sex-role attitudes and self-actualization of adult women following a consciousness-raising group. *Sex Roles,* 1977, *3,* 329-336.

Kirkpatrick, M. J. A report on a consciousness raising group for women psychiatrists. *Journal of American Medical Women's Association,* 1975, *30,* 206-212.

Kirsh, B. Consciousness-raising groups as therapy for women. In V. Franks & V. Burtle (Eds.), *Women in therapy.* New York: Brunner/Mazel, 1974.

Klein, M. H. Feminist concepts of therapy outcome. *Psychotherapy: Theory, Research, and Practice,* 1976, *13,* 89-95.

Kravetz, D. Consciousness-raising groups and group psychotherapy: Alternative mental health resources for women. *Psychotherapy: Theory, Research, and Practice,* 1976, *13,* 66-71.

Kravetz, D. Consciousness-raising groups in the 1970s. *Psychology of Women Quarterly,* 1978, *3,* 168-186.

Lange, A., & Jakubowski, P. *Responsible assertive behavior: Congnitive/behavioral procedures for trainers.* Champaign, Ill.: Research Press, 1976.

Lerman, H. What happens in feminist therapy. In S. Cox (Ed.), *Female psychology: The emerging self.* Chicago: Science Research Associates, 1976.

Lieberman, M. A., Yalom, I. D., & Miles, M. B., *Encounter groups: First facts.* New York: Basic Books, 1973.

Lieberman, M. A., & Bond, A. R. The problem of being a woman: A survey of 1,700 women in consciousness-raising groups. *The Journal of Applied Behavioral Science,* 1976, *12,* 363-379.

Mander, A. V., & Rush, A. K. *Feminism as therapy.* New York: Random House, 1977.

Marecek, J., & Kravetz, D. Women and mental health: A review of feminist change efforts. *Psychiatry,* 1977, *40,* 323-329.

McShane, C., & Oliver, J. Women's groups as alternative human service agencies. *Journal of Sociology and Social Welfare,* 1978, *5,* 615-626.

Meador, B., Solomon, E., & Bowen, M. Encounter groups for women only. In N. A. Solomon & B. Berzon (Eds.), *New perspectives on encounter groups.* New York: Jossey-Bass, 1972.

Micossi, A. Conversion to women's lib. *TransAction,* 1970, *8,* 82-90

Moreland, J. R. Facilitator training for consciousness-raising groups in an academic setting. *The Counseling Psychologist,* 1976, *6,* 66-68.

Morgan, R. Introduction: The women's revolution. In R. Morgan (Ed.), *Sisterhood is powerful: An anthology of writings from the women's liberation movement.* New York: Vintage Books, 1970.

Nielsen, J. M., & Doyle, P. T. Sex-role stereotypes of feminists and nonfeminists. *Sex Roles,* 1975, *1,* 83–95.

Phelps, S., & Austin, N. *The assertive woman.* San Luis Obispo, Cal.: Impact, 1975.

Piliavin, J. A., & Martin, R. R. The effects of the sex composition of groups on style of social interaction. *Sex Roles,* 1978, *4,* 281–296.

Rawlings, E. I., & Carter, D. K. (Eds.). *Psychotherapy for women: Treatment toward equality.* Springfield, Ill.: Charles C. Thomas, 1977. (a)

Rawlings, E. I., & Carter, D. K. Feminist and nonsexist psychotherapy. In E. I. Rawlings & D. K. Carter (Eds.), *Psychotherapy for women: Treatment toward equality.* Springfield, Ill.: Charles C. Thomas, 1977.(b)

Rogers, C. R. The necessary and sufficient conditions of therapeutic personality change. *Journal of Consulting Psychology,* 1957, *21,* 95–103.

Sanger, S. P., & Alker, H. A. Dimensions of internal–external locus of control and the women's liberation movement. *Journal of Social Issues,* 1972, *28,* 115–129.

Susan, B. About my consciousness raising. In L. B. Tanner (Ed.), *Voices from women's liberation.* New York: New American Library, 1970.

Tennov, D. *Open rapping.* Pittsburgh: KNOW, 1973.

Truax, C. B., & Carkhuff, R. R. *Toward effective counseling and psychotherapy.* Chicago: Aldine, 1967.

Warren, L. W. The therapeutic status of consciousness-raising groups. *Professional Psychology,* 1976, *7,* 132–140.

Whiteley, R. M. Women in groups. *The Counseling Psychologist,* 1973, *4,* 27–43.

The Women and Mental Health Project. Women-to-women services. *Social Policy,* 1976, *7,* 21–27.

Wyckoff, H. Radical psychiatry in women's groups. In J. Agel (Ed.), *The radical therapist.* New York: Ballantine, 1971.

Wyckoff, H. *Solving women's problems through awareness, action, and contact.* New York: Grove Press, 1977.

Yalom, I. D. *The theory and practice of group psychotherapy.* New York: Basic Books, 1975.

Zweig, M. Is women's liberation a therapy group? In J. Agel (Ed.), *The radical therapist.* New York: Ballantine, 1971.

CHAPTER 12

Minority Women: Social–Cultural Issues

DORIS Y. WILKINSON

Introduction

For more than a decade, following from the impetus of the women's liberation movement, there has been an increased interest in the mental health needs of women (President's Commisson on Mental Health, 1978). This movement, with roots in the civil rights revolution (LaRue, 1976), has pointed toward the necessity for an examination of the emotional problems of all women. At present, researchers and practitioners are directing attention not only to the causes and consequences of these problems but also to the effects of varying treatment modalities, sex-role stereotyping, and sex bias in therapy with women (APA Task Force, 1975; Broverman, Clarkson, Rosenkrantz, & Vogel, 1970; Chesler, 1972; Stricker, 1977) and to the role of gender in therapy as it affects input, process, and outcomes. Some researchers and clinicians have offered a rationale and/or framework for a feminist therapy (Holroyd, 1976; Johnson, 1976; Klein, 1976; Marecek & Kravetz, 1977; S. A. Thomas, 1977). Overall, there has been a proliferation of discourse, research, and conceptual models focusing on psychotherapy with women (Chesler, 1971; Fabrikant, 1974; Hare-Mustin, 1978; Levine, 1974; Orlinsky & Howard, 1976).

While there has been a plethora of clinical, social science, and behavioral science research and critical literature on women, mostly white, there exists a significant hiatus in examinations of the therapeutic process and outcomes with minority women (i.e., American Indian, black or African-American, Mexican-American, and Puerto Rican). Most studies of racial and ethnic minorities have not been sex-specific and have centered primarily on intrapsychic factors as giving rise to their emotional problems. Further, emphasis has been placed on structural var-

Doris Y. Wilkinson. Department of Sociology, Howard University, Washington, D.C.

iables as causal factors, such as racial discrimination (Morales, 1971), the distribution of disorders (Pasamanick, 1963), utilization of psychiatric facilities (Kramer, Rosen, & Willis, 1973; Meyer, 1977; Milazzo-Sayre, 1977), and rates of mental disorders (Fischer, 1969; Taube, 1971).

Moreover, there is a paucity of data on the cultural and social-psychological dimensions of the race of counselors and therapists and the impact of this variable on therapeutic relationships. Further, studies designed to measure the interactive effects between the gender and race of a therapist *and* the dynamics and parameters of therapist–client interaction when the client is a minority female are virtually nonexistent. This chapter will focus specifically on literature pertinent to an understanding of the psychotherapeutic encounter with minority women.

The interest in the minority female sector, in particular, is, to a large extent, a consequence of growing concerns with the roles, statuses, and health needs of women in general. This interest manifests itself most clearly in the economic, educational, and political spheres. In addition, there is a greater awareness of the mental health problems and needs of minority women as well as the functions of gender and race as culturally conditioned variables affecting the judgments of counselors, psychiatrists, diagnosticians, and therapists (W. M. Banks, 1972; W. M. Banks & Martens, 1973; Bernard, 1972; Goldberg, 1972; Lane, 1968). Another issue which relates to the emphasis on minority women is their disproportionate concentration in clinical diagnostic categories with severe disorders. For example, data on the diagnostic distribution of admissions to inpatient services of state and county mental hospitals show that, in 1975, 50% of nonwhite females were diagnosed as schizophrenic, while 38% of white females were similarly diagnosed. For nonwhite females, the age-adjusted rate was approximately two-and-one-half times greater than the rate of white females (Meyer, 1977; Wilkinson, Note 1). Although such data do not enable us to uncover the extent to which racial values and gender of therapists affect clinical diagnoses and therapeutic interactions, it has been documented that growing racial conflicts, independent of gender, impede the interracial therapeutic experience (Butts, 1969; Friedman, 1966; Milliken, 1965; Pinderhughes, 1969; Sattler, 1970; Taylor, 1971; Vontress, 1971).

This discussion incorporates a recognition of the interface between societal beliefs and customs and the social psychology of the therapeutic context involving a white male therapist and a minority female client. Therapists and social and behavioral scientists are products of their cultures. This means that despite professional training, they are socialized in the beliefs, values, customs, and attitudes of the society (Patterson, 1958; Saxe, 1970; Szasz, 1966; Wilkinson, 1971, 1974). Available literature indicates that this is clinically relevant in the cross-gender and inter-racial therapeutic situation, since each participant in individual, group, or family therapy has been conditioned to the norms and values of his or her culture (Baratz, 1967; Carkhuff & Pierce, 1967; Gallahorn, Cushing, & Brody, 1965; Jackson, 1973; King, 1973; Vontress, 1969).

This chapter has several objectives. The first is to review selected works which provide a general picture of the state of the art of psychotherapy with minority women. Another objective is to discuss potential limitations of present-day psychotherapy with women of racial and ethnic groups other than white. Results from my own research on psychiatrists as these pertain to the topic under discussion will be presented. In conjunction with this, an extensive set of references is provided for those seeking to critically evaluate psychotherapeutic practices and for others interested in engaging in research. Finally, some suggestions will be offered for research and training which would improve psychotherapy and enhance the sensitivity of therapists to the mental health needs of minority women. The premise of this review of conceptual and theoretical frameworks and empirical studies is that racial and ethnic beliefs serve to reduce objectivity and sensitivity and affect not only the etiology and content of emotional problems but also the therapeutic effort (Burgest, 1973; Edgerton & Karno, 1971; Forster, 1962; Lambley & Cooper, 1975; McLean, 1949; Miranda & Castro, 1977; Olmedo & Parron, in press; Toker, 1966; Wolkon, Moriwaki, & Williams, 1973).

Research on the Modal Minority Group

Most of the literature on minority women and psychoanalysis, counseling, and psychotherapy focuses on black Americans (Backner, 1970; G. Banks, Berenson, & Carkhuff, 1967; King, 1973; Vail, 1970; Watson, 1974; Williams & Kirkland, 1970; Stembridge, Note 2). This is understandable in view of the fact that the black population, which represents the largest racial/ethnic minority population, approaches nearly 27 million. Moreover, the civil rights revolution of the 1960s ushered in a widespread concern for the health—physical and mental—of the poor (Chu & Trotter, 1974) and, specifically, black Americans. Emphasis in research on therapeutic interactions involving Asian, Mexican-American, Puerto Rican, Alaskan native, and American Indian women as clients is thus relatively new. Only recently has there been a concerted effort to focus attention on their mental health needs (Ruiz, 1977; True, Note 3), such phenomena as clinical stereotypes of Chicanos (Lopez,

1977; Simmen, 1971), and the linguistic and cultural barriers which impede successful therapy in the white therapist–minority client situation (Arkoff, Thaver, & Elkind, 1966; G. Banks, 1971; Burgest, 1973; Edgerton & Karno, 1971; Martinez, 1977; Pinderhughes, 1973; Taylor, 1971; A. Thomas, 1962; Torrey, 1969; Vontress, 1971; Wesson, 1975; Yamamoto, James, & Palley, 1968). There is little in the existing literature on mental health issues specifically confronting American Indian women, although it has been acknowledged that black and Hispanic Americans, American Indians, and Alaskan natives are "among the undeserved so far as their mental health needs are concerned" (Thackeray, Skidmore, & Farley, 1979, p. 47). The rationale for discussing extensively therapeutic experiences of black American women is based on (1) their unique and harsh historical, cultural, and social experiences; (2) their differential position in the economic order; (3) the differential labeling and negative stereotyping of black as a color in our society's ideological system and, hence, in the cognitive and perceptual systems of all its members; and (4) the availability of a larger body of data and literature, although basically stereotypical, on their self-concepts, personalities, and behaviors, as well as their emotional problems (W. M. Banks, 1972; Gordon, 1976; Helms, 1979; Jefferies, 1976; Nobles, 1973; Spurlock, 1971; St. Clair, 1951; Willie, Kramer, & Brown, 1973).

Moreover, few of the stereotypes ingrained in the culture about African or black American males and females are characteristic of Asian, American Indian, Mexican-American, and Puerto Rican males and females (Baldwin, 1979; Beale, 1970; Butts, 1969; Carter & Haizlip, 1972; Comer, 1969; Helms, 1979; Rodgers, 1960; Szasz, 1971; A. Thomas & Sillen, 1972; C. S. Thomas & Comer, 1973; Welsing, 1974a, 1974b; Wilkinson & Taylor, 1977). Thus, in examining pertinent literature on the topic under discussion, one finds that most of the research essays and critiques on therapist–client interaction are devoted to white therapist–black client exchanges (P. Adams, 1970; W. A. Adams, 1950; Baratz, 1967; Cohen, 1974; Curry, 1964a, 1964b; Fibush, 1965; Heine, 1950; Kennedy, 1952; Lewis, Balla, & Shanok, 1979; Sager, Brayboy, & Waxenberg, 1972; Sattler, 1977; Schachter & Butts, 1968; Waite, 1968; Wesson, 1975).

A Legacy of Myths

Myths about racial and sex differences are relevant in any therapeutic context, since effectiveness in the process is the ultimate goal. Stereotypes about minority women have not been dissected with the thorough analytic sensibilities required. However, it is recognized that "myths about racial differences have made many psychiatrists uncomfortable with cross-cultural psychiatry" (Carter & Haizlip, 1972, p. 866). These ideas extend to psychotherapy, since such myths are part of the ideology permeating any interracial liaisons and thus would reduce the capability of a white male psychotherapist to fully comprehend the influence of his socialization on the therapeutic exchange with minority female clients (Arkoff *et al.*, 1966; Bernard, 1953; Bloombaum, Yamamoto, & James, 1968; Helms, 1979; Frogg, Note 4).

One of the most resourceful works on clinical practice, psychiatry, and psychoanalytic theory is *Racism and Psychiatry* (A. Thomas & Sillen, 1972). In this penetrating and informative scrutiny, numerous myths with scientific legitimation are traced and perceptively evaluated. By uncovering racially biased premises espoused from the early 1800s to the present, the authors expose a number of assumptions on which psychoanalysis and psychotherapy rest. Among these are racialistic concepts and axioms, integrated in theoretical frames of reference, which bear on this discussion: "the genetic fallacy," the preoccupation with minority psychopathology in research and theory, and the "mark-of-oppression" thesis, which postulates that black males and females have been permanently damaged by a racist social system. Further, "deficit models" focusing on alleged cultural, cognitive, intellectual, and linguistic deprivation and the myth of the pathological character of an alleged matriarchal structure are exposed. Myths about "the racism of sex" and the "sexual mystique" are probed in conjunction with denials of the existence of racism and its impact on psychoanalytic theory, research, and practice (Wilkinson, 1973). A prominent myth which affects the psychotherapeutic process and outcomes is the misconception that sexual conflict is the "root cause of racism." According to the authors, failure on the part of psychiatrists to "grasp the social context of behavior results in interpreting behavior as deviant when it is realistic and normally adaptive" (A. Thomas & Sillen, 1972, pp. 57–58). This inability also serves to inhibit therapists from understanding their own racial, ethnic, and sexual attitudes, thereby reducing their effectiveness (Ganter, 1977a, 1977b; Jackson, 1973; Pinderhughes, 1973; Torrey, 1969). According to Jefferies (1976), the dominant emphasis on deficit models, rather than strengths of black women, creates limitations in the therapeutic context.

Critical evaluations of psychoanalysis and psychotherapy prior to the 1960s were directed at works such as *The Mark of Oppression* (Kardiner & Ovesey, 1951) which stressed solely the psychopathology of blacks. In dissecting this work, one commentator (Brown, 1951) asserted that psychoanalysis has established a pseudoscientific rationale for the economic structure and its consequences. The profession was described as incorporating a "reactionary ideology used against black people," and it was concluded that the study represented a "perversion of scholarship, being a product of and rationale for the oppressing system of white supremacy" (Brown, 1951, p. 16). Brown further contended that the work was representative of the field of psychoanalysis and reflected class biases and chauvinistic attitudes toward black Americans, who are defined in theories and conceptual paradigms as having personalities deviant from those of white behavioral standards. His assessment has implications for understanding the interactive effects between the race or ethnicity of a psychotherapist and the therapeutic experiences of minority women.

Rosen and Frank (1962) have stressed that a model therapeutic encounter to study is that which occurs between a black patient and a white therapist, since this interactional situation embodies deeply rooted racial beliefs and attitudes. They argue that this pairing in individual therapy, or even in group therapy, is determined by the cultural attitudes of whites and blacks toward each other, as well as by their personality configurations. Predictably, however, the authors proceed to a lengthy discussion of the relevance of minority status to the psychopathology of black patients and the role of catalytic incidents in the onset of severe psychotic or neurotic symptoms. In conventional stereotypical fashion, they claim that while blacks exhibit adjustment problems similar to those observed in other ethnic minorities such as the Irish, Italians, Poles, and Jews, as well as poor whites, for blacks these "problems are apt to be more intense and pervasive because they wear with the color of their skin an undisguisable sign of their minority status" (Rosen & Frank, 1962, p. 456). Further, they assert that as a consequence of their ascriptive status, black clients and patients bring predisposing attitudes to the therapeutic relationship: "self-hatred," resentful anxiety, and distrust. According to the authors, distrust, observed frequently in therapeutic contexts, is a greater impediment in group than in individual therapy. They add that the therapist, however, is not free from prejudice, although such an attitude may be operative at the unconscious level. Rosen and Frank (1962) contend that unconscious prejudices are manifested through behaviors such as insecurity, reaction formation, guilt feelings, and rejection. On the other hand, according to the authors, if the therapist is black, overidentification with the black patient may be the consequence. This discussion represents the kind of negative evaluation of blacks in psychotherapy wherein emphasis is placed on minority status as the dominant factor determining the therapeutic process.

One prevailing theme in the research literature is the matriarchal conception of black American families, a subjective model also applied to other ethnic family structures. This sustained and reinforced misconception has permeated psychological literature on black women and behavioral and social science theory and research on black families (Wilkinson, 1972), as well as psychoanalytic theory and psychotherapy. It is the one myth which clearly demonstrates the interaction of sex and race in psychotherapeutic philosophy, research, and practice. Although this value-based thesis recently has come under close scrutiny (Staples, 1977; Ten Houten, 1970; A. Thomas & Sillen, 1972, pp. 89–100), it is nevertheless ingrained in psychotherapy theories, diagnostic patterns, and clinical assessments. Critics of the thesis have focused on its culturally biased dimensions, its failure to incorporate class variations in family structure, and its lack of scientific validity. Further, it has been stated that "to view the black mother only as a repressor of rebellion and aggressivity is... to adopt a stereotype" (A. Thomas & Sillen, 1972, p. 95). This kind of biased perspective affects the objectivity, empirical validity, and clinical usefulness of theoretical paradigms pertaining to black women.

Attitudes, Beliefs, and Behaviors of Therapists

With respect to the prevalence of racial myths and stereotypical thinking, the following question has been posed: "Can a white therapist, operating against the background of a three hundred year history of discrimination and deprivation, and within the context of today's tense racial situation, engage a poor black person in therapy?" (Sager *et al.*, 1972, pp. 415–416). With this question, race and class are linked (Wolkon *et al.*, 1973). Yet the question can be rephrased to focus on whether a white male therapist can develop an effective therapeutic situation with the requisite rapport and empathy when working with an American Indian, Asian, African or black American, or Hispanic female. According to Sager *et al.* and others, "to regard skin color as irrelevant to treatment overrides the central importance the patient's blackness has for him" (Sager *et al.*, 1972, p. 416). This predictable orientation needs to be refocused on the meaning of *whiteness* and *blackness* in the perceptual and cognitive systems of white therapists (Burgest, 1973; Butts, 1969, 1971; Welsing, 1974b). The history of racial ideologies and the structuring of interracial relationships in the society itself have consequences for the patient *and* therapist (Harrison & Butts, 1970). Sattler (1977) notes, in this connection, that the combination of black male client and white female therapist represents the most problematic therapeutic relationship.

Earlier works which addressed the impact of same race, sex unspecified, on effectiveness in psychotherapy (G. Banks *et al.*, 1967) demonstrated that black clients have been found to show a preference for black therapists (Wolkon *et al.*, 1973). Trust, and concomitant attitudes and behaviors surrounding its perceived absence or presence, is a salient variable in the therapeutic process. "The conditions which foster trust at the beginning of the relationship must be explored and then exploited to improve the effectiveness of therapy" (Wolkon *et al.*, 1973, p. 316). "Since most forms of psychotherapy are predicated on achieving absolute openness on the patient's part . . . fradulence provides a shaky substructure for the therapeutic process" (Sager *et al.*, 1972, p. 416).

Grier (1967) has stressed the role of race in the transference process in the *black therapist–white patient* encounter. In his discussion, emphasis is placed on the psychodynamics characterizing this infrequent arrangement (P. Adams, 1970). Case studies are presented in which the racial factor is shown as intensifying the processes of sexualization in transference and those in which it affects maternal transference. It was observed that "the therapist's race presents a situation from the outset which evokes a response in the unconscious of the white patient" (Grier, 1967, p. 1587). Modes of adaptation of the patient range from seeing the black male therapist as having low esteem to viewing him as having unusual powers and thus deserving of special admiration. Ironically, it is claimed that "the racial factor makes white patients easier to cure" (Grier, 1967, p. 1591).

A few years following Grier's observations on the black male psychiatrist and white patient, a number of expositions appeared focusing on the therapeutic relationship and the relevance of race independent of sex (Taylor, 1971). Again, however, the major thrust was on the patient as the unit of analysis. In contrast to the foregoing interpretations, Riess (1971) posed a crucial question which has a direct bearing on the thesis of this discussion: "What happens in therapy interactions when the patient is black and the therapist white?" (Riess, 1971, p. 71). Using selected observational data, he concluded that there is a "need for therapists to examine themselves when they practice across racial lines and to test the validity of their assertion that the problem with interethnic therapy lies solely in the struggle of the patient for identity and equality" (Riess, 1971, p. 72). The question posed by Riess was analyzed thoroughly by Gardner (1971) in his study of factors intervening in therapeutic interactions under two racial situations: white therapist–black client and black therapist–white client, with sex unspecified. Several countertransference patterns, observed in the analysis, suggest variables which would influence input and outcomes in the white male therapist–minority female client situation. These include the need to relieve racial guilt on the part of the therapist, the need for a dominant role, the need for affection and vicarious gratification through the sexual experiences of clients, and the desire for a broadening of social experiences (Gardner, 1971, p. 81). With respect to these psychosocial needs, it was noted that "effective psychotherapy with black clients requires dealing with intense feelings about race and experiences of discrimination" (Gardner, 1971, p. 82).

While similar factors impinge on the therapeutic relationship involving a black therapist and a white client, the needs demonstrated above have been found to become transposed. Interestingly, however, patients' responses to black psychiatrists are seen as more "intense by white psychiatrists" and therapists than the reverse (Harrison & Butts, 1970). Nevertheless, it is surprising that there has been as much research as exists on black therapist–white client encounters, since these are so infrequent (Calnek, 1970; Curry, 1964a; Gardner, 1971; Grier, 1967). Obviously, if color is a key aspect of the transracial clinical context, as researchers have indicated, it is more salient and significant in its consequences when the client is a minority female and the therapist is a white male. One probable outcome of a failure to recognize cultural and personality facets of race and gender has been, in some circumstances, high attrition rates attributable to the therapist's racial ethnocentricity (Gardner, 1971, p. 80; Krebs, 1971; Silverman, 1971; Yamamoto, James, Bloombaum, & Hattem, 1967).

A study of 16 psychotherapists conducted a decade ago revealed that of the responses received in structured interview sessions, approximately 23% were ethnically and racially stereotypical. More significant was the finding that 79% of those studied indicated the presence of latent stereotypical attitudes toward Mexican, black or African, Japanese, Chinese, and Jewish Americans. The findings led to the conclusion that "psychotherapists may be said to reflect the general culture of which they are a part and are therefore not to be considered immune to cultural conditioning" (Bloombaum *et al.,* 1968, p. 99). Broverman *et al.* (1970) and others have also suggested that as a result of socialization to sex-role stereotypes, therapists should be concerned about the potential influence these exert in reinforcing intrapsychic and social conflict.

More recently, an African-American psychologist has pointed to the linguistic, behavioral, and attitudinal differences which permeate the white clinician–black client exchange where social class is an intervening variable. Presenting a hypothetical situation in which a white therapist is confronted with the ghetto idiom, it is stated that "without a knowledge of black life and black jargon, the clinician [will] make a futile attempt to evaluate the 'problem'" (Wesson, 1975, p. 15). But what represents a problem, in the author's view, is the experiential gap between the races. Wesson asserts that the cultural meanings assigned to race thus prevent white therapists from effectively treating black patients.

> American standards are not used in dealing with Chinese culture, and it would be an exceptionally disastrous state of affairs should a white psychologist (or even a black one) audaciously entertain the notion that he could possibly deal effectively with Chinese problems in an appropriate fashion. (Wesson, 1975, p. 17).

The author, however, concedes that white clinicians are not totally responsible for the ideological and value systems in which they operate, since they are "partially innocuous victim[s] caught up in the racist structure; and [since] clinical training deals with no reasonable approaches or meaningful solutions that will help" (Wesson, 1975, p. 14) them develop empathic and intimate relationships with racial and ethnic minority patients or clients.

Further, the research in social and behavioral science does not provide objective information on racism—its history, ideological dimensions, and behavioral consequences. Rather, such research serves primarily to further prejudice white clinicians. Green, however, views psychology as having the "potential for helping combat racial, economic, and sex discrimination and exploitation" (Green, 1975, p. 35).

Psychiatrists' Views of Psychotherapy: An Exploratory Study[1]

In an attempt to ascertain the racial and sexual perceptions and beliefs of psychiatrists as these influence therapeutic philosophy and practice with minority women clients, specifically, African-American women, I conducted a survey of practicing psychiatrists during the summer and fall of 1975. The general purpose of the exploratory study was to determine and describe racial and sexual attitudes and beliefs of a representative sample of psychiatrists practicing in the United States. Unlike the large number of studies and expositions emphasizing the mental health and personality attributes of patients or the demographic and social correlates with mental disorders (Edgerton & Karno, 1971; Forster, 1962; Lambley & Cooper, 1975; McLean, 1949; Toker, 1966), this study was designed to focus solely on those who engage in diagnosis and

[1]This research was supported by a grant awarded in 1975 from the Social Science Research Council.

therapy. With respect to this emphasis, Sattler (1977) notes that clinical judgment examinations and studies of diagnostic decisions made by mental health professionals for black clients constitute important research topics.

Underlying the larger project were the following questions: (1) What are the sexual and racial beliefs of psychiatrists? (2) How do psychiatrists, and especially those engaged in therapy, perceive the role of these beliefs and attitudes in the therapeutic context? (3) Do these beliefs and attitudes influence diagnostic and therapeutic processes? (4) Can a white male psychiatrist or psychotherapist be color- and gender-blind in a race- and sex-conscious society?

The sampling frame consisted of practicing analysts and therapists who identified themselves as psychiatrists in the 1973 biographical *Directory of the Fellows and Members of the American Psychiatric Association.* At the time of the survey, 20,184 psychiatrists were members of the Association. The sample, based on a 10% probability design, was selected in one stage. With the assistance of a clinical psychologist, an instrument was constructed to elicit information about racial and sexual perceptions and beliefs. Data were obtained by means of a mailed questionnaire consisting of demographic items, items pertaining to type of work setting and occupational position, a series of open-ended attitudinal and belief questions on race and sex, and structured items designed to elicit data about the therapeutic encounter with male and female, black and white clients. A total of 188 responded, of whom 164 were male and 24 female. Of the total, 178 were white, 5 black, 3 naturalized United States citizens who identified themselves as white, and 2 Asian. Thirty-two percent were in private practice and 13% in public institutions. Only 151 white males turned in usable questionnaires. Results from selected items bearing on the scope of this literature examination will be presented.

All items in the instrument were derived from the literature. The two focusing on race as a variable influencing the therapeutic relationship were as follows: (1) *The race of the patient is a key problem in a white therapist's relationship with a black patient.* (2) *Do you think a white therapist can relate to a black patient and treat him or her effectively?* These items yielded the following data: Of the white male psychiatrists responding to item 1 (n = 131), 56% agreed, while 44% disagreed. Of these responding to item 2 (n = 131), 94% indicated "yes" and 2% indicated "no," with 4% expressing reservations.

Several structured items comprised the Race Stereotyping section of the questionnaire. Among these were three bearing on this discussion; respondents were asked whether they agreed or disagreed with the following statements: (3) *Due to racial attitudes toward them, most blacks tend to have impaired self-images.* (4) *There is a noticeable self-hatred among blacks.* (5) *The matriarchy structure of the black family contributes to identity problems for the black male.* Sixty-five percent of the white male psychiatrists agreed that as a consequence of racial attitudes toward blacks, most tend to have impaired self-images. Forty-three percent further indicated that there is a noticeable self-hatred among blacks. When these two items were cross-tabulated, 84% agreed with items 3 and 4. This agreement was statistically significant, $p < .001$. In responding to item 5, which incorporated a combined race/sex-role stereotype, the psychiatrists' responses reflected conventional racial attitudes. Despite both data and compelling arguments which refute the matriarchal thesis, 78% of the white male psychiatrists agreed that the matriarchy structure of the black family contributes to identity problems for the black male (Wilkinson, 1977).

Research Needs and Priorities

This brief review of pertinent literature on the general subject of the state of the art of psychotherapy with minority women has placed special emphasis on the social and cultural factors which influence perceptions and attitudes of therapists. As a consequence of the preoccupation with the personalities, behaviors, and emotional disorders of blacks in therapy, most of the available literature on the topic discussed has centered on black Americans (Sattler, 1977). Although research conducted on race and mental disorders has not been sex-specific, one implication of this review is that there is a need for systematic studies which take into account the combined *clinical significance of race and/or ethnicity and the sex of those who formulate theories and engage in clinical practice.* A second implication is that there is a need to train and retrain therapists in such a way that they will become cognizant of the sociocultural factors influencing their *interactions with and judgments of* the emotional difficulties encountered by minority females who become their clients. As Gardner (1971) notes, there is no evidence in the psychological and psychoanalytic literature that the training of white therapists comprises in-depth self-disclosure and introspective analysis of their own racial and sexual prejudices. This is a significant omission, since the history, structure, and socialization processes of our society are "characterized by an almost universal tendency to unconscious racial bigotry" (Gardner, 1971, p. 78). Familiarity with this history—its myths and stereotypes—is a necessary principle for .effective psychotherapy with black women (Helms, 1979).

Moreover, it has been observed that "when the therapist is white and the client is black [for example], due consideration must be given to the complicating aspects of culturally conditioned interaction tendencies which will influence transference and countertransference phenomena" (Gardner, 1971, p. 80). Therefore, it is imperative that white therapists be trained to understand the multicultural history of the society and to cope with racial and ethnic biases and race/sex-role stereotypes, since these have an impact on the therapeutic experiences of minority women. Misconceptions about ethnic and/or racial differences, in conjunction with gender differences, function as initial inputs in the interracial or interethnic therapeutic encounter and may preclude success in outcomes. As Sager *et al.* (1972) note, even those whites most sympathetic to the minority condition cannot fully identify with the minority experience.

While this literature review has focused primarily on African-American women, the discussion has emphasized those factors likely to affect the dynamics characterizing psychotherapeutic contexts with other racial/ethnic minority women. The various selections have pointed to the need to study therapeutic transitions and outcomes in terms of the interaction between the status attributes of race and ethnicity *and* the behaviors of clients as well as therapists (Orlinsky & Howard, 1975). At present, there are no systematic outcome studies on racial and ethnic minority women in psychotherapy. Although racial similarity is considered a positive status feature in therapeutic relationships, there is no way to ascertain with certainty, from existing case studies and surveys reviewed here, whether, for example, black therapists are more effective than white therapists with black clients (Sattler, 1977, p. 284). However, the data that we do have indicate the need for descriptive and explanatory research designs which identify those status variables and racial and ethnic biases likely to affect clinical and diagnostic judgments of therapists and, hence, successes or failures in therapy. Further, research designs are needed which would enable researchers to delineate and analyze those aspects of patient transitions which can be attributed to specific status dimensions and behaviors of therapists.

As previously indicated, cultural conditioning to racial beliefs and attitudes does have an impact on therapists; and such conditioning pervades therapeutic contexts in which minority women are clients. In fact, racial beliefs, attitudes, and customs of the larger society may be reinforced by current clinical theories and practices. In view of this, carefully structured examinations of evaluation criteria used in therapy and anticipated outcomes are imperative (Orlinsky & Howard, 1978). Sattler's (1977) excellent overview, for example, incorporates a number of studies of differential treatment of black and white clients in various facilities (e.g., outpatient psychiatric clinics, inpatient hospitals, and community mental health centers). His documentation points to the need for systematic and objective research on the following questions: (1) What factors account for black and other racial/ethnic minority clients perceiving the effects of therapy less positively than white clients? (2) How prevalent is the practice of assigning black clients to less individual therapy than white clients (Yamamoto *et al.*, 1968), and what are the clinical implications and potential consequences of this practice for minority women in therapy? (3) What social and cultural variables are operative in therapeutic contexts in which black patients are more likely to be given drugs than white patients (Singer, 1967)? (4) What racial and cultural attitudes of white therapists may be operative in the assignment of black females to crisis therapy rather than long-term treatment (Krebs, 1971)? (5) What aspects of therapists' attitudes, beliefs, and behaviors might account for higher dropout rates for black than for white female clients (Krebs, 1971; Raynes & Warren, 1971; Salzman, Shader, Scott, & Binstock, 1970)? These are among the many questions which require study; and, according to Sattler (1977), research is needed on every facet of interracial and interethnic therapy.

In summary, this discussion has highlighted both research and training needs. Specifically, generalizable and useful data are needed in the following areas: (1) the effects of race/sex-role biases and stereotypes on psychotherapists and others in clinical fields; (2) construction of reality-based theoretical paradigms on the experiences and behaviors of minority women seeking therapy; (3) racial/ethnic beliefs, attitudes, values, and personalities of white psychotherapists, whether or not their clients will be minority women; (4) psychological functions of negative labeling of minority women and their families (Berk & Hirata, 1973; Karno & Edgerton, 1969; Krush & Bjork, 1963; Scheff, 1974; Welsing, 1974a; Wilkinson, 1974, 1978; Wilkinson & Taylor, 1977); and (5) multicultural and multilingual differences (Valentine, 1971; Vontress, 1969; Walton, 1962; Wesson, 1975; Yamamoto *et al.*, 1968) and the relevance of these to clinical theory, research, and practice and to an understanding of the life experiences and psychology of minority women.

Recently, subpanels of the President's Commission on Mental Health (1978) emphasized that increasing the pool of multicultural and multilingual clinical personnel is essential (Miranda & Castro, 1977; Schorr, 1979; Stembridge, Note 2; Frogg, Note 4). Thus, given the various reports to the Commission and the content of this review, it would be a serious impediment to the production of qualified personnel in psychotherapy to ignore the significance of the sociocultural parameters of race, ethnicity, and sex as influences on clinicians' behaviors, as well as on theory, research, and, hence, therapeutic inputs, processes, and outcomes (J. A. Banks & Gramb, 1972; Bell, 1971; Butts, 1971; Franklin,

1971; Gordon, 1976; Green, 1975; Gunnings, 1971; Jones, Lightfoot, Palmer, Wilkerson, & Williams, 1970; Nobles, 1973; A. Thomas, 1962; Torrey, 1969; Vontress, 1969). In this connection, it has been aptly observed that "clinicians undoubtedly exert an influence on social standards and attitudes beyond that of other groups" (Broverman *et al.*, 1970, p. 6). Thus, psychotherapy curricula and research must be designed to enable white therapists to enhance their therapeutic skills, to develop a knowledge and understanding of their own socialization and beliefs as well as of the multicultural nature of the society, and to increase their effectiveness in therapy with minority women as well as minority men.

Reference Notes

1. Wilkinson, D. Y. *Labelling and psychiatry: Explanations of non-white admissions.* Paper presented at the U.S. Civil Rights Commission, Washington, D.C., April 1977.
2. Stembridge, B. J. *Some preliminary ideas with respect to research needs on Black female mental health.* Paper prepared for the President's Commission on Mental Health, Howard University, 1977.
3. True, R. *Mental health issues among Asian-American women.* Paper presented at the Asian and Pacific Women's Conference, sponsored by the National Institute of Education, San Francisco, August 1976.
4. Frogg, W. *Mental health and American Indian women.* Paper prepared for the President's Commission on Mental Health, National Indian Board on Alcoholism and Drug Abuse, Turtle Lake, Wis., 1977.

References

Adams, P. Dealing with racism in biracial psychiatry. *Journal of the American Academy of Child Psychiatry*, 1970, *9*, 33–43.

Adams, W. A. The Negro patient in psychiatric treatment. *American Journal of Orthopsychiatry*, 1950, *20*, 305–310.

American Psychological Association Task Force. Report of the Task Force on Sex Bias and Sex-Role Stereotyping in Psychotherapeutic Practice. *American Psychologist*, 1975, *30*, 1169–1175.

Arkoff, A., Thaver, F., & Elkind, L. Mental health and counseling ideas of Asian and American students. *Journal of Counseling Psychology*, 1966, *13*, 219–223.

Backner, B. L. Counseling black students; Any place for whitey? *Journal of Higher Education*, 1970, *41*, 630–637.

Baldwin, J. A. Theory and research concerning the notion of Black self-hatred: A review and reinterpretation. *The Journal of Black Psychology*, 1979, *5*, 51–77.

Banks, G. The effects of race on one-to-one helping interviews. *Social Service Review*, 1971, *45*, 137–146.

Banks, G., Berenson, B. G., & Carkhuff, R. R. The effects of counselor race and training upon counseling process with Negro clients in initial interview. *Journal of Clinical Psychology*, 1967, *23*, 70–72.

Banks, J. A., & Gramb, J. D. (Eds.). *Black self-concept:Implications for educational and social science.* New York: McGraw-Hill, 1972.

Banks, W. M. The differential effects of race and social class in helping. *Journal of Clinical Psychology*, 1972, *28*, 90–92.

Banks, W. M., & Martens, K. Counseling: The reactionary profession. *Personnel and Guidance Journal*, 1973, *51*, 457–462.

Baratz, S. S. Effects of race of experimenter, instructions, and comparison population upon level of reported anxiety in Negro subjects. *Journal of Personality and Social Psychology*, 1967, 7, 194–196.

Beale, F. Double jeopardy: To be Black and female. In T. Cade (Ed.), *The Black woman: An anthology*. New York: New American Library, 1970.

Bell, R. L. The culturally deprived psychologist. *Counseling Psychologist*, 1971, *2*, 104–106.

Berk, B., & Hirata, L. C. Mental illness among the Chinese: Myth or reality? *Journal of Social Issues*, 1973, *29*, 149–166.

Bernard, V. W. Psychoanalysis and members of minority groups. *Journal of the American Psychoanalytic Association*, 1953, *1*, 256–267.

Bernard, V. W. Interracial practice in the midst of change. *American Journal of Psychiatry*, 1972, *128*, 978–984.

Bloombaum, M., Yamamoto, J., & James, Q. Cultural stereotyping among psychotherapists. *Journal of Consulting and Clinical Psychology*, 1968, *32*, 99.

Broverman, I. K., Broverman, D. M., Clarkson, F. E., Rosenkrantz, P., & Vogel, S. R. Sex-role stereotypes and clinical judgments of mental health. *Journal of Counseling and Clinical Psychology*, 1970, *34*, 1–7.

Brown, L. Psychoanalysis vs. the Negro people. *Masses and Mainstream*, 1951, *4*, 16–20.

Burgest, D. R. The racist use of the English language. *The Black Scholar*, 1973, *5*, 37–45.

Butts, H. F. White racism: Its origins, institutions and the implications for professional mental health practice. *International Journal of Psychiatry*, 1969, *8*. 914–944.

Butts, H. F. Psychoanalysis and unconscious racism. *Journal of Contemporary Psychotherapy*, 1971, *3*, 67–81.

Calnek, M. Racial factors in the countertransference: The Black therapist and the Black client. *American Journal of Orthopsychiatry*, 1970, *40*, 39–46.

Carkhuff, R. R., & Pierce, R. M. The differential effects of therapist race and class upon patient depth of self-exploration in the initial clinical interview. *Journal of Consulting Psychology*, 1967, *31*, 632–634.

Carter, J. H., & Haizlip, T. M. Race and its relevance to transference. *American Journal of Orthopsychiatry*, 1972, *42*, 865–871.

Chesler, P. Women as psychiatric and psychotherapeutic patients. *Journal of Marriage and the Family*, 1971, *33*, 746–759.

Chesler, P. *Women and madness*. Garden City, N.Y.: Doubleday, 1972.

Chu, F., & Trotter, S. *The madness establishment*. New York: Grossman, 1974.

Cohen, A. I. Treating the Black patient: Transference questions. *American Journal of Psychotherapy*, 1974, *28*, 137–143.

Comer, J. P. White racism: Its root, form, and function. *American Journal of Psychiatry*, 1969, *126*, 802–806.

Curry, A. E. Myth, transference and the Black therapist. *Psychoanalytic Review*, 1964, *51*, 7–14. (a)

Curry, A. E. The Negro worker and the white client. *Social Casework*, 1964, *45*, 131–136. (b)

Edgerton, R. B., & Karno, M. Mexican-American bilingualism and the perception of mental illness. *Archives of General Psychiatry*, 1971, *24*, 286–290.

Fabrikant, B. The psychotherapist and the female patient: Perceptions, misperceptions, and change. In V. Franks & V. Burtle (Eds.), *Women in therapy*. New York: Brunner/Mazel, 1974.

Fibush, E. The white worker and the Negro client. *Social Caseworker*, 1965, *46*, 271–277.

Fischer, J. Negroes and whites and rates of mental illness: Reconsideration of a myth. *Psychiatry*, 1969, *32*, 428–446.

Forster, E. B. The theory and practice of psychiatry in Ghana. *American Journal of Psychotherapy*, 1962, *16*, 7–51.

Franklin, A. J. To be young, gifted and black with inappropriate professional training: A critique of counseling programs. *Counseling Psychologist*, 1971, *2*, 107-112.

Friedman, N. James Baldwin and psychotherapy. *Psychotherapy: Theory, Research, and Practice*, 1966, *3*, 177-183.

Gallahorn, G., Cushing, J., & Brody, E. Anti-Negro prejudice before, during, and after an acute schizophrenic episode in a white woman. *American Journal of Psychotherapy*, 1965, *19*, 650-652.

Ganter, G. Racism and white clinicians: The relevance of social definition. *Voices*, 1977, *13*, 63-66. (a)

Ganter, G. The socio-conditions of the white practitioner: New perspectives. *Journal of Contemporary Psychotherapy*, 1977, *9*, 28-31. (b)

Gardner, L. H. The therapeutic relationship under varying conditions of race. *Psychotherapy: Theory, Research, and Practice*, 1971, *8*, 78-87.

Goldberg, M. The black female client, the white psychotherapist: An evaluation of therapy through clients' retrospective reports (Doctoral dissertation, California School of Professional Psychology, 1972). *Dissertation Abstracts International*, 1973, *33*, 3302B. (University Microfilms No. 72-33, 287)

Gordon, V. V. The methodologies of Black self-concept research: A critique. *Journal of Afro-American Issues*, 1976, *4*, 373-381.

Green, R. L. The social responsibility of psychology. *The Black Scholar*, 1975, *6*, 32-35.

Grier, W. H. When the therapist is Negro: Some effects on the treatment process. *American Journal of Psychiatry*, 1967, *123*, 1587-1591.

Gunnings, T. Preparing the new counselors. *Counseling Psychologist*, 1971, *2*, 100-101.

Hare-Mustin, R. T. A feminist approach to family therapy. *Family Process*, 1978, *17*, 181-194.

Harrison, P., & Butts, H. F. White psychiatrists' racism in referral practices to Black psychiatrists. *Journal of the National Medical Association*, 1970, *62*, 278-282.

Heine, R. W. The Negro patient in psychotherapy. *Journal of Clinical Psychology*, 1950, *16*, 373-376.

Helms, J. E. Black women. *Counseling Psychologist*, 1979, *8*, 40-41.

Holroyd, J. Psychotherapy and women's liberation. *Counseling Psychologist*, 1976, *6*, 22-28.

Jackson, A. M. Psychotherapy: Factors associated with the race of the therapist. *Psychotherapy: Theory, Research, and Practice*, 1973, *10*, 273-277.

Jefferies, D. Counseling for the strength of the black woman. *Counseling Psychologist*, 1976, *6*, 20-22.

Johnson, M. An approach to feminist therapy. *Psychotherapy: Theory, Research, and Practice*, 1976, *13*, 72-76.

Jones, B. E., Lightfoot, O., Palmer, D., Wilkerson, R. G., & Williams, D. H. Problems of Black psychiatric residents in white training institutes. *American Journal of Psychiatry*, 1970, *127*, 798-802.

Kardiner, A., & Ovesey, L. *The mark of oppression.* New York: Norton, 1951.

Karno, M., & Edgerton, R. B. Perception of mental illness in a Mexican-American community. *Archives of General Psychiatry*, 1969, *20*, 233-238.

Kennedy, J. Problems posed in the analysis of Negro patients. *Psychiatry*, 1952, *15*, 313-327.

King, M. C. The politics of sexual stereotypes. *The Black Scholar*, 1973, *4*, 12-23.

Klein, M. Feminist concepts of therapy outcome. *Psychotherapy: Theory, Research, and Practice*, 1976, *13*, 89-95.

Kramer, M., Rosen, B. M., & Willis, E. M. Definitions and distributions of mental disorders in a racist society. In C. V. Willie, B. M. Kramer, & B. S. Brown (Eds.), *Racism and mental health.* Pittsburgh: University of Pittsburgh Press, 1973.

Krebs, R. L. Some effects of a white institution on Black psychiatric outpatients. *American Journal of Orthopsychiatry*, 1971, *41*, 589-596.

Krush, T., & Bjork, J. Mental health factors in an Indian boarding school. *Mental Hygiene*, 1963, *49*, 94-103.

Lambley, P., & Cooper, P. Psychotherapy and race: Interracial therapy under apartheid. *American Journal of Psychotherapy,* 1975, *29,* 179–184.

Lane, E. A. The influence of sex and race on process-reactive rating of schizophrenics. *Journal of Psychology,* 1968, *68,* 15–20.

LaRue, L. The Black movement and women's liberation. In S. Cox (Ed.), *Female psychology: The emerging self.* Chicago: Science Research Associates, 1976.

Levine, S. V., Kamin, L. E., & Levine, E. L. Sexism and psychiatry. *American Journal of Orthopsychiatry,* 1974, *44,* 327–336.

Lewis, D. O., Balla, D. A., & Shanok, S. S. Some evidence of race bias in the diagnosis and treatment of the juvenile offender. *American Journal of Orthopsychiatry,* 1979, *49,* 53–61.

Lopez, S. Clinical stereotypes of the Mexican-American. In J. L. Martinez, Jr. (Ed.), *Chicano psychology.* New York: Academic Press, 1977.

Marecek, J., & Kravetz, D. Women and mental health: A review of feminist change efforts. *Psychiatry,* 1977, *40,* 323–329.

Martinez, J. L., Jr. (Ed.). *Chicano psychology.* New York: Academic Press, 1977.

McLean, H. The emotional health of Negroes. *Journal of Negro Education,* 1949, *18,* 283–290.

Meyer, N. G. *Diagnostic distribution of admissions to inpatient services of state and county mental hospitals, United States, 1975. (Mental Health Statistical Note No. 138).* Washington, D.C.: Department of Health, Education and Welfare, 1977.

Milazzo-Sayre, L. *Admission rates to state and county psychiatric hospitals by age, sex, and race, United States, 1975 (Mental Health Statistical Note No. 140).* Washington D.C.: Department of Health, Education and Welfare, 1977.

Milliken, R. L. Prejudice and counseling effectiveness. *Personnel and Guidance Journal,* 1965, *43,* 710–712.

Miranda, M. R., & Castro, F. G. Culture distance and success in psychotherapy with Spanish-speaking clients. In J. L. Martinez, Jr. (Ed.), *Chicano psychology.* New York: Academic Press, 1977.

Morales, A. The impact of class discrimination and white racism in the mental health of Mexican Americans. In N. Wagner & M. Hang (Eds.), *Chicanos: Social and psychological perspectives.* St. Louis, Mo.: C. V. Mosby, 1971.

Nobles, W. W. Psychological research and the Black self-concept: A critical review. *Journal of Social Issues,* 1973, *29,* 11–31.

Olmedo, E. L., & Parron, D. L. Mental health of minority women: Some special issues. *Professional Psychology,* in press.

Orlinsky, D. E., & Howard, K. I. *Varieties of psychotherapeutic experience.* New York: Teachers College Press, 1975.

Orlinsky, D. E., & Howard, K. I. Female clients' perceptions of psychotherapy process. *Psychotherapy: Theory, Research, and Practice,* 1976, *13,* 82–88.

Orlinsky, D . E., & Howard, K. I. The relation of process to outcome in psychotherapy. In S. Garfield & A. Bergin (Eds.), *Handbook of psychotherapy and behavior change.* New York: Wiley, 1978.

Pasamanick, B. Some misconceptions concerning differences in the racial prevalence of mental disease. *American Journal of Orthopsychiatry,* 1963, *33,* 72–86.

Patterson, C. H. The place of values in counseling and psychotherapy. *Journal of Counseling Psychology,* 1958, *5,* 216–223.

Pinderhughes, C. A. Understanding Black power: Processes and proposals. *American Journal of Psychiatry,* 1969, *125,* 1552–1557.

Pinderhughes, C. A. Racism and psychotherapy. In C. V. Willie, B. M. Kramer, & B. S. Brown (Eds.), *Racism and mental health.* Pittsburgh: University of Pittsburgh Press, 1973.

President's Commission on Mental Health. *Report of the special populations sub-panel on women (Task Panel Reports, III).* Washington, D.C.: U.S. Government Printing Office, 1978.

Raynes, A. E., & Warren, G. Some distinguishing features of patients failing to attend a psychiatric clinic after referral. *American Journal of Orthopsychiatry*, 1971, *41*, 581–588.

Riess, B. F. Observations of the therapist factor in interethnic psychotherapy. *Psychotherapy: Theory, Research, and Practice*, 1971, *8*, 71–72.

Rodgers, T. C. The evolution of an active anti-Negro racist. In W. Muensterberger & A. H. Esman (Eds.), *The psychoanalytic study of society.* (Vol. 1). New York: International Universities Press, 1960.

Rosen, H., & Frank, J. D. Negroes in psychotherapy. *American Journal of Psychiatry*, 1962, *119*, 456–460.

Ruiz, P. Culture and mental health: A Hispanic perspective. *Journal of Contemporary psychotherapy*, 1977, *9*, 24–27.

Sager, C. J., Brayboy, T. L., & Waxenberg, B. R. Black patient–white therapist. *American Journal of Orthopsychiatry*, 1972, *42*, 415–423.

Salzman, C., Shader, R. I., Scott, D. A., & Binstock, W. Interviewer anger and patient dropout in walk-in clinic. *Comprehensive Psychiatry*, 1970, *11*, 267–273.

Sattler, J. M. Racial "experimenter effects" in experimentation, testing, interviewing and psychotherapy. *Psychological Bulletin*, 1970, *73*, 137–160.

Sattler, J. M. The effects of therapist–client racial similarity. In A. S. Gurman & A. M. Razin (Eds.), *Effective psychotherapy: A handbook of research.* New York: Pergamon Press, 1977.

Saxe, J. A review of Black rage. *The Black Scholar*, 1970, *1*, 58–62.

Schachter, J., & Butts, H. Transference and countertransference in interracial analysis. *Journal of the American Psychoanalytic Association*, 1968, *16*, 792–808.

Scheff, T. J. The labelling theory of mental illness. *American Sociological Review*, 1974, *39*, 444–452.

Schorr, A. L. The President's Commission on Mental Health as a Symptom. *American Journal of Orthopsychiatry*, 1979, *49*, 388–391.

Silverman, D. The influences on the Negro patient dropping out of psychiatric treatment. *Psychiatric Opinion*, 1971, *8*, 29.

Simmen, E. *The Chicano: From caricature to self-portrait.* New York: New American Library, 1971.

Singer, B. D. Some implications of differential psychiatric treatment of Negro and white patients. *Social Science and Medicine*, 1967, *1*, 77–83.

Spurlock, J. A reappraisal of the role of Black women. *Journal of the National Association of Private Psychiatric Hospitals*, 1971, *3*, 8–16.

Staples, R. The myth of the Black matriarchy. In D. Y. Wilkinson & R. L. Taylor (Eds.), *The black male in America: Perspectives on his status in contemporary society.* Chicago: Nelson-Hall, 1977.

St. Clair, H. R. Psychiatric interview experience with Negroes. *American Journal of Psychiatry*, 1951, *108*, 113–119.

Stricker, G. Implications of research for psychotherapeutic treatment of women. *American Psychologist*, 1977, *32*, 14–22.

Szasz, T. S. Psychotherapy: A socio-cultural perspective. *Comprehensive Psychiatry*, 1966, *7*, 217–223.

Szasz, T. S. The Negro in psychiatry: An historical note on psychiatric rhetoric. *American Journal of Psychotherapy*, 1971, *25*, 469–471.

Taube, C. A. *Admission rates to state and county mental hospitals by age, sex, and color, United States, 1969 (Statistical Note No. 41).* Washington D.C.: National Clearinghouse for Mental Health Information, Survey and Reports Section, 1971.

Taylor, J. The interface between racism and psychopathology: An approach through psychotherapy. *Psychotherapy: Theory, Research, and Practice*, 1971, *8*, 73–77.

Ten Houten, W. The Black family: Myth or reality. *Psychiatry*, 1970, *33*, 145–173.

Thackeray, M., Skidmore, R. A., & Farley, O. W. *Introduction to mental health: Field and practice.* Englewood Cliffs, N.J.: Prentice-Hall, 1979.

Thomas, A. Pseudo-transference reactions due to cultural stereotyping. *American Journal of Orthopsychiatry,* 1962, *32,* 894–900.

Thomas, A., & Sillen, S. *Racism and psychiatry.* New York: Brunner/Mazel, 1972.

Thomas, C. S., & Comer, J. Racism and mental health services. In C. V. Willie, B. M. Kramer, & B. S. Brown (Eds.), *Racism and mental health.* Pittsburgh: University of Pittsburgh Press, 1973.

Thomas, S. A. The theory and practice in feminist therapy. *Social Work,* 1977, *22,* 447–454.

Toker, E. Mental illness in the white and Bantu populations of the Republic of South Africa. *The American Journal of Psychiatry,* 1966, *123,* 55–65.

Torrey, E. F. The case for the indigenous therapist. *Archives of General Psychiatry,* 1969, *20,* 365–373.

Vail, S. The effects of socioeconomic class, race, and level of experience on social workers' judgments of clients. *Smith College Studies in Social Work,* 1970, *40,* 236–246.

Valentine, C. A. Deficit, difference, and bicultural models of Afro-American behavior. *Harvard Educational Review,* 1971, *41,* 137–157.

Vontress, C. E. Cultural barriers in the counseling relationship. *Personnel and Guidance Journal,* 1969, *48,* 11–17.

Vontress, C. E. Racial differences: Impediments to rapport. *Journal of Counseling Psychology,* 1971, *18,* 3.

Waite, R. R. The Negro patient and clinical theory. *Journal of Consulting and Clinical Psychology,* 1968, *32,* 427–433.

Walton, H. Psychiatric practice in a multiracial society: Modifications required in clinical approach. *Comprehensive Psychiatry,* 1962, *3,* 255–267.

Watson, Y. Self-concept formation and the Afro-American woman. *Journal of Afro-American Issues,* 1974, *2,* 226–236.

Welsing, F. C. The conspiracy to make Blacks inferior. *Ebony,* 1974, *29,* 85; 88; 92. (a)

Welsing, F. C. The Cress theory of color confrontation. *The Black Scholar,* 1974, *5,* 32–40. (b)

Wesson, K. A. The Black man's burden: The white clinician. *The Black Scholar,* 1975, *6,* 13–18.

Wilkinson, D. Y. Coming of age in a racist society: The whitening of America. *Youth and Society,* 1971, *3,* 100–118.

Wilkinson, D. Y. Racism and American sociology: The myth of scientific objectivity. *Sociological Abstracts,* 1972, *20,* 1888.

Wilkinson, D. Y. Review of *Racism and psychiatry* by A. Thomas & S. Sillen. *Contemporary Sociology,* 1973, *2,* 192–194.

Wilkinson, D. Y. Racial socialization through children's toys: A sociohistorical examination. *Journal of Black Studies,* 1974, *5,* 96–109.

Wilkinson, D. Y. The stigmatization process: The politicization of the Black male's identity. In D. Y. Wilkinson & R. L. Taylor (Eds.), *The Black male in America: Perspectives on his status in contemporary society.* Chicago: Nelson-Hall, 1977.

Wilkinson, D. Y. Toward a positive frame of reference for analysis of Black families: A selected bibliography. *Journal of Marriage and the Family,* 1978, *40,* 70–71.

Wilkinson, D. Y., & Taylor, R. L. (Eds.). *The Black male in America: Perspectives on his status in contemporary society.* Chicago: Nelson-Hall, 1977.

Williams, R. L., & Kirkland, J. The white counselor and the black client. *Counseling Psychologist,* 1970, *2,* 114–117.

Willie, C. V., Kramer, B. M., & Brown, B. S. (Eds.). *Racism and mental health.* Pittsburgh: University of Pittsburgh Press, 1973.

Wolkon, G. J., Moriwaki, S., & Williams, K. J. Race and social class as factors in the orientation toward psychotherapy. *Journal of Counseling Psychology,* 1973, *20,* 312–316.

Yamamoto, J., James, Q., Bloombaum, M., & Hattem, J. Racial factors in patient selection. *American Journal of Psychiatry,* 1967, *124,* 630–636.

Yamamoto, J., James, Q., & Palley, N. Cultural problems in psychiatric therapy. *Archives of General Psychiatry,* 1968, *19,* 45–49.

PART FOUR

Intervention in Crises

CHAPTER 13

Reproductive Crises

MALKAH T. NOTMAN

CAROL NADELSON

Introduction

A growing body of recent research in areas such as contraception, pregnancy, abortion, sterilization, rape, menopause, and sexual functioning has challenged widely held myths and provided new insights and information, but major questions are yet to be answered. These include the ways in which these data can be applied to psychotherapeutic approaches.

In the 1930s, Horney (1931/1967) and Frank (1931) published separate papers on premenstrual tension and Benedek and Rubenstein (1939/1952) first published their work correlating ovarian activity and psychodynamic processes. Lindemann, in 1938, reported on pre- and postoperative evaluations of women following hysterectomy. His emphasis on the specific meaning of the loss of the uterus was an impetus for investigations of women's responses to the range of physiologic and pathologic conditions involving reproductive organs. This work was expanded when Renneker and Cutler (1952) stressed the meaning to women of the loss of the breast and reported on the postmastectomy mourning process. A vast literature has been developed in this area, with several textbooks devoted to specific psychological phenomena related to women and their anatomy, physiology, and pathology (Howells, 1972; Kroger, 1962; Norris, 1972). However, very little that is unbiased, definitive, and based on solid or extensive data has been written about the links between mental health and reproductive and sexual issues for women.

There is evidence from recent critical discussions by Parlee (1976, 1978), Lennane and Lennane (1973), Glasser and Pasnau (1975), and

Malkah T. Notman. Department of Psychiatry, Harvard Medical School and Beth Israel Hospital, Boston, Massachusetts.
Carol Nadelson. Department of Psychiatry, Harvard Medical School and Tufts–New England Medical Center, Boston, Massachusetts.

Bart and Grossman (1978) that many of the data on which attitudes and recommendations have been based and which have been cited in the past as substantive are questionable. For instance, the concept that a depression inevitably follows an abortion, which was widely believed, has been shown to be incorrect (Payne, Kravitz, Notman, & Anderson, 1976). The implications of these data for therapeutic approaches and for success of treatment will be of crucial importance.

Crisis-intervention techniques are clearly more applicable if abortion is seen as a life crisis similar to other experiences, whereas if abortion is seen as a major loss, or if guilt and ambivalence related to aggressive and/or sexual impulses are important factors, then long-term intensive psychotherapy might be the treatment of choice. Furthermore, one must consider the consequences of viewing the woman who has an abortion as a normal person under a stress which demands adaptation and working through, as opposed to viewing her as, inevitably, a "patient."

The past years have seen major social changes affecting women and families. Birth rates have declined, families are smaller, and more women choose not to marry, to marry late, and/or to remain childless. An increasing number of young women are seeking sterilization, and many of them are nulliparous and in their early 20s (Lindemayer, cited in Roche Report, 1976; Kaltreider & Margolis, 1977). Sexual relations outside of marriage are more widespread. Lesbian relationships are more open, some as an expression of political ideology or as an expression of alternative patterns of intimacy (DeFries, 1976). New realities also include the possibility of venereal disease in a wide cross section of patients and requests for contraceptive and sexual counseling for unmarried couples.

Some of these changes have been accompanied by relevant research. Other areas have been neglected. We are not attempting an exhaustive review in this chapter of all of the research data which have accumulated, nor of all areas relating to reproductive crises, but we will review and exemplify specific areas and needs. Several issues clearly stand out. There are few long-term well-controlled studies which provide information on the long-range impact of medical procedures and decisions and their emotional consequences. That these are highly significant, and that the period of observation has to extend beyond what was previously considered adequate, namely, to span several generations, has been demonstrated by the experience with long-range effects of diethylstilbestrol (DES) and with difficulties in assessing the effects of oral contraceptives. In both cases, medical consequences have become apparent many years following administration of the drugs. Furthermore, the psychological impact of a history of DES ingestion on families and offspring, and the possible kinds of therapeutic approaches to these people, both those aimed at prevention and those aimed at treatment, have barely begun to be investigated.

Another issue which must be considered is how values and attitudes of investigators and subjects influence measured behaviors and functions, both biologic and psychological, and how this influence, in turn, relates to the treatment interventions offered. One example of the way in which the context affects the experience is to be found in those studies on the menstrual cycle which indicate that reported symptoms varied if the subject was aware of the purpose of the study (Wilcoxon, Shrader, & Sherif, 1976). Another example is the difference in the patient's perception of an abortion when it is performed as an accepted medical procedure as compared to when it is illegal and not condoned (Marder, 1970). That values and attitudes inevitably affect choices of treatment and outcome has been discussed by many contributors to this volume; these issues apply in the same way in the area of reproductive crises.

Contraception

Current concern about contraception covers several areas. Recent data linking use of oral contraceptives to blood clotting in women over 35, particularly smokers, have highlighted ongoing concerns about long-term effects of these methods. They have been the subject of some controversy ever since their initial trials and the controversial experiment by Goldziener (cited in Katz, 1972) in which, in an attempt to assess side effects, control subjects were not informed about the ineffectiveness of their placebos, resulting in a number of unwanted pregnancies.

Reactions to contraceptive pills have involved physical effects and emotional effects, and although both have been studied, Winokur (1973) and others (Bardwick, 1971) have urged further exploration of the interaction between personality traits and contraceptives. There is some agreement (Grounds, Davies, & Mowbray, 1970; Warnes & Fitzpatrick, 1979); that some psychological symptoms result from the use of some pills by some patients.

It has not been easy to sort out the contributions of hormonal effects, the psychological consequences of changes in menses, the effects of changes in contraceptive safety, the effects of being regulated by a "foreign" substance which is ingested daily, and the effects on sexual behavior, and opinions are not conclusive at present. Nor have the variables of a woman's age, sexual experience, current relationships, and feelings about her femininity and sexuality been fully assessed in relation to the use of contraceptives.

Certain populations, such as adolescents, are notorious in their nonuse of contraception, even when it is available (*Bulletin of Planned Parenthood League of Massachusetts,* 1978; Goldsmith, Gabrielson, Matthews, & Potts, 1972; Notman, 1975). Social, psychological, and family factors are as important as information (Morgenthau, Rao, Thornton, & Cameron, 1977) in determining whether or not contraceptives will be used, as are peer pressures and other motivations toward pregnancy. Effective methods of teaching contraceptive responsibility and planning have not been developed for the teenagers (Anderson & Smith, 1975; Morgenthau *et al.,* 1977).

Although obvious at some levels, it is difficult to assess the relationship of nonuse or ineffective use of contraception to a motivation for pregnancy, especially since the latter is often ambivalent, multideter-mined, and unconscious. Research which would develop safer, more effective, and more accessible contraceptives while further clarifying internal impediments to their use, and which would lead to programs, would be important.

Another area which is of recent interest, although still in the experimental stage, is the development of reversible, effective, and safe contraceptives for men. Although there is evidence that men in well-established couples participate strongly in fertility decisions (Lidz, 1978), it is difficult for teenage men or those first exploring relationships to take responsibility for contraceptive methods equal in effectiveness to those available to women. Condoms are the most widely used and are difficult for anxious or impatient young people to use consistently. Further research on effective, safe techniques is needed, as well as studies on the more complex interactions of personality, reality situation, and contraceptive use.

Psychotherapeutic implications include the attempt to reach individuals whose personal situation, ignorance, or anxiety prevents their use of effective contraceptive methods and the development of approaches which support planning and the possibility of exercising conscious choices.

Abortion

In order to provide a perspective on the issue of abortion, it is necessary to review both the medical and psychological aspects, since both factors are often cited as reasons for "damage."

Medical Aspects

The incidence of serious medical complications of abortion ranges from 1 to 20%, depending upon the data set surveyed, the skills of those performing the procedure, and the setting and stage of pregnancy. Fewest complications occur in early pregnancy terminated by suction or curettage. Later abortion, done by means of intrauterine injection of an abortifacient agent, increases the rate of complications about threefold, and threefold further if hysterotomy is required (Friedman, 1978). This procedure is necessary when intrauterine injection fails to effect an abortion. The recent introduction of intraamniotic prostaglandin injection has reduced the risks associated with the use of saline, most particularly, blood-clotting defects. Problems associated with midtrimester abortions induced by prostaglandins, including hemorrhage and infection, are small but substantial in number and must be considered. At present, the risk of death from oral contraceptives for certain groups of women, such as those over 35 who smoke, far exceeds that from abortion (Beral & Kay, 1977; Vessey, McPherson, & Johnson, 1977).

The incidence of morbidity from thromboembolic disease, hypertension, and hepatomas is clearly increased with the use of oral contraceptives. Thus, while abortion is not recommended as an alternative to contraception, it may in certain circumstances be less dangerous. This makes it clear that, in evaluating interventions of any kind, it is necessary to understand the relative risks and the availability of alternative resources, including contraceptives, the physical reactions, and the implications of abortion for different socioeconomic and cultural groups.

Emotional Impact

Recent controversy concerning abortion has renewed claims that it is a psychologically damaging procedure (Pasnau, 1972). This view was prevalent before 1960, when guilt and shame resulting from abortion were felt to lead to serious depression and disturbance in relationships (Deutsch, 1945). The guilt and shame in reaction to an abortion were confused with reactions to committing a socially stigmatized and usually illegal act. The myth of inevitable psychological damage persisted, despite the results reported from Ekblad's 1955 study of 479 women who had legal abortions in Sweden for psychiatric reasons. His was the first report to provide evidence that abortion was not necessarily detrimental to emotional health. He found that 14% of women having abortions experienced some regret, and only 11% continued to regret having had an abortion. Of the 1% who had demonstrable emotional consequences, all had had previous histories of emotional disorders. Ekblad concluded that there was little evidence that abortion had serious negative effects on the mental health of women. Furthermore, he emphasized that the problem is more often one of judging the effect of the addition of another child to a household or mother or both, under stress, than of predicting the likelihood of mental decompensation (Ekblad, 1955).

While Ekblad's was not a carefully controlled psychological study, it clearly provided evidence which suggested further inquiry. However, this report did not evoke much interest until 1963, when Kummer surveyed 32 psychiatrists in the United States who frequently saw women postabortion. Of the psychiatrists surveyed, 75% stated that they had never seen severe emotional sequelae, and 25% stated that severe psychological complications rarely occurred. While this study also raised obvious methodologic problems, subsequent studies with better methodologies challenged pervasive views that abortion was damaging. Peck and Marcus (1966) reported that women who had previously been diagnosed as psychologically ill benefited from the procedure. They found that symptoms of depression and anxiety, precipitated by the pregnancy, were relieved, and new symptoms were mild and self-limited. Another study by Simon, Senturia, and Rothman (1967) reported that women who were psychologically healthy, as well as those who were ill, responded to abortion with transient symptoms but were generally improved following the procedure. In fact, they found an increased risk of neurotic or depressive illness if an unwanted pregnancy was not terminated.

A 1969 review by the Group for the Advancement of Psychiatry noted the lack of serious postabortion psychological complications and recommended that during the preabortion period, motivation for the decision should be explored and counseling provided when indicated. Others also emphasized the need to clarify motivation for the termination of pregnancy (American Psychiatric Association, 1970). Evidence has accumulated indicating that it is not possible to predict which women will suffer from emotional disturbances if therapeutic abortion is denied, since the reasons for not wanting another pregnancy have not been differentiated from the manifestations of emotional stress (Sloane, 1969; Whittington, 1970).

Studies from Great Britain following the liberalization of their abortion law refocused the issue on the stress of bearing an unwanted child. The studies reported that psychiatric symptoms were more likely to occur in the overburdened multipara and the single woman without support than in those having abortion, and women who had a pregnancy terminated were found to have little lasting psychiatric disturbance (Pare

& Raven, 1970). Marder (1970) observed that negative attitudes on the part of hospital personnel and inadequate counseling contributed directly to the incidence of postabortion guilt, remorse, and depression. Others reported that for most women, abortion was, in fact, therapeutic when they had made the decision that it was the best course of action for them (C. Ford, Atkinson, & Bugonier, 1971; H. Osofsky & Osofsky, 1973; J. Osofsky & Osofsky, 1972; Payne *et al.*, 1976). One study found that "tired mothers" who often requested sterilization particularly benefited from abortion. These women reported that they found new meaning in life when they were no longer in the position of having obligatory pregnancies (C. Ford, Castelnuovo-Tedesco, & Long, 1971).

Another study pointed out that under legal conditions requiring documented severe prior psychiatric illness, one would find a group least likely to respond favorably to abortion as a therapeutic procedure (Partridge, Spiegel, Rouse, & Ewing, 1971). Of the 207 women followed in this study (average age, 18), the reasons for seeking abortion included depressive feelings (most frequently), guilt, anxiety, fears (hurting parents, having and raising a child), social stigma, rejection, malformed fetus, and loss of job. Seventy-four of the pregnancies in this group resulted from contraceptive failures. Naiveté (i.e., the idea that one cannot become pregnant the first time one has sexual intercourse) was prominent in many. The reports of the women in this study indicated that 98% felt that their general health was the same or better, and 94% felt that their emotional health was the same or better, after the abortion. Most of the symptoms reported (depression, anxiety, and guilt) decreased with time. The authors found that very few of the women required psychiatric treatment. In fact, a history of previous psychiatric symptoms or illness did not predict those who had a negative emotional response to abortion.

In a 1976 report (Payne *et al.*, 1976) which developed and validated scales to measure anxiety, depression, anger, guilt, and shame preabortion and postabortion, the investigators found that the pattern of response was similar to that of other instances of crisis reaction and crisis resolution. During the 24-hour postabortion period, relief and feelings of well-being predominated. Over a 6-month period, the absence of grief, sadness, or depression suggested that abortion was not experienced as a major loss by most women. Those women who were most vulnerable to conflict following abortion were those with (1) a previous history of mental illness or serious emotional conflict; (2) immature interpersonal relationships or unstable, conflictual relationships with men; (3) negative relationships with their mothers; (4) strong ambivalence or uncertainty and helplessness with regard to abortion; and/or (5) religious or cultural background in which there were negative attitudes toward abortion. In addition, single women, especially those who had not borne children, were more susceptible to conflict following abortion. The authors cautioned, however, that these factors were not to be interpreted as contraindications to abortion. They pointed out that women in the vulnerable groups believed, at their 6-month follow-up evaluation, that their decision for abortion was the right one. The authors concluded that the opportunity to play an active role in resolving the crisis of an unwanted pregnancy and to choose or reject abortion promotes successful adjustment and maturation. Thus, rather than making a decision for or against abortion on tenuous grounds, the woman seeking an abortion may benefit from a variety of crisis-intervention and therapeutic techniques, and the evidence for long-term negative consequences requiring treatment does not exist.

In another report, Freeman (1977) considered the implication of abortion from another perspective. She found that the women she studied did not perceive themselves to be active and instrumental in their own lives and thus chose abortion out of "necessity." Postabortion, however, these women felt that the experience resulted in a "different awareness about themselves," especially since for many, it was their first experience with a major individual decision the consequences of which were important and affected others as well as themselves. Gilligan (1977) has also reported the importance for psychological maturation of the woman's perception of herself as active and affecting her own future in plans about the decision for abortion. Another important outcome is the evidence that contraceptive use increases postabortion (Dauher, Zalar, & Goldstein, 1972; Margolis, Rindfuss, Coghland, & Rochat, 1974; Smith, 1973; Tietze, 1975).

An important aspect of this issue, one which is rarely addressed and on which there are currently no substantive data, is the outcome of alternatives to abortion. Comparative longitudinal studies of women making different choices are necessary if we are to adequately evaluate this complex factor. Bremer's (1977) report, for example, that the incidence of pueperal psychosis is greater than that of postabortion psychosis must be considered in any attempt to define psychological outcomes. Another area which is rarely considered from the perspective of the choice of abortion versus keeping an unwanted child (the most prevalent alternative currently chosen) is the consequences to the unwanted child. While data on child abuse and neglect abound, there are few studies which seriously weigh the outcome to the unwanted child over time.

Caplan (1954) reported that special problems were apt to develop between mother and child when an unsuccessful attempt at abortion had been made during the pregnancy. This study has not been replicated in the United States, but since demographic data and follow-ups are more available in Scandinavian countries, most of the work has been reported from these countries. Hook (1963) studied 213 children born to women who had been refused therapeutic abortion and found that these unwanted children were both physically and mentally impaired. In their classic study, Forssman and Thuwe (1966) followed, for 21 years, 120 children who were born after an application for a therapeutic abortion had been refused. These children were matched with controls of the same sex born in the same hospital or district on the same day. The results indicated that the unwanted children fared worse in almost every way. They had a higher incidence of psychiatric disorder, delinquency, criminal behavior, and alcoholism. They were more often receiving public assistance, they were often exempted from military service, and they had less schooling than the control group. The study concluded that the very fact that a woman applies for a legal abortion means that the prospective child will have greater difficulty surmounting social and mental handicaps than his peers. While this study has been criticized because it does not control for illegitimacy, it should be replicated in the current social context so that more substantive data can be brought to bear on policy decisions.

At present, abortion is rarely regarded as "therapeutic," but it is seen as a matter of choice with multiple alternatives. Research directions with psychotherapeutic implications are many. The impact, for example, of giving up a baby for adoption, an option frequently suggested as an alternative to abortion, is not clear, nor are there data comparing the outcomes of these options and their effects on mothers and children. Methodologically, these studies are complex, and they raise ethical problems. In the face of the current controversy about abortion, the importance of this issue has increased. It is clear, however, that policy recommendations cannot be made in the absence of outcome data which supply multiple variables longitudinally on large populations across socioeconomic, cultural, and geographic lines.

Pregnancy and Childbirth

Pregnancy

Pregnancy can be seen as a normal condition with special characteristics that make it similar to other "developmental crises" of the life cycle (Bibring, 1959), that is, puberty and menopause. These crises require adaptation. They confront the individual with new conflicts and also precipitate the reemergence of earlier unsettled conflicts. As with other crises, they offer the individual the possibility of further growth and maturation through mastery of both current and past issues.

While pregnancy has been considered a state of fulfillment and a creative act (Deutsch, 1945), it may also be a stressful time, requiring that the woman meet it and emerge with some solutions. Bibring, Dwyer, Huntington, and Valenstein (1961) point out that pregnancy, like puberty and menopause, involves both physical and psychological changes that are immutable.

When a woman recognizes that she is pregnant, regardless of whether or not the pregnancy was desired, anxiety and ambivalence may be experienced, in the same way one would expect with any new and major life change. The beginning is simple, but the implications are lifelong, and the changes are progressive and permanent and progressive. Areas that had previously seemed conflict-free may no longer be seen in the same way. Anxiety may arise about future role and responsibility, about marriage and/or career plans, etc.

Other feelings which are basic to the experience of pregnancy are those concerning the woman's early relationships with her own mother and the experience of having been "mothered." A necessary change must occur in the relationship of the woman to her mother as roles change and the woman herself becomes a mother. Old identifications and past difficulties may cause feelings of guilt, anger, ambivalence, and remorse (Bibring, 1959; Bibring *et al.,* 1961; Bibring & Valenstein, 1976; Deutsch, 1945). Pregnancy also has multiple meanings for both prospective parents together, as well as for each of them individually. They must conceptualize themselves as parents and deal with their ambivalence, their sense of separateness, and the shared aspects of their new roles. In addition, the father may feel threatened if he views the child as a potential competitor (Daniels & Lessow, 1964). The child's sex or position in the family may also have particular meaning. Sexual problems may be manifested for the first time, related to feelings about the current pregnancy or future pregnancies or because of the physical and psychological changes which occur during this period. Bearing a child may also represent a premature pressure toward adulthood (Nadelson & Notman, 1977). Therapeutic implications involve helping the parents work through earlier unresolved conflicts and differentiate them from the current concerns. The recognition of the normality of ambivalence and anxiety is an important aspect, since the expectation of this period as an idyllic one prevails. There are few research data available on therapeutic interventions from this perspective.

In addition to these psychosocial aspects, there are psychophysiologic aspects of pregnancy which have not been well defined. For example, Chertok (1972) points out that there is no clear agreement on the causes of some of the symptoms which appear during pregnancy (e.g., nausea and vomiting). Some researchers focus on psychological factors (e.g., ambivalence about the pregnancy) as causal, and others emphasize the hormonal determinants of the symptoms (Lennane & Lennane, 1973).

Other changes must also be studied. For example, late in the second trimester, women begin to report increased feelings of dependency, passivity, and a desire to be alone. These feelings peak in the third trimester and do not disappear until sometime during the postpartum period (Caplan, 1957). They may occur, in part, for physiologic reasons, and they also involve psychological issues, for example, the relationship of the mother to an unseen baby and the development of a new identification as a mother.

As the pregnancy nears term, women have reported many increased anxieties and fears (Nadelson & Notman, 1977). They are concerned about the realities of becoming a mother and the changes in marital and family relationships which necessarily occur. They are concerned about the process of labor and the difficulties they may experience with delivery. This is especially prominent if they have had a previous experience with pregnancy or a stillbirth. The sex and health of the infant and possibilities of death and/or injury to mother and/or child preoccupy a woman during an often sleepless and restess period in the last trimester. Since these are seen as "normal," little has been done regarding therapeutic interventions, especially for women who are more vulnerable.

Childbirth

The issue of whether pain is intrinsic to childbirth is often answered by attempts to extrapolate from the experiences of women in "primitive" societies. It appears, however, that despite our romantic fantasies, these groups also vary with regard to how pain is experienced or dealt with (Seiden, 1978). There do appear to be sociocultural differences reported in this regard, although anxiety and fear play a large role in the experience of what may be perceived as pain (Mead & Newton, 1967; Wolff & Langley, 1968; Zobrowski, 1962; Zola, 1966). This may relate to changes in one's body and self-image, fears of loss of control, and fears about adequacy and damage. All of these data have clear implications for interventions.

While there is no doubt that pain in childbirth is experienced, it is affected by preparation and understanding of the process involved. The effect of the context on the experience is analogous to the difference between suturing a 3-cm chin laceration on an 18-year-old football player and repairing the same-sized wound on a confused and frightened 4-year-old (Shaffer, 1969). Similarly, a woman's attitude about her pregnancy and approaching motherhood may be important. The pain of childbirth can be compared to a pain in the side of the chest when one is running a winning race, and it can be associated with a sense of pride and mastery rather than with the feeling of humiliating dependency which cries to be relieved (Seiden, 1978).

Bradley (1965) has observed that women may be made more vulnerable to obstetric pain because of their socialization. Their views about their body and its functions may discourage them from being sufficiently insistent on their own comfort or may make them feel ashamed of bodily exposure or function. Since the anxiety and discomfort of labor are potentially intensified by stress and fear, obstetric pain may be relieved to some extent by measures aimed at removing the fear response. Childbirth preparation has occupied much attention in recent decades. Its history has, unfortunately, been marked by exaggerated enthusiasm countered with vehement skepticism. There can be little doubt that the approach has been demonstrated to be effective (Friedman, 1978). The experience of pain appears to be diminished by familiarizing the pregnant woman with the process of childbearing and by fostering self-confidence and active mastery.

The theoretical basis of this response, however, is unclear. The techniques used are based on concepts of conditioning. They aim at providing information in advance of as well as during labor, accompanied by physical and emotionally supportive components. There are no entirely objective criteria for evaluating pain scientifically, and, therefore, the results of these approaches have not been subjected to investigational scrutiny regarding the degree of pain. However, it has been amply demonstrated that preparation diminishes the need for anesthesia in many women (Enkin *et al.*, 1972). Recent neurophysiologic research indicating that the human brain is able to synthesize and release analgesic substances (endorphins) is interesting in this regard. It may be that we will be able to "learn" to release and utilize intrinsic rather than extrinsic factors for pain relief (Snyder, 1978). Furthermore, it is possible that this physiologic mechanism is an aspect of the response to pain which accounts for the success of prepared childbirth. It is clear that research in this area is important and promising. Aside from the response to pain itself, prepared childbirth has psychological benefits in permitting active participation and mastery and some control, thereby diminishing feelings of helplessness (Bradley, 1965; Dick-Read, 1944/ 1972; Lamaze, 1958; Vellay, 1960).

RECENT DEVELOPMENTS IN DELIVERY

Recently introduced Leboyer principles are based on the theoretical concept that the infant at birth may suffer both physically and psychologically from the shock of the birth process and the sudden, startling exposure to the light, noise, and cold of the environment. The recommended approach is to effect delivery in a warm, quiet, and darkened room in an atmosphere of calm and tranquility, where there is opportunity for immediate mother–infant contact and gradual exposure of the infant to the world (Leboyer, 1975).

While babies delivered under such circumstances appear comfortable and content, there has been some concern that the lack of stimulation may inhibit respiration and crying, an effective means of clearing mucus and amniotic fluid from the newborn's lungs. Moreover, it is difficult to observe the baby's condition in a darkened room, making observation of adequate oxygenation difficult. This problem also applies to observing the parturient woman, especially with regard to vaginal bleeding and repair of injuries. These, Friedman (1978) observes, are not insurmountable obstacles. At this time, there are no data substantiating the benefits of this method to the baby, but its innocuous nature, coupled with the apparent positive psychological impact on the parents, suggest that it may become more widely used (Friedman, 1978).

PUERPERIUM

Outgrowths of "natural-childbirth" programs are the concepts of rooming-in and family-centered maternity care. The psychological implications of the separation of mother from baby, as occurs in some hospitals, can result in less than optimal bonding (Klaus, Jer Auld, Kreger, McAlpine, Steffa, & Kennell, 1972; Klaus & Kennell, 1976). While we do not know to what extent inadequate bonding occurs because human mothers and infants lack dependable "instinctual" bonding repertoires, nor to what extent social learning and current obstetric/ pediatric practice interfere with otherwise adequate responses, we have reason to make procedural changes to facilitate this important early step. We do have evidence indicating that even in lower primates, so-called "instinctual nurturant behavior" is heavily dependent upon the mother's prior life experience, that is, learning, and that mammalian mothering behavior is obliterated by decortication of the mother and, in some instances, of the child (C. S. Ford & Beach, 1951; Harlow, Harlow, & Hansen, 1966). Thus, drugs used in labor may interfere with cortical functioning in a way which may be similar to the effect of temporary decortication (e.g., barbiturates, scopolamine, analgesics) or suppress activity in those neural circuits most likely to be involved in instinctual behaviors (e.g., phenothiazines). These drug effects appear to last longer in the infant than in the mother and have been shown in the human infant to alter electroencephalogram-recorded brain activity. Thus, there is a high potential for interference with the baby's initial response to the mother when drugs are used during labor (Brazelton, 1970). Moreover, medication-induced sucking depression, especially when combined with mother–child separation during the early hours of life, can delay the development of adequate sucking until after engorgement of the breast has occurred. Thus, the infant may fail to receive colostrum, and lactation can be delayed or even prevented (Haire, 1973). Data on the maternal response to the infant reveal that it is highly dependent upon the infant's response to the mother, and there is evidence suggesting that a critical period occurs during the first hour postpartum (Klaus *et al.*, 1972).

Thus, there is reason to question practices which sedate infant or mother immediately postpartum or which separate the pair or impair contact. These procedures risk impairing initial bonding, thus producing a less dependable beginning of the mother–child relationship (Robson & Moss, 1970).

Since, as noted above, the major approaches to prepared or natural childbirth do reduce the need for analgesic medication during normal births, and since studies indicate that the preparation itself, and not merely the selection of women or their general education about birth, is an important factor, these methods must be further studied and developed (Bradley, 1965; Dick-Read, 1944/1972; Doering & Entwisle, 1975; Enkin *et al.*, 1972; Vellay, 1960). This may be especially important for those women who are at higher risk by virtue of age, illness, or ambivalence about pregnancy or womanhood. Furthermore, the data on bonding suggest that infants who are unwanted or who are to be adopted need to be provided with early substitute care. Research on therapeutic interventions in this area is almost nonexistent and clearly imperative.

There appear to be many changes in practices which have been insufficiently evaluated over time in well-controlled settings. Research in this area suffers from sufficient observer bias and other methodologic defects, so that conclusions are difficult to draw. For example, data on early mother–child bonding exclude the significance of father–child bonding or the relationship between the parents, either because the investigators believe that only the mother–child interaction is critical or because of their desire to be methodologically "clean." Thus, we know little of the more complex interactions in families which could lead to interventions. Furthermore, cultural and ethnic variables have been largely ignored. The cognitive labeling approach to the study of emotions, described by Schacter and Singer (1962), is important in this context, since it suggests that subjects in a bodily state different from their "normal" one (in this case, pregnancy, labor, etc.) explain or interpret their feelings by relying on cues from their environment. The applicability of this approach to the study of pregnancy and psychotherapeutic interventions is clear. In the reproductive areas, a chicken–egg problem exists: Physiologic processes affect psychological processes, and vice versa. There are few data which take into account these complex interactions.

Postpartum Reactions

There is considerable controversy in the literature about whether postpartum psychosis is a specific syndrome or a reaction to the psychological and physical changes of childbirth. While there is no resolution of this issue at present, many investigations do distinguish postpartum reactions from other stress responses.

The incidence of severe emotional illnesses following childbirth is approximately 1–2 per 1000 births (Normand, 1967). Less severe postpartum emotional disorders, referred to as "transient mild depression" or "postpartum blues," are said to occur in over 50% of parturient women (Pitt, 1973). The problem is therefore an extremely important one despite the relative dearth of literature in the field.

Definition

Most often these disorders develop in the period beginning with parturition and ending with the involution of the uterus. Certain investigators extend this period and include disturbances associated with the stresses of early infant care. Others consider disorders seen in adoptive mothers, husbands, and grandparents. Confusion of definition abounds, so that one is often unclear about the terms being used, the specific nature of the syndromes, and the clinical picture being discussed. The generally recognized clinical varieties of postpartum disorders are as follows (Weintraub, 1978):

1. transient mild depression or postpartum blues
2. postpartum confusional states
3. postpartum affective disorders
4. postpartum schizophrenia
5. postpartum neurotic reactions

Although pregnancy and childbirth are undoubtedly associated with major endocrinologic changes, there is relatively little clear evidence to explain why some women develop these syndromes and others do not. Specific vulnerability and/or other factors have not been clearly delineated.

The evidence that endocrinologic and psychological mechanisms are inexplicably linked comes from the kind of study conducted by Yen and Quesenbery (1976). They reported elevated labels of specific hormones in a woman with pseudocyesis which fell immediately, as did the abdominal distension, when the diagnosis was revealed. The authors concluded: "Pseudocyesis is a classic example of the dominating role of the central nervous system in the control of ovarian function" (Yen & Quesenberry, 1976, p. 132).

Postpartum Neurotic Reactions

The most common neurotic symptomatology reported during the postpartum period is obsessive–compulsive reactions. These often take the form of ruminations about the safety of the baby and intense preoccupation with the details of his or her care. These reactions may evolve into schizophrenic or depressive psychosis. Neurotic depressive reactions occur in approximately 10% of women, generally lasting weeks or months, and must be distinguished from the more common and benign postpartum blues (Hamilton, 1962).

The prognosis of this heterogeneous group of neurotic disorders depends upon the clinical picture, the amount of time that has elapsed postpartum before the episode develops, and the previous history of mental illness. Generally, women who develop postpartum illnesses shortly after childbirth have a poorer prognosis than those who develop symptoms later in the postpartum period. Women with a history of treatment for psychiatric illness prior to their pregnancies also have a poorer prognosis (Wilson, Barglow, & Shippman, 1972).

Women who have had a postpartum reaction are at risk for similar reactions following future pregnancies. It is estimated that approximately one out of four women with a history of postpartum psychosis will develop a similar disorder after subsequent pregnancies. Women with manic–depressive psychoses are a particularly vulnerable group (Kane, Lachenbruch, & Lokey, 1971; Reich & Winocur, 1970).

Research Issues

There are a number of problems with existing research in this area, some of which have been noted. The greatest problem is the lack of integration of attention to methodology with the interaction of psychological and organic variables. When one tries to identify the causes of postpartum syndromes, it is clear that hormonal changes have not been carefully correlated with pregnancy, although new biochemical assay techniques now make this more possible.

Furthermore, the definition of the postpartum period is inconsistent, and clinical pictures and symptoms and specificity are variable. Methodologic approaches differ widely. Some investigators use objective tests, others use self-reports, and still others use interviews to determine the existence of symptoms. These symptoms, in turn, are seldom defined in the literature. The incidence of postpartum reactions is difficult to estimate because of the variation in definition and in populations studied. There are few data correlating sociocultural and biologic factors. Kane *et al.* (1971), for example, suggest that there are differences between black and white women. Some of these may be socioeconomic rather than racial variables. Another problem in assessing incidence is that sampling techniques vary, and some investigators use women with pathologic diagnoses while others use "normals." It is obvious that well-controlled comparative studies are necessary to understand the prognosis of this group of disorders and the reasons for the risk factors.

Therapeutic and preventive approaches are hampered by the difficulty in arriving at consistent definitions and conceptions of causes. Results are generally similar to those for similar syndromes in the non-postpartum patient. In recent years, some attention has been devoted to the family and milieu and to organic methods of treatment.

The roles of the husband and the baby in the treatment of the woman with puerperal psychosis are controversial. Because the mother almost always harbors feelings of hostility toward the baby, some clinicians have advocated separation for the duration of the acute episode.

Recently, attempts have been made to hospitalize the baby, and even the husband, with the mother in order to encourage the resolution of interactional conflicts and to facilitate the development of a supportive environment. Although the results of this approach are not uniformly favorable, several authors have reported success (Grunebaum & Weiss, 1963; Luepker, 1972). Since some of these data indicate that the maturity and psychological stability of the husband are important factors in the successful outcome of conjoint hospitalizations, research in this area should be pursued.

Dalton (1971a, 1971b) recommends an organic approach. She reports favorable responses to treatment of postpartum blues with progesterone. Since this disorder tends to be self-limited, and since progesterone may affect the resumption of menstruation as well as breastfeeding, this approach must be viewed cautiously and with full concern for the wishes of the mother.

Emotional Impact of Hysterectomy

The number of hysterectomies performed in the United States has been increasing; the frequency of this procedure is now greater than that of any other major operation performed on women. The National Center for Health Statistics (cited in Bunker, 1976) estimates that in 1973, 690,000 hysterectomies were performed in the United States. Bunker (1976) estimates that this represents a rate of 647.7 per 100,000 and, if the rate continues, might result in loss of the uterus by half of the female population by age 65. During the late 1960s, the hysterectomy rate in the United States was two times that in England and Wales. Obviously, the indications for this procedure are neither firmly established nor universally agreed upon.

The psychological impact of hysterectomy is complex. It is, in part, the consequence of biologic reality and its meaning, namely, ending reproductive possibilities and causing the cessation of menstruation. It is also, in part, the result of social factors such as the way in which a woman without a uterus is regarded and responded to. Finally, the psychological impact is the result of factors such as the symbolic and unconscious significance of the uterus for an individual woman. In addition, the experience of undergoing the surgery, including the way in which the surgical procedure is presented by the physician and perceived by the woman, affects the outcome to some extent. The actual surgical procedure performed will have a major influence, that is, removal of only the uterus, as opposed to removal of the uterus plus ovaries, resulting in surgical castration. In earlier studies, these populations were frequently grouped, resulting in difficulty differentiating the effects of surgical menopause from those of hysterectomy.

For some women, the procedure ushers in the end of an era of "youth" and the beginning of middle age with its impact on self-concept and life planning and its implications for psychotherapy. An assessment of this complex problem is further complicated by the fact that social changes have been very rapid, and the expectations and opportunities for women have expanded. Therefore, the meaning of a hysterectomy marking the end of childbearing possibilities may now have different real consequences from those of some years ago, when a woman's identity was more closely linked with her reproductive role.

It is important to distinguish the effects of surgery itself from those of the particular procedure and, further, to separate concerns about the underlying pathology from reactions to the procedure. Surgery for malignancy is obviously different from an elective procedure for fibroids. For the sake of survival, sacrifice of an organ is more readily accepted. However, there are potential reactions to the loss of the organ itself, even though these may be masked by the concerns about the disease.

The three components of a woman's traditional identity in our society, that is, femininity, sexuality, and motherhood, are related to the uterus (Roeske, 1978). Even though a woman may know rationally that a hysterectomy will not affect her day-to-day life or her sexual functioning, she may still be worried about these issues until informed and reassured explicitly by the surgeon. She may be concerned even afterwards. For example, women reveal their underlying response to the significance of the experience when they talk about the hysterectomy as, "Everything was taken out," or, "I lost my nature." It is not clear whether hysterectomy does or does not affect sexual functioning. If the vagina is shortened, it may do so (Morgan, 1978). However, many women report no changes (Masters & Johnson, 1966; Roeske, 1978). Since sexuality is multidetermined, here, too, integrated research is necessary. Therapy aimed at improving sexual relationships may be helpful even in the face of anatomic changes.

An additional source of fantasy and nonrational perceptions about hysterectomy derives from the hidden location of the uterus in contrast to the visible genitals of the male. Thus, female fantasies about normality cannot be tested against reality as they can in the male.

Symptom Formation

There are a number of ways in which emotions may affect symptoms. Pelvic symptoms, particularly pelvic pain, may represent a displacement from other problems such as sexual conflicts and problems concerning femininity and childbearing (Castelnuovo-Tedesco & Krout, 1970). Although this phenomenon is widely recognized, it has been insufficiently studied and remains a puzzling clinical problem for gynecologists who tend to treat the physical symptom specifically or turn it over to a consultant (Pasnau, 1975). The pain threshold may be lowered due to current emotional stress, so that discomfort which might otherwise be tolerated becomes intolerable. For instance, dysmenorrhea, which may ordinarily be experienced as moderate, may become a major problem, and the patient pursues treatment more actively. Other types of symptom formation include conversion reactions or the somatic symbolic repression of an emotional conflict. Some individuals express most of their emotional problems somatically. This is particularly true for depression (Lipowski, 1974, 1975). The treatment implications require that the therapist be aware of the data on hysterectomy and the complex meanings of reproduction for women, especially in the current cultural context.

Posthysterectomy Depression

All through life, an individual must confront and master losses. Losing a part of one's body must also be mastered by the same psychological process of mourning. Some people ward off and deny their losses and may respond to all potentially depressing experiences in the same way. Relief of the symptoms and relief that the surgery is over or relief of the anxiety about sex or surgery may mask this transient depression, which then emerges later. Preparation and support are extremely helpful and permit some mourning to take place in advance. When a hysterectomy is performed in a premenopausal woman, the loss of menses may also be perceived as a loss (Morgan, 1978; Roeske, 1978), since menstruation is a sign of active feminine function.

The reactions to the surgery reflect, to a large extent, the individual's characteristic mechanisms for coping with any stress and clearly vary with each person and the circumstance (Barber, 1968; Janis, 1958; Richards, 1973). However, certain recurrent issues emerge. In attempting to understand the response, it is important to include the patient's reaction to the process of diagnosis and the physician's recommendation (Notman, 1979). When the surgeon explains the procedure to the patient, he or she often seeks to convey to the patient that she will not be missing a significant organ by explaining that after reproductive life, the uterus has no function and is an "empty bag." This is meant to be reassuring but can be experienced as devaluing, since it means that part of oneself is useless or diseased. The uterus has psychological significance beyond its actual reproductive function, for a woman's sense of bodily intactness, completeness as a woman, and even her sexual desirability is closely associated with her uterus by her and possibly by others.

The loss of her uterus may also be an abrupt reminder that her reproductive identity is over, whether she greets this with dismay or relif.

In many cultural groups in the United States, and in other cultures as well, a woman without her uterus is regarded as being "damaged goods" and not worth as much by men, not even in her own eyes (Lidz, 1978). Although women have many other sources of identity and self-esteem, their reproductive potential has been an important component, with menstrual bleeding as a periodic reminder, so that the end of this function represents a challenge to that source of self-esteem.

Methodologic Problems in Research

Posthysterectomy depression has been difficult to evaluate because of all of the issues discussed above, and the research has suffered from many methodologic problems (Meikle, Brody, & Pysh, 1977). The incidence of posthysterectomy depression appears to be greater among women under 40, those with dysfunctional uterine bleeding, those with no pathology noted in the uterus, and those with a prior history of depression (Barber, 1968; Polivy, 1974; Richards, 1973). Also, women with disrupted relationships posthysterectomy have a greater incidence of depression.

Some women experience relief and a welcome end to burdensome childbearing. For most women, it is probably a manageable stress (Meikle *et al.*, 1977; Roeske, 1978). Current social changes, with the shift away from the domestic and childbearing roles as the central source of status and self-esteem for women, may bring changes in some of the implications of hysterectomy and, thus, changes in posthysterectomy depression. However, the deep-seated and unconscious meanings of uterus, reproduction, and self-esteem are not necessarily as easily reached by attitudinal changes derived from social change and need to be considered. Preexisting psychological pathology must be considered as well (Meikle, 1977).

Careful research that differentiates the effects of hysterectomy from those of the surgical procedure must be well designed, prospective, and controlled, so that indications for the surgery age and socioeconomic variables are possible to assess. In addition, the use of hysterectomy as a means of contraception, the differences between effects of hysterectomy alone and when accompanied by ovariectomy, which precipitates a surgical menopause, and the consequences of surgical menopause for women at various ages have not been fully researched. Other treatments for conditions usually treated by hysterectomy, for example, fibroids, have not been fully studied. The therapeutic implications of these problems are clear. Therapy addressed to role issues and their changes and effects on self-image, the sense of damage, and possible sexual consequences is important. It is also important to involve sexual partners and families where appropriate, both in preparation, including education about effects, and in postsurgical aspects.

Psychosocial Consequences of Mastectomy

The significance of her breasts to a woman goes beyond realistic considerations alone and remains throughout her life. The physician may not be sensitive to the degree of their symbolic importance. For instance, a 48-year-old woman who consulted a doctor with a small lump was told, "Your breasts are no longer functional," with the implication that she need not hesitate to have them removed. Women with potential malignancies often do delay seeking medical attention (Gates & Burnwall, 1978).

Breast cancer has been a major form of cancer in women, and, in spite of much research, the cure rate has not increased dramatically (Tishler, 1978). Denial of the feared diagnosis extends to all forms of potential malignancy but is accentuated for women with breast disease, because until recently, there were no medically acceptable choices except for mutilating radical mastectomy. The controversy about survival rates with varying treatments has increased in recent years (Tishler, 1978), with current opinion casting doubt on the success of radical mastectomy compared with more conservative procedures, including the use of radiation and chemotherapy combined with less extensive surgery. The confusion and controversy surrounding optimal treatment puts the individual patient under considerable stress, since she must make choices, at a time of considerable anxiety, in areas in which she has no expertise.

The impact of a mastectomy raises a number of issues: those relating to confrontation with a life-threatening illness, those deriving from the loss of a body part, and the specific concerns related to the breast itself. These issues are similar to those raised by major illness in other parts of the body which have similar special significance, such as the uterus (Asken, 1975; Polivy, 1977).

For the surgeon, the dominant aspect is usually the life-threatening illness. Appropriately, he or she is first concerned with the patient's survival, then the patient's physical and emotional response to the whole experience. Many physicians feel that they protect the patient by not fully communicating their concern to her. There may be a discrepancy between what the physician knows and what is told to the patient and family, and, therefore, what the patient must deal with. A discrepancy also exists between the doctor's idea of what he or she is doing, namely, helping the patient and treating the illness, and the patient's perception of the physician's actions, namely, not only as a helpful procedure for her survival and cure, but also as an attack. Some women feel that their survival is worth the loss. Others hesitate. For optimal treatment, the patient needs to have some idea of the choices available. Psychotherapeutically, an opportunity to investigate the experience is very important. Action may not be as urgent as the surgeon thinks. There currently has been a shift of emphasis, with the recommended procedure being a biopsy with very careful pathologic examination of the nature of the cancer and its extent and then a discussion of recommended treatment. This procedure can sometimes involve a therapist to help the patient assess alternatives and make decisions. The role of family members is not always clear. They sometimes cannot confront the patient, even if they know the extent of illness.

Family doctors are extremely important in the patient's reaction to mastectomy. The stability of a marriage, sexual reassurance, and the capacity of family members to tolerate the truth and the anxiety of uncertainty about the future are pivotal in the amount of support the patient has in regaining her emotional balance (Asken, 1975). The capacity to offer support varies, of course, with the personal experiences of each individual member as well as with the family's pattern of response to crisis and loss. The role of the ill member in the family will also determine the reaction of the other family members and may mobilize ambivalence in others which is particularly hard for them to tolerate. Absence of the mother, or her depression, is a major life crisis for young children, which is accentuated if there is no other family member who is able to be supportive. A husband's anxiety over how to treat his wife and how to deal with his own conflicting feelings leads to withdrawal, which the patient interprets as rejection.

Gates and Burwell (1978), in a review of psychological aspects of breast cancer, describe the broad range of psychological responses observed clinically immediately postmastectomy: "Shock, guilt, anger, denial, loss of feminine self-image, and occasional depression" were reported. They stress the paucity of research differentiating the loss of the breast from the impact of the diagnosis of breast cancer. They also emphasize the impact of mastectomy on total self-concept, rather than only on body image. Breast reconstruction (Gifford, 1976) offers a restored sense of self-assertiveness and confidence, rather than just an increased sense of femininity.

The acuteness of the situation precipitated by the diagnosis of breast cancer has a considerable effect on the trauma a mastectomy represents. A sudden change from a state of apparent good health to one in which a major loss has occurred creates greater potential for disorganization, and crisis-intervention therapeutic techniques may be most helpful.

Research Issues

Research on the psychological consequences of various procedures, and on the readiness to report lesions if the expected treatment is less mutilating, needs to be expanded. The importance of the recommendation for surgery as an indication of the physician's concept of the treatability of the lesion may be an important component in the patient's view of her disease.

Further studies of family consequences of mastectomy are important, including focusing on the patient's sisters and daughters, since the incidence of breast cancer is known to be influenced by a great number of familial factors. Family reactions which are negative or ambivalent, such as depression, withdrawal or guilt over the inability to be supportive, may affect the patient's recovery but also require that attention be paid to the family member who is reacting in these ways. Most optimal ways of reaching these issues, for example, individual approaches or examining the influence of the patient's awareness on therapeutic techniques, need further study.

Psychotherapy aims at a realistic approach to what may be an ambiguous situation, and the effects of approaches permitting active mastery need further assessment. Self-help groups such as Reach to Recovery are sometimes merely tolerated by physicians, sometimes actively involved collaboratively. The polarizations between consumer-based self-help groups and professionals can be undermining of optimal care.

Menopause

Many symptoms occurring in women during midlife have been thought to be related to menopause, and menopause has been stereotyped as dominating this life period. In reality, this does not appear to be the case. Only recently have studies attempted to differentiate life-cycle developmental changes of the midlife period (Barnett & Baruch, 1978; Bart & Grossman, 1976) from menopausal effects. In addition, symptoms which may represent the response of a particular individual to menopause appear to be related to a considerable degree to that person's adaptive and responsive style and not to hormonal changes alone. Symptomatology attributed to menopause has included depression, irritability, insomnia, headache, dizzy spells, palpitations, weight increases, hot flashes and flushes, night sweats, and a variety of other symptoms.

Research in this area has been relatively sparse and uneven. It has been criticized methodologically for sloppiness of definitions, sampling, and approach. McKinlay and Jeffreys (1974) and Parlee (1976) further point to the general lack of attention to menopause in the medical literature. Their criticisms focus on the failure to develop consistent objective definitions of menopause and of menopausal symptomatology; the use of retrospective data, case histories, and clinical impressions; and the analysis of data obtained from selected samples of women who are under the care of gynecologists and psychiatrists. Those studies which are considered more reliable show that psychosomatic and psychological complaints were not reported more frequently by so-called "menopausal" than by younger women (Neugarten & Kraines, 1965).

Some researchers attribute flashes to psychological factors such as anger, anxiety, or excitement or to activities giving rise to excess heat production or retention, such as a warm environment, muscular work, or eating hot food (Perlmutter, 1978; Reynolds, 1962). However, the symptoms may arise without any clear psychological or heat-stimulating mechanism. Other symptoms which have been attributed to the menopause have included a wide variety of complaints. These do not seem to be directly attributable to the actual menopause. Using menstrual histories as an index of menopausal status, Neugarten and Kraines (1965) studied 100 women 43–53 years of age. They found menopausal status to be unrelated to a wide array of personality measures. They also found that there were very few significant relationships between the severity of somatic and psychosomatic symptoms and personality variables, although they were consistent with an individual's tendency to somaticize. Kraines (1963) found that menopausal status was not a contributing factor in self-evaluations of middle-aged women. She also found, as one might expect, that women who previously had low self-esteem and low life satisfaction were likely to have difficulties with menopause. These and other data do indicate that women's reactions to menopause are consistent with their reactions to other important transition points in their lives, such as menarche and pregnancy (McKinlay & McKinlay, 1973). Thus, menopause can be considered as one of the important experiences for women (Benedek, 1950) but one that is best understood in the context of their lives, their particular experiences and adaptive responses, and their sociocultural environment with its value systems.

Women's sexual interest and responsiveness do not necessarily diminish at midlife. Many women report increased sexual satisfaction as they are freed from anxiety about pregnancy. Masters and Johnson (1966) and others document the existence of full sexual activity in middle-aged and older women, and, although changes in patterns of response occur with age, particularly for men, they stress that the idea that sexual functioning is inevitably diminished with age is a myth (Masters & Johnson, 1966).

Concomitant family experiences are important in determining the outcome of this period. The midlife transition for men, often the husbands of menopausal women, brings new stresses (Levenson, Darrow, Klein, Levenson, & McKee, 1978) as men reassess their own lives. For men, this period has been reported to be accompanied by sexual problems, sometimes leading to affairs, marital disruption, and the abandonment of their wives. Adolescent children may be sexually and aggressively provocative, challenging, or disappointing. There have been important class differences in the readiness to have affairs and the availability of divorce (Rainwater, 1966). The increasing work opportunities for women have probably stimulated more women who are dissatisfied with their marriages to seek divorces than in the past.

Research Issues

The origin, nature, and possible therapeutic approaches to menopausal symptoms need further clarification. Current data on the possible carcinogenicity of estrogen-replacement treatment make alternative modes of therapy particularly important. Hypnosis and relaxation techniques for treatment of symptoms are important possibilities. Facilitating the development of alternatives to childbearing and reproductive roles for women as they approach midlife is another significant area for therapeutic intervention. The development of competence, as well as efforts to counter the social stigma surrounding the menopausal woman, will help diminish the stresses of this period. Some of the more malignant postmenopausal physical illnesses, such as rapidly progressive osteoporosis, are at present poorly understood and treated. Clearly, more research is needed on menopausal concomitants and midlife development for women.

Recommendations for Further Research

From our overview of a number of important reproductive crises, it is possible to select several critical research areas which require integration and correlation between fields and researchers in order to point more clearly toward appropriate intervention strategies.

1. On the biologic level, research is needed on the specific biochemistry and physiology accompanying normal reproductive functioning. For example, we must understand normal menarche and menopause if we are to assess what aspects of symptoms are biologically determined and to what extent psychogenic factors play a role.

2. The long-term and short-term detrimental effects of various procedures and medications need clarification. These include reported psychological side effects of oral contraceptives and the impact on mother and child of analgesics during delivery.

3. We need to develop good follow-up data on certain phenomena (e.g., teenage pregnancy) and on the impact of various interventions (including abortion with and without family, group, or individual treatmnet) or educational programs, with or without psychotherapy, on these youngsters.

4. Psychological research should be integrated with endocrinologic and other biologic findings. A prospective design incorporating multiple variables would be most valuable, making planning for intervention possible.

5. There is a need for careful descriptive detailing of responses to a number of procedures and experiences, for example, the effects on the individual and family of procedures such as amniocentesis, genetic counseling, gynecologic surgery, and fetal monitoring. Information as to which interventions are beneficial or detrimental is at present sketchy.

6. Personality and trait studies using adequate controls must be put in a contextual perspective and used appropriately, not globally, with careful analyses of alternative therapeutic interventions.

References

American Psychiatric Association. Postition statement on abortion. *American Journal of Psychiatry*, 1970, *126*, 1554.

Anderson, J. E., & Smith, J. C. Planned and unplanned fertility in a metropolitan area: Black and white differences. *Family Planning Perspectives*, 1975, *7*, 281–285.

Asken, M. Psychoemotional aspects of mastectomy. *American Journal of Psychiatry*, 1975, *132*, 56–59.

Barber, M. Psychiatric illness after hysterectomy. *British Medical Journal*, 1968, *2*, 91–95.

Bardwick, J. The effects of body state on the psyche. In J. Bardwick (Ed.), *Psychology of women*. New York: Harper and Row, 1971.

Barnett, R., & Baruch, G. Women in the middle years: A critique of research and theory. _Psychology of Women Quarterly,_ 1978, _3_(2), 187–197.

Bart, P., & Grossman, M. Menopause. _Women and Health,_ 1976, _1_(3), 3–11.

Bart, P., & Grossman, M. Menopause. In M. Notman & C. Nadelson (Eds.), _The woman patient: Medical and psychological interfaces._ New York: Plenum Press, 1978.

Benedek, T. Climacterism: A developmental phase. _Psychoanalytic Quarterly,_ 1950, _19_(1), 1–27.

Benedek, T., & Rubenstein, B. Correlations between activity and psychodynamic processes. In T. Benedek (Ed.), _Studies in psychosomatic medicine: Psychosexual function._ New York: Roland, 1952. (Originally published, 1939.)

Beral, V., & Kay, C. R. Mortality in women on oral contraceptives. _Lancet,_ 1977, _2,_ 1276–1277.

Bibring, G. Some considerations of the psychological processes in pregnancy. _Psychoanalytic Study of the Child,_ 1959, _14,_ 113–121.

Bibring, G., Dwyer, T., Huntington, D., & Valenstein, A. A study of the earliest mother–child relationship. _Psychoanalytic Study of the Child,_ 1961, _16,_ 9–72.

Bibring, G., & Valenstein, A. Psychological aspects of pregnancy. _Clinical Obstetrics and Gynecology,_ 1976, _19_(2), 357–371.

Bradley, R. A. _Husband-coached childbirth._ New York: Harper and Row, 1965.

Brazelton, T. B. Effects of prenatal drugs on the behavior of the neonate. _American Journal of Psychiatry,_ 1970, _126,_ 1261–1266.

Bremer, C. Incidence of post-abortion psychosis: A prospective study. _British Medical Journal,_ 1977, _1,_ 476–477.

Bulletin of Planned Parenthood League of Massachusetts. March 1978.

Bunker, J. Elective hysterectomy: Pro and con. _New England Journal of Medicine,_ 1976, _296,_ 264–266.

Caplan, G. The disturbance of the mother–child relationship by unsuccessful attempts at abortion. _Mental Hygiene,_ 1954, _38,_ 67–80.

Caplan, G. Psychological aspects of maternity care. _American Journal of Public Health,_ 1957, _47,_ 25–31.

Castelnuovo-Tedesco, P., & Krout, B. Psychosomatic aspects of chronic pelvic pain. _Psychiatry in Medicine,_ 1970, _1_(2), 109–126.

Chertok, L. The psychopathology of vomiting of pregnancy. In J. G. Howells (Ed.), _Modern perspectives in psycho-obstetrics._ New York: Brunner/Mazel, 1972.

Dalton, K. Prospective study into puerperal depression. _British Journal of Psychiatry,_ 1971, _118,_ 689–692. (a)

Dalton, K. Puerperal and premenstrual depression. _Proceedings of the Royal Society of Medicine,_ 1971, _64,_ 1249–1252. (b)

Daniels, R. S., & Lessow, H. Severe postpartum reactions: An interpersonal view. _Psychosomatics,_ 1964, _5,_ 21–26.

Dauher, H., Zalar, M., & Goldstein, P. Abortion counselling and behavioral change. _Family Planning Perspective,_ 1972, _4_(2), 23–27.

DeFries, J. Pseudo-homosexuality in feminists. _American Journal of Psychiatry,_ 1976, _133_(4), 400–404.

Deutsch, H. _Motherhood_ (Vol. 2). New York: Grune and Stratton, 1945.

Dick-Read, G. _Childbirth without fear_ (4th ed.). New York: Harper and Row, 1972. (Originally published, 1944.)

Doering, S. G., & Entwisle, D. R. Preparation during pregnancy and ability to cope with labor and delivery. _American Journal of Orthopsychiatry,_ 1975, _45,_ 825–837.

Ekblad, K. Induced abortion on psychiatric grounds. _Acta Psychiatrica Scandinavica, Supplementum_ 99, 1955, 1–238.

Enkin, M., Smith, S., Dermer, S., & Emmett, J. An adequately controlled study of the effectiveness of P.P.M. training. In M. Norris (Ed.), _Psychosomatic medicine in obstetrics and gynecology: Proceedings._ Basel: S. Karger, 1972.

Ford, C., Atkinson, R., & Bugonier, J. Therapeutic abortion: Who needs a psychiatrist? *Obstetrics and Gynecology,* 1971, *38,* 206-213.

Ford, C., Castelnuovo-Tedesco, P. & Long, K. Is abortion a therapeutic procedure in psychiatry? *Journal of the American Medical Association,* 1971, *218,* 1173-1178.

Ford, C. S., & Beach, F. A. *Patterns of sexual behavior.* New York: Harper and Row, 1951.

Forssman, H., & Thuwe, I. On hundred and twenty children born after application for therapeutic abortion refused: Their mental health, social adjustment and educational level up to the age of 21. *Acta Psychiatrica Scandinavica,* 1966, *42,* 71-88.

Frank, R. Hormonal causes of premenstrual tension. *Archives of Neurological Psychiatry,* 1931, *26,* 1053-1057.

Freeman, E. Influence of personality attributes on abortion experiences. *American Journal of Orthopsychiatry,* 1977, *47*(3), 503-513.

Friedman, E. A. The physiological aspects of pregnancy. In M. Notman & C. Nadelson (Eds.), *The woman patient: Medical and psychological interfaces.* New York: Plenum Press, 1978.

Gates, C., & Burwell, B. Psychological aspects of breast cancer. In B. Wolman (Ed.), *Psychological aspects of gynecology and obstetrics.* Oradell, N.J.: Medical Economics, 1978.

Gifford, S. *Emotional attitudes toward cosmetic breast surgery: Loss and restitution of the ideal self in plastic and reconstructive surgery of the breast.* Boston: Little, Brown, 1976.

Gilligan, C. In a different voice: Women's conception of the self and morality. *Harvard Education Review,* 1977, *47*(4), 481-517.

Glasser, M., & Pasnau, R. The unwanted pregnancy in adolescence. *Journal of Family Practice,* 1975, *2,* 91-94.

Goldsmith, S., Gabrielson, I., Matthews, V., & Potts, L. Teenagers, sex, and contraception. *Family Planning Perspectives,* 1972, *4*(1), 32-38.

Grounds, D., Davies, B., & Mowbray, R. The contraceptive pill, side effects, and personality. *British Journal of Psychiatry,* 1970, *116,* 169-172.

Group for the Advancement of Psychiatry. *The right to abortion: A psychiatric view* (Vol. 7, No. 75, pp. 197-227). New York: Mental Health Materials Center, 1969.

Grunebaum, H., & Weiss, J. Psychotic mothers and their children: Joint admission to an adult psychiatric hospital. *American Journal of Psychiatry,* 1963, *119,* 927-933.

Haire, D. The cultural warping of childbirth. *Environmental Child Health,* 1973, *19,* 171-191.

Hamilton, J. *Postpartum psychiatric problems.* St. Louis, Mo.: C. V. Mosby, 1962.

Harlow, H., Harlow, M., & Hansen, E. The natural affectional system in rhesus monkeys. In H. Rheingod (Ed.), *Maternal behavior in mammals.* New York: Wiley, 1966.

Hook, K. Refused abortion: A follow-up study of two hundred and forty-nine women whose applications were refused by the national board of health in Sweden. *Acta Psychiatrica Scandinavica, Supplementum* 168, 1963, *39.*

Horney, K. Premenstrual tension. In H. Kelman (Ed.), *Feminine psychology.* New York: Norton, 1967. (Originally published, 1931.)

Howells, J. G. (Ed.). *Modern perspectives in psycho-obstetrics.* New York: Brunner/Mazel, 1972.

Janis, I. *Psychological stress.* New York: Wiley, 1958.

Kaltreider, N., & Margolis, A. Barren by choice: A clinical study. *American Journal of Psychiatry,* 1977, *134*(2), 179-182.

Kane, F., Lachenbruch, P., & Lokey, L. Post-partum depression in southern black women. *Disease of the Nervous System,* 1971, *32*(7), 486-489.

Katz, J. The atrocity of the investigator, subject and state in the human experimentation process. In J. Katz (Ed.), *Experimentation with human beings.* New York: Russell Sage Foundation, 1972.

Klaus, M., Jer Auld, R., Kreger, N., McAlpine, W., Steffa, M., & Kennell, J. Maternal attachment: Importance of the first post-partum days. *New England Journal of Medicine,* 1972, *286,* 460-463.

Klaus, M., & Kennell, J. *Maternal–infant bonding: The impact of early separation or loss on family development.* St. Louis, Mo.: C. V. Mosby, 1976.

Kraines, R. *The menopause and evaluations of the self.* Unpublished doctoral dissertation, University of Chicago, 1963.

Kroger, W. (Ed.). *Psychosomatic obstetrics, gynecology and endocrinology.* Springfield, Ill.: Charles C. Thomas, 1962.

Kummer, J. Post abortion psychiatric illness: A myth? *American Journal of Psychiatry*, 1963, *119*, 980–983.

Lamaze, F. *Painless childbirth.* London: Burke, 1958.

Leboyer, F. *Birth without violence.* New York: Knopf, 1975.

Lennane, K., & Lennane, R. Alleged psychogenic disorders in women: A possible manifestation of sexual prejudice. *New England Journal of Medicine*, 1973, *288*(6), 288–292.

Levenson, D., Darrow, C., Klein, E., Levenson, M., & McKee, B. *The seasons of a woman's life.* New York: Knopf, 1978.

Lidz, R. Conflicts between fertility and infertility. In M. Notman & C. Nadelson (Eds.), *The woman patient: Medical and psychological interfaces.* New York: Plenum Press, 1978.

Lindemann, E. Hysteria as a problem in a general hospital. *Medical Clinics of North America*, 1938, *22*, 591–605.

Lipowski, A. Current trends in psychosomatic medicine: I. *Psychiatry in Medicine*, 1974, *5*, 303–610.

Lipowski, Z. Current trends in psychosomatic medicine: II. *Psychiatry in Medicine*, 1975, *6*, 3–336.

Luepker, E. Joint admission and evaluation of postpartum psychiatric patients and their infants. *Hospital Community Psychiatry*, 1972, *23*(9), 284–286.

Marder, L. Psychiatric experiences with a liberalized therapeutic abortion law. *American Journal of Psychiatry*, 1970, *126*, 1230–1236.

Margolis, A., Rindfuss, R., Coghland, P., & Rochat, R. Contraception after abortion. *Family Planning Perspective*, 1974, *6*, 55–60.

Masters, W., & Johnson, V. *Human sexual response.* Boston: Little, Brown, 1966.

McKinlay, S., & Jeffreys, M. The menopausal syndrome. *British Journal of Preventive and Social Medicine*, 1974, *28*(2), 108–115.

McKinlay, S., & McKinlay, J. Selected studies of the menopause: An annotated bibliography. *Journal of Biosocial Science*, 1973, *5*, 533–555.

Mead, M., & Newton, N. Cultural patterning of perinatal behavior. In S. Richardson & A. Guttmacher (Eds.), *Childbearing: Its social and psychological aspects.* Baltimore: Williams and Wilkins, 1967.

Meikle, S. The psychological effects of hysterectomy. *Canadian Psychological Review*, 1977, *13*(12), 128–141.

Meikle, S., Brody, H., & Pysh, F. An investigation into the psychological effects of hysterectomy. *Journal of Nervous and Mental Disease*, 1977, *164*(1), 36–41.

Morgan, S. Sexuality after hysterectomy and castration. *Women and Health*, 1978, *3*(1), 5–9.

Morgenthau, J., Rao, P., Thornton, J., & Cameron, O. Adolescent contraceptors: Follow-up study. *New York State Journal of Medicine*, 1977, *77*, 928–931.

Nadelson, C., & Notman, M. *Emotional aspects of the symptoms, functions, and disorders of women in psychiatric medicine.* New York: Brunner/Mazel, 1977.

Neugarten, B., & Kraines, R. Menopausal symptoms in women of various ages. *Psychosomatic Medicine*, 1965, *27*, 266–273.

Normand, W. Post-partum disorders. In A. Freedman & H. Kaplan (Eds.), *Comprehensive textbook of psychiatry.* Baltimore: Williams and Wilkins, 1967.

Norris, M. (Ed.), *Psychosomatic medicine in obstetrics and gynecology.* Basel: S. Karger, 1972.

Notman, M. Teenage pregnancy: The non-use of contraception. *Psychiatric Quarterly*, 1975, *2*, 23–27.

Notman, M. What to tell your hysterectomy patient. *Modern Medicine*, 1979, *2*, 112–118.

Osofsky, H., & Osofsky, J. *The abortion experience: Psychological and medical impact.* Hagerstown, Md.: Harper and Row, 1973.

Osofsky, J., & Osofsky, H. The psychological reaction of patients to legalized abortion. *American Journal of Orthopsychiatry,* 1972, *42*(1), 48–60.

Pare, C., & Raven, H. Follow-up of patients referred for termination of pregnancy. *Lancet,* 1970, *1,* 635–638.

Parlee, M. Social factors in the psychology of menstruation, birth, and menopause. *Primary Care,* 1976, *3,* 477–490.

Parlee, M. Psychological aspects of menstruation, childbirth, and menopause: An overview with suggestions for further research. In V. Sherman & F. Denmark (Eds.), *The psychology of women: Future directions of research.* New York: Psychological Dimensions, 1978.

Partridge, J., Spiegel, T., Rouse, B., & Ewing, J. Therapeutic abortion: A study of psychiatric applicants at North Carolina Memorial Hospital. *North Carolina Medical Journal,* 1971, *32,* 132–136.

Pasnau, R. Psychiatric complications of therapeutic abortion. *Obstetrics and Gynecology,* 1972, *40,* 252–256.

Pasnau, R. Psychiatry and obstetrics–gynecology: Report of a five-year experience in psychiatry liaison. In R. Pasnau (Ed.), *Consultation–liaison psychiatry.* New York: Grune and Stratton, 1975.

Payne, E., Kravitz, A., Notman, M., & Anderson, J. Outcome following therapeutic abortion. *Archives of General Psychiatry,* 1976, *33,* 725–733.

Peck, A., & Marcus, H. Psychiatric sequelae of therapeutic interruption of pregnancy. *Journal of Nervous and Mental Disease,* 1966, *143,* 417–425.

Perlmutter, J. A gynecological approach to menopause. In M. Notman & C. Nadelson (Eds.), *The woman patient: Medical and psychological interfaces.* New York: Plenum Press, 1978.

Pitt, B. Maternity blues. *British Journal of Psychiatry,* 1973, *122,* 431–433.

Polivy, J. Psychological reactions to hysterectomy: A critical review. *American Journal of Obstetrics and Gynecology,* 1974, *118*(3), 417–426.

Polivy, J. Psychological effects of mastectomy on a woman's feminine self concept. *Journal of Nervous and Mental Disease,* 1977, *164,* 77–87.

Rainwater, L. Some aspects of lower class sexual behavior. *Journal of Social Issues,* 1966, *22*(2), 96–108.

Reich, T., & Winocur, G. Postpartum psychosis in patients with manic depressive disease. *Journal of Nervous and Mental Disease,* 1970, *151,* 60–69.

Renneker, R., & Cutler, M. Psychological problems of adjustment to cancer of the breast. *Journal of the American Medical Association,* 1952, *148,* 833–838.

Reynolds, S. Physiological and psychogenic factors in the menopausal flush syndrome. In W. Kroger (Ed.), *Psychosomatic obstetrics, gynecology and endocrinology.* Springfield, Ill.: Charles C. Thomas, 1962.

Richards, D. Depression after hysterectomy. *Lancet,* 1973, *2,* 429–433.

Robson, K., & Moss, H. Patterns and determinants of maternal attachment. *Pediatrics,* 1970, *77,* 976–985.

Roche Report. *Frontiers of Psychiatry,* June 15, 1976.

Roeske, N. Hysterectomy and other gynecological surgeries: A psychological view. In M. Notman & C. Nadelson (Eds.), *The woman patient: Medical and psychological interfaces.* New York: Plenum Press, 1978.

Schacter, S., & Singer, J. Cognitive, social and physiological determinants of emotional state. *Psychology Review,* 1962, *69,* 379–399.

Seiden, A. The sense of mastery in the childbirth experience. In M. Notman & C. Nadelson (Eds.), *The woman patient: Medical and psychological interfaces.* New York: Plenum Press, 1978.

Shaffer, I. Naturally it hurts—but not that much. *Medical World News*, 1969, *10*(40), 17–18.

Simon, N., Senturia, A., & Rothman, D. Psychiatric illness following therapeutic abortion. *American Journal of Psychiatry*, 1967, *124*, 59–65.

Sloane, R. The unwanted pregnancy. *New England Journal of Medicine*, 1969, *22*, 1206–1213.

Smith, E. A follow-up study of women who request abortion. *American Journal of Orthopsychiatry*, 1973, *43*(4), 574–585.

Snyder, S. The opiate receptor and morphine-like peptides in the brain. *American Journal of Psychiatry*, 1978, *135*(6), 645–652.

Tietze, C. Contraceptive practice in the context of a non-restrictive abortion law. *Family Planning Perspective*, 1975, *7*(3), 197–202.

Tishler, S. Breast disease. In M. Notman & C. Nadelson (Eds.), *The woman patient: Medical and psychological interfaces*. New York: Plenum Press, 1978.

Vellay, P. [*Childbirth without pain*] (D. Lloyd, trans.). New York: E. P. Dutton, 1960.

Vessey, M., McPherson, K., & Johnson, B. Mortality among women participating in the Oxford Family Planning Association Contraceptive Study. *Lancet*, 1977, *2*, 731–733.

Warnes, H., & Fitzpatrick, C. Oral contraceptives and depression. *Psychosomatics*, 1979, *20*(3), 182–194.

Weintraub, W. Postpartum reactions. In G. Balis, L. Wurmser, E. McDaniel, & R. Grenell (Eds.), *Psychiatric problems in medical practice*. Boston: Butterworths, 1978.

Whittington, H. Evaluation of therapeutic abortion as an element of preventive psychiatry. *American Journal of Psychiatry*, 1970, *126*, 1224–1229.

Wilcoxon, L., Shrader, S., & Sherif, C. Daily self-reports on activities, life events, moods, and somatic changes during the menstrual cycle. *Psychosomatic Medicine*, 1976, *38*(6), 399–416.

Wilson, J., Barglow, P., & Shippman, W. The prognosis of post-partum mental illness. *Comprehensive Psychiatry*, 1972, *13*, 305–316.

Winokur, G. Depression in the menopause. *American Journal of Psychiatry*, 1973, *130*(1), 92–93.

Wolff, B., & Langley, S. Cultural factors and the response to pain: A review. *American Anthropological Society*, 1968, *70*, 494–501.

Yen, R., & Quesenberry, N. Pituitary function in pseudocyesis. *Journal of Clinical Endocrinology and Metabolism*, 1976, *43*, 132–136.

Zobrowski, M. Cultural components in response to pain. *Social Issues*, 1962, *8*, 16.

Zola, I. Culture and symptoms: An analysis of patients presenting complaints. *American Sociological Review*, 1966, *31*, 615–630.

CHAPTER 14

Battered Women

LENORE E. WALKER

A man chases a woman until she catches him, then they are
married and live happily ever after.

The foregoing has been the popular view of how men and women enter
into relationships. Women have traditionally been seen as the sex needing the stability of marriage or a marriage-like relationship and having
the power to achieve such coupling. In addition to the research that has
shown that marriage does not facilitate the mental health of women
(Radloff, 1975), there is a growing body of literature that indicates that
physical and psychological abuse rather than "happily ever after" may be
that relationship's ending (Straus, Gelles, & Steinmetz, 1980; Walker,
1979). The plight of the battered woman has received more media attention than any other social problem during the past few years. Why this is
so is not clear. However, it has spurred development of a grass-roots
woman-dominated movement to provide alternative services and shelter
for battered women and has castigated the mental health profession for
not recognizing or treating the millions of women in the United States
and throughout the rest of the world who are beaten each year by men
who love them.

Few psychologists or other mental health professionals were ever
trained to recognize or treat battered women and their families. The
professions also reflect traditional cultural norms that allowed that violence in the marital relationship was the mutually caused product of two
emotionally disturbed individuals. With today's knowledge, psychology
can no longer accept the rationale of the masochistic woman or
psychopathic man as an appropriate answer. Rather, practitioners have
to wrestle with the uncomfortable knowledge that they may have inadvertently victimized a battered woman a second time by their inability to

Lenore E. Walker. Department of Psychology and Battered Women Research Center—
Domestic Violence Institute, Colorado Women's College, Denver, Colorado.

focus on her being a victim of the violence in her relationship. Fortu-
nately, the feminist movement and our social consciousness have now
encouraged us to expose the shameful secrets of marital violence.

Prevalence

The history of wife abuse is ancient: Brownmiller's (1975) research on
the history of rape, which is one form of violence against women,
suggested that from biblical days women traded freedom for security. In
many societies, men were not considered manly if they did not beat their
wives. Women were treated as men's property. As married men became
responsible for their wives' behavior, laws were passed that permitted
husbands to discipline their wives also. Thus, men's physical, economic,
and legal strength reinforced women's acceptance of the so-called "right
to discipline."

Talking about such assaults, reporting them to police, discussing
them in psychotherapy sessions, or even conducting research on wife
abuse has not been popular until the past 5 years. Recently, these battered women have been breaking this taboo of silence and are now
admitting to being abused by their mates or partners. Interestingly
enough, their stories directly conflict with the previous stereotypes of the
battered woman as an economically, socially, educationally disadvantaged person (Walker, 1979).

Attempts to estimate the prevalence of battered women in our society have been fraught with difficulties, not the least of which is the need
to deny the reality of wife abuse by many of the victims. Concealing such
violence behind closed doors has traditionally been an important survival technique for battered women. It is estimated that only one out of
ten battered women has reported her abuse to the police. In 1975, the
FBI crime reports recorded 20,510 murders in the United States. It is
estimated that two-thirds of all murders are committed by friends or
relatives of the victim. Spousal murders accounted for over half of the
deaths. In Kansas City, Missouri, analysis of the homicide patterns indicated that in 85% of the murders, police had been called to the home
from one to five times previously. The estimate of number of women
who have been physically assaulted ranges from 20 to 60%.

Definitions and sample selection of battered women vary from study
to study, which accounts for the wide variance in statistics. Studies based
on police and agency reports will necessarily be limited to particular
subsections of the entire population of battered women. The definition
of a "battered woman" at the Battered Women Research Center in Den-

ver, Colorado, is the following: a woman who is serously psychologically or physically battered at least twice by a man with whom she has an intimate marital or marital-like relationship. The definition of "serious psychological abuse" is still under study but usually includes a component of an expectation that includes physical or life-threatening abuse. From my research, I estimate that 50% of women will be battered by men who love them at sometime in their lives (Walker, 1979).

Sociologists (Straus *et al.*, 1980) who conducted the most recent national epidemiologic survey of domestic assault in the United States conclude that physical violence occurs between family members more often than it occurs between any other individuals or in any other setting except for wars and riots. In their survey, they found that 28% of their sample, or an estimated 13 million American couples, engaged in physical assaults against one another in 1 year. Over 2 million children in the United States used a gun or knife on a sister or brother; almost 2 million adults used lethal weapons in attacking their spouses; and over 1 million young children were assaulted by their parents using those same weapons (Straus *et al.*, 1980). This violence occurred in families across all demographic characteristics: all ages, races, ethnic groups, socioeconomic levels, and educational levels. The rape research also indicates a higher percentage of violent acts committed between people who know each other rather than between strangers (Chappell, Geis, & Geis, 1977). Despite the television and movie version of violence as street shoot-outs between men, the data indicate that these scenes are rarely repeated in real life. It is much more likely that the most unsafe place to be is in one's own home, especially for a woman.

Connection with All Forms of Domestic Violence

While the data have not yet demonstrated a direct link between wife abuse and child abuse, the general consensus of researchers in the field is that such a connection exists. The medical model that has permeated the child abuse field has been broadened to link sociological variables such as unemployment or unusual stress with intrapsychic problems of the abuser (Helfer & Kempe, 1974) but still utilizes a medical pathology model to understand the offenders. In an attempt to move away from such a pathology model, Gelles (1974) has placed child abuse on one extreme of a continuum that anchors normal child discipline on the other end. The emphasis is on a sociological model of analysis, with norms changing for various cultures.

Social-learning theorists have demonstrated that witnessed aggression causes an increase in aggressive thoughts and behavior in a variety of settings (Bandura, 1973). Even when there is no overt physical trauma, watching their father beat up their mother is probably the most insidious form of child abuse that children experience. Besherov (1978), the former director of the National Center for Child Abuse and Neglect, testified before the United States Congress that in homes where there is known wife abuse and child abuse, the man is the abuser of both in 70% of reported cases. Although women more frequently neglect their children, the more serious physical abuse is inflicted by men. Besherov's data indicate a 20% overlap of child and wife abuse cases. According to recent studies, the number may be larger. In any event, researchers in the field seem to agree that there is some kind of generational cycle whereby the use of violence in family relationships is passed down from one generation to another.

Connection with Violence against Women

For a feminist, the issue of domestic violence takes on a special perspective. By definition, a feminist psychologist and researcher would be especially sensitive to identifying inequality between men and women if it occurs within a specific area such as family violence. While all the forms of domestic assault have a commonality in the acts of violence which are committed, a feminist perspective notes that there is also commonality in the presence of sexism. Expressing such discrimination based on gender can cripple the emotional growth of boys and girls. Leidig (Note 1) has described numerous acts of violence committed by men against women. In addition to the battering of women, these include rape, girl-child incest, pornography, prostitution, and sexual harassment on the job and in the professional's office. Leidig asserts that all men benefit from violence against women even if they do not engage in it themselves, since it encourages women to seek men's protection. Both Leidig and Walker (in press) document the occurrence of subservient behavior, passivity, decreased mobility, and dependence on a man for survival. Many researchers studying wife abuse have presented detailed evidence of how a patriarchal society actually facilitates women being beaten (Chapman & Gates, 1978; Dobash & Dobash, 1977–1978; Fields, 1978; Martin, 1976). Police, courts, hospitals, and social services have all refused to provide adequate protection to battered women. Psychologists, too, have learned how to keep the family together at all costs—even if the individual's mental health or life is at stake. Thus, battered women have been subjected to a second assault by the institutions designed to protect people.

Feminists have been resistant to link all forms of domestic violence together because of the inference that child abuse deserves more attention, since women, as adults, are thought to be more able to protect themselves than are children. While it is important to understand how this is not true, how often women are at the mercy of men who are physically strong, it is also important to be careful not to infantilize women. Current childrearing patterns probably do train little boys in misogyny and do not give little girls the needed coping skills to prevent their own abuse. For feminists, all violence in the family will not be eliminated until profound changes are made in our social structures and childrearing patterns, eliminating sexism as well as violence.

Theoretical Explanations of Causation

Numerous theories of causation of spouse abuse have been proposed in the literature. Some have looked toward historical roots (Flick, Note 2) and patriarchal (Dobash & Dobash, 1977–1978) and religious (Davidson, 1978) ideology; facilitative cultural values (Martin, 1976; Pizzey, 1974) and institutional sanctions (Fields, 1978; Roy, 1978; Kremen, Note 3); sociological factors (Gelles, 1974; Steinmetz, 1977–1978; Straus, 1978); masochism and other intrapsychic personality characteristics (Gayford, 1975; Shainess, 1979; Snell, Rosenwald, & Robey, 1964; Starr, 1978); learned helplessness (Walker, 1977–1978); intermittent reinforcement in a cycle of violence (Walker, 1978, 1979); cognitive distortion through causal attribution (Frieze, Note 4); and reciprocity of coercive behaviors (Margolin, 1979).

These theoretical orientations develop different approaches that often reflect the biases and training of their proponents. Data come from epidemiologic studies as well as from individual interviews, organizational analysis, reviews of historical literature, and treatment programs. Analysis has been both deductive and inductive, often using nonrandom empirical date to provide both checks and balances. Nevertheless, these approaches represent a welcome creativity in a field that formerly has yielded little understanding that could be translated into applied programs to eliminate violence from family life. The sexist biases apparent in many of our established theoretical orientations have been documented (Groth, Note 5; Walker, Note 6) and suggestions made that all models for understanding violence need a feminist scrutiny.

A multideterministic theoretical orientation for explaining causality probably makes good common sense, given the overlap of so many theories. Indeed, most current writers propose an interactionist model.

For the purpose of this discussion, I will group the various theoretical orientations into the following distinct models: feminist–political, sociocultural, and psychological theories. It is understood that no combinations and interactions should be excluded by this arbitrary classification.

Feminist-Political Theories

The theoretical orientation most clearly associated with the feminist-political stance is that all violence is a reflection of unequal power relationships, the most unequal of all occurring between men and women. Thus, power is seen to be at the root of all violence. Some writers hold this stance to the exclusion of others (Dobash & Dobash, 1977–1978; Pleck, Pleck, Grossman, & Bart, 1977–1978). It appears that such a militant position has been taken because of political considerations, which include the need for women to be taken seriously and the fear that confused data can and have been used against needed social reform programs.

Most feminists stress the historical legal precedent of male supremacy. Prior to patriarchal religion, women and men were thought to have lived in equality (Davidson, 1978). As men assumed the role of protector of their women and assumed responsibility for paternity of their children, they were given the right to discipline and chastise their property. Laws remaining until recently gave a man the right to beat his woman provided that he use a stick no wider than his thumb, hence the "rule-of-thumb" law (Martin, 1976). When those laws were eliminated from our legal code, an informal system of benign neglect and different standards for prosecution were the substitution.

The inability of the criminal justice system to provide consequences for men's violent behavior toward women has caused an additional amount of stress on the woman and reinforces the man's belief that he can legitimately use such violence to control his woman's behavior. The woman sees herself as powerless and caught in a system which gives a double message: Violence against another person is unlawful and is a punishable offense, except against a wife. Current research at the Battered Women Research Center is looking at whether early sex-role socialization that supports such inequality in power relationships plays a role in maintaining such violence. It is possible that the woman's inability to resist being intimidated by the man's initial coercive threats may actually facilitate the violent attack, even though she is not responsible for causing it.

Sociocultural Theories

Sociologists have long been involved in the search to understand domestic and other criminal violence. The sociological analyses of Straus, Steinmetz, and Gelles have been the pioneering research on battered women. Straus began writing about the kind of sociocultural conditions that facilitate domestic violence. He saw sex-role stereotyping and sexism, as well as cultural acceptance of violence in the name of discipline, as underlying factors (Straus, 1978). Because of the deeply embedded nature of domestic violence in our society, Straus calls for a program of primary prevention as an important step in elimination of the problem. Gelles (1974) does the same for both wife abuse and child abuse. He demonstrates how the cultural standard of discipline permits different cultures to tolerate various degrees of violence against children and, like Straus, calls for prevention strategies to ensure that we do not raise a new generation committed to physical coercion as a way of resolving problems. Steinmetz (1977–1978) has moved from wife abuse to a concern with sibling violence and children's violence against their parents. She draws parallels between all forms of abuse within the family context and cites learning theory principles to explain why different forms of abuse occur in the same family. The opportunity for modeling is clear, and the message is passed on: The people who love you have the right to hurt you in the name of discipline.

Steinmetz (1977–1978) has speculated that the number of men who are battered by their wives is as high as the reverse. This unfortunate and unfounded argument was originally based on 4 out of 60 men in an unrepresentative sample who reported having been battered (Steinmetz, 1978). The sociocultural theories are very skeptical of the concept that battered men exist within the same context as do battered women and children. It is essential, however, to accept their premise that living together as a family legitimizes the use of violent behavior that would not be tolerated in any other setting.

Sociologists also have looked at several theories other than cultural legitimization of violence in the family. The whole body of literature which analyzes the uses and abuses of power has had interesting applications to the understanding of power dynamics between members of violent couples (Rounsaville, 1978; Stahly, 1977–1978; Nielsen, Eberle, Thoennes, & Walker, Note 7). Arguments documented by limited empirical data state that men who beat their wives have fewer resources than do the women, and so ruling by physical strength allows them one way of equalizing the power balance (Gelles, 1974). The limited fund of resources attributed to these men includes poorer verbal skills, less education, lower salaries, greater stress in the outside world, more sexual dysfunction, and fewer friends than their wives. Preliminary analyses of the data at the Battered Women Research Center do not support this resource theory (Nielsen *et al.,* Note 7). Needless to say, none of these deficits justifies the use of coercive behavior. Furthermore, such a theory is pejorative to men, implying that they do not have adequate behavioral control when adverse social conditions occur. Abusers do have control in limiting the amount of violence they inflict upon their victims. Such violence is generally meted out, moving from less to more abuse over time (Nielsen *et al.,* Note 7). It is hoped that the movement to understand male sex roles will shed more understanding on how men are socialized into violent behavior patterns.

Psychological Theories

The early studies on domestic violence were concerned with the strength of.bonding between the men and women involved. After observing that women repeatedly return to receive more violence, psychologists concluded that there must be a flaw in the personality development of such women (Snell *et al.,* 1964). It is possible that the intense bonding and sexuality often seen in these couples, combined with the simultaneously experienced feelings of love, fear, anger, hatred, and pain, may have encouraged psychoanalysts to attribute causation to what they labeled as women's inherently masochistic nature (Shainess, 1979). As a result of inaccurately labeling battered women as masochistic, psychoanalysts reinforced these women's self-blame and low self-esteem, which further robbed them of the psychological energy needed to escape from the violent situation. With the blame placed on the victims, the men who beat them were not held responsible for their own behavior. Men also were not held accountable for their behavior by being declared mentally ill, usually psychopathic (Gayford, 1975), although recent clinical observations indicate that those batterers who have come to a mental health center for psychotherapy are more likely to be diagnosed as a schizoid personality, paranoid, or depressed with suicidal features (Walker, 1979). The batterer's responsibility may be further compromised by attempts to blame his violent behavior on excessive alcohol abuse or too much stress, or even to assign him a "Saturday-night-brawler" label (Steinmetz, Note 8), all of which imply that this man should not be treated too harshly because the rest of the time he behaves appropriately.

The search for a mental illness explanation to domestic violence is still popular today, despite greater public understanding of the complexity of the problem. If we could find the cause of this disease, then a cure might more easily follow. Most clinicians who have been working in this field no longer hold out such hopes, understanding instead that when one-third of the population exhibits a behavior, the underlying causes are psychosocial and epidemiologic, rather than intrapsychic and disease-focused. Although typologies of battered women and their abusers have been offered (Starr, 1978), it is generally recognized that symptoms are usually the results of living in violence, and not the cause. The early reports of dramatic changes in the behavior of battered women when they live in shelter, separated from their batterers, support the "state," not "trait," designation of personality characteristics associated with these (CAABW, 1979).

Theorists with a systems orientation have attempted to look at the reciprocal nature of coercive behavior in a dyadic relationship. Both partners are seen as having mutual responsibility for the causation of violence. This view is based on the philosophy that while each person has an individual responsibility for his or her own feelings, thoughts, and behavior, the way one partner responds to the other's actions in a relationship is equally important in the causation and maintenance of domestic violence (Margolin, 1979). While this perspective adds an important dimension in understanding an individual couple's violent behavior, it has some serious limitations which need further study. For example, the assumption of mutual responsibility usually attributes equal power to the man and woman in negotiating in their relationship. The feminist–political arguments outlined earlier would challenge that assumption.

Cycle Theory of Battering

Understanding the family as a system with properties that extend beyond the characteristics of each individual member has been a valuable contribution of the marriage and family therapy theorists. It appears that such distinct characteristics occur in violent relationships, lending credence to the arguments stated earlier that an individual pathology model is inadequate for understanding or treatment purposes. My early interviews with battered women revealed that the violence is neither constant nor does it occur in a consistent manner in these families. Rather, it occurs in a predictable cycle with three distinct phases (Walker, 1979). The first phase is one in which tension builds and minor battering incidents occur. The woman accepts spouse abuse in the hopes of averting another acute battering incident, which becomes the explosive sec-

ond phase of the cycle. Following the acute battering incident, the batterer becomes sorry and frightened that his behavior might cause him to
lose his wife. He becomes kind and loving, often contrite, and tries to
make it up to her by showering her with lots of gifts and love. Sometimes
he fears that she will not forgive him, and then he may threaten to
commit suicide. Threats of homicide and further violence may also be
used as a way to keep the relationship together. His mental health status
may be viewed by others as borderline or worse. Psychosis and death are
both likely outcomes if the woman does not quickly forgive and forget.
This third phase may last for awhile, but soon minor incidents begin to
recur, tension builds, and the cycle starts anew.

Relationship of Learned Helplessness, Depression, and Battering

In moving beyond the psychopathology model to understand the psychology of battering, it seems useful to search for a theoretical explanation that is psychological and sociological in its tenets and considers the
interaction of causative approaches previously discussed. Such a model
has been constructed and is presently being tested at the Battered
Women Research Center. It is based on social-learning theory and explains behavior which previously was thought to be innate or pathologi-
cally deviant. The learned-helplessness theory adapted from the work of
Seligman (1975) and his colleagues, who began their experiments in
animal laboratories, provides a framework from which to build this
model. It is firmly based in learning theory and explains the emotional,
cognitive, and behavioral deficits seen in battered women. The model
would work if the women were subjected to unpredictable and uncontrollable violence directed against them for a variety of behaviors that
varied from time to time. Furthermore, the learned-helplessness model
calls for prior faulty learning patterns which make the women more
susceptible to being unable to develop adequate coping strategies or to
escape from the violence. These prior faulty learning patterns could
come from the sex-role socialization patterns for little girls. Thus, it has
been hypothesized that little girls who learn rigid sex-role-stereotyped
behavior are more likely to succumb to learned helplessness if they became battered women. This model probably could be applied to the
batterer as well, but it has not been tested as yet.

There have been attempts to link exogenous depressions with
learned helplessness. Results from the area of motivational and behavioral deficits were first reported from animal research, and then the
experiments were replicated using human subjects. The cognitive and

emotional deficits seen in depressed people were then studied. In the laboratory, college students showed motivational deficits similar to those observed in animals; the cognitive ability to perceive success was distorted, and emotional responses were heightened, when subjects were exposed to inescapable, random, variable aversive stimuli (Seligman, 1975).

Although there has been limited acceptance of the connection between depressions and learned helplessness, there are many competing theories of depression, such as cognitive disturbances (Beck, 1972) and attribution (Weiner, Frieze, Kukla, Reed, Rest, & Rosenbaum, 1971). Recent reformulations have taken into account the competing theories (Abramson, Seligman, & Teasdale, 1978; Costello, 1978; Rizley, 1978), but the issue is far from resolved. It seems probable from these recent reformulations that learned helplessness has much in common, but is not synonymous, with cognitive and attribution theories of depression. Rather, it may be that learned helplessness is a process the complete outcome of which would be a depression.

Thus, learned helplessness would not be the depressed condition itself, but rather the detailed behavioral explanation for how the process of exogenous depression occurs. The cognitive distortions that are present in learned helplessness make it more difficult for the individual to learn that responses do produce certain outcomes. These distortions may be the beginnings of faulty cognitive patterns which are manifested in the clinical core of symptoms labeled "depression." This would help to explain some of the inconsistencies of the learned-helplessness theory. If the inconsistencies are taken into account, however, the effectiveness of various therapeutic modalities could be studied.

The application of the learned-helplessness model to battered women is in the area of vulnerability. If, through faulty socialization patterns, a woman learns that she cannot control aversive outcomes such as being beaten by a man who loves her, yet, at the same time, also learns that she cannot live without that man to love and care for her, then learned helplessness that slowly becomes depression and paralysis can be the result. The cognitive attributions, motivational deficits, including a lowered rate of behavioral responses, and emotional responses of battered women are quite similar to those of subjects in learned-helplessness experiments. The unpredictability, randomness, and variability with which the battering takes place and the woman's perceptions of lack of control over the aversive events (even though she may overestimate her own role when the beating is successfully avoided) are similar to Rizley's (1978) experiments. As the woman becomes more tangled in the battering relationship, her fall into learned helplessness becomes more complete. The process becomes self-perpetuating, and the outcome looks more like serious pathology, including typical diagnoses of depression, paranoia, and passive–aggressive character disorders. Reversal of the learned-helplessness process may be necessary for elimination of these symptoms, at least initially. Social-learning therapeutic approaches would have the most promise of accomplishing this reversal.

Maintenance of the violent relationship needs explanations beyond the responses predicted by learned-helplessness and attribution theories. The bonding that exists in families where domestic violence occurs is unique and powerful. Learning theory would suggest random, variable, intermittent reinforcement as a factor. The cycle of violence, with its three phases (Walker, 1979), appears to be just that kind of reinforcement. The same behavior elicits a different response depending on which phase of the cycle the couple is in. The reward for keeping the relationship together occurs during the third phase of the cycle, when behavior becomes kind, nurturing and loving and meets each person's expectations of the other's ability to satisfy his or her needs. Faulty logical explanations that the man gives the woman to explain the violence cause confusion at first and, ultimately, cognitive distortions that may generalize into other areas in their lives beyond the relationship.

It has been argued that women are more susceptible to learning independent response/outcome from the rewards and punishments they receive while being socialized. It is also probable that learned helplessness is learned on a continuum. Radloff (1975) suggests that analysis of sex-role stereotypes, psychological theories of depression, and epidemiologic studies of marital status need to be integrated. There may be different levels of learned helplessness that a woman learns from the interaction of traditional female role standards in individual personality development. The male/female dyadic relationship is probably a specific area that is affected by this interactive developmental process. Battered women seem to be the most affected by feelings of helplessness in their relationships with men. This is true for battered women who are housewives as well as for those with responsible jobs and careers. Many battered women are well educated and ambitious and function in a superior manner in high-status positions. The average educational level of the first 106 cases analyzed at the Battered Women Research Center was 12.8 years of schooling, certainly well above the educational level predicted by the myths. However, when it comes to their marriages or other social relationships with men, battered women resort to traditional female sex-role-stereotyped behavior. They typically defer to men to make decisions, even if they have manipulated the choices behind the scenes. Direct communication is conspicuously absent from the battering relationships studied to date (Nielsen *et al.*, Note 7).

Psychotherapy and Battered Women

Battered women and their families in the United States have traditionally sought the services of psychotherapists, yet there are no research studies in the literature which evaluate psychotherapy process or outcome with such abusive families. In a preliminary analysis of our data, we found that a large percentage of women interviewed sought psychotherapy (Nielsen *et al.*, Note 7). As was true for other helpers, professional psychotherapists were reported to be inadequate in helping the battered women. The women who were interviewed reported that most therapists refused, directly or indirectly (usually by omission), to deal specifically with the acute battering incidents. Instead, therapists tended to concentrate on the psychological consequences that such incidents produced. It is to be expected that women who have been abused repeatedly will have enough psychological symptoms to keep a therapist busy. The question of whether these symptoms are transient and will disappear if the violence stops or indicative of more serious personality traits is not resolved by empirical evidence. Our preliminary interview data suggest the former, although detailed comparative analysis may show differences for age, time in the relationship, or other variables.

Battered women have related stories of being treated as though they were exaggerating or engaging in "crazy" behavior. They have told of seeking psychotherapy for their batterers, only to be told that the problem was theirs. Many battered women's coping techniques, learned to protect themselves from further violence, have been viewed as evidence of severe intrapsychic personality disorders. Some women were diagnosed as paranoid schizophrenic, evidenced by their suspiciousness and lack of trust in people, whom they feared might say the wrong thing to their batterers. In a paranoid way, they concealed their actions, wrote and stashed away messages on tiny pieces of paper, and constantly worried about manipulating other people's behavior so as not to upset their batterers and thus encourage another beating.

Other women told of their frustration in being unable to communicate the depth of their batterers' psychological torture and lies to them. Their difficulty in coping with men who can smile and be charming in public one minute, and then turn and whisper some hateful message privately the next, leaves them vulnerable to accusations of being crazy. Rarely do these women report to their therapists that they have been brutally beaten at home. In some cases where women reported that battering behavior became a topic of discussion in their treatment, they said that the therapist's purpose seemed to be to discover what they were doing to provoke this kind of abuse. The assumption was always that if the woman could change her behavior, then the man would learn to control his. When they tried as hard as they could and this still did not happen, the battered women felt guilty and suffered further loss of self-esteem.

Many of our women reported being treated for their serious depressions, which, no doubt, served to protect them from the constant level of stress in their unpredictable lives. For too many women, their justified and perhaps motivating anger was mellowed by indiscriminate use of tranquilizers. Flitcraft (1978) currently is studying battered women's use of drugs and alcohol. She postulates that many a battered woman's dependence upon drugs and alcohol may have been unwittingly started or enhanced by emergency room physicians who gave her drugs and sent her home after treating her injuries from an acute battering incident. The acute stress reaction that battered women often experience is usually diagnosed as a more serious emotional disturbance. Perhaps the most difficult behavioral pattern to treat is displayed by the woman who is labeled "passive–aggressive with hysterical features." This particular battered woman is most likely to frustrate helpers because of her inability to express anger directly. She needs to acquiesce and please people openly but then expresses indirectly the hostility that she feels at giving up her power. The swiftness and tenacity with which this previously passive anger is expressed takes unsuspecting professionals by surprise. If it is reacted to with anger, then this type of battered woman often becomes frantic, exhibiting the exaggerated and labile behavior of the classic hysteric. This frequently is evident in court proceedings, much to the woman's detriment in convincing judges, juries, or court-appointed evaluation teams of her emotional stability.

Once the survival component of this kind of behavior is understood, then psychologists are less likely to react personally. Furthermore, there is preliminary evidence that suggests that this is not a character disorder but rather a temporary state which becomes less salient as the externally imposed stress from the batterer recedes (CAABW, 1979). Others, such as Shainess (1979) and Starr (1978), would argue that this is a more stable personality pattern, the change of which necessitates long and arduous psychotherapy. Despite the controversy over diagnosis, no process or outcome research can be found. This is unfortunate, as it might help to clarify the temporary or stable nature of the mental health symptoms.

Treatment Recommendations

Psychotherapeutic approaches have evolved from the various theoretical approaches already discussed. A central issue for therapists has been the opposing theories of the psychological development of aggression. These are represented by the innate deterministic and the learned behavioral points of view. Psychoanalytic, dynamic, and insight-oriented therapies tend to subscribe to the perspective that aggressive impulses will occur naturally and that they need to be discharged periodically in small doses and in a safe manner, for example, in athletic activities. Social-learning-based therapies would be founded on the belief that aggression is learned behavior which results from an inability to deal effectively with angry feelings. The former, then, would be more likely to design therapeutic strategies for violent couples that teach them to express their aggressive impulses in a more acceptable way, such as the fair-fighting techniques developed by Bach and his colleagues (Bach & Wyden, 1968). The social-learning approach would be more likely to stress elimination of aggressive behavior by the use of behavioral techniques to obtain effective anger management (Margolin, 1979). These therapeutic approaches could be applied to various modalities, including individual, group, or couple therapy. Comparison of the effectiveness of each has no empirical basis, but the recent research discussed does demonstrate the efficacy of the social-learning model in anger control.

Interestingly enough, the most successful form of treatment to date seems to be the grass-roots woman-dominated system of shelters for battered women. These shelters and safe homes have sprung up all over the United States, literally on shoestring finances (CAABW, 1979). Their only measure of process or outcome success, however, is the numbers of women who use the services as each opens in a new community. For example, there are five shelters for battered women in the metropolitan Denver, Colorado, area, and in 1978, their records showed that 1500 women and children were turned away for lack of space. From a national survey conducted during 1977 (CAABW, 1979), it was reported that 47,000 women and 15,000 children used services for battered women in the United States. These facilities are just beginning to document their program effectiveness with an evaluation component. They have developed a paraprofessional and peer counseling model for therapeutic intervention which is rooted in crisis-intervention philosophy.

Crisis Intervention

Crisis-intervention techniques are often very appropriate for intensive therapy after an acute battering incident in view of the high risk of lethality. Battered women or batterers are usually concerned about their lack of control and want to understand and change their behavior. Crisis therapy usually focuses on a specific critical incident. The goal then is to teach the client how to resolve possible future crises by applying conflict-resolution techniques to the present crisis situation while motivation is still high. It is most important to assess immediately the potential lethality in the relationship. It is also essential to determine whether or not the woman wants to leave the relationship during the present crisis situation. Most battered women express ambivalence at this time. Behavioral rehearsal of how to make contact with agencies that can provide safety and emergency services is an important part of such crisis-intervention counseling. Although some battered women are ready to use crisis therapy to help them separate permanently, most need more time.

Individual Psychotherapy

According to their own accounts, the only evidence currently available, battered women find individual psychotherapy to be most useful. Therapeutic goals directed toward strengthening the battered woman's independence, whether or not she chooses to remain with the batterer, are important. Career goals need to be explored, reinforcing the positive in the battered woman's life. The recommended procedure seems to be the use of successive approximations from minimum to maximum independence. Individual therapy concentrating on the present and possibly using the past to promote understanding of the current situation is recommended. The therapy is more action-oriented than analytical, as psychoanalysis was not reported to help resolve the battered woman's situation. In fact, in most reported instances, psychoanalytic emphasis on self-analysis served to perpetuate the woman's victimization. Feminist therapy has been reported as most useful (Walker, Note 6). Cognitive restructuring is a necessary component to therapy if changes brought about in therapy are to be maintained. As therapy progresses, other adjunctive therapies can be recommended, such as assertiveness training, parent education, vocational counseling, and, in some cases, couples therapy.

Group Therapy

Group therapy is another common therapeutic format used with battered women. It has some reported benefits over individual therapy. Battered women are usually isolated and rarely meet other battered women. They have few friends with whom they can confide. A group composed solely of battered women can be a therapeutic experience, as it combines the best features of consciousness-raising groups with the expertise of therapists who are familiar with group process. It facilitates the learning of new cognitions, since the women also learn from each other. It is often necessary to provide individual appointments for group members during crises. Women describe having derived a sense of strength from the other group members that is more difficult to provide on an individual basis. Again, action-oriented therapy is recommended, with a focus on changing behavior. Group norms that are established encourage positive behavior change in order that the battered woman continues to feel supported by the other women in the group. This may partially explain the success of battered women's shelters even when there is no formal therapeutic program.

It has been found that two different kinds of groups are needed when working with battered women (Jens & Museo, Note 9). These groups have been identified as first-stage and second-stage groups, each needing different therapeutic techniques and having different therapeutic goals. First-stage groups tend to be more crisis-oriented in nature. They generally include women who are beginning to think of leaving the relationship with their batterers or women just recently separated. First-stage groups usually meet over a period of several months. Members depend on each other for emotional as well as informational support. It is common for one member to advocate for another member in the criminal justice and social service agency procedures. Second-stage groups are more concerned with issues common to most women in a life-transition stage. Dating men and relating to women and men in an assertive manner are the two critical issues unique to ex-battered women in these groups. For some, learning new parenting techniques that encourage less punitiveness in discipline is also important. The women report this to be the most useful time to explore their own role in their victimization. Again, no empirical studies could be found to support these clinical reports. They come from battered women and their helpers and are most often available in an anecdotal, unpublished format.

Couples Therapy

There has been a controversy about the use of couples therapy in battering relationships. Although the issue of inappropriately expressed anger has typically been one of the major focuses of marital and family therapies, most of the reports of successful interventions with violent couples come from the therapists and not the battered women themselves. Typically, the follow-up period in these cases is 6 months or less. In the few instances where there was a longer follow-up after the termination of therapy, recurrence and escalation of the violent behavior were reported (Walker, 1979). In cases where reduction in the intensity and frequency of the violent behavior was successful as a result of therapy, two cotherapists, usually a male/female team, were involved, and individual therapy on a crisis or regular basis and/or group therapy were also available.

The theoretical rationale discussed earlier helps to explain some of the difficulties with couples therapy as a treatment of choice. A battered woman does not enter the therapeutic relationship free from the terror that what she says or does during the session will earn her another beating. Thus, she may be more likely to minimize or deny her needs when contingency contracting or negotiations get under way. She usually has experienced her batterer's promises to express his displeasure in nonviolent ways, only to have these promises broken when his internal anxiety state so dictates. She accurately perceives that the therapist does not have the ability to protect her from another beating and so finds it difficult to enter into a therapeutic alliance, even when the couple seem to be dependent upon the therapist. It is critical for the therapist to be aware of the lethality risks when interfering in this system. The system's resistance to positive change seems greater than the resistance encountered when working with its individual members. While eventually it will be necessary for the woman to analyze her participation in the maintenance of her batterer's violent behavior, using such an approach initially does not allow for the development of the more adequate coping skills she needs to keep her safe. Thus, other therapeutic modalities discussed are recommended as an initial strategy wherever possible.

There are times when couples therapy is the only means of offering assistance. Thus, effective strategies need further exploration, and there are some reports beginning to appear in the therapy literature. Saunders (1977) reports success using couples therapy in a social service agency setting, and he is beginning to collect impressive data to support his clinical impressions. Prior to his death, Morton Flax and I were in the process of developing a therapeutic model for couples therapy which incorporated much of the theoretical rationale stressed in this chapter (Walker, 1979; Flax, Note 10). A similar model, applying social-learning techniques to marital discord, is reported by Margolin (1979), although it differs in some important aspects, including her acceptance of the violence as a mutual problem. She reports success, with a 4 month follow-up period, and advocates the use of this model with couples who are not seriously abusive. Unfortunately, there are no criteria offered to identify couples who are not seriously abusive. Research at the Battered Women Research Center suggests that violent behavior escalates over time, beginning with minor psychological and/or physical abuse. Serious battering incidents do not always result in observable injuries that would suggest the violent nature of the abusive incident. Thus, caution is urged until more is known about how to differentiate levels of seriousness in abusive relationships.

I have not found any literature on couples who have successfully terminated serious battering behavior without terminating their relationship. In fact, even when the relationship is terminated, the battering behavior often continues. Because violent couples often have children together, which mandates that they remain in some contact even after separation and divorce, it would be useful if there were therapy techniques that were successful with these couples. At present, teaching the woman strategies to effectively cope with the man's violent behavior offers the most promise with the least potential for negative consequences.

Psychotherapy and the Abuser

Psychotherapy with the male offender has been reported to have a positive effect on the woman's mental health, since she transfers some of her erroneously perceived responsibility for his mental health to his therapist. Many batterers will enter therapy under some coercive threat such as the fear that their wives will leave them if they do not seek help. Couples therapy seems to be the most popular treatment modality requested by the men, although there is some question as to its efficancy for either the man or the woman, as discussed above. Saunders (1977) is one of the few who reports some limited success with the man. Ganley and Harris (Note 11), Boyd (Note 12), Klingbeil (Note 13), and Walker (Note 14) report a preference for treating the man and the woman separately. Conferees at an invitational conference on intervention programs for spouse abusers debated this issue (*Belmont Conference*, Note 15). Therapy techniques which help the batterer to learn better arousal cues, as well as those which improve his anger reduction and management strategies, are advocated. Again, no empirical evidence has been collected, although clinical impressions support individual treatment programs rather than a family systems approach. The greatest reported deterrent to psychotherapy with the abuser was the difficulty in getting him to attend therapy sessions.

Research Recommendations

It is apparent from this chapter that providing psychotherapy which deals directly with violence for battered women, abusers, and their children is a very recent addition to the field of psychology. The knowledge reported here is new enough to still be in the process of being disseminated to service providers. Empirical research on the process or outcome of psychotherapy with these special clients needs to be done. Several cautions can be stated conceiving the methodology used to conduct these studies. At an HEW-funded invitational conference held in Denver, Colorado, in June 1978, domestic-violence service providers and researchers discussed the methodology they felt was best suited to collecting useful data. The complete report can be found in a monograph detailing the results of the entire Colorado study on services to battered women in the United States (CAABW, 1979). Excerpts are presented here, as this study raised some fundamental research problems.

The need to gather data in a more systematic and controlled way was acknowledged by all who participated in this study. Disagreement and confusion existed, however, over not only the kinds of questions to be asked but also who should do the asking. It was concluded that research is perhaps the most divisive issue today among those who are working in the area of domestic violence. Since the participants were skilled researchers, heads of government funding agencies, and service providers, their comments are particularly relevant. One area of conflict was the conceptualization of the problem of battering. Rather than looking at negative personality characteristics of battered women, it was suggested that strengths and coping skills be evaluated. Another area of conflict was sampling errors. It was suggested that generalization of data obtained from a narrow sample to the entire population resulted in misinformation that stereotyped battered women and batterers. Stratification of research subjects to include all socioeconomic levels and representative minorities was urged, and grass-roots women's groups would pledge cooperation only if sensitivity to poor and third-world women's needs were met and exploitation avoided. In fact, this last issue was so emotionally charged that it threatened to disrupt the entire conference at several times (personal observation).

The desire for research with a tight methodologic design was another area of conflict. Conferees felt that it was difficult to control variables in violent homes where complex, multilevel interactions naturally occur. Holding some variables constant while measuring the effects of others may not be realistic in a constantly changing situation. However, utilization of more sophisticated statistical techniques to help untangle these interactions is possible with flexibility of experimental design. Longitudinal studies which observe and collect information from the same persons over a long period of time, cross-sectional studies which measure the information obtained from many persons at different chronologic points in their lives, and epidemiologic studies which sample the entire population are essential to ensure reliability and accuracy. Locating funding sources to support this kind of research concerned all participants, including the heads of funding agencies present.

Finally, those surveyed in this study evidenced distrust of professional researchers as political people. Grass-roots service providers (and probably professionally trained clinicians, too) did not subscribe to the researcher's maxim that science needs to be advanced for its own end. Those who provide services to battered women and their families place higher priority on influencing public policy in order to raise the level of funding for battered women's programs. There is little patience for evaluation research, although its need is acknowledged, unless the immediate outcome will be beneficial to the people who need the services being evaluated. Basic research was thought to be desirable but not essential. These emotional responses were in direct conflict with the cognition that all kinds of research were important. Research that evaluated sexism, classism, racism, and violent behavior was seen as the most beneficial to the battered women's movement.

In reviewing the literature on psychotherapy research, I have found it to be influenced by similar concerns, although not stated in the same terms. When measuring the effects of interventions for people who are in crisis, the morally and ethically correct priority is saving the person—collecting the data only as it does not interfere with the primary task. Certainly, the human rights assurances that researchers must make to government funding sources support this philosophy. Nevertheless, there are important questions that need the researcher's scrutiny. I suggest a few:

1. What differences and similarities are there in psychotherapeutic techniques which impact on the treatment of battered women and their families?
2. Can batterers be rehabilitated and the violence stopped, in the original relationship or in new relationships, through the use of psychotherapeutic techniques?
3. What are the effects on children who live in a violent home? What is the impact of psychotherapy with them? Research in this area is affected by mandatory child abuse report laws in effect in many states.
4. What is the relationship among all forms of domestic violence? Is psychotherapy useful in preventing the spread of more violence? These areas call for evaluation of the process of therapy as well as outcome studies.

5. How do battered women's programs compare with traditional mental health services in their impact on the violent family? A systematic means of evaluating diverse programs needs to be applied here.

6. Are there gender and attitude differences among therapists who provide services to battered women and their families?

7. How does living with stress and violence affect physical and psychological health? Does it affect the course of diseases such as hypertension, heart disease, and cancer? Are biochemical changes temporary or permanent, and how do they impact on body structure? What impact can psychotherapy have on reversal of psychophysiologic damage?

8. Can psychotheraphy with women impact on the effects of sexism, classism, racism, and other stereotyped behavior in our society? How can psychotherapy influence power relationships between men and women so as to get at the roots of domestic violence?

Summary

It is an understatement to say that research into the effectiveness of psychotherapy with the special population of battered women is insufficient to draw definitive conclusions. Planning more effective psychotherapy research requires a great deal of time and energy so as to design effective conceptualization and methodologic strategies. On the other hand, there is much clinical evidence to suggest that the crisis-intervention model of the shelter or safe-house system is quite effective. This model stresses grass-roots paraprofessional counseling, with referral to more highly trained professionals according to individual need. Women whose lives are not in as great danger have been seen in outpatient psychotherapy. Based on battered women's self-reports and utilization records, individual and group treatment modalities offer the most benefit. There is more controversy concerning the effectiveness of couples therapy, and less is known about effects of treatment with the abusers and the children. As the issue of domestic violence gains greater acceptance, treatment plans that deal directly with the abusive behavior will become more widely available, and then process and outcome measures will be forthcoming. At present, providing such psychotherapy is still a specialized service.

ACKNOWLEDGMENT

The author's research reported in this chapter has been partially funded by grant 1 R01 1MH30146 from the National Institute of Mental Health.

Reference Notes

1. Leidig, M. *Psychology and violence against women: An overview.* Paper presented at the meeting of the American Psychological Association, Toronto, September 1978.
2. Flick, D. *Historical precedents for current attitudes regarding violence against women.* Paper presented at the meeting of the American Psychological Association, Toronto, September 1978.
3. Kremen, E. *The discovery of battered wives: Consideration for the development of a social service network.* Paper presented at the meeting of the American Sociological Association, New York, August 1976.
4. Frieze, I. H. *Social-psychological theory and problems of wifebeating.* Unpublished manuscript, University of Pittsburgh, 1977.
5. Groth, G. *Sexism in psychology: Theorizing about violence against women.* Paper presented at the meeting of the American Psychological Association, Toronto, September 1978.
6. Walker, L. E. *Feminist therapy and battered women.* Paper presented at the meeting of the American Psychological Association, Division 29 Mid-Winter, Scottsdale, Ariz., March 1978.
7. Nielsen, J., Eberle, P., Thoennes, N., & Walker, L. *Why women stay in battering relationships: Preliminary results.* Paper presented at the meeting of the American Sociological Association, Boston, August 1979.
8. Steinmetz, S. *Spousal abuse: An interdisciplinary perspective.* Paper presented at the meeting of the American Psychological Association, New York, September 1979.
9. Jens, K. S., & Museo, L. *Group therapy with battered women.* Paper presented at the Colorado Mental Health Conference, Vail, Colo., September 1977.
10. Flax, M. L. *Couples therapy in battering relationships.* Paper presented at the Colorado Women's College Conference, Denver, April 1977.
11. Ganley, A., & Harris, L. *Domestic violence: Issues in designing and implementing programs for male batterers.* Paper presented at the meeting of the American Psychological Association, Toronto, September, 1978.
12. Boyd, V. D. *Domestic violence: Treatment alternatives for the male batterer.* Paper presented at the meeting of the American Psychological Association, Toronto, September 1978.
13. Klingbeil, L. *A treatment program for male batterers.* Paper presented at the meeting of the American Psychological Association, Toronto, September 1978.
14. Walker, L. E. *Male batterers and their families: Treatment implications.* Paper presented at the meeting of the American Psychological Association, Toronto, September 1978.
15. *Belmont conference on the male abuser.* Law Enforcement Assistance Agency Special Programs Division, Washington, D.C., May 1979.

References

Abramson, L. Y., Seligman, M. E., & Teasdale, J. A. Learned helplessness in humans: Critique and reformulation. *Journal of Abnormal Psychology,* 1978, *87,* 49–74.

Bach, G. R., & Wyden, P. *The intimate enemy.* New York: Avon, 1968.

Bandura, A. *Aggression: A social learning analysis.* Englewood Cliffs, N.J.: Prentice-Hall, 1973.

Beck, A. *Depression: Causes and treatment.* Philadelphia: University of Pennsylvania Press, 1972.

Besherov, D. Testimony presented to the Congressional Committee on Science and Technology, Subcommittee on Domestic and International Scientific Planning, Analysis and Cooperation. *Research into violent behavior: Domestic violence.* Washington, D.C.: U.S. Government Printing Office 27-090-0, February 14, 1978.

Brownmiller, S. *Against our will: Men, women and rape.* New York: Simon and Schuster, 1975.

Chapman, J., & Gates, M. (Eds.). *The victimization of women.* Beverly Hills: Sage, 1978.

Chappell, D., Geis, R., & Geis, G. (Eds.). *Forcible rape: The crime, the victim and the criminal.* New York: Columbia University Press, 1977.

Colorado Association for Aid to Battered Women (CAABW). *Services to battered women in the U.S.* (DHEW Monograph). Washington, D.C.: Ù.S. Government Printing Office, 1979.

Costello, C. G. A critical review of Seligman's laboratory experiments on learned helplessness and depression in humans. *Journal of Abnormal Psychology,* 1978, *87,* 21–31.

Davidson, T. *Conjugal crime.* New York: Hawthorn, 1978.

Dobash, R. E., & Dobash, R. P. Wives: The "appropriate" victims of marital violence. *Victimology: An International Journal,* 1977–1978, *2* (3–4), 608–622.

Fields, M. *Wifebeating: Government intervention policies and practices in battered women issues of public policy* (Consultation sponsored by the U.S. Commission on. Civil Rights). Washington, D.C.: U.S. Government Printing Office, 1978.

Flitcraft, A. Battered women: An emergency room epidemiology with a description of a clinical syndrome and critique of present therapeutics. Testimony presented to the Congressional Committee on Science and Technology, Subcommittee on Domestic and International Scientific Planning, Analysis and Cooperation. *Research into violent behavior: Domestic violence.* Washington, D.C.: U.S. Government Printing Office 27-090-0, February 15, 1978.

Gayford, J. Wife battering. A preliminary review of 100 cases. *British Medical Journal,* 1975, *1,* 94–197.

Gelles, R. *The violent home.* Beverly Hills: Sage, 1974.

Helfer, R. E., & Kempe, C. H. *The battered child* (2nd ed.). Chicago: University of Chicago Press, 1974.

Margolin, G. Conjoint marital therapy to enhance anger management and reduce spouse abuse. *American Journal of Family Therapy,* 1979, *7*(2), 13–24.

Martin, D. *Battered wives.* San Francisco: Glide, 1976.

Pizzey, E. *Scream quietly or the neighbors will hear.* London: Penguin, 1974.

Pleck, E., Pleck, J., Grossman, M., & Bart, P. The battered data syndrome: A comment on Steinmetz' article. *Victimology: An International Journal,* 1977–1978, *2*(3–4), 680–683.

Radloff, L. Sex differences in depression: The effects of occupation and marital status. *Sex Roles,* 1975, *1*(3), 249–265.

Rizley, R. C. Depression and distortion in the attribution of causality. *Journal of Abnormal Psychology,* 1978, *87,* 32–48.

Rounsaville, B. J. Theories in marital violence: Evidence from a study of battered women. *Victimology: An International Journal,* 1978, *3*(1–2), 11–31.

Roy, M. *Battered women: A psychosociological study.* New York: Van Nostrand, 1978.

Saunders, D. G. Marital violence: Dimensions of the problem and modes of intervention. *Journal of Marriage and Family Counseling,* January 1977, 43–52.

Seligman, M. *Helplessness: On depression, development and death.* San Francisco: Freeman, 1975.

Shainess, N. Vulnerability to violence: Masochism as process. *American Journal of Psychotherapy,* 1979, *33*(2), 174–189.

Snell, J., Rosenwald, R., & Robey, A. The wife beater's wife: A study of family interaction. *Archives of General Psychiatry,* 1964, *11*(2), 107–112.

Stahly, G. B. A review of select literature of spouse abuse. *Victimology: An International Journal,* 1978, *2*(3–4), 591–607.

Starr, B. Comparing battered and non-battered women. *Victimology: An International Journal,* 1978, *3*(1–2), 32–44.

Steinmetz, S. The battered husband syndrome. *Victimology: An International Journal,* 1977–1978, *2*(3–4), 499–509.

Steinmetz, S. Testimony presented to the Congressional Committee on Science and Technology, Subcommittee on Domestic and International Scientific Planning,

Analysis and Cooperation. *Research into violent behavior: Domestic violence.* Washington, D.C.: U.S. Government Printing Office 27-090-0, February 14, 1978.

Straus, M. Sexual inequality, cultural norms, and wife-beating. In J. Chapman & M. Gates (Eds.), *The victimization of women.* Beverly Hills: Sage, 1978.

Straus, M., Gelles, R., & Steinmetz, S. *Behind closed doors: Violence in the American family.* New York: Doubleday, 1980.

Walker, L. E. Learned helplessness and battered women. *Victimology: An International Journal,* 1977-1978, 2(3-4), 525-534.

Walker, L. E. Treatment alternatives for battered women. In J. Chapman & M. Gates (Eds.), *The victimization of women.* Beverly Hills: Sage, 1978.

Walker, L. E. *The battered woman.* New York: Harper and Row, 1979.

Walker, L. E. Sex roles and clinical issues: Battered women. *Professional Psychology,* in press.

Weiner, B., Frieze, I., Kukla, A., Reed, L., Rest, S. A., & Rosenbaum, R. M. *Perceiving the causes of success and failure.* New York: General Learning Press, 1971.

CHAPTER 15

Women in Marital Transition

SARAH LYNNE McMAHON

Introduction

Marital transition is one of the most stressful events a woman can expect to encounter in her lifetime. Whether experienced as a divorce or as a husband's death, this transition is felt as disruptive and disorienting. Moreover, the force of numbers affected alone makes marital transition a social crisis as well as a personal one. Each year in the United States, more than one million women experience divorce. Four out of every five married women will confront widowhood. That so many American women experience the personal and social disruptions of marital transition makes this a particularly important issue for a volume on women and psychotherapy.

And yet when this issue is examined in the literature, there are problems. The many descriptions of service programs and theoretical discussions of crisis intervention contrast with the absence of assessments of services that are responding to the crisis nature of women's experiences. Although crisis-intervention theory provides a valuable perspective for understanding marital transition, no studies evaluate crisis-intervention models represented by divorce adjustment groups, family crisis counseling, and traditional psychotherapy. This may reflect the general bias of therapists toward saving marriages and two-parent families (Gettleman & Markowitz, 1975). Surveys and epidemiologic studies of marital transition often report the results without taking into account the impact of sex bias in institutions and stereotypical sex-role expectations on the findings.

Although either sex can be widowed or divorced, the sex-segregated nature of American life means that the transitions are experienced quite

Sarah Lynne McMahon. Women in Transition, West Philadelphia Mental Health Consortium, Philadelphia, Pennsylvania.

differently by men and women. Even though they share similar problems and feelings and must negotiate the same transitional stages, a
woman experiences marital transition as more disruptive of her basic
self-identity than does a man. This is underscored by the fact that most
single-sex services have been designed for women by women with life
experience in marital transition, or by feminist practitioners. From the
experiences of such groups as Women in Transition (WIT), and from
the issues and problems described in the literature, it appears that crisis-
intervention services for women offer a potentially powerful source of
help to women in crisis.

   This view is based, in part, on the proliferation of such services. The
experiences of WIT, an organization based in Philadelphia, Pennsylvania, are a prime example. Since its inception in 1972, WIT has conducted peer support groups for nearly 1000 women and has consulted
with women's groups in many states. In the Philadelphia area, training
workshops have made the crisis model available to women in eight wom-
en's centers and four community health systems. Program descriptions
in the literature further suggest that the peer support approach to crisis
intervention is nationwide. One would think that the rapid increase and
duration of these services would lead to evaluative efforts. That this has
not happened, or has not been reported, is disappointing and suggests
larger problems such as conflicts between service delivery and program
evaluation. Crisis-intervention services which have the potential of helping thousands of women must be submitted to rigorous evaluative efforts. These efforts, moreover, must be conducted where the services are
being offered, where the women are coming for help.

   In order to establish a basis for evaluating crisis-intervention
models, the first section of this paper presents a crisis framework for
viewing divorce and widowhood. A summary of literature follows which
more specifically describes women in marital transition in terms of features, problems, and needs. Next, a crisis-intervention model is presented which contains major features of models described in the literature and developed by women's groups. The final section discusses the
problems of program evaluation research and suggests research
priorities.

Marital Transition: An Adult Situational Crisis

Increasingly, professionals have focused attention on the nature of adult
situational crises and the needs of persons experiencing them (Parad,
1965). A situational crisis such as separation or bereavement refers to the
event that precipitates a state of distress so extreme that it is beyond the in-

dividual's normal resources and coping skills (Rapoport, 1965). The crisis state varies in degree of intensity and length of duration, although any divorced or widowed person will experience the event as a crisis.

Widowhood and divorce precipitate a period of emotional and social adjustment during which a woman attempts a transition from her role as part of a mutually interdependent couple to her new role of an independent single woman. It may take 2 years, or longer, for a woman to complete the transition and rebuild her life (Silverman, MacKenzie, Pettipas, & Wilson, 1975). The crisis period, however, refers to the early stages of the process and is of shorter duration. Crisis-intervention models, therefore, are designed to help women in the early stages of crisis.

It is important to review the major assumptions of crisis theory (Pasewark & Albers, 1972; Rapoport, 1965) before applying them specifically to divorce and widowhood.

1. A situational crisis is not pathological, although previously unresolved developmental issues may be brought to the surface. During the acute phase of the crisis, women may feel crazy and manifest symptoms associated with more severe mental disturbances. Nonetheless, the crisis is not mental illness nor are those undergoing the crisis to be treated as mentally ill.
2. Crises follow predictable stages, and each type has its own distinct reaction patterns. Individuals, however, may vary in the length of time spent in each stage and, indeed, may experience aspects of more than one stage simultaneously.
3. Omission of any stage has the effect of prolonging the transition period.
4. Crises are resolved at either a higher or lower level of functioning. The crisis period provides a unique and potentially positive opportunity to reexamine one's previous behavior and value structure. It is possible, therefore, to have a prolonged positive effect with relatively little intervention during the crisis period.
5. There are three major stages to a transitional crisis: (a) The crisis is precipitated by a stressful event that leads to a level of *disequilibrium* for which the woman does not possess adequate coping mechanisms. (b) Following the precipitation of the crisis, a period of *disorganization* occurs when emotions and behaviors are most unstable. (c) After disorientation, a period of *reorganization* follows. The individual begins to adapt to the new situation and gain control of her life. *Reintegration* has occurred when the new behaviors, values, decisions, and feelings become a stable part of the woman's responses.

Stages of Separation and Divorce

The crisis stages of separation and divorce are sometimes difficult to discern because the process may begin years before the public act of separating occurs. Bohannan (1970) suggests six dimensions of divorce that may overlap and come in different order: (1) emotional divorce, (2) legal divorce, (3) economic divorce, (4) coparental divorce, (5) community divorce, and (6) psychic divorce. The following synthesis of the ideas of Weiss (1976), Smart (1977), and Wiseman (1975) provides a framework for understanding the crisis.

Stage I: Alienation (months to years). The erosion of love and commitment and the concomitant continuation of attachment to the partner takes place while the couple is still together. This stage is characterized by denial and feelings of fear, anxiety, and ambivalence.

Stage II: Separation (months). The most emotionally difficult stage of the process generally occurs at the time of actual physical separation. Wild mood swings, from extreme distress to euphoria, are coupled with somatic symptoms and unusual behavior. If the woman takes responsibility for the separation, she may feel guilty; otherwise, she feels abandoned. Anger is frequently used to maintain the separation and overcome the grief and mourning, while legal and economic issues complicate the interactions between the couple. Relationships with friends, children, and family may be disrupted for a time.

Stage III: Reorientation (2–4 years). Changing habits and redirecting energies are a major part of building a new identity as a single woman. The woman must take new risks, learn and experiment with new behaviors, until she accepts her new status. New patterns of interaction develop that are satisfying and that do not include the ex-spouse.

Widowhood: Stages of Grief and Mourning

Unlike separation and divorce, a woman may become a widow with no forewarning or emotional preparation. The mourning process may begin with the knowledge that her husband is terminally ill. The literature on death and dying suggests that the emotional adjustment process following death can be divided into three distinct phases (Kubler-Ross, 1974; Silverman *et al.,* 1975; Temes, 1977).

Stage I: Initial Shock (weeks). The first stage of the adjustment process is characterized by feelings of numbness, shock, and denial. During this initial phase, family, friends, and clergy play an active role in the life of the new widow. Ironically, the widow may need to insulate herself emotionally until she can begin to assimilate the full impact of the loss.

Stage II: Disorganization (months). Recognizing that she is alone marks the beginning of the widow's second phase of mourning. At this time, widows report experiencing strong feelings of abandonment, fear, loneliness, guilt, anger, and despair. The widow may have somatic reactions to her grief. Although the ability to participate in the outside world returns increasingly during these months, the widow feels disoriented by the many changes in her position. One or two months after the death, when she is ready to reach out, friends and family have moved back into their own lives. She needs to ventilate her feelings in order to acknowledge the impact of her loss.

Stage III: Reorganization (months). The beginning of the recovery period is the readiness to reorient her life to the present and future. She feels more at peace with herself and the past relationship with her spouse. The widow then lets go of the past and learns how to live her life as a single person.

Widows and Divorcées

"Women in transition" essentially defines the loss of a primary relationship and, at the same time, encompasses two distinct groups: divorced and widowed. As women in crisis, they face similar problems and experience similar feelings. Because of the work of Kubler-Ross (1974), many persons working with divorce emphasize the similarities of the processes of divorce and widowhood, particularly grief and mourning. Gettleman and Markowitz (1975), however, point out how professionals have oversimplified the divorce process by the easy analogy with death. Real differences dictate viewing them as separate processes and thus approaching them with different models.

1. The death of a marriage relationship usually takes place over many years, and at the moment of separation the affections are already alienated (Weiss, 1976). Separation by death can take place without warning, within seconds.
2. During a divorce, the legal relationship dies but the spouse is very much alive and a different type of relationship must be developed. In widowhood, the spouse dies but the relationship may be very much alive.
3. The element of control and choice separates widows and divorcées. Widows point out that they had no choice in becoming single and often blame women who choose to leave their marriage or suspect a woman of not trying hard enough if her husband leaves her.

4. Separating and divorcing women are in the process of coming to terms with the conflicting aspects of their marriage; thus, feelings of anger, bitterness, and resentment may, for a time, dominate. One of the pitfalls of the mourning process is the idealization of the dead spouse or the marriage (Silverman *et al.*, 1975). Deprocessing the marriage, that is, coming to terms with the positive and negative aspects of the relationship, usually takes place in the second stage of the mourning process.

5. The stigmas attached to widows differ from those of divorcées. The divorced woman is stigmatized by being a failure in her major function as wife and mother, the stablizing influence in the family. Friends may shun her because of conflict in their own marriages or because she is now "available." The widow is shunned because of unresolved feelings about one's own death; she is, in effect, tainted by death. Many times she is expected to remain loyal to her dead husband, a throwback to more primitive mourning rites.

6. If the widow had fantasized about being divorced or if there were conflicts in the marriage, the guilt may be so overwhelming that some denial is required until the shock has passed. Divorcing women sometimes are so distressed by feelings of anger and ambivalence in dealing with their spouses that they wish they had been widowed.

7. Divorce is increasingly viewed as an acceptable process for seeking a more rewarding life; death of a spouse is not.

8. Few feminist groups have reached out to widows because most widows are older than the feminists. Feminists have been more absorbed with self-actualization and with freeing themselves of past socialization strictures. Because of the perception of feminists as anti-male and anti-marriage, widows have not brought their needs to the attention of women's programs as have other groups. Most feminists have not yet experienced widowhood, but that is changing.

Review of the Literature

The literature on marital transition shows a clear relationship between marital transition and increased stress. Holmes and Masuda (1973) assigned the following stress points to life changes: marital separation 65, divorce 73, and death of spouse 100. When marital transition is coupled with other changes, as it inevitably is, the stress points frequently reach near the danger point of 300.

Brown and Manela (1976) and Halpern (1973) found that divorcing persons were in crisis; likewise, death of the spouse precipitated stress. Marital crisis frequently results in somatic symptoms and severe expressions of despair due to loss (Weiss, 1976). Increased stress results in increased risk of psychiatric disorders, homicide, suicide, motor vehicle accidents, and various forms of disease morbidity and mortality (Bachrach, 1975; Glick & Norton, 1973). In a review of the effects of bereavement (Conroy, 1977; Epstein, Weitz, Roback, & McKee, 1975), studies indicate marked physical symptoms, increased mortality rate, and higher rates of hospitalization for mental disorders. At every age, widowed persons have a higher mortality rate than married persons of the same age, even higher than divorced persons (Kraus & Lilienfeld, cited in Epstein *et al.*, 1975).

Since women in transition experience more stress, they are more likely to seek help (Epstein *et al.*, 1975; Kessler, 1978; Kressel & Deutch, 1974). Psychological stress may be compounded by survival issues. One out of three families headed by a woman is living at or below the poverty line (McEaddy, 1976). Thus, for many women, the crisis of marital separation is accompanied by the stigmas of single parenthood and low socioeconomic status (Bould, 1977). The following sections address the identification of problems and issues for divorcing women and widows. Differences by sex, race, and socioeconomic group are briefly reviewed. The needs of women in transition are considered together.

Separation and Divorce

Recent changes in attitudes toward divorce can be partially attributed to the rapidly increasing divorce rate. Divorces in the United States totaled over one million during the 12 months ending with January 1979, an increase of almost 4% over 1978 (Vital Statistics Report, cited in *Marriage and Divorce Today*, 1979). Although the increased incidence of divorce occurs at all socioeconomic levels, the rates remain higher for the economically disadvantaged groups. The 1970 United States census showed that women 35–44 years of age with low incomes and low educational attainment were more likely to have been divorced (Glick & Norton, 1976). Although blacks and whites display generally similar patterns of divorce by social and economic characteristics, the incidence of both divorce and separation is uniformly higher for blacks than for whites.

EFFECTS OF SEX ROLES

Role loss appears to be a critical aspect of a woman's experience of separation and divorce (Chiraboga & Cutler, 1977). Bernard (1972) states that since women have internalized the cultural message that marriage and motherhood are the most acceptable roles for women, considerable anxiety results when the marriage is dissolved. A man is more likely to find continuity through his work. Raschke (1974) further points out that sex-role socialization gives men experience in modes of behavior, such as autonomy and assertiveness, that facilitates their participation in new roles. Interviews with 309 newly separated men and women were conducted to investigate the effects of sex and age on morale and psychological well-being (Chiraboga, Roberts, & Stein, 1978). Although men reported being more unhappy, women seemed to experience greater emotional turmoil. Increased age correlated with decreased happiness.

Brown and Manela (1978) conducted interviews with 253 women in the process of divorce to investigate the relation between sex-role attitudes and distress. The outcomes suggest that women who hold nontraditional sex-role attitudes, or who become more nontraditional during the transition, experience less distress. The nontraditional group also showed more personal growth and higher self-esteem than women who maintained traditional sex-role attitudes over the process of divorce. Herman (1977), Carter (1977), and Morris and Prescott (1975) cite self-esteem as a special problem of divorcing women and relate its cause, in part, to sex-role socialization. Although the clinical experiences of Weiss (1975) support this view, the relation of sex-role attitudes to crisis management needs further investigation.

Cultural expectations still dictate that the woman assume major responsibility for the children. At the same time, the single-parent family is stigmatized as a broken home (Gettleman & Markowitz, 1975). Research (Brandwein, Brown, & Fox, 1974) indicates that an interpersonal network of support is of critical importance to the divorced mother's adjustment, yet institutions and agencies appear to add to her problems rather than provide needed supports. The woman is inequitably burdened with the economic responsibility for the family at the same time that a double standard for sexual activity can jeopardize her custody of the children (Women in Transition, 1975).

LOW-INCOME AND MINORITY WOMEN

A greater percentage of minority women are single heads of households (Bequaert, 1976). A black woman may share her residence with her husband at the same time that she is divorced in every aspect except legally. A low-income woman may have to put survival issues above her emotional needs. Her economic security and that of her children depend on her ability to relate to agencies and institutions (Weiss, 1975). White working-class women, who hold the most traditional role values, may face the equally objectionable choices of going on welfare or leaving their children for low-paying jobs.

Widowhood

The stereotype of the widow is a grandmother—old and gray, resigned and accommodating. The average age of American widows is 56, and there are twice as many widows as there are divorced or separated women (Bequaert, 1976). More than half of the women over 65 are widowed (Temes, 1977).

Studies that look at differences between widows and widowers note that the mortality risk is higher for men at all ages (Epstein *et al.*, 1975). However, a survey of 78 widows and 41 widowers conducted at 13 and 16 months after bereavement found that widowers were significantly better adjusted than widows (Carey, 1977). Further, women were more concerned than men about money, even after adjustment for income differences. Carey discovered the obvious: It is easier for a widower to remarry. According to Carey (1977), this "suggests that women do not work through their grief as quickly as men" (p. 130). This may be an oversimplification. There are fewer men available to women in the older age range, and men have social sanctions to marry younger women, while women do not have approval to marry younger men.

OBSTACLES TO CRISIS RESOLUTION

There are many obstacles that inhibit a widow from finishing her grief work. Studies by Maddison (cited in Epstein *et al.*, 1975) suggest predictors of poor risks for resolving bereavement crises. The high-risk widow is young with dependent children living at home. Evidence of difficulties in the marriage, avoidance of affect, and survival issues can increase the burdens of widowhood. Most important, high-risk widows tend to be dissatisfied with the lack of support available to them during the crisis. Widows who resolve the crisis perceive that their social relationships provide support during mourning.

Few widows, however, receive the help they need to complete the mourning process. In one study, Silverman and Cooperband (1975) find that many widows get stuck in the second stage because they have not received the support which allows them to talk out their grief and envision a new future. The widow's failure to complete the mourning process may result in emphasizing the widowhood role, idealizing the past and the marital relationship, and refusing to take responsibility for her new life.

Carey (1977) found that the amount of forewarning was the second main predictor of adjustment to grief for widows. This was especially true when the widow had experienced a prolonged death of her spouse or when there had been unhappiness in the marriage. This suggests that anticipated grief may be particularly important to women (Kubler-Ross, 1974).

In records from the Widow Service Line (Abrahams, 1972), 73% of the 570 callers stated that loneliness and isolation were their main problems. Analysis of the records indicated that 90% of the callers were women (the program was designed for widowers, too), and widows' needs were differentiated by age. Lopata (1973) noted that 50% of the widows she surveyed felt like a "fifth wheel," and middle-class women, especially, felt that friends had withdrawn. Lower-class women had fewer friends to begin with and relied on relatives. In black and ethnic ghettos, few lower-class widows had family to help them.

One of the few studies (Lopata, 1973) investigating class and race differences was conducted in the Chicago, Illinois, area. Interviews with 301 widows (244 whites and 52 blacks) showed that black women were less likely (76%) than white women (94%) to idealize their husbands and less likely to idealize marriage in general. Black women were more likely to be accustomed to making decisions: 61% of the white women stated that decision-making was difficult as compared to 37% of black women. The freedom and independence of widowhood was appreciated more by black women, although 54% of the sample felt that the changes in themselves toward independence were mostly beneficial. Lopata stated that class has direct bearing on widowhood. Working-class women ranked the mother role over the wife role and had less identification with the working and social worlds of their husbands. Although higher educated women were eventually more independent, their lives were more disrupted by their husbands' deaths because of shared activities and interests.

ECONOMIC HARDSHIP

Although widowhood is an experience shared by the majority of women, few women are economically prepared for the financial hardships that accompany it. Two-thirds of all widows live at or below the poverty line

(Bequaert, 1976). For many women, the change from middle-income to low-income status is abrupt and devastating. In a survey of 30 support group members at Women in Transition, widows identified the following practical concerns: information on and assistance with financial matters (80%); information on employment (80%); and legal assistance (70%).

In summary, societal attitudes toward death and widows, plus survival concerns, obstruct the widow's recovery from this crisis. As Lopata (1973) asserted, widows have almost an invisible status, a characteristic of other oppressed minority groups:

> They are women in a male-dominated society. They are old in a society that venerates youth. Many are grieving and lonely in a country that would deny and ignore such unhappy emotions. They are without mates in a social network of couples. Many are members of ethnic or racial minority groups and already face prejudice on that basis. (For example, about one and a half million of our female elderly are foreignborn.) They are poor in a wealthy land, and they tend to be ignorant and uneducated in a society that increasingly demands knowledge and skills. (p. 92)

Needs of Women in Marital Transition

For a woman to resolve a marital crisis effectively, she needs (1) a realistic perception of her situation and what to expect, (2) adequate environmental support, and (3) appropriate coping skills (Rapoport, 1965). The literature indicates that continued stereotyping of women's roles, inadequate access to economic and legal support, social isolation, and certain personality traits associated with women make marital transition particularly difficult for women. The crisis-intervention models need to address the following issues for divorcing and recently bereaved women.

REALISTIC PERSPECTIVE

An important reality check is the realization that there are stages to marital transition. Habib and Landgraf (1977) and Silverman and Cooperband (1975) maintain that the woman who views herself as an isolated, sick patient has a lower self-image than the woman who sees herself solving a life crisis similar to that faced by other women.

Carter (1977) and Riessman (1976) advocate cognitive restructuring as an avenue for helping the woman discriminate between her individual problems and the social and cultural values and institutions that affect all women. Defazio and Klenbort (1975) stress that during the second stage of transition, the role of the helper is to emphasize the real aspects of the divorce process.

ENVIRONMENTAL SUPPORT

Women need support for working through the stages of separation and divorce and grief and mourning (Carter, 1977; Silverman & Cooperband, 1975; Weiss, 1975). An adequate support system recognizes that feelings of anger, ambivalence, loneliness, and grief are intrinsic to the crisis experience. The traditional support network of family and friends may not recognize the psychological stress of loneliness (Miles & Hays, 1975).

COPING MECHANISMS

As Riessman (1976) points out, support is not sufficient for the person in crisis. For maximum empowerment, individuals must be shown specifically how they can actively shape their lives. To complete the transition process through problem-solving skills, women in marital transition need practice in assertive behavior (Kessler, 1978; Morris & Prescott, 1975; Weiss, 1975). Single parents need skills to manage their new role (Gettleman & Markowitz, 1975). Women need to be trained in the practical concerns of home management frequently left to their husbands (Schlesinger, 1977). Single-again women may need to replace stereotypical female behaviors and develop career goals (Aslin, 1976).

Crisis-Intervention Models

Many types of services exist for individuals who have been widowed or divorced. Group and individual psychotherapy, marriage counseling, and family therapy provide traditional approaches to dealing with the stress of marital transition. These, however, are not specifically within the scope of this chapter. The discussion of crisis-intervention models excludes other services and programs: educational models that rely on films, lectures, and discussion (Welch & Granvold, 1977); resocialization or rap groups; mixed-sex programs; and single-parent organizations. The scope of this section is limited to services that are designed with a crisis-intervention perspective and, whenever possible, with a specific focus on the needs of women.

Possibly the best-known project for women in transition is the Widow-to-Widow program at the Laboratory of Community Psychiatry, Harvard Medical School, Boston, Massachusetts. The publications growing out of this project (Silverman et al., 1975) have spawned many other programs. McCourt, Barnett, Brennen, and Becker (1976), Hiltz (1975), and Abrahams (1972) describe other programs for widows. Counseling services for separating and divorcing women are described by Carter (1977), Habib and Landgraf (1977), Brown (1976), and Pincus, Radding, and Lawrence (1974). Although no empirical data exist on the effects of these programs, most at least attempt to collect and report results of client feedback. Although outreach, hotlines, and home visitations can appropriately be labeled crisis interventions, and are helpful to many persons, anonymity of clients and the sporadic nature of the client–counselor interaction make it difficult to assess their effectiveness systematically. The crisis-intervention group appears to be a promising psychotherapeutic approach to marital transition. Viewed together, crisis-intervention services for women in marital crisis are diverse in philosophy, staffing, client characteristics, and methods; nonetheless, they share important characteristics.

Peer Support Groups

The group model is characterized by nonsexist, self-help, and feminist features (Marecek & Kravitz, 1977; Rawlings & Carter, 1977). The support group offers women an opportunity to deal with the problems of role change and social reorientation and with financial and legal issues in an atmosphere of tolerance for diversity and respect for individual preferences, including differences of race, ethnic origin, class, and sexual preference.

1. It is assumed that transitional crises are a normal and natural part of adult life. The needs of the woman in crisis are met without psychiatric labeling (McCourt *et al.*, 1976).
2. The peer self-help approach assumes that women, some professionally trained and some not, can help other women (Silverman *et al.*, 1975).
3. Group members are assumed to be able to learn about themselves and their life options and, therefore, to be able to make responsible decisions for their lives.
4. It is assumed that a relationship exists between a woman's individual problems and the society in which she lives. A woman is encouraged to develop a conscious insight into the sex-role expectations she has internalized so that she can gain better control of her life and perceive the variety of options available to her.

SUPPORT GROUP FORMAT

The peer group provides a supportive environment where women with similar concerns come together for eight to ten topic-oriented, structured sessions. The structure and content are designed to work with either a heterogeneous or homogeneous group membership.

Unlike educational models, crisis-intervention models use group dynamics to facilitate individual growth. The topics are sequentially arranged to increase group intimacy and risk-taking behavior. The amount of structure decreases as members take increased responsibility for content and group maintenance functions.

GROUP FACILITATORS

The use of female facilitators is a key ingredient in a peer support model (Carter, 1977; Krause, 1971). They function as role models, initiate discussion of nontraditional options, and confront sex-stereotyped assumptions. WIT uses co-facilitators who are paired to represent different life-styles, ages, or ethnic/racial background. Further, as co-facilitators, they model a cooperative rather than competitive relationship between women in a leadership role. This also allows the pairing of former clients with professionally trained women.

GROUP PARTICIPANTS

Not all women are appropriate for a peer support group. Women with severe psychological problems, women with drug or alcohol problems that are not under control, and intellectually limited women would not be suitable for this type of service. In order to benefit from a support group, a woman must be able to listen as well as to verbalize her own feelings, provide support for others as well as receive support from the group, and be willing to examine her life from a new perspective in order to change and grow. Women may, however, use both individual therapy and a support group to maximize therapeutic input.

Suggestions and Priorities

Services for women in marital transition are largely alternative services and, as such, are not reported in the research literature on program outcomes. The topic of this chapter is not adequately addressed in the research literature.

The following recommendations for research priorities are based on the review of the literature which presents the needs of women in marital transition as critical and suggests that crisis-intervention groups may provide a vehicle for meeting those needs. The first group of suggestions applies to crisis theory and the second to crisis-intervention models. More specific questions are formulated for widows and divorced or separated women.

Crisis theory as it attempts to explain the experience of marital transition needs more investigation. Lopata (1975) suggests that an ideologic adherence by professionals to crisis stages can be counter-productive and inhibit an individual's process of bereavement. Although the stages of crisis provide a general framework for working with women, not enough is known at this time about specific factors that contribute to or detract from successful crisis resolution. The following questions arise:

1. What are the effects of previous life crises on marital transition?
2. Which aspects of female socialization are negatively and positively related to successful crisis resolution?
3. What is the effect of anticipatory grief on the process of grief work? The literature is somewhat contradictory on this issue (Clayton, Halikas, Maurice, & Robins, 1973).
4. What is the effect of physical abuse on marital transition? How do such variables as length of marriage, severity of violence, frequency of violence, and socioeconomic factors contribute to the crisis?

The basic question is whether crisis-intervention models are cost-effective compared to other treatments or no treatment. Therefore, the first priority is that program evaluations investigate the following: (1) participants in crisis-intervention groups versus a control group and (2) participants in crisis-intervention groups versus those in individual therapy. Next in importance for a research agenda are long-range studies that investigate the effect, over time, of participation in a crisis-intervention group on the quality of crisis resolution. Studies should be designed to investigate change from several perspectives: (1) standardized measures, (2) self-report inventories, (3) behavior change assessed during the group and followed up at 6- and 12-month intervals, and (4) perceptions of group facilitators.

Program evaluation studies should take into consideration such questions as the following:

1. Does participation in a group effect change in sex-role attitudes, locus of control, self-esteem, severity of symptomatology, evidence of assertive behavior, and problem-solving skills?
2. Does participation affect such factors as remarriage, the development of new social networks, or economic independence?

3. What are the predictors of client change?
4. What impact does the model have on minority women, rural populations, and working-class women?
5. What are the limitations of the model?
6. What are the perceived effects, if any, of using female facilitators, peer facilitators, and co-facilitators?
7. What is the effect of previous psychotherapy experience on the participant's response to the group?

Although research may be conducted in various settings—women's programs, universities, community mental health centers—the following guidelines for funding agencies and researchers are recommended:

1. Research should be conducted where an established program exists with at least 2 years' experience in providing services.
2. Priority should go to those groups with a client population that includes minority women, low-income women, and a broad age range.
3. Priority should go to groups that have supporting program components, that is, hotlines, outreach, referrals, and linkages to other institutions.
4. The service agency should be able to demonstrate a clear commitment to nonsexist, specialized services to women.

A review of the literature on crisis intervention and women in marital transition contributes to an understanding of the impact of this life experience on women. Crisis theorists have charted the similarities and differences between widows and divorcées and have listed the tasks to be accomplished by women seeking to reorient their lives. The descriptions of experiences, feelings, and problems of women in crisis suggest guidelines for the development of services. Although few empirical data have been reported, the literature and experience of women's services sketch the salient features of a peer support crisis-intervention model. The model was described to suggest features that should be considered in program evaluation efforts. Crisis groups appear to be therapeutic; the research community and service agencies still need to combine their expertise to find out how and why.

ACKNOWLEDGMENT

The author acknowledges the contributions of Bette Begleiter and Nancy Walsh to the research and ideas in this chapter.

References

Abrahams, R. B. Mutual help for the widowed. *Social Work,* 1972, *17,* 54–61.

Aslin, A. L. Counseling "single-again" (divorced and widowed) women. *Counseling Psychologist,* 1976, *6,* 37–41.

Bachrach, L. L. *Marital status and mental disorder: An analytical review* (DHEW Publication No. [ADM] 75-217). Washington, D.C.: U.S. Government Printing Office, 1975.

Bequaert, L. H. *Single women.* Boston: Beacon Press, 1976.

Bernard, J. *The future of marriage.* New York: World 1972.

Bohannan, P. (Ed.). *Divorce and after.* Garden City, N.Y.: Doubleday, 1970.

Bould, S. Female headed families: Personal fate control and the provider role. *Journal of Marriage and the Family,* 1977, *39,* 339–349.

Brandwein, R. A., Brown, C. A., & Fox, E. M. Women and children last: The social situation of divorced mothers and their families. *Journal of Marriage and the Family,* 1974, *36,* 498–514.

Brown, E. M. Divorce counseling. In D. H. Olson (Ed.), *Treating relationships.* Lake Mills, Ia.: Graphic, 1976.

Brown, P., & Manela, R. Changing family roles: Women and divorce. *Journal of Divorce,* 1978, *1,* 315–328.

Carey, G. The widowed: A year later. *Journal of Counseling Psychology,* 1977, *24,* 125–131.

Carter, D. K. Counseling divorced women. *The Personnel and Guidance Journal.* 1977, *55,* 537–541.

Chiraboga, D. A., & Cutler, L. Stress responses among divorcing men and women. *Journal of Divorce,* 1977, *1,* 95–105.

Chiraboga, D. A., Roberts, J., & Stein, J. A. Psychological well-being during marital separation. *Journal of Divorce,* 1978, *2*(1), 21–36.

Clayton, P. J., Halikas, J. A., Maurice, W. L., & Robins, E. Anticipatory grief and widowhood. *British Journal of Psychiatry,* 1973, *122,* 47–51.

Conroy, R. C. Widows and widowhood. *New York State Journal of Medicine,* 1977, *3,* 357–360.

Defazio, V. J., & Klenbort, I. A note on the dynamics of psychotherapy during marital dissolution. *Psychotherapy: Theory, Research, and Practice,* 1975, *12,* 101–104.

Epstein, G., Weitz, L., Roback, H., & McKee, E. Research and bereavement: A selective and critical review. *Comprehensive Psychiatry,* 1975, *16,* 537–546.

Gettleman, S., & Markowitz, J. *The courage to divorce.* New York: Ballantine Books, 1975.

Glick, P. C., & Norton, A. J. Perspectives on the recent upturn in divorce and remarriage. *Demography,* 1973, *10,* 301–314.

Glick, P. C., & Norton, A. J. Marital instability: Past, present and future. *Journal of Social Issues,* 1976, *32,* 5–20.

Habib, M., & Landgraf, B. J. Women helping women. *Social Work,* 1977, *22,* 510–512.

Halpern, H. A. Crisis theory: A definitional study. *Community Mental Health Journal,* 1973, *9,* 342–349.

Herman, S. J. Women, divorce, and suicide. *Journal of Divorce,* 1977, *1,* 107–117.

Hiltz, S. R. Helping widows: Group discussions as a therapeutic technique. *The Family Coordinator,* 1975, *24,* 331–336.

Holmes, T., & Masuda, M. Life change and illness susceptibility. In J. P. Scott & E. C. Senay (Eds.), *Separation and depression: Clinical and research aspects.* Washington, D.C.: American Association for the Advancement of Science, 1973.

Kessler, S. Building skills in divorce adjustment groups. *Journal of Divorce,* 1978, *2,* 209–216.

Krause, C. The femininity complex and women therapists. *Journal of Marriage and the Family,* 1971, *33,* 476–482.

Kressel, K., & Deutch, M. Divorce therapy: An in-depth survey of therapists' views. *Family Process*, 1974, *16*, 413–443.

Kubler-Ross, E. *Questions and answers on death and dying.* New York: Macmillan, 1974.

Lopata, H. Z. Living through widowhood. *Psychology Today*, July 1973, pp. 87–92.

Lopata, H. Z. On widowhood: Grief work and identity reconstruction. *Journal of Geriatric Psychiatry*, 1975, *8*, 41–55.

Marecek, J., & Kravitz, D. Women and mental health: A review of feminist change efforts. *Psychiatry*, 1977, *40*, 323–329.

Marriages, divorces, January 1979. *Marriage and Divorce Today*, May 1979, p. 4.

McCourt, W. F., Barnett, R. D., Brennen, J., & Becker, A. We find each other: Primary prevention for the widowed. *The American Journal of Psychiatry*, 1976, *133*, 98–100.

McEaddy, B. J. Women who head families: A socioeconomic analysis. *Monthly Labor Review*, 1976. Washington, D.C.: U.S. Dept. of Labor.

Miles, H. S., & Hays, D. R. Widowhood. *American Journal of Nursing*, 1975, *2*, 280–282.

Morris, J. D., & Prescott, M. R. Transition groups: An approach to dealing with post-partnership anguish. *The Family Coordinator*, 1975, *24*, 325–330.

Parad, H. J. (Ed.). *Crisis intervention: Selected readings.* New York: Family Service Association of America, 1965.

Pasewark, R. A., & Albers, D. A. Crisis intervention: Theory in search of a program. *Social Work*, 1972, *17*, 70–77.

Rapoport, L. The state of crisis: Some theoretical considerations. In H. J. Parad (Ed.), *Crisis intervention: Selected readings.* New York: Family Service Association of America, 1965.

Pincus, C., Radding, N., & Lawrence, R. A professional counseling service for women. *Social Work*, 1974, *19*, 197–194.

Raschke, H. *Social and psychological factors in voluntary postmarital dissolution adjustment.* Unpublished doctoral dissertation, University of Minnesota, 1974.

Rawlings, E. I., & Carter, D. K. *Psychotherapy for women: Treatment toward equality.* Springfield, Ill.: Charles C. Thomas, 1977.

Riessman, F. How does self-help work? *Social Policy*, 1976, *7*, 41–47.

Schlesinger, B. The crisis of widowhood in the family circle. *Essence*, 1977, *77*, 147–155.

Silverman, P., & Cooperband, A. On widowhood: Mutual help and the elderly widow. *Journal of Geriatric Psychiatry*, 1975, *8*, 9–26.

Silverman, P., MacKenzie, D., Pettipas, M., & Wilson, E. (Eds.). *Helping each other in widowhood.* New York: Health Sciences, 1975.

Smart, L. S. An application of Erikson's theory to the recovery-from-divorce process. *Journal of Divorce*, 1977, *1*, 67–80.

Temes, R. *Living with an empty chair: A guide through grief.* Amherst, Me.: Mandala, 1977.

Weiss, R. S. *Marital separation.* New York: Basic Books, 1975.

Weiss, R. S. The emotional impact of marital separation. *Journal of Social Issues*, 1976, *32*, 135–145.

Welch, G. J., & Granvold, D. K. Seminars for separated/divorced: An educational approach to post-divorce adjustment. *Journal of Sex and Marital Therapy*, 1977, *3*, 31–39.

Wiseman, R. S. Crisis theory and the process of divorce. *Social Casework*, 1975, *6*, 205–212.

Women in Transition. *A feminist handbook on separation and divorce.* New York: Charles Scribner's Sons, 1975.

PART FIVE

Conclusion

CHAPTER 16

Psychotherapy and Women: Priorities for Research

ANNETTE M. BRODSKY

RACHEL T. HARE-MUSTIN

A number of researchers (e.g., Bergin & Strupp, 1972; Parloff, 1979) have pointed out that the fundamental questions asked by psychotherapists are: What kind of changes are affected by which techniques, and how do they differ with regard to therapists, patients, and conditions? Parloff (1979) concludes, "No single study, no matter how carefully designed and executed, can hope to control for or investigate systematically the plethora of variables whose influences on outcome may be confounded with and obscure the effects of treatments" (p. 303). It is this dilemma that makes it necessary to establish priorities for psychotherapy research in any area. With regard to treatment of women, the issues are even more in need of study, since only recently have they emerged as worthy of scientific investigation.

As the *Report of the President's Commission on Mental Health* (1978) has pointed out, women are the primary users of all health care services in a system controlled and administered largely by men. In the area of psychotherapy, women have represented the majority of patients and the minority of therapists. Yet, in spite of the number of female consumers of psychotherapy, problems specific to women and the woman's point of view in the development of theory and the practice of psychotherapy have suffered wide-ranging neglect. Such neglect is not a result of conscious discrimination, but a concomitant of prevailing attitudes toward women.

Along with the neglect of women's issues in clinical practice, there has been an even greater neglect of women's issues in psychotherapy re-

Annette M. Brodsky. Department of Psychology, University of Alabama, Tuscaloosa, Alabama.
Rachel T. Hare-Mustin. Program in Counseling and Consulting Psychology, Graduate School of Education, Harvard University, Cambridge, Massachusetts.

search. Part of this difficulty is due to a lack of development of services which meet needs *specific* to women. Thus, evaluation of programs and techniques that might address treatment issues for women is hampered by the absence of long-term experience with such techniques and programs. Existing services for women have been criticized for many reasons, among them the tendency to make outmoded assumptions about what women want and/or need, ignoring differences among women such as those due to age, and ignoring the impact of such services on the total life context of women. Although such new approaches as feminist therapy, self-help groups, and crisis intervention for rape, battering, and marital transition have been used by women, they have not received the attention of empirical researchers that the more traditional therapies have received. The changing roles and needs of women demand new methods of research and evaluation of results to meet the criticisms of feminist and traditional researchers alike.

Research on the Influence of Gender

Subsumed under the main question "Are there gender differences in the treatment of men and women?" are three basic questions regarding gender differences in psychotherapeutic practice: (1) What is the influence of gender on therapist attitudes toward male and female clients; (2) how are the processes in therapy affected by gender of therapist and client; and (3) how do therapist and patient gender variables affect the outcome of treatment?

Therapist Attitudes

Studies stimulated by the women's movement have provided evidence demonstrating that clinicians, particularly men, engage in sex-role stereotyping. As reviewed by Sherman, these empirical findings, whether from surveys of clinician ratings of adjectives to describe self and clients or from analogue studies, all point to the existence of stereotyped attitudes and behavior. The more recent studies indicate a moderating of such stereotyping. The reduction in stereotyping has been variously interpreted as being due to a change in clinician attitudes, more appropriate training, artifacts of unrepresentative sampling, or socially desirable responding as awareness of discrimination against women has increased. However, while there is increasing awareness that women's issues are salient, there is evidence that therapists' information on the issues that impact on women is quite inadequate.

The development of a conceptual framework to guide research in the field is a priority issue. Many studies have explored random variables or those of doubtful relevance to the question of sex-role stereotyping. The measurement of stereotyping and bias is particularly difficult, because subjects may deny their biases in any but the most effectively disguised experimental designs. Therefore, measures to minimize socially desirable responding are needed.

There is also a need for clearer conceptualization of the possible effect of sex-role stereotyping on the outcome of treatment. With regard to research on this issue, there are virtually no data on the relationship of therapist stereotyping to patient outcome. In general, studies suggest that therapists' judgments of clients' needs for treatment appear to be modified by the therapist's own gender and attitudes about sex roles. However, practitioners have apparently become more liberal over time in their attitudes toward women's career aspirations and related areas, but these findings are based mainly on analogue studies.

Studies of sex-role stereotyping in clinical judgments have shown that women qua women have not been discriminated against in terms of judgments of severity of diagnosis, maladjustment, or prognosis. These studies, however, have been primarily analogue studies. Such analogues may not adequately reflect complex therapy situations in which mental health workers may experience pressures to conform to traditional practices.

Process Variables

There are very few "true" process studies in this area, that is, analyses of material from actual therapy sessions. Thus, as Marecek and Johnson suggest, there exists no solid basis for stating whether gender differences influence process. Among the questions related to gender influences on the process of therapy are: What are the effects of various gender pairings of patient and therapist on these variables, and how do variables such as age, marital status, and client personality interact with gender to affect process as well as outcome? Significant effects of variables that interact with gender may be missed by studies that do not take gender into account. It should also be pointed out that certain populations of female patients are rarely studied: female children and adolescents, working mothers, elderly women, hospitalized psychotic women, and minority women.

Another question that may relate to the process of therapy concerns how therapy clients are selected. The literature suggests that women in general, and married women in particular, are preferred as clients by therapists of both sexes. A problem in determining the validity of these findings derives from the popular method of defining therapist preference on the basis of caseload information. Since most therapists in psychology and psychiatry are male and most clients are female, the apparent preference for females may not be surprising. The major question still to be answered regarding preferences of therapists in selection of clients is: What effect does therapist preference for gender of client have on the therapists' differential treatment of men and women? Also of interest are ways in which the development of the therapeutic relationship during the process of therapy might moderate or alter initial attitudes or behavior toward the client. Assessment of actual therapist behavior is clearly needed.

With regard to client preference for a male or female therapist, the modal client does not appear to have a preference, although in the past, there was a preference for male therapists. Of those who do express a preference, recent research indicates that clients who are young, well educated, and female tend to prefer female therapists. There has been an increase over the last several years in preference for female therapists by all groups of clients. The motives underlying this increased preference for female therapists are unclear, but they may be of interest in understanding the therapy process.

What variables are associated with entering treatment and with length of treatment for women? There is no evidence that given comparable levels of distress, women are more likely to enter therapy than men, although data exist that indicate that women seek help more readily than do men. Some theoretical orientations have been criticized as fostering dependency, and thus longer-term treatment, in female clients. The majority of studies found no difference between men's and women's length of stay in therapy, while a substantial minority of studies found that, indeed, women did stay longer in therapy. A more basic question that such studies have not addressed is how or why such differences in length of therapy occur. Who initiates termination and for what reason? It cannot be assumed that termination is always a result of dissatisfaction. The data on effects of gender of therapist and client on early termination of therapy are equivocal and require further study.

Another question that has been raised concerns the relationship between the gender of the therapist and empathy. There appear to be distinct differences in this area between the results of analogue studies and those of naturalistic studies, with the analogue studies suggesting that female therapists are more emphatic than males and the naturalistic studies implying that gender matching and experience level of therapist are more important determinants of empathy than gender per se.

One way of investigating the effects of sex-role stereotyping on the process of therapy would be to study the manifest content of therapists' interventions with male and female clients. Although this issue has been raised in various contexts during the last several years and was identified as a high-priority area for research in 1974 at the Society for Psychotherapy Research workshop in Denver, Colorado, only one relevant study has been reported in the intervening 6 years (Shapiro, 1977). Female therapists were found to give more positively reinforcing responses and show less sex-role stereotyping in their choice of cues to reinforce than males. However, counselor sex-role attitudes failed to predict responses to the stereotypical and counterstereotypical cues. The need for more empirical work in this area is urgent.

Do clients' perceptions of therapists show gender differences? The data are fragmentary and the studies inconsistent or lacking in positive results. However, at least one study found that in cotherapy with opposite-sex group leaders, males are perceived as leaders and females as providers of warmth in the group (Wright & Gould, 1977).

Critics of psychotherapy have pointed to reports indicating that a small percentage of therapeutic interventions include sexual intimacy, particularly between male therapists and female clients. Although such practices are unethical, sufficient empirical data on the degree or extent of deleterious consequences of such practices do not exist.

There are few process studies using actual therapy session material, since such studies require privileged access, painstaking analysis, and often prohibitive cost in research time and dollars. Questionnaire data are numerous and analogue data requiring interviews or experimental sessions less frequent. The closer a study approaches actual therapy, the more difficult the material is to obtain, but the more desirable the design in terms of generalizable results. Thus, one must be cautious about accepting the validity of results from many of the available studies. Data are also needed on differences between therapists who are willing to be studied and those who are not.

Outcome Variables

Outcome studies are the bread and butter of psychotherapy research. What matters in the end is whether whatever is being studied will make a difference in the behavior, feelings, or well-being of the client. In order to assess that difference, the client needs to be studied before, during, and at intervals after therapy. The criteria for determining adequate outcome are, of course, the central issue. The questions to be asked are: What is therapy? What should it accomplish? When is a person improved? How is that improvement to be measured or, for that matter, communicated? Who determines improvement? Is it the same for all people or all women? Who decides the answers to these questions?

In seeking to answer these questions, one becomes impressed with the complexity of the conceptual issues involved, as discussed by Orlinsky and Howard. In evaluating the effectiveness of treatment outcome, two cognitive tasks emerge:

1. The descriptive task is to demonstrate a causal link between therapeutic intervention and behavioral changes in the client.
2. The value task is to identify standards which can be used to assess the importance and benefits of the changes in question.

The available literature on gender effects on the outcome of therapy is riddled with inconsistencies. These inconsistencies, however, may be more a result of the confounding of salient variables that interact with gender than support for the nonexistence of gender effects. Gender rarely appears as a significant main effect in most of the studies in which it is analyzed, but it is often found to have significant impact on outcome in interaction with other therapist and patient variables. For example, one study found that patients who were married women perceived experienced male therapists as most helpful, while young, unmarried women saw female therapists as most helpful (Orlinsky & Howard, 1976).

One possible approach that has been suggested repeatedly for studying the effects of gender on psychotherapy outcome is the reanalysis of old data. Many investigators of large-scale projects might undertake retrieval of sex-difference data without collection of new material. However, caution is needed in the interpretation of sex-difference findings from reanalyzed data. If the original study is more than a few years old, what does the reanalysis tell us about current gender influences? The impact of the women's movement on sex-role behavior for both men and women has been significant in many contexts, making most previous data useful only for historical purposes. What is needed now is a knowledge of the current differences between men and women in psychotherapy. In addition, relying on data collected for other purposes may not assure appropriate measures for identifying sex bias and stereotyping, the inclusion of both female and male raters, or control for the bias of investigators regarding these issues. It seems more important that new studies be undertaken which include a priori provisions to examine gender as a variable.

The matter of identifying value biases in both the measurement and interpretation of changes in men and women clients is a broader problem. Disagreement over the meaning of specific findings has resulted in some studies being used to support both the existence and nonexistence of gender bias. Thus, the development of measures for outcome criteria that are not subject to gender bias of the therapist, client, or researcher remains a priority for researchers.

In summary, the area of sex differences in psychotherapy is understudied at present, but of critical concern. The available literature is sometimes confused and frequently flawed, and results are generally confounded by the many variables that interact with gender. Priority should be given to the development of clearer conceptualizations of the issues and the elimination of contamination by value biases in the judgment of outcome. Encouragement of work in this area by established researchers of psychotherapy and guidance for new researchers as to the nature of the variables involved are seen as priorities. Researchers need to explore such questions as: How do the sex-role attitudes and gender of the therapist and client, and their interaction in therapy, affect the therapeutic process and outcome?

Disorders of High Prevalence

Certain disorders are of particular concern to the treatment of women because of their association with the female gender, either in terms of the large numbers of women affected, as in depression and eating disorders, or because of the specific relationship of the disorder to women's role issues, as in hysteria. The disorders identified for closer examination in this volume were depression, anxieties such as agoraphobia and hysteria, eating disorders, and marital and family conflict.

Some features common to all disorders of high prevalence are important for researchers. One of the questions that the higher prevalence rates raise is, Are the demands of traditional sex roles more maladaptive for women than men? The literature spawned by the Broverman studies (Broverman, Broverman, Clarkson, Rosenkrantz, & Vogel, 1970) indicates that clinicians consider "feminine" characteristics less healthy, but it is not clear what the behavioral consequences are for women who adhere closely to the feminine ideal. Certain variables associated with women's sex roles may have an impact on the development of mental illness: nonexpression of negative feelings, taking roles which satisfy a male partner, passivity, learned helplessness, exaggerated femininity, and "other-directedness." Thus, women's traditional ways of relating to others, particularly to men, may predispose women to mental illness. Studies need to be conducted on the kinds of relationship problems women bring to psychotherapy, the changing roles in marriage, and assumptions about the relationship of marital status to women's well-being.

Depression

Over the last two decades, there has been considerable research on depression and on the efficacy of various treatments. Key publications on therapeutic evaluation have appeared, including guidelines for the principles and problems in establishing the efficacy of psychotropic drugs, guides for designing clinical trials of psychotherapy, and catalogues of standardized change and outcome measures. Despite the considerable research on efficacy of treatment, gaps still exist in our understanding of the right treatment for the right person.

According to Weissman, there is substantial evidence that depression is more common among women than men. Some evidence has been presented for a sex-linked genetic factor operating in certain types of depressive disorders. Reproductive system factors such as hormones may also be associated with depression, although here the evidence is less clear. For example, while the risk of postpartum depression does seem high, depression does not appear to be significantly associated with menopause, contrary to popular myth. Psychosocial reasons have been offered as explanations for the high prevalence of depression among women, with some authors suggesting that women experience more stresses than men. One line of investigation has attempted to demonstrate that depression exists equally in men but is less visible due to the tradition which allows women to reveal feelings.

The higher rate of depression among women does not appear to be an artifact, but rather a true sex difference in prevalence. There is evidence that certain psychosocial factors are associated with depression in women, such as low social status, legal and economic discrimination, and role expectations leading to learned helplessness. Perhaps the most compelling evidence is found in the data that suggest that marriage has a protective effect for men but a detrimental effect for women in terms of rates of depression.

The questions that remain significant ones for researchers in the treatment of depression are: Why are women at higher risk than men? How do role expectations and behaviors contribute to depression? Which subtypes of depressed women are best treated by which combinations of drugs and psychotherapy? Comparisons of married and single women as well as working and nonworking women are needed in relation to rates of depression and outcomes of treatment.

Some treatments may well have an inoculating effect on women by providing increased coping skills. Research that examines the preventive as well as therapeutic effects of behavioral marital therapy, assertiveness training, and training in communication skills may give valuable answers to the question of which skills are helpful to keep women functioning adequately regardless of family, career, and life stresses.

Hysteria

Why are women more likely to show hysterical traits than men? Does treatment result in improvement? Since the term "hysteria" has been used to define exaggerated femininity, it may represent a caricature of women's traditional role, rather than a disease entity. Are more women diagnosed as hysterical because hysteria describes women's role attributions? Hysteria is also often used as a pejorative term. Improved diagnostic criteria are needed if adequate research is to be done in this area.

One methodologic problem for researchers has been the fact that hysterical patients do not typically present for psychological treatment. Our understanding of the phenomenon is still based on those few women who enter therapy voluntarily and on the anecdotal reports of clinical cases. The single-case design may provide data about these women at this stage of development of the concept, but empirical evidence of treatments that lead to improvement is the ultimate research goal.

Agoraphobia

The questions germaine to improved understanding of this disorder of high prevalence among women are: How is the etiology related to women's experience? Do the criteria for improvement consider the long-term as opposed to short-term gains? There is evidence that agoraphobia is determined by multiple factors and is learned as part of the sex-role socialization of some women. Separation anxiety appears to be one of the central issues in agoraphobia, but treatment for this aspect of the disorder is as yet unresearched, according to Chambless and Goldstein. Both clinical impressions and research findings suggest that improvement that may be obtained with *in vivo* exposure (to the anxiety-arousing situation) frequently is precarious. Relapse continues to be a significant problem and appears to be linked to marital conflicts that reemerge with the agoraphobic partner's improvement. Research is needed that looks at long-term effects, rather than episodic improvement, as well as age-related factors before claims of successful treatment can be considered valid. The use of multifaceted treatment designs, rather than studies of single treatment approaches, is suggested on the basis of clinical observations.

Eating Disorders

Wooley and Wooley point out the obsessional nature of our cultural prescriptions for ideal weight, particularly for women. The treatment questions related to eating disorders involve the social pressures on many women to achieve unrealistic standards of slimness. The pressures in certain occupations that require women to maintain weights at anorexic levels are also part of the clinical considerations in treatment and research. Women with anorexia nervosa apparently learn to starve themselves through positive reinforcement from their employers, parents, and peers and then lose perspective of the original goal and of their own body image.

Researchable questions in the area of weight control include: What is the relationship of weight to psychological well-being under different conditions of social acceptance? How do dieters differ from nondieters in their images of body and self? What is the effect of treatments that utilize shame, that imply lack of motivation where weight loss is insufficient for the therapist's goals, or that result in maintenence levels of constant hunger? What treatments that are effective in the short run are also effective in long-term weight control and in improving body image? What are the psychological implications of repeated failure to lose weight?

We know little about why women differ in their degree of comfort with their bodies and what personal characteristics predict problems with weight control. The psychodynamics of eating disorders appear to be contaminated with misinformation about obesity and anorexia on the part of the treating therapists and primary physicians as well as the patients.

Marital and Family Conflict

As Gurman and Klein indicate, the question of the prevalence of marital and family conflict is extremely complex, since there are many ways to define the phenomenon. Although the rates of some manifestations of marital conflict such as divorce are fairly well known, the rates of other expressions of marital and family conflict are not clear. Recent surveys suggest that rates of marriage postponement, divorce, and remarriage are on the increase. What concepts adequately describe dysfunctional patterns of interaction? What are appropriate criteria of "normal" marital or family interactions? How are a woman's relationships in the family associated with her relationships to the rest of the world? What is the impact of feminism on families? These questions have been raised in the context of our current knowledge and concern about treatment of women in marital and family conflict.

Marriage postponement, divorce, and remarriage are increasing, and rates of divorce are widely used as an indication of marital conflict. Research has not, however, focused on the effects on women and men of marital conflicts that do not end in divorce. There is evidence that married women are at higher risk for depression than single women. Thus, the use of marital stability as the major criterion for successful marital treatment is questioned. As values concerned with the family are changing, assumptions about appropriate family organization are being challenged, particularly regarding the roles of wife and mother. There is need for careful examination of outcome criteria in evaluating marital and family therapy.

There is also a great need for more adequate ways to assess marital and family conflict. The newer feminist perspectives on marriage are just now beginning to be investigated. Studies are emérging on role sharing, paternal parenting, and conflict resolution. To aid the research in this area, measurement strategies are needed that can address both the level of total family functioning and the relative costs and benefits of such functioning for the woman as an individual. At present, researchers cannot properly investigate the differences between individual improvement in the conflict situation and personally harmful accomodation by the individual to family expectations. Research is needed to determine when the choice of marital or family therapy is not in the woman's best interest. Techniques such as cotherapy or couple and multifamily groups need to be examined for their effects on female clients.

As a further note on the high-prevalence disorders of women, mention needs to be made of the specific groups that are understudied: the aged, poor, handicapped, severely disturbed, ethnic minorities, and rural populations. One of the biases against researching these populations has been attributed to the difficulty in transporting subjects to service or research agencies. Thus, there are insufficient data on who may be suitable for which particular kind of treatment because of the difficulty in reaching those subjects who do not present as regular clients.

Another deficit in the research literature that cuts across all the high-prevalence disorders is the lack of long-term follow-up of treatment research. Since disorders like depression and agoraphobia tend to run a recurring, episodic course, assessing outcome for a single episode does not represent an accurate picture of the consequences of the treatment for the total life process. A high priority is the examination of temporal patterns of treatment outcome, with attention to life stresses, situational factors, and cyclical remission and decompensation.

Traditional Approaches

Traditional approaches to the treatment of women have been criticized for encouraging women to conform to prescribed roles and unhealthy life circumstances and, in some approaches, for defining the patients' problems as intrapsychic rather than taking into account the influence of situational stresses. In examining the treatment of women in psychotherapy, the most valuable questions for research include: How do the theory's assumptions about women and men, in terms of sex-role expectations and general behavior, affect the therapy? Who sets the goals for therapy, and what is the process by which these goals are sought? How and when is termination agreed to for men and women? Are the processes and goals different for men and women? Is change conceived of as internally or externally produced? How does the prescribed relationship between therapist and client affect outcome? How do the theory's concepts concerning power, anger, and other sex-role-related conditions affect the therapeutic process differentially for men and women? Does the theory encourage the use of psychotropic drugs as an adjunct to therapy for the purpose of dealing with power and anger in women?

The data for answering these questions are sparse at present. For example, the impression among feminists that psychodynamic approaches foster dependency and self-blame in women is based on survey questionnaires and reports of therapists and clients. Another problem is that most studies attempt to measure goal-setting and therapy process by examining facets of one particular theoretical approach rather than comparing across theoretical approaches. To date, claims that cognitive, behavioral, or similar specific approaches are more beneficial to women than are other approaches are not supported by objective, empirical data. Thus, our knowledge about the contributions of different theoretical orientations to sex bias is extremely limited.

One priority for all theoretical orientations is an area repeatedly focused on by clinicians but rarely studied by researchers—that of validating a woman's sense of personal competency. Proponents of most therapeutic schools agree that competency and worth in women are desirable, but one does not find these concepts defined as central issues, with the exception of the recent focus on assertiveness training and overcoming learned helplessness for women.

Part of the difficulty in exploring the effects of traditional therapeutic approaches is due to the questionable usefulness of some of the conventional measuring devices for assessing women's experience. Since research relies heavily on appropriate dependent measures, there is a need for systematic appraisal for sex bias in tests utilized to assess therapy outcomes.

The use of prescription drugs in psychotherapy becomes a salient issue in the treatment of women clients because of the comparatively greater frequency reported for medicating women. Because women's socialization leads them to be more dependent on authorities, they may be more likely to accept drug treatment without genuine involvement in that decision. Research is needed to discover the relation of gender to the extent of use, side effects, and patient satisfaction with drug treatment. The use of more extreme procedures such as electroshock therapy also needs investigation in terms of the impact of differential prescriptions for women and men.

Psychodynamic Perspectives

Psychodynamic theory has tended to center around the understanding of transference relationships. As pointed out by Kaplan and Yasinski, male–male and cross-sex relationships have been of interest to researchers in the past, but female–female relationships have been examined only recently with respect to their centrality in women's lives. If the therapeutic relationship is assumed to be a curative element, better ways need to be developed to measure its effect.

It has been suggested that differential labeling of identical behaviors performed by both men and women disadvantages women, as the more pejorative terms are usually reserved for describing women. It would be especially important to examine the connotative use of specific labels, such as "aggressiveness," that are related both to traditional gender stereotypes and to traditional theories of psychopathology. Research is needed on the extent to which certain theoretical approaches differentially encourage or disallow the expression of behaviors such as anger for women and men.

Behavior Therapies

The research needs with regard to behavioral approaches include the assessment of the influence of cognitions on behaviors, particularly in light of the changes of attitudes that may have been fostered by the women's movement. In addition, the behavior modifications that have been applied in institutions such as schools and work settings often are not evaluated for their impact on women's lives, and yet, as Blechman mentions, it is known that systems changes affect the environment to which individual psychotherapy clients will have to adapt. Researchers are also concerned that subpopulations of women or women at different points in the life span have not been considered in the planning of evaluation procedures. Behavior-modification techniques may be particularly clear in defining a specific goal or method and in involving the client in determining goals, but we do not know whether, in practice, individual goals tend to be different for men and women and whether there is sex bias in selecting such goals.

In general, research on the traditional theories and orientations of psychotherapy has not addressed the impact of these approaches on women in the context of changing roles occasioned by the advent of the new feminist perspective. Even the basic question of which therapeutic goals may be applied differentially to males and females is essentially unanswered today for therapeutic approaches developed in the past.

Alternative Approaches

Alternative approaches to psychotherapy are those that are not found within the traditional schools of psychotherapeutic persuasion and that exist separately, either because of political differences from traditional approaches, as in feminist therapy or treatment of ethnic minorities, or because of nonprofessional leadership, as in consciousness-raising groups and self-help groups. These alternative approaches for women who might otherwise find themselves in traditional therapy make some common assumptions about the treatment of women: Therapists should be familiar with research on the psychology of women; they need to be aware of the importance of therapist–client similarity of values; and they need to be aware of the importance of social change in considering therapeutic goals for women. Other important areas include the need to be aware of the heterogeneity of women, the psychological consequences of economic, political, and social inequality between men and women, and the resulting effect on the capacity of women to produce change in their own behalf.

The questions to be addressed in order to evaluate the effectiveness of alternative approaches focus on the understanding of the processes of such approaches, the comparison with traditional approaches, and the outcome for different populations of women clients. Specifically, the questions for research include: Which women are likely to use alternative systems for treatment? What are their demographic and personality characteristics, and what motivates them to seek help? What transpires in the treatment sessions, and what are the outcomes, behaviorally and by self-report? The evidence that bears upon these questions can be viewed more clearly by separately considering feminist therapy and consciousness-raising groups.

Feminist Therapy

The common goal agreed upon by most feminist therapists is to develop autonomous individuals with personal strength, independence, and trust in self and in other women. To achieve this goal, feminist therapy, according to Gilbert, aims at clarifying the distinction between the internal and the situational or societal sources of problems. It confirms and validates the positive features of the female experience. Emphasis on an egalitarian relationship means that the values and attitudes of therapist as well as client are open to examination. Change in self and environment is sought, as opposed to adjustment to existing conditions; clients identify their therapists as agents of change. Feminist therapy accepts the expression of anger against previous discrimination or oppression, with the eventual assumption of personal power.

There is some evidence that women entering feminist therapy as opposed to traditional therapies do not differ in age, education, employment status, occupational level, marital status, level of pretherapy stress, or presenting complaints. Differences that do appear in some of the early investigations are that feminist therapy clients are more likely to be child-free and politically radical. Although characteristics of feminist therapists have been largely unexplored, such therapists tend to be more liberal, active, dominant, aggressive, and self-actualized, as well as higher in self-esteem, self-confidence, and independence, than nonfeminists. When feminists of both sexes have been studied, males and females did not differ. Feminist therapists highly value similarity between therapist and client and have been found to rate clients as stronger and healthier than do nonfeminists. The outcome evidence for feminist therapy is very sparse, but it appears that feminist therapy is equally effective for both feminist and nonfeminist clients, while traditional therapy seems to be less effective for feminist than for nonfeminist clients, particularly where therapy emphasized adjustment to traditional expectations.

Consciousness-Raising Groups

The critical aspects of consciousness-raising groups as a therapeutic technique include the relationships between members in the consciousness-raising group and goals of the' group. The structure is an egalitarian one, with no designated leader and sanctions against dominance by a single individual or a few individuals. The group aims for the personal growth of its members. Members serve as advocates for one another in some cases; they also attempt to produce social change in the environment. Most groups function outside of established institutions and do not consider themselves as treatment-oriented, in the sense that the members are not mentally disturbed. Consciousness-raising focuses on the sharing of thoughts and feelings in the group and increasing awareness of oneself and of women's problems in general while gaining personal support from others.

Knowledge about the effects of consciousness-raising groups on women who participate in them is emerging from recent research, as Kravetz points out. Data suggest that therapeutic effects may include an altered view of the world encompassing an understanding of the political–social aspects of women's experience; changes in identity, particularly with regard to body image and sexuality; enhanced self-acceptance; change in the primary reference group from men to women; and development of egalitarian relationships with men. These changes appear to be greater than the changes in political beliefs that may also occur.

Many questions remain concerning the relation of consciousness-raising groups to various forms of psychotherapeutic treatment. When is consciousness-raising an appropriate treatment? What are the behavioral and personality changes that occur after consciousness-raising? How do outcomes differ for different types of women? How are the new insights applied to various roles and relationships? What is the impact of consciousness-raising on family and significant others? What is the relation of consciousness-raising to mental health?

Minority Women

Very little attention has been directed to the process and outcome of therapy with minority women, that is, black or African-Americans, native Americans, Mexican-Americans, Puerto Ricans, and other Hispanic groups. Although there has been an increasing awareness of the needs of minorities in general in society, the focus has been on economic and social influences rather than on psychotherapy as a treatment approach.

As Wilkinson observes, what literature does exist on minority treatment does not address issues of race *and* gender.

A prominent theme in the research literature that needs to be questioned is the matriarchal conception of black American families. The extent to which this view of minority women prevails in the attitudes of therapists and influences the treatment process with minority women needs examination. Social-class variables also need to be partialed out in research on race and gender.

The range of questions raised regarding gender and psychotherapy needs to be raised again for minority clients: What are the influences of therapist gender, race, and attitudes on psychotherapy with minority women? What are the effects of therapist and client race and gender on outcome? Are minority women likely to be diagnosed differently or assigned to crisis therapy more often than other women or men? As data accumulate on the life experiences and psychology of minority women, such knowledge needs to be applied to issues in psychotherapy with minority women.

The alternative therapeutic approaches require the development of new outcome measures that are not sex-biased, that reflect increased social awareness, that consider minority women, and that directly address some of the goals of these approaches, such as power, competence, and independence. Revision of existing instruments to incorporate these concepts has been suggested. Research programs are needed to evaluate alternatives to medically oriented and other traditional treatments.

Intervention in Crises

Crisis-intervention models have only recently been applied to women's issues. Rape centers have tried to treat one type of violence toward women, while battering, incest, and other types of violence are only beginning to be systematically studied. In reproductive crises, the physical aspects of pregnancy, childbirth, menopause, and surgical intervention have received more attention than the social-psychological context in which they occur. The questions related to crises and crisis treatments include: Have treatment approaches been developed that respond adequately to crises that differ for women and men? How does treatment reflect the fact that a particular event may impact more on women than men because of women's socialization to be dependent on others, particularly men? Do therapists and patients label potential crises differently for women and men?

Almost no research has focused on these questions. Research in related areas, however, points to additional issues to be considered in studying crisis treatment for women. Data indicate that women tend to organize their emotional supports around relationships, while men organize around work. Also, there is some evidence that men and women cognitively label events differently, that men depersonalize more, feel less guilt, and express anger and rage outwardly. Perhaps most relevant, however, is the research on learned helplessness that suggests that women characteristically feel that they have less control over life events than do men, and that this feeling is often based on realistic perceptions.

Lack of control over critical experiences in their lives is a perceived or real condition common to women in different crises. Thus, therapy outcome studies need to measure the variables of regained control, mastery, power, and integration of the crisis event into the total life situation. Prevention of further mental health disorders is also seen as a task of crisis intervention, one that is not often assessed in the evaluation of outcome. Focus on the traumatic event may obscure important information about the woman's background that should be addressed in therapy and in the evaluation of outcome.

Reproductive Crises

Historically, Western culture has considered the primary value of women to be their ability to reproduce and care for children. The impairment or loss of this ability has precipitated major crises for women, and the damage to the female reproductive organs by disease, surgery, or injury has occasioned mental anguish out of proportion to the physical trauma endured. As is clear from Notman and Nadelson's chapter, there is almost no research addressing psychologically based treatments during such crises. There also has been little attention paid to stresses associated with normal reproductive functions such as the menstrual cycle, pregnancy, and lactation. It is unclear whether the lack of attention is due to the fact that these stresses are regarded as normal states or as unique to women and, therefore, less important.

A major consideration in the psychotherapeutic treatment of women during reproductive crises is the need to expand the knowledge on which treatment is based. For example, much more basic research is needed on the effects of the menstrual cycle on women, particularly the psychological impact of menarche on the young girl and menopause on the older woman. What are the interaction effects between life-cycle stage, demographic variables, and social situation? How do such variables as cognitive labeling, perceptions, and expectations of women influence the extent to which a crisis is perceived? The dynamics of reproductive change or loss of function also need exploration.

Treatment research is needed on variables occurring in conjunction with the crisis event and their influence on a woman's ability to cope, length of recovery, and receptivity to a psychotherapeutic relationship. For example, what is the effect of a waiting period between discovery of a malignancy and surgical intervention in mastectomy or hysterectomy? Does age or stage in the life cycle make a difference in treatment outcome? Can psychotherapeutic crisis intervention moderate recovery time and influence the spread of disease, pain control, and satisfaction with one's situation in life?

The various types of crises share some common research priorities. The threat of loss during the crisis, the experience of lack of control as a result of the event, the mechanisms best suited to gain mastery over the experience, and the process of reintegration are all theoretically proposed aspects that have received clinical, but not research, attention. These aspects need systematic study.

Violence against Women

The questions specific to crises of violence against women are: Is fear of violence a normal expectation for women? How does fear of potential violence affect the way women live? Does such a fear motivate women to enter psychotherapy, apparently for other reasons? What are the coping tasks for victims of rape, incest, or battering that should be a focus of therapy, and are they the same tasks? Are minority women more vulnerable to violence? How does treatment handle the impact of rape, incest, and battering on women's future lives? Is self-disclosure easier in individual treatment or in groups of victims? How do concerns for ethical issues in treating crisis victims, such as confidentiality, affect services offered?

The evidence from crisis settings indicates that there are wide individual differences in how the stress or life event is appraised by the victim. Rape is usually experienced as a single traumatic event, but, as Walker points out, wife battering, marital rape, and girl-child incest are typically repeated traumas inflicted on women by men who may also love them. Incest victims seem to experience conflicts of divided loyalty and role confusion. Rape victims who are attacked by trusted persons have longer recovery times than those raped by strangers. Very few empirical data exist on the efficacy of psychotherapy during and after such crises. In fact, one of the questions to be answered is whether or not psychotherapy is the best therapeutic intervention. For example, in the case of battering victims, is marital or family therapy more beneficial to the batterer than to the female victim? Does the presence of a male-female cotherapy team mitigate potential bias against women? When is divorce an appropriate outcome? Certainly, studies that compare treatments between groups are desirable, but a model of randomized clinical trials, including control conditions, raises ethical issues of withholding treatment, even of marginally known benefit, from victims of violence. Since these situations are often life-threatening, particularly in chronic battering relationships, treatment by primary-care providers such as general practitioners or therapists needs evaluation.

Marital Transition

The women's movement literature points out that the traumas of divorce and widowhood differentially affect women and men. Although women traditionally have dealt with marital transitions in psychotherapy, there is little if any research on the crises of divorce and widowhood or on whether they are resolved more beneficially through therapy than through alternative interventions. Some of the questions that arise regarding psychotherapeutic treatment of women in marital transition are: Is previous therapy useful when transitional life crises arise? Do specialized therapeutic interventions generalize to other crises? Is there such a phenomenon as too much or too little therapy? How do therapist values influence decision-making during crises? Does group participation facilitate passage through marital crises? How do different therapeutic approaches affect remarriage, independence, and problem-solving? Are different needs associated with widowhood and divorce, and how does treatment address them?

According to McMahon, there is evidence that when crisis services are offered to separating and divorcing individuals, they are well utilized by women. This is not true for widows, with the exception of programs like Widow-to-Widow that utilize peer leaders. The early evidence from organizations such as Widow-to-Widow indicates that support groups are catalysts for resocialization of women. However, the evaluation of crisis-intervention services for marital transition suffers from a lack of institutional support for grass-roots alternatives. Rape centers have experienced a variation of this problem recently, with available monies designated for research but almost no funding allocated to maintain services after completion of the project. Thus, it becomes difficult, if not impossible, to evaluate alternative treatments when they do not have support for basic services. In addition, because such services tend to exist only in well-supported, urban communities, research on violence against women and on marital transition may follow the path of other alternative treatments—a dearth of attention to women's experiences among underserved, rural, and inaccessible populations.

Conclusions

Several common themes run through the recommended directions for research on psychotherapy for women. First, an overriding need exists for conceptualization to integrate the literature on isolated variables which may have an impact on the treatment of women. It is hoped that established researchers in psychotherapy, as well as those particularly concerned with these issues, will attend to this need. Systematic research will serve to demystify the field and avoid conflicting, contradictory findings currently characteristic of research on sex differences.

There is a need for increased sophistication in the models and methods of research in this area. The evidence that gender in interaction with other variables yields greater statistical significance than does gender alone suggests that simple comparisons are not going to be fruitful for this field. The quality of the research is of crucial importance. Although other areas of research include weak studies, it is more harmful to this field, as the subject matter is emotional and skeptics are quick to show intolerance of its rough beginnings. Thus, the encouragement of research should no longer include the uncritical acceptance of inadequate work, no matter how relevant the content. There is a greater need for theoretical and methodologic soundness than for the discovery of one more relationship of gender to some psychotherapy variable.

Another recurring theme speaks to the development of measures, particularly on outcome, that do not bias the interpretation of results. Currently used instruments need to be evaluated for their relevance to women and for possible sex bias before they can be adopted as measures of outcome. For example, the goals of marital stability, adjustment to outdated lifestyles, and the role of woman as nurturer and childrearer can no longer be accepted as positive outcomes without consideration of their impact on women's lives. Concepts of improvement must themselves be examined.

An issue that affects many areas of treatment of women involves the concept of mastery over situations. This concept emerges most clearly in relation to recovery from crisis situations but also emerges as an important goal in alternative therapies of a non-crisis nature and in the treatment of chronic neuroses and depression. In the light of recent critiques, outcome research that does not consider a woman's sense of mastery or control over her life and does not include long-term follow-up may be considered deficient in its conceptualization of therapy goals.

An overriding concern about the current status of research on psychotherapy and women involves the lack of resources allocated to the area. While part of the problem stems from the disinclination of established psychotherapy researchers to include gender variables in their projects, the greater concern expressed by leaders in research on women and psychotherapy involves the lack of encouragement of younger researchers to pursue gender-related questions. It is not known whether younger researchers fear that such research will be regarded as trivial by colleagues and superiors or have personal priorities to become involved more in service delivery than in research in crisis and alternative programs. Agency support of both service and research components of newer, alternative programs may be the only reasonable direction in which to move. When outside funds for feminist research are available, the discrimination against academics involved in such research may be considerably reduced, and professional advancement, which often depends on acquiring outside money, will be possible for feminist researchers.

Additionally, there is need for a mechanism for the dissemination of skills in writing grants and in presenting research for publication, skills which have traditionally been passed on by mentors to selected prodigies. Such skills cannot be readily learned in a short-term course given at a convention or weekend workshop, although the interchange at a working conference can be a vital educational experience, particularly for new researchers. A communications network with a publication to encourage interchange of ideas and ongoing research might well be conceived of and funded by the National Institute of Mental Health as a service to the field concerned with the emerging body of knowledge on women and psychotherapy.

Finally, the importance of the conference on which this book is based lies not solely in the background papers, report, or recommendations that were generated. Probably of equal value were the interchanges initiated at the conference, the professional growth of investigators in the field, and the identification of a bank of talent in this area of research. Participants became aware of resources among themselves and generated ideas that will further communications in the field, all of which should have an important impact on future research strategies and priorities. Thus, continued support from the National Institute of Mental Health for such research conferences is regarded as one of the most cost-effective mechanisms to stimulate future progress in this area.

Recommended Priorities for Research on Women and Psychotherapy

1. Research on women and psychotherapy shares a major concern with research on all issues related to the psychology of women: the need for a conceptual framework within which sex-role variables may be systematically integrated. At present, such a conceptual framework is not yet available to the field as a whole. The development of theories to explain the causes of sex-role stereotypes and sex-role biases is in a beginning stage. Research that can integrate the diverse findings reported in the literature into testable models is a major priority.

2. Research on issues specific to women's needs for and use of psychotherapy is needed.

a. Certain personality traits and emotional states are strongly associated with women's sex roles and disorders of high prevalence among women. Research is needed to identify predisposing factors of such disorders and the effectiveness of treatment for women who exhibit extremes of passivity, learned helplessness, exaggerated femininity, inhibition of negative feelings, control of sexuality, role-taking to satisfy a male partner, fearfulness, and other-directedness.

b. Research is needed on the relation of marriage to women's mental health and on the appropriateness of family adjustment, marital stability, and divorce as therapeutic goals for women.

c. Research is needed on psychotherapy for problems associated with women's unique reproductive functions.

d. Research is needed on the efficacy of short-term psychotherapy and group interventions for women in crises, whether due to rape, battering, incest, or marital and other life-cycle transitions.

3. Research is needed to develop measures for evaluating the process and outcome of psychotherapy that reflect current knowledge of the psychology of women and that are not subject to gender bias of therapist, client, or investigator.

a. Research is needed on criteria that define healthy functioning for women and on measures for assessing healthy functioning before and after psychotherapeutic intervention. Mastery, competence, independence, and coping skills are among the concepts that need empirical definition.

b. Research is needed on progress at different points in therapy and on follow-up over different time periods, particularly in the treatment of depression, phobias, and eating disorders, where short-term gains have not assured long-term effects.

c. Standardized diagnostic criteria, clinical assessments, and operational definitions of improvement for women are needed in order to provide researchers with guidelines for the methodology to document which treatments are useful with which patients.

d. Research on alternative psychotherapeutic interventions with women and on prevention in the social context should be given high priority, especially with regard to the evaluation of cost-effectiveness of the therapeutic outcome of feminist therapy, self-help groups, crisis intervention for women, and consciousness-raising groups.

e. Research is needed on therapist variables and their effect on outcome, particularly with regard to how different theoretical orientations influence goals, termination, limitation of accessibility to treatment, and attitudes toward women and traditional roles.

f. Research is needed on the differential effects of male–female and all-female psychotherapy groups and on the use of various cotherapy combinations for female clients.

4.   Priority should be given to research designs that explicate the factors that interact with gender variables.

a. All psychotherapy and treatment research should include gender as a variable unless there is clear documentation that gender effects do not exist with regard to the dependent variables studied.

b. Research priority in psychotherapy should be given to multivariate designs and analyses that explicate a number of factors that interact with gender.

c. Research is needed on psychotherapy with different age cohorts of women at different points in the life cycle.

d. Longitudinal studies are needed on the relation of gender to help-seeking patterns, depressive episodes, and reaction to change in marital status.

e. Research is needed on psychotherapy with special subpopulations of women, for example, those who are hospitalized, severely ill, living in rural or other inaccessible areas, or members of ethnic monirity groups.

5.   The National Institute of Mental Health should take leadership in supporting and encouraging research on women and psychotherapy.

a. Psychotherapy research supported by the National Institute of Mental Health should include variables relating to sex differences and sex-role attitudes wherever feasible. Applicants for funds and reviewers of grants and contracts should be sensitized to this need.

b. The National Institute of Mental Health should develop and disseminate to the professions and the general public strategies to deal with the problems of sex bias and sex-role stereotyping that may lead to the misdiagnosis and thus the mistreatment of women patients. Continuing education should focus on such strategies as a priority.

c. The National Institute of Mental Health should take the lead in developing data banks and communications networks on clinical interventions with women and make known their availability.

d. The Division of Manpower and Training should develop research training grants to support training of researchers in psychotherapy with women.

e. The National Institute of Mental Health should periodically prepare publications for the general public on women's issues in psychotherapy.

f. The National Institute of Mental Health should sponsor periodic conferences to assess progress in the field of women and psychotherapy and to set further priorities for the field.

ACKNOWLEDGMENT

This chapter is based in part on the report *Women and Psychotherapy: Priorities for Research*, NIMH contract 278-78-0063(ER), 1979.

References

Bergin, A., & Strupp, H. *Changing frontiers in the science of psychotherapy.* New York: Aldine-Atherton, 1972.

Broverman, I. K., Broverman, D. M., Clarkson, F. E., Rosenkrantz, P. S., & Vogel, S. R. Sex-role stereotypes and clinical judgments of mental health. *Journal of Consulting and Clinical Psychology,* 1970, *34,* 1–7.

Orlinsky, D. E., & Howard, K. I. The effect of sex of therapist on the therapeutic experiences of women. *Psychotherapy: Theory, Research, and Practice,* 1976, *13,* 82–88.

Parloff, M. Can psychotherapy research guide the policymaker? A little knowledge may be a dangerous thing. *American Psychologist,* 1979, *34,* 296–306.

Report of the President's Commission on Mental Health. Washington, D.C.: U.S. Government Printing Office, 1978.

Shapiro, J. Socialization of sex roles in the counseling setting: Differential counselor behavioral and attitudinal responses to typical and atypical female sex roles. *Sex Roles,* 1977, *3,* 173–184.

Wright, F., & Gould, L. J. Recent research on sex-linked aspects of group behavior: Implications for group therapy. In L. R. Wolberg & M. L. Aronson (Eds.), *Group therapy '77: An overview.* New York: Stratton Intercontinental Medical Book Corp., 1977.

Author Index

Subject Index